1995

The Moment of Decision

The Moment of Decision

BIOGRAPHICAL ESSAYS ON AMERICAN CHARACTER AND REGIONAL IDENTITY

EDITED BY

Randall M. Miller & John R. McKivigan

Contributions in American History, Number 156

Jon L. Wakelyn, *Series Editor*

GREENWOOD PRESS

Westport, Connecticut · London

Library of Congress Cataloging-in-Publication Data

The moment of decision : biographical essays on American character and regional identity / edited by Randall M. Miller and John R. McKivigan.
    p.   cm. — (Contributions in American history, ISSN 0084–9219 ; no. 156)
    Includes bibliographical references (p.   ) and index.
    ISBN 0–313–28635–3 (alk. paper)
    1. United States—History—1815–1861—Biography. 2. United States—History—1849–1877—Biography. 3. Decision-making—Social aspects—United States—History—19th century. 4. Social reformers—United States—Biography. 5. Intellectuals—United States—Biography. 6. United States—Social conditions—To 1865.
I. Miller, Randall M. II. McKivigan, John R.
III. Series.
E415.8.M66   1994
973'.099—dc20   93–30981

British Library Cataloguing in Publication Data is available.

Library of Congress Catalog Card Number: 93–30981
ISBN 0–313–28635–3
ISSN 0084–9219

First published in 1994

Greenwood Press, 88 Post Road West, Westport, CT 06881
An imprint of Greenwood Publishing Group, Inc.

Printed in the United States of America

The paper used in this book complies with the Permanent Paper Standard issued by the National Information Standards Organization (Z39.48–1984).

10 9 8 7 6 5 4 3 2 1

To

MERTON L. DILLON

Teacher, Scholar, Friend

Contents

Preface

This collection of original chapters centers on the theme of the "historical moment" in the lives of several representative nineteenth-century, and one family of twentieth-century, Americans, each of whom experienced a "moment of decision" (or a series of such moments) that directed the courses and identities of those individuals in important ways thereafter. The authors identify critical moments when individuals were converted to action by an idea, an event, or an experience, but their concerns are not solely biographical. All the chapters examine moments of decision within regional and social contexts, suggesting that the range of individual decision was constrained by the particular historical world in which those people lived.

The book principally focuses on decisions related to nineteenth-century social reform, political, or intellectual issues, though it also offers some observations on the significance of moments of decision generally. As such, it presents an extended discussion of the relationship between personal decision and public action. The authors in no way claim to have canvassed the subject of historical moments in any comprehensive way, and, indeed, some of the moments described in this volume are subtle and disguised, even denied, by the biographical subjects. However limited in focus, the authors' attention to moments of decision reminds us that history did not just happen. Neither personal lives nor American development was predestined. People made choices within the particular historical contexts in which they lived — choices that in some instances altered or redirected those contexts thereafter. Understanding the dynamics of decision promises to reveal the range of choices available to Americans at any given time. It also invites further consideration of the ways in which thought begets action and personal experience shapes public identity.

The chapters are divided into three sections. Section I looks primarily at the role of identity within the southern regional context. In chapters variously weighing the burdens of southern history, the authors explore the ways in which family, law, religion, politics, and slavery shaped southerners' decisions about personal and public morality and obligation and, in the case of David Walker, led to a direct challenge to the assumptions and institutions undergirding the conservative social order of the Old South. That the white southerners studied in these chapters risked less than the black one speaks to the powerful, if also paradoxical, cultural and social restraints on southern intellectuals such as the Percy family of Mississippi, lawyer James Petigru of South Carolina, and educational reformer and proslavery apologist Calvin Wiley of North Carolina.

Section II surveys antislavery and moral reform within the antebellum northern regional context. What emerges from studies of abolitionists William Lloyd Garrison and Wendell Phillips, colonizationist Leonard Bacon, and "true woman" editor Sarah Josepha Hale is an appreciation of the varieties of reform sensibility and interest and of the reformer personality. Despite very different individual family and life histories, Garrison and Phillips found common ground in an ardent abolitionism that sought not only to liberate slaves but also to free the United States itself from a history of moral corruption. By temperament and association, Bacon recoiled from abolitionist vehemence, even as he preached antislavery colonization. Likewise, Hale emphasized the importance of historical memory (for example, in pushing for a Bunker Hill monument and for a national Thanksgiving day) in building a stable social order, even as she expanded the roles of women to include support for patriotic memorials and involvement in public education.

Section III examines the responses of several individuals to the facts of emancipation. For General George Thomas, the needs of battle and military Reconstruction forced him to rethink and finally abandon his prewar racial prejudices and also to accept a larger role for the military in political administration than he earlier would have tolerated. For abolitionist James Redpath, the need to provide schooling for the freedmen led him to reconsider his preemancipation assumptions about the pace of black adjustment to freedom and American social responsibility. For Massachusetts historian George Moore, the need to write an honest history based on primary sources and new concepts of historical writing caused him to revise his own state's claims to moral superiority and antislavery prominence. Except for abolitionists like Walker, Garrison, Phillips, and, to some extent, Redpath, the "reformers" studied in all these chapters were reconcilers in their approaches to reform and history, revealing a conservative trend among American reform that often has been obscured by contemporary emphasis on, and historians' interest in, the front-line abolitionists who would be heard and would not compromise.

The chapters in this book were written in honor of Merton L. Dillon, recently retired from Ohio State University, whose own work often turned on the historical moment in an individual reformer's life. The authors include friends and former students of Dillon who share his lifelong interest in antislavery reform, the Old South and slavery, and the Civil War and its aftermath. All also have learned from Merton Dillon in various ways to appreciate the importance of individual choice within particular historical contexts. Dillon's own work moved from close biographical studies of such antislavery reformers as Benjamin Lundy and Elijah P. Lovejoy to more general considerations of the abolitionists, whom Dillon styled a "dissenting minority." Although Dillon never wholly retreated from an early argument that the antislavery movement had failed, because slavery ended in war rather than through the moral persuasion or political mobilization of antislavery ideas, by shifting the focus of his research from northern antislavery to southern slaves, he began to show the vulnerability of slavery. Indeed, in his most recent book, *Slavery Attacked: Southern Slaves and Their Allies 1619–1865* (1990), Dillon wrote about the slaveholders' failure and the ultimate success of slaves and their antislavery friends, who by constant pressure from within and without brought ruin to the slave-owning South. Still, for Dillon, there was nothing inevitable about slavery's demise or its resilience over two centuries in North America. Slavery's end came from individuals' actions, just as its persistence rested on decisions by those without slaves not to act against slavery and by those with them to act for it. The contingency of human action explained the outcomes. This collection of chapters in Dillon's honor attempts to recognize his own major contributions to the debates on antislavery character and southern interests by exploring some of the ways in which Americans confronted their society and themselves and, in so doing, remade history.

Acknowledgments

A cooperative enterprise such as this book succeeds because many hands help the editors and authors. Our effort received immediate support from the department of history at Ohio State University, especially Warren Van Tine, who, as departmental chair, encouraged the project when it was proposed in 1991, and Janice Gulper, who, as departmental secretary, responded promptly and kindly to our requests for information. At Saint Joseph's University, Stephanie McKeller-Auer smoothed the administrative process with her usual intelligence and efficiency.

The idea for the book received support from Betty Fladeland, David D. Lee, Patricia W. Romero, Richard H. Sewell, and Robert Sayre. The book itself profited from a close reading by Paula Benkart, who made numerous useful criticisms about content and style in the introduction and several of the contributions.

Special thanks are due to Cynthia Harris at Greenwood Press for her constant nudging us along and for believing in the project from its inception. Thanks, too, to Jon Wakelyn for seizing on the suggestion of a collection of essays on "the moment of decision" and inviting us to include the book in his series at Greenwood Press.

Finally, thanks are due to Merton L. Dillon, whose own work as a teacher and scholar inspired so many of us and taught us so much about the importance of argument and narrative in writing history. Although Merton Dillon knew nothing about this book, written to honor him, his presence is everywhere in it. We dedicate this book to him.

The Moment of Decision

Introduction

Randall M. Miller

Late in the evening of November 7, 1837, a mob surrounded a warehouse in Alton, Illinois, where Presbyterian minister and antislavery editor Elijah P. Lovejoy and several others stood guard over a printing press Lovejoy intended to use to publish his newspaper, the Alton *Observer*. Twice before, antiabolition mobs had destroyed presses owned by Lovejoy, and prominent Alton citizens repeatedly had complained that Lovejoy's "unwise agitation" threatened the town's commercial relations with southerners downriver and encouraged blacks to become restive everywhere. However, Lovejoy persisted in his antislavery witness. When the local community acted to uphold its interest, Lovejoy did not retreat. On that fateful November night he would die in defense of his press, when he was shot five times after coming out from the warehouse that the mob had set afire.[1]

Lovejoy's murder shocked the nation. Across the North, news of Lovejoy's death excited immediate anger and fed growing resentments toward a supposed "slave power conspiracy" that even reached its tentacles into northern communities to strangle basic freedoms. In mass meetings, funeral sermons, and public memorials, northerners protested the "bloodthirstiness" of the slave power and demanded that Americans uproot the cause of such violence. Probably no other event until the Kansas-Nebraska Act in 1854 and then John Brown's own martyrdom in 1859 so galvanized northern antislavery feeling as did Lovejoy's murder. Thoughtful southerners, too, saw Lovejoy's death as a cause around which abolitionists might rally northern sentiment by shifting their focus from the wrongs done to the slave to the threat slavery posed to civil liberties. The entire debate on slavery seemed to enter a new phase of urgency as a consequence.

Many contemporaries to the event and its aftermath would recall Lovejoy's death as a defining moment in the antislavery struggle. John Quincy Adams, among others, went further by describing it as "an epochal in the annals of human liberty" that might determine the course of freedom everywhere.[2] Nevertheless, others, both then and later, would dispute the centrality of Lovejoy's murder in human history, or even in the course of the slavery issue in the United States, by pointing to different defining moments.

To many observers, for example, 1831 had marked a more profound shift in public thinking about slavery. In that year the appearance in Boston, Massachusetts, of William Lloyd Garrison's *Liberator*, pledged to be "as harsh as truth and as uncompromising as justice" in its insistence on immediate abolition, was followed by Nat Turner's insurrection in Southampton County, Virginia, that left almost threescore white men, women, and children dead and the South trembling with rumors of slave revolts and by the slavery debates in the Virginia legislature that signaled the last gasp of public antislavery discussion in the Upper South and in 1832 brought forth Thomas R. Dew's unapologetic defense of slavery. Massachusetts and Virginia once had stood together at the creation of the republic; now they pointed the United States in two opposing directions.[3] Meanwhile, Great Britain had claimed the mantle of liberty's champion by emancipating its slaves in 1831. Whether one fixed on 1831, 1837, or the crises of the 1850s, however, contemporaries to those events and many later historians shared a common belief that a defining moment was significant in symbolizing and shaping a people's identity and destiny.

American history often has been written as a series of such moments. Indeed, Americans as a whole have constructed their popular memory of the past in an episodic fashion, endowing particular events such as Lexington and Concord, Gettysburg, and Pearl Harbor with providential meaning. From the memorials and myths that make up America's public history echoes a simple refrain: a chosen people endured because they acted bravely in crises. They seized the historical moments.[4]

Embedded in such a history was a particular conception of time that governed American thought during the nineteenth century. Although Americans increasingly conceived of time as a straightforward progression, many clung to notions of time borrowed from Scripture. Scriptural time was God ordained, with a beginning and an end but also with interruptions in chronology during which a wayward Israel, and in the New Testament all humankind, was to reflect on their place in history and to chart a new course. The biblical prophets demanded no less. A scriptural sense of imminence, or "the time is at hand," colored Americans' thinking about their individual and collective responsibilities to the world and its maker from the beginning of their identity as a people. To the American mind, the Revolution had been such a historical moment, indeed, one that promised to redeem first the American people and then the world. *Common Sense* and the Declaration of Independence implied no less. After the Revolution, the American belief that history turned on such moments of decision became still more pronounced as the Enlightenment yielded to evangelicalism and romanticism during the nineteenth century.[5]

Abraham Lincoln, for one, invoked the combined scriptural and Revolutionary understanding of defining moments in many of his public statements. He did so before the Civil War broke out in his famous "House Divided" speech and in his statement that if war must come to save the Union, it had best come now, and he did so again during the war in his justification for emancipation — "The moment came when . . . slavery must die that the nation might live." Likewise, southern fire-eaters in late 1860 and early 1861 had insisted that secession must not wait on Lincoln's inauguration. In reaching a moment of decision, northerner and southerner alike believed that to tarry was to lose God's favor, to lose everything.[6]

In the nineteenth-century United States, especially, private moments of decision demanded public expression. Public acts had moral weight. They revealed the private self and affirmed one's place in the larger community. Just as that community itself — a new republic awash in a swirl of changes caused by industrialization, urbanization, immigration, and migration — sought common patriotic symbols, individual acts of public affirmation served to bind together an invertebrate society of few and plastic national institutions set against strong local and regional loyalties. While secret lodges and societies, communitarian groups, and P. T. Barnum flourished, Americans were growing suspicious of the world behind the veil. Fears of conspiracy that had lurked deep in the American psyche since the days of the American Revolution burst forth during the nineteenth century into an almost paranoid style in politics, propelling anti-Masonry, anti-Catholicism, nativism, both sides in the slavery debate, and populism.[7]

Collective insecurity and fear of conspiracy focused special attention on public acts. To be a member of the community, it was necessary to come out in support of that community, to decide — and to declare — which side you were on. Young men were expected to volunteer for service during the Civil War, as they had been expected to stand with the Minutemen and militia during the Revolution or as they later would be expected to join vigilantes, mobs, and other extralegal groups, including the Ku Klux Klan, when "lawlessness" or invasion threatened one's community.

During the nineteenth century, religion and politics were especially important in identifying those who belonged to a community. The dominant evangelical culture of the age demanded a public profession of faith, an admission before a congregation or a camp meeting that one had got right with God and joined others in Christian fellowship. The proliferation of competing denominations added to pressures to become a member of some church. So, too, democratic politics in the age before the secret ballot required visible support for party and candidates in rallies and parades and on election day. Whether stepping up to the anxious bench to proclaim one's salvation or to the labeled ballot box to proclaim one's partisan loyalties, the nineteenth-century American had to stand up to be counted. Not to do so signaled a failure of character and an estrangement from community.[8]

First, however, the community had to be defined. For most nineteenth-century Americans, the communities that counted most in their lives were local and formed concentric circles that spread out from family to church to town or county. Yet, the emerging market economy, the founding of national organizations (for example, religious denominations and reform societies), and both sectionalism and nationalism increasingly pulled Americans outward to new conceptions of community, which, however abstract or distant, were no less real and inescapable.

The Lovejoy murder proved a defining moment just for that reason. It pitted different definitions of community against one another. Lovejoy's antislavery arguments were premised on a common interest with friends of antislavery elsewhere and, in a broader sense, with humanity everywhere. Like most reformers, Lovejoy appealed to his followers' sense of common humanity and their need to rise above parochialism and self-interest. To his thinking, Alton's commercial ties to the South via the Mississippi River counted less than its obligations to humanity generally. From an Alton point of view, however, Lovejoy was himself an outsider — a New Englander by birth living in a town largely settled by southerners that was dependent on southern trade and suspicious of "Yankee" reformers. He seemed to personify the external threats to the local community that many in Alton felt when shifts in national transportation began to siphon off trade and when reform and national publications began to convey alien ideas into homes and churches. Simply forcing people to choose sides in a debate in which most people in Alton preferred not to engage made Lovejoy a flashpoint for a host of deeper concerns about identity and destiny. Lovejoy's presence, and then his death, forced Altonites, and then Americans generally, to ponder the nature of their community, locally and nationally.[9]

Such reflection occurred wherever reformers acted, be it in petition campaigns abolitionists conducted across the North or in demands for temperance or public education other reformers carried across the nation. The frequency and intensity of such reflection did not diminish the significance of a defining moment such as Lovejoy's death or John Brown's raid. Far from it. Such particular events acquired almost sacred meaning in part because they provided a way to order the rush of events and to untangle confused ideas about identity and interest.

Defining moments also forced individuals to discover their true selves. Whether it was Wendell Phillips making his famous leap onto the stage at a mass meeting following Lovejoy's death to come out boldly for abolitionism or a Civil War soldier overcoming fear in the first flush of battle, moments of crisis brought forth heroic acts of self-definition. For most Americans, such moments were more private, though often no less heroic in their meaning.

During the nineteenth century, the rituals attending the life cycle often became defining moments for both participants and witnesses. Ritual had become increasingly important and self-conscious during the century. Advice books on the sacramental aspects of the marriage ceremony and the importance of baptism and proper burial proliferated while the public processions memorializing fallen heroes joined the staged political events of holiday parades and campaign speeches as occasions that emphasized the importance of ritualized moments in defining self and society. For individuals, marriage and rituals surrounding the death of a loved one especially called for self-reflection and renewal and for dedication to a higher purpose.

Consider the case of John Hartwell Cocke (1780–1866), a wealthy Virginia slaveholder who became a temperance advocate, crusader against tobacco, and colonizationist. As a young man, Cocke had assumed a prominent place in local affairs by virtue of his wealth and Cavalier genealogy, which ran back to the seventeenth century, but he was unusual among his fellow planters in eschewing public office. After rising from the rank of captain to brigadier general of Virginia troops during the War of 1812, he left public life to cultivate his fields, breed horses, and build the pisé Greek Revival mansion and outbuildings at his Fluvanna County plantations that would win him the admiration of contemporaries and architectural historians alike. Because Cocke shared with his friend Thomas Jefferson a republican inclination born of the Enlightenment, he joined the Sage of Monticello in drafting the plans for the University of Virginia. Scientific farming and improved transportation also became Cocke's interests. However, his vision remained largely parochial. He clashed with Jefferson over the direction of the university, wanting a religious influence there instead of Jefferson's nonsectarian liberalism. In most of his early public activities, Cocke's sense of social responsibility derived from the expectations of his class and family and entailed little personal risk.[10]

Two personal crises redirected Cocke's life outward and fired him with a zeal theretofore lacking. In 1816, at the deathbed of his first wife, Anne "Nancy" Barraud Cocke, he found religion. During the long illness that led to her death, Cocke began to search his own soul for purpose. His diary, which for years had revealed little of his inner self amid a daily refrain on the weather and farm affairs, became his solace, wherein he agonized over the meaning of his beloved Nancy's decline and death. Ultimately, Cocke concluded that her death, which came two days after Christmas and their wedding anniversary in 1816, was a providential sign that he must live an active Christian life. The rituals of nursing his wife during her illness, comforting her friends and family and being comforted by them in turn, and, finally, laying her to rest quickened Cocke's appreciation for his need to redirect his life outward. Cocke's religious resolve following his wife's death led directly to his decision to bring the Gospel to his slaves. He built chapels for the slaves on his property and taught them to read the Bible. In 1821 Cocke's marriage to Louisa Maxwell Holmes, a strong Christian woman, led him to rededicate his own life to Christ and to play a more energetic, visible role in church affairs and social reform. The marriage ceremony reminded him of his earlier vows and of the promise to begin life anew. Although Cocke did not take his public temperance pledge until 1828 and did not conceive his plan to free his slaves until 1831, the two personal defining moments in 1816 and 1821 had set the course of his life and bound him morally and emotionally, through the rituals of marriage and burial, to keep his promises of Christian witness and social responsibility.[11]

Public crises forced Cocke to confront other moments of decision. The Nat Turner rebellion and the Virginia debates on slavery in 1831 awakened Cocke to slavery's wrong. Cocke interpreted the Nat Turner uprising as a warning that God had grown impatient with America's slow progress toward freedom and the failure of masters to do their Christian duty in uplifting the slaves. It was time to act. Cocke pledged himself to a plan of gradual emancipation of his slaves, who would earn their freedom through self-purchase and Christian self-discipline and then be sent to Liberia. Cocke embraced colonization as the best way to relieve America of the burden of racial divisions and to extend Christian witness and American commerce to "benighted Africa." In a series of letters written to friends North and South in 1831 and 1832, he urged others to mount a concerted effort to save America from an angry God by ridding it of slavery, and the slaves, in a responsible, nondisruptive way and by practicing temperance and self-control.[12]

A final moment of decision for Cocke came during the Civil War. Staggered, in 1861, by his son Philip St. George Cocke's suicide and influenced, in 1863, by the jeremiads from southern ministers on the South's lost soul following the Confederate defeats at Gettysburg and Vicksburg, Cocke began a long, reminiscent essay on slavery and his own life in August 1863. Cocke did not go so far as his distant relative and fellow Virginian Edmund Ruffin, who saw the South's failures as the end of any life worth living, but he viewed the war as a punishment for the failure of reasonable men to act in earlier crises. In his bitterness over the loss of his son and the collapse of his own plans for emancipation and colonization of slaves, which had produced the manumission of only a few families, Cocke blamed both Puritan Yankees and fire-eating secessionists for America's troubles and lamented that slavery had ever come to America. Because responsible Americans had failed to act forthrightly on slavery in the republic's moments of decision during the Revolutionary era or again in 1831, fanaticism had come to rule the issue. The end was civil war and God's wrath.[13]

Cocke's story reveals several important aspects of personal defining moments. One is that such moments might not be momentary. The death of Nancy Cocke after a protracted illness, for example, was but the most dramatic part of a series of actions, the final act in a process, and the one validated by ritual. Another aspect of a personal defining moment is its centrifugal force that thrusts the individual away from self-indulgence in personal grief or triumph to some kind of social purpose. Moving outside of oneself becomes the heroic act. Finally, the personal defining moment must at some point converge with a public one to give it transcendent, even sacred, meaning as part of a larger shared experience. It is not just that the boy becomes a man in battle but that so many others do likewise and that the nation remembers by celebrating the action of so many as good and true and also as central to the nation's own defining moment, whether in victory or defeat.

Perhaps no other people have been so sensitive to defining moments in their individual and collective lives as have Americans. Americans are an invented people, self-conscious about their newness in history and the need to define national character. An American was one in the process of becoming. As J. Hector St. Jean de Crèvecoeur observed in *Letters from an American Farmer* (1782), a classic statement on American nationality, the American was a "new man," an amalgam of many peoples, "who leaving behind him all his ancient prejudices and manners, receives new ones from the new mode of life he has embraced, the new government he obeys, and the new rank he holds."[14] The American could be whatever he or she wanted to be — or so said Benjamin Franklin and countless other autobiographers retailing accounts of personal progress from rags to riches or even slavery to freedom. Especially during the nineteenth century, one was an American by an act of will. Freedom came from the decision to be free — coming to America, fleeing bondage, heading west, or getting control over one's personal self. Reformers, especially, harped on themes of defining moments that might transform individual conscience and behavior and redeem the nation. But Americans generally understood the importance of seizing the historical moment.

The chapters in this book examine the lives of a variety of nineteenth-century Americans, many of them reformers, whose sense of themselves individually, and their place in history, came from their responses to critical moments in their lives and in their relationship with their larger community. Whether it was the death of a father, a crisis of conscience, a political or military crossroads, or a meditation on the past, they all recognized that history had thrust upon them a particular responsibility to act honestly and forthrightly. They were much like Ralph Waldo Emerson's proverbial hero, the man of thought who was also the man of action. Several of the individuals described in this book sometimes proved unheroic — having failed to escape the burden of their family or personal history or to put aside self-interest — and some of their actions described in this book were hardly dramatic. Still, they all understood that if their lives were to have meaning, they must recognize and seize those moments in history when destiny beckoned. Being American demanded no less.

NOTES

1. The best account of Lovejoy and the riots at Alton remains Merton L. Dillon, *Elijah P. Lovejoy, Abolitionist Editor* (Urbana, 1961), especially 143–79. On the moral significance of Lovejoy's death, see Edward Beecher's powerful, insightful contemporary account, *Narrative of Riots at Alton: In Connection with the Death of Rev. Elijah P. Lovejoy* (1838; New York, 1965), and Robert Meredith's excellent "Introduction" to the 1965 edition.

2. John Quincy Adams, "Introduction," in Joseph C. Lovejoy and Owen Lovejoy, *Memoir of the Rev. Elijah P. Lovejoy: Who Was Murdered in Defence of the Liberty of the Press, at Alton, Illinois, Nov. 7, 1837* (New York, 1838), 12.

3. The literature on the crises of Union and the changing thinking about slavery in the United States, symbolized in the different courses taken by Massachusetts and Virginia, is large; so, too, are accounts of the origins of antislavery reform, the Nat Turner revolt, and the South's turning inward after 1831. For a revealing portrait of the complicated, and often contradictory, relationships of a United States that was coming apart even as it was growing more interconnected, see Robert Wiebe, *The Opening of American Society: From the Adoption of the Constitution to the Eve of Disunion* (New York, 1984). Wiebe's book informs much of my chapter. See also David Potter, *The Impending Crisis 1848–1861* (New York, 1976), especially chapters 1, 2, 14, and 17, and, for the southern route, William W. Freehling, *The Road to Disunion: Secessionists at Bay 1776–1854* (New York, 1990).

4. The literature on the patterns of American historical thinking and writing is too vast to list here. My own thinking has been influenced by such recent work as David Thelen, "Memory and American History," *Journal of American History* 75 (1989): 1117–29, a good introduction to the literature on collective memory; the March 1989 issue of the *Journal of American History* devoted to that topic; Edward T. Linethal, *Sacred Ground: Americans and Their Battlefields* (Urbana, 1991); and, for more recent writing, Peter Novick, *That Noble Dream: The "Objectivity Question" and the American Historical Profession* (Cambridge and New York, 1988).

5. The revivalistic and millennial cast of much of American religion especially urged Americans toward views of time that stressed imminence; so, too, did the so-called Protestant ethic, embodied in Benjamin Franklin, with its emphasis on time as money. On such matters, see, for example, Richard D. Brown, *Modernization: The Transformation of American Life, 1600–1865* (New York, 1976), especially his comments on time-thrift and clocks. On time in Western thought, see, for example, David Landes, *Revolution in Time: Clocks and the Making of the Modern World* (Cambridge, 1983); E. P. Thompson, "Time, Work-Discipline, and Industrial Capitalism," *Past and Present* 38 (December 1967): 56–97; and for literary expressions of time, Samuel L. Macey, *Clocks and the Cosmos: Time in Western Life and Thought* (Hamden, 1980).

6. On Lincoln, see Stephen B. Oates, *With Malice Toward None: The Life of Abraham Lincoln* (New York, 1977); LaWanda Cox, *Lincoln and Black Freedom: A*

Study in Presidential Leadership (Columbia, 1981), who shows Lincoln's overall caution but also his firm resolve once the moment for emancipation came; and James McPherson, *Abraham Lincoln and the Second American Revolution* (New York, 1991), especially chapters 2, 3, and 5. For the Lincoln quotation, see Francis B. Carpenter, *Six Months at the White House with Abraham Lincoln* (New York, 1866), 76–77. On southerners' crisis of fear in 1860–61, see Michael S. Greenberg, *Masters and Statesmen: The Political Culture of American Slavery* (Baltimore, 1985), 107–46; Steven A. Channing, *Crisis of Fear: Secession in South Carolina* (New York, 1970); William L. Barney, *The Secessionist Impulse: Alabama and Mississippi in 1860* (Princeton, 1974); Michael P. Johnson, *Toward a Patriarchal Republic: The Secession of Georgia* (Baton Rouge, 1977); and Potter, *Impending Crisis*, 448–84.

7. Historians from Richard Hofstadter to Bernard Bailyn have noted the fears of conspiracy and paranoid style of American politics and culture. For a brilliant short treatment of one of its principal antebellum manifestations, see David Brion Davis, *The Slave Power Conspiracy and the Paranoid Style* (Baton Rouge, 1969). On the violence such fears begat in antebellum America, see, for example, Michael Feldberg, *The Turbulent Era: Riot and Disorder in Jacksonian America* (New York, 1980); and Dallin H. Oaks and Marvin S. Hill, *Carthage Conspiracy: The Trial of the Accused Assassins of Joseph Smith* (Urbana, 1975).

8. On the public and populist nature of nineteenth-century American religion, see Nathan O. Hatch, *The Democratization of American Christianity* (New York, 1989).

9. On antiabolitionist fears, see Leonard L. Richards, *"Gentlemen of Property and Standing": Anti-Abolition Mobs in Jacksonian America* (New York, 1970), especially 30, 101–10 for Alton and Lovejoy.

10. On Cocke, see Clement Eaton, *The Mind of the Old South* (rev. ed., Baton Rouge, 1967), 23–43; and M. Boyd Coyner, "John Hartwell Cocke of Bremo: Agriculture and Slavery in the Ante-Bellum South" (Ph.D. diss., University of Virginia, 1961).

11. John Hartwell Cocke diaries, especially November 1816–January 1817 and 1821, in the John Hartwell Cocke Papers (Alderman Library, University of Virginia). In his unfinished manuscript biography of Cocke, in the Armistead C. Gordon, Jr., Papers (Alderman Library, University of Virginia), Armistead Gordon speculated that the loss of Nancy Cocke shook Cocke more profoundly than any other event in his life. For a recent analysis of Cocke's relationship with Nancy, see Melinda S. Buza, "'Pledges of Our Love': Friendship, Love, and Marriage among the Virginia Gentry, 1800–1825," in *The Edge of the South: Life in Nineteenth-Century Virginia*, eds. Edward L. Ayers and John C. Willis (Charlottesville, 1991), 25–29.

12. On Cocke's emancipation plans and the responses of the slaves and exslaves to them, see Randall M. Miller, *"Dear Master": Letters of a Slave Family* (1978; rev. and enlarged ed., Athens, 1990). On his growing conviction that slavery was wrong, see, for example, Cocke to [unknown], 23 September 1831 (see also Cocke to Elliott Cresson, letter enclosed with the 23 September 1831 letter); Cocke to J. C. Cabell, 31 January 1832; Cocke manuscript entitled "Wilberforce" (1832), all in Cocke Deposit, Cocke Papers; and Cocke to J. C. Cabell, 14 February 1832, Cabell Family Papers (Alderman Library, University of Virginia). See also Coyner, "Cocke," chap. 8 and 9.

13. John Hartwell Cocke Journal, 1863–64, especially 1–15, 16–22, 31–32, 51–79, Campbell Deposit, Cocke Papers. The essay begins in August 1863 under the title, "Earliest Recollections of Slavery."

14. J. Hector St. Jean de Crèvecoeur's discussion of American character and nationality is in his *Letters from an American Farmer*, eds. Albert Boni and Charles Boni (New York, 1925), "Letter III. What Is an American."

I

REFORM AND IDENTITY
IN A
SOUTHERN CONTEXT

1

The Percy Family, the "Adamses" of the Deep South: A Study of Creative Melancholy

Bertram Wyatt-Brown

> We tell you, tapping our brows,
>   The story as it should be, —
> As if the story of a house
>   Were told or ever could be.

—"Eros Turannos," E. A. Robinson (1916)

At the center of the peaceful cemetery of St. James Episcopal Church in Greenville, Mississippi, stands a bronze figure of a knight bearing the inscription "Patriot." The figure marks the grave of Senator LeRoy Percy, who died in 1929. Sometime in the early 1930s the monument was erected at the behest of the senator's son, William Alexander Percy, adoptive father of the novelist Walker Percy and attorney, poet, and author of a classic southern memoir, *Lanterns on the Levee* (1941). On the reverse side of the stela of white marble behind the statue is carved a stanza from "The Last Word," a poem by Matthew Arnold. The last three lines read, "Let the victors, when they come, / When the forts of folly fall, / Find thy body by the wall !"[1]

Will Percy, as he was popularly known, had many friends in the art world of New York. No doubt they recommended the sculptor, Malvina Hoffman, for the work he had in mind. At that period of his bachelor life, Percy had been unusually restless and wretched. In 1929 he had lost not only his father, whom he worshipped, but also his mother, Camille, and a favorite cousin, LeRoy Pratt Percy, the novelist Walker Percy's father. As soon as he had made arrangements with the eccentric, chain-smoking Hoffman, Will Percy had sailed for Bora Bora in the South Seas for a much-needed rest from the sorrows he could not easily put behind him.[2]

His choice of artist had been excellent; Hoffman had a facility for interpreting the dynamics of human movement. Her success was most evident in her studies of the commanding motions of the Russian ballerina Pavlova, her rumored lover.[3] In this case, a sense of kinetic energy lies beneath the tension of the muscles in the knight's face and in his frozen stance. Will Percy could not have been more gratified with the result. It expressed in the bitterest terms his sense of the world's injustice. In 1911, under the leadership of the racist demagogue James K. Vardaman, a sweeping majority of white farmers and laborers had defeated Will's father, Senator LeRoy Percy. Filling an almost-expired term, the senator represented the old order of southern noblesse oblige as well as the rising corporate elite of New South industry and commerce. Smarting from the humiliation, in 1922 he won belated retribution against a collarless mob, as the family viewed the Mississippi Democracy, when he and his son Will narrowly emerged victorious over the Ku Klux Klan in a local election that caught national attention. However, the triumph seemed transitory, and Will Percy grieved. Even if small victories might create social peace for a time, the decline of old-fashioned southern chivalry and sense of civic obligation would continue apace. "The good die when they should live, the evil live when they should die; heroes perish and cowards escape," Will Percy lamented in *Lanterns on the Levee*; "noble efforts do not succeed because they are noble, and wickedness is not consumed in his own nature."[4] The statue was meant to convey these thoughts to the pensive onlooker.

A specialist in bronze, Malvina Hoffman became the heir to the tradition of Augustus Saint-Gaudens, who had created the famous, shrouded figure of "Grief," as it is called, in the Rock Creek Cemetery of the national capital. In 1888 Henry Adams had commissioned the statue to memorialize the grave of his wife, "Clover" Hooper, who had killed herself in 1885. Like Will Percy, Adams would be best known for an autobiography, *The Education of Henry Adams* (1906), that mourns the passing of an era of familial greatness. As Will Percy was later to do, Adams promptly departed in his grief for the South Seas. Saint-Gaudens should design a figure, he directed before he left, to be emblematic of contemplation — gaunt, anonymous, timeless, cryptic. So it was. According to Ernest Samuels, Adams's biographer, "the statue became a touchstone of aesthetic and philosophical insight, his private challenge to a money-grubbing world." The grieving husband detected a hidden intractability or defiance in the face that gratified him, but the resistance seems passive and doubting. Having no other model available at his Manhattan studio, Saint-Gaudens had thrown a blanket over an Italian immigrant boy's head and shoulders. The result conveyed an hermaphroditic quality. Baffled, Theodore Roosevelt had ventured that the hooded figure was a woman, but Adams, who was greatly pleased with the work, disabused his friend. He declared that the sculptor "wanted to exclude sex and sink it in the idea of humanity.

"Grief" by Saint-Gaudens

"Patriot" by Hoffman

The figure is sexless."[5] Adams considered the statue an expression of his sorrow, even self-pity, not of his wife's character, but it was also to signify enigma and uncertainty of human existence.[6]

Although, like "Grief," the "Patriot" represents melancholy, Hoffman's creation is far from being abstract, sexless, and timeless; rather, it is masculine and martial. His thick, mailed hands rest on an unsheathed broadsword. In contrast to the lean and passive Saint-Gaudens statue, Senator LeRoy Percy's protector is stocky, concrete, oddly short. Although the battle is over and the specter of defeat hangs heavy, the mood is anything but submissive. Rage is gathering beneath the immobile features. Defiance sets the jaw. In having his father represented by so grim a pose, Will Percy wanted no sign of androgyny to cast doubt on family manhood. Despite his love of classical culture, he chose no Greek motif, no slim Ganymeade, no knight of the Gabriel Rossetti school, with long, rolled locks and sensuous mouth, to guard the grave. Instead, he had the New York sculptor create a barbaric figure, North European gothic. The warrior could be imagined as a legendary founder of the noble House of Percy — Algernon, for instance, who was the first of the lineage at Alnwick Castle in Northumberland to protect the realm of Harold from Scottish marauders, and then, with a fortuitous switch of sides, hailed the new regime of his fellow Norman, William.[7]

These two representations in bronze may symbolize key elements in the Percy and Adams families and the sectional cultures to which they made such remarkable contributions. Both families, in European societies, would have gained titles or have been accorded the sobriquet of aristocratic, but in the United States, monuments of stone — or of printed words — would have to suffice. Yet, in a sense the significance of the two clans is not comparable despite the power they both exercised in separate domains. Members of the Adams family twice occupied the White House, sat in Congress and in cabinets, represented the United States in Petersburg and London, taught at Harvard University, presided over national corporations and railroads, and wrote works of fiction, history, and biography that still earn the respect of scholars and remain in print for general readership. For three generations early in American history they were at the vortex of policy making, refusing always to stoop to the low arts of the politician, a matter of considerable pride but of doubtful electoral utility. Although in Walker Percy the family produced a figure of national rather than purely regional or local reputation, his predecessors on the genealogical tree, four southern nineteenth-century female writers of fiction and poetry, produced only one bestseller among the 20 works they published, and none of the publications deserves a late resurrection.[8] All in all, the contribution of the Percys was proportionately small, but location and opportunity, more than differences in intelligence or shrewdness, separated the trajectories of family careers.

Despite these disparities, much can be learned about the sense of identity that families can create and carry forward from generation to generation by exploring these two extraordinary lines and how that collective image may be shaped by internal factors of emotional legacies and external ones of regional influences. The most salient feature that draws together the Percys and Adamses is a common problem of deep suffering. The melancholy moods into which some members of the two families fell proved to be severe, but such affliction was also the very source of their creativity, imagination, and philosophical explorations. After showing how the annals of Percys and Adamses were marked by problems of genetic depression, other commonalities — and subtle differences based on regional variation — will emerge as well.

Unlike the Adamses, the Percys inhabited a relatively underpopulated and understudied region of the country, where, until the latter half of the nineteenth century, most of them led private lives. Also unlike the Calvinistic Adamses, the early Percys did not preserve family documents in a systematic way and wrote nothing introspective about their swings of temperament or existential problems for the edification of themselves and descendants. Each generation of Percys had to reinvent itself, because history, it seemed, periodically wiped the slate clean. When disappearance, early death, or suicide removed fathers, their sons and daughters had to become sui generis even as they replicated in their lives the heritage of family pride and integrity.

In contrast, the Adamses knew exactly who they were. They came from plain stock, ordinary farmers, who left England in the 1630s. One Henry Adams, yeoman, married into wealth on this side of the Atlantic.[9] No less important for the establishment of their rank in society, the Adamses could depend upon a sturdy cultural order in the environs of Boston and Cambridge. They always lived at the centers of national power — Boston and Washington — with lengthy sojourns in the capitals of Europe. The Percys remained in the backwater of the Lower South. However, many of the Percys, made rich from slaveholding and cotton planting, were quite at home in Europe, spoke French fluently, and had a refinement of taste equal to that of the Adamses. They had to reside far from their habitat to gain a college education — at Princeton, Harvard, the University of Virginia, or, closer to home, the University of the South, Sewanee, Tennessee. The early nineteenth-century women in the clan attended Madame Sigoigne's or Madame Grelaud's French-speaking academies in Philadelphia.[10]

When compared with the Adamses, whose origins were so easily traced to the seventeenth century in Massachusetts, the Percy family's roots were obscure, even troubling. The first American Percy, Charles, was an eighteenth-century rogue, an intellectual of sorts, and a self-promoting Irishman with doubtful claims to nobility. After arriving out of the mists of the Caribbean in 1775 to settle in British West Florida, he boasted to have been an officer in the King's Army, although no record of his regiment or rank has ever appeared. He also named his chief plantation "Northumberland House," a reference to the enormous palace on the Strand where the dukes of Northumberland resided when in London.[11]

Charles Percy's pretensions to gentility were designed to hide the fact that sometime in the 1770s he had left one wife, Margaret, in London, when in 1780 he married his third wife, Susan Collins, in what had recently become Spanish Louisiana. (The second wife, a Miss Burroughs, on an island in the Bermuda, had conveniently died after learning that Charles had a living spouse and even more conveniently had left no offspring to run him to ground later.) Nemesis, however, arrived in 1790 at Northumberland House in the form of a handsome 28-year-old lieutenant in the Royal Navy. Five years after his mother Margaret's death in the stews of London, Lieutenant Robert Percy crossed the Atlantic and confronted his father, who confessed his paternity but denied that he had ever been married to Margaret. Upon retirement from the service in 1803, Robert settled his Scottish wife and family on a large plantation near St. Francisville, Spanish Louisiana, within a score of miles of his half-brothers and sisters to the north. As a result, two Percy families lived side by side, including the "illegitimate" descendants of Susan Collins, some of whom died very young. The survivors of this third Percy union will be the chief concern here.[12]

Charles Percy did not live to witness the curious turn of fate that brought his two families into such proximity. Afflicted with a psychotic episode of depression, in 1794 he had tied an iron kettle to his neck and plunged into the creek that ran near Northumberland House. In the twentieth century, Will Percy, Walker, his ward, and other family members from the Susan Collins line rather enjoyed the problematic character of their progenitor. After gleefully reporting the manner of his death, Will Percy concluded in *Lanterns on the Levee*, "He was not exactly a credit to anybody, but, as ancestors go, he had his points." In fashioning the character of Dr. Tom More, a mad, saturnine, and charming lothario, in *Love in the Ruins* and *The Thanatos Syndrome*, Walker Percy borrowed something from this suicidal ancestor in whom he took considerable interest.[13]

Genial but passive in character, the family thought Susan and Charles's only surviving son, Thomas George, rather humdrum by comparison. During the years that John Adams at Braintree was corresponding with Thomas Jefferson at Monticello and his son John Quincy Adams was struggling in Washington with the Jacksonian majority in Congress, Thomas George Percy was merely raising cotton on his large plantation near Huntsville, Alabama. He left political ambitions to his best friend and brother-in-law, Senator John Williams Walker of

Alabama, whose patronym would figure in the Christian names of the Percy family for 150 years thereafter. Will Percy remarked that Squire Thomas Percy "cut no great figure in the world. He isn't a demanding ancestor."[14] One of Squire Percy's sons, William Alexander of Greenville, Mississippi, made the law a family vocation, as it was for some of the Adamses (notably John, John Quincy, and Charles Francis). After service in the Confederate Army as a colonel, the "Gray Eagle of the Valley," as this Percy was dubbed for his heroic exploits in the Shenandoah, was elected speaker of the Mississippi House of Representatives at a crucial moment in Reconstruction history.[15]

Early death for males inhibited the family's opportunity for more than local prominence, the average age at death being 39 from the eighteenth century to 1942, when Will Percy died at age 57. A number of male descendants of Charles Percy died in their early thirties.[16] Still more important, the Percys had no grand beginnings, as the Adamses had, with the American Revolution as the stage for their progenitor's contribution to the new republic. By the time the Percys' political moment had come in 1865, the world they inhabited had crashed in ruins. Former slaves had gained the franchise, and the recapturing of old seats of power meant no advancement to national prominence but simply a chance to rule over tenants and undeveloped wastelands. Even so, according to his many political friends, the brilliant attorney William Alexander Percy might have climbed the ladder to political prominence, even winning a seat in a Democratic cabinet, had death not cut him short in 1888 at the age of 53. The American male Percys, like the earls of Northumberland, were seldom destined to live a full span because of their inherited predisposition to ill health.[17]

In addition to a poor record of mortality, melancholia hobbled the Percys' ambition. Melancholia, of itself, was not necessarily an obstacle to political prominence. Abraham Lincoln, Jefferson Davis, Alexander Stephens (vice-president of the Confederacy), Robert Toombs (one-time secretary of state of the Confederacy), and others struggled with episodes of depression, and its ravages could be seen in their poor health, bouts of insomnia, and foul temper. Only Lincoln was able to master the last manifestation in self-deprecating humor.[18]

Affective disorder, as current medical language describes the condition, can be completely debilitating. So it was in the case of the Gray Eagle's brother, LeRoy Pope Percy, a doctor without a regular practice who in 1882 overdosed himself with laudanum. Will Percy later attributed his great uncle's melancholy to his worry over the impending death of a niece, 23 and newly married, whom he had been privately treating at Eureka Springs, Arkansas. She died the day after her uncle killed himself. The next generation also was ill-fated. In 1917 Walker Percy, Senator LeRoy Percy's brother and the nephew of the suicidal physician, placed a shotgun against his chest and fired. His son and law partner, LeRoy Pratt, ran to the gun room, but it was too late. On

July 9, 1929, LeRoy Pratt Percy followed his father's example, blasting himself with a shotgun charge under the chin.[19] Thus, from 1794 to 1929, every generation of the family included one male suicide.

Female members of the family suffered from the illness as well. Although Thomas George Percy was the only son who had been spared the illness, his sister Sarah lost her reason and had to be admitted to the Pennsylvania Hospital in Philadelphia in 1819. Her tragedy, when she was 39, was the result of a postpartum depression that came simultaneously with the birth of her second child in a second marriage. She remained under close supervision in the hospital until 1831, when Colonel Nathaniel Ware, her emotionally distant husband, had her discharged and placed in the hands of Sarah's eldest son. She died in 1835 at his plantation house in Natchez, never having recovered her mind. Sarah Ware's eldest daughter, Mary Jane Ellis LaRoche, was likewise afflicted with melancholia immediately after the birth of a son, Percy LaRoche. She died of consumption in 1844 under the care of a Philadelphia physician.[20]

The Adamses were almost as well-acquainted with this form of mental suffering as the Percys. Alcoholism often is a factor in the disease, and both families had difficulties along these lines. Two of John Quincy Adams's brothers and one of his three sons were alcoholics. Despite his artistic and literary talent, another son, George Washington Adams, also a heavy drinker and frequently in debt, sank under the weight of John Quincy Adams's expectations for him to rise, possibly, to the presidency himself. At the same time the young Adams had to witness the humiliating defeat that his father underwent in the election of 1828. In spring 1829 George Adams also learned that he had made a serving girl pregnant. Bearing these travails, he threw himself into the waters of New York harbor.[21] In his anguish, the surviving father felt "deserted by all mankind." He kept rehearing a phrase from a favorite French opera, *Richard Coeur de Leon*: "O, Richard! O mon Roi! L'Univers t'abandonne." Charles Francis was the only one of the former president's sons left to carry on the family line and its traditions.[22]

The same pattern could be found in the Percy family. John Walker Percy, brother of the Gray Eagle and LeRoy Pope, was reputed to have problems with alcohol. Heavy drinking may have been a factor in the early death in 1912 of William Armstrong Percy of Memphis, Senator LeRoy and Walker's eldest brother. Jay Tolson explains in his biography of the novelist Walker Percy that Walker's father LeRoy's "drinks before dinner may have exacerbated his bad moods."[23]

The demon of depression did not choose between the achievers and those of mediocre talent in either family. The condition induces feelings of inanition and worthlessness no matter how substantial the reality of success might be. The Adamses made no secret of their inner despair and the "painful greatness" that weighed upon their shoulders. "The history of my family," lamented Charles Francis Adams, "is not a pleasant one to remember. It is one of the great triumphs in the world but deep groans within, one of extraordinary brilliancy and deep corroding mortification." Although President John Adams apparently never was driven to attempt suicide (Abigail would never have permitted it), he sometimes fell into what a biographer calls "a dark tide of paranoia" that rendered him "depressed, hostile, and suspicious."24

Such a cast of mind resembled that of Senator LeRoy Percy after his election defeat in 1911. The senator developed a credo of Ciceronian honor, hard though it was to maintain. He turned reclusive and despairing after his wife Camille's death in 1929 and died several weeks later. Will Percy took his father's defeat as if he himself had been the loser, just as George Washington Adams had felt the world collapsing when his father lost in 1828 to the Jacksonians.25 Like his own father John, John Quincy Adams also struggled for control of his volatile feelings, fearful that, as he put it, "I have not enough of the Stoic in my Soul." According to Paul Nagel, Charles Francis Adams, Lincoln's representative at the Court of St. James, struggled from time to time with "loss of memory, lethargy, and depression." The U.S. minister could make one feel, Carl Schurz remarked, "as though the temperature of the room had dropped several degrees."26

The cold Adams demeanor, so in keeping with the Calvinistic heritage of New England, was not to be found among the Percys, a sociable and warrior breed, who hid their despondency behind the masks of conviviality and bellicosity, hunting trips, and visits in the 1880s to the mulatto Eliza Compton's house in Greenville for champagne parties lasting into the midnight hours. By contrast to the dour Adamses of Quincy and Washington, Will Percy had a presence that at once commanded positive notice. Walker Percy recalled that his guardian radiated "that mysterious quality we call charm, for lack of a better word, in such high degree that what comes to mind is not that usual assemblage of features and habits which make up our memories of people but rather a quality, a temper, a set of mouth, a look through the eye." However, Percy admitted that Will had a fierce temper and fiery look that always astonished and awed him.27 In fact, Will Percy was not as cheerful as his graciousness suggested. Beneath his wit and careful regard for others lay a deep sorrow that bordered on hopelessness. He was concerned that he could never become the man he thought his father was or the kind of man his father would admire. From Will's perspective, the formidable Delta attorney and senator "was kin to Hotspur and blood-brother to Richard Couer de Lion." One could tell Will Percy's unhappy state of mind by the eyes, Walker Percy remembered. "They were beautiful and terrible eyes, eyes to be careful around. Yet now, when I try to remember them, I cannot see them otherwise than as shadowed by sadness."28

People challenged by depression are attracted to those with similar difficulties. Walker Percy's troubled father, attorney LeRoy Pratt, married a woman of great charm, beauty, and intelligence in Martha Susan Phinizy, but she also began to reveal hints of melancholia after her husband's death in 1929. Her accidental death in 1932 involved feelings she little understood. She and the boys had joined Will Percy, her husband's first cousin once removed, in Greenville in autumn 1931. Gifted and determined as an instructor of family lore and values, Will Percy monopolized her sons, without indicating any interest in her as a woman. Her situation was anomalous. On April 2, the Saturday before Easter Sunday, she, with her youngest son Phinizy, age ten, drove her roadster over a railless bridge into a rain-swollen creek. While the car began to sink, she clutched at her son, making it impossible for him to wriggle out of the back window. She finally let him go; he escaped, reached shore, and ran for help, but by the time it arrived, she had drowned.[29]

Tragedy of a similar nature also had struck Henry Adams. Henry Adams's wife, Marian Hooper, known as "Clover," had an artistic temperament and showed great skill as a photographer. Like the Percys, the Hooper family had to cope with serious mental problems of a genetic character. Adams had been warned about the perils of marriage into that family. His brother Charles Francis Adams, Jr., had exclaimed on hearing of the engagement, "Heavens! — no — they're all crazy as coots. She'll kill herself, just like her aunt!" The aunt in question had fatally dosed herself with arsenic at the age of 28. Another aunt, Caroline Sturgis, who became fascinated with psychic phenomena, was thought, perhaps unfairly, to be mentally unstable. Aunt Carrie had deeply resented her brothers' education at Harvard when, according to the custom of the day, she was denied such intellectual stimulation and pathway to career, a complaint that Clover Hooper never voiced but must have felt. In 1887, two years after Clover's death, her sister, whose mind was said to have been as brilliant as hers, took her own life under the wheels of a locomotive.[30]

Indeed, Boston, like Greenville, Mississippi, seemed to have a disproportionate share of mentally unstable residents among its upper ranks. Hearing that yet another Boston matron had committed herself to the sanatorium at Somerville, Clover Adams remarked to a friend, "The insane asylum seems to be the goal of every good and conscientious Bostonian, babies and insanity the two leading topics. So and so has a baby. She becomes insane and goes to Somerville, baby grows up and promptly retires to Somerville." The reference to infants was not casual. She and Henry were childless. When she had to face the loss of her father, her misery and sense of worthlessness reached a climax. Like so many suicides, she briefly presented an outward appearance of serenity and improved health. On December 6, 1885, the kind of cold and gloomy day she always dreaded, Clover swallowed a phial of potassium cyanide, a chemical used in her photographic work. Henry reached her almost at once, but it was still too late for any rescue to succeed.[31]

Suicide was both a cause and an effect of the depression that ran in the two families. When Senator LeRoy Percy died on Christmas Eve, 1929, after giving up on life and refusing to eat, Will Percy fell into a deep despondency, as if he were somehow responsible for his dispirited father's death. A few years later, Will had finally reconciled himself to the loss of the individual who meant most to him in life, perhaps because he could never win LeRoy Percy's unqualified approval. The senator had always considered his son a disappointment — effeminate in manner and unlikely to produce heirs. Will Percy repressed the pain that knowledge of LeRoy's dissatisfaction constantly gave him. Grieving for himself as well as his parent, he remarked to a friend that gradually one learns "to endure the dark and the solitude with an incredible sort of dignity."[32]

Henry Adams reacted similarly to the loss of Clover, who had come to mean more to him than anyone else. "I am weary of the world's cackle and bustle, and the dreary recurrence of small talk," Henry lamented. Gradually, like Will Percy, he recovered. Yet, close to the end of his life he wryly recorded, "Thank God, I never was cheerful. I come from the happy stock of the Mathers, who, as you remember, passed sweet mornings reflecting [on] the goodness of God and the damnation of infants." Following a stroke, Henry Adams twice tried to fling himself from his sickroom window.[33]

Henry Adams had little of the amiability and good humor that Will Percy possessed, but with regard to inner feelings, they shared much in common. Neither could break the habit of self-deprecation or overcome the episodes of despondency that began in their earliest years. Henry Adams remembered his childhood as a time of learning his deficiencies. He did not grow at the pace of his elder brothers; he was no good in fistfights. "The habit of doubt; of distrusting his own judgment" and "the horror of ennui" were common to most New Englanders of his time, he recalled, but he experienced these feelings with greater acuteness. "His brothers were the type; he was the variation," he said, putting his thoughts and feelings in the distant third person. Likewise, Will Percy remembered sadness as a constant companion in childhood. Nain, his 16-year-old black nurse, used to sing a song that made him "feel so lost and lonely that tears would seep between my lids," until Nain would ask, "What's de madder Peeps? Whut you cryin' fur?" These and other memories meant little in themselves, but they suggested that Will Percy felt his parents' unarticulated dismay and further sensed that nothing he could say or do would alter their attitude.[34]

In young manhood, matters did not necessarily improve for either Will Percy or Henry Adams. At several points in his early life, Henry Adams contemplated suicide in a despondency over career. Like Will

Percy, he loved his parents but felt them distant and alien. Each time, he pulled himself together, and then, after the last bout of worry after the Civil War, he embarked on literary and scholarly pursuits and settled down in the late 1860s in Washington with Marian Hooper. He had overcome his sense of unworthiness in comparison with his accomplished father, but he remained in the shadow of the great name of Adams. Even when he published *The Education* late in life, he asserted to Charles Milnes Gaskell that "the volume is due to piety on account of my father and John Hay." To Henry James he wrote that its appearance was "a mere shield of protection in the grave."[35] Both remarks reflected an inner mood and were not, as might appear, signs of false pride or sly modesty to garner praise. That was the way he genuinely felt, although a fierce sense of privacy and reticence was involved as well. The first publication of *The Education* in 1906 was restricted to 100 copies, solely for friends.[36]

To Will Percy, the shackles that the past placed upon his life were even more inhibiting than those that Henry Adams faced. The New Englander eventually surmounted his, but Percy never did. He looked upon his forebears, especially the Gray Eagle and his own father LeRoy, as demigods whom he could never dare to match. He feared his father's contempt, but in fact, what haunted him most was his own sense of shame, for those in the South with homoerotic leanings had to be extremely circumspect. For instance, in 1895 a case of premeditated murder erupted out of a male sexual encounter at the state Democratic convention in Jackson. T. Dabney Marshall, a wellborn young legislator from Vicksburg, probably inebriated, made advances upon his hotel roommate, R. M. Dinkins. Humiliated by the gossip that threw into question his heterosexuality and manhood, Marshall gathered some kinsmen, accosted Dinkins at a train station, and killed him with two bullets. When arrested, Marshall pleaded justifiable homicide. "The man had done me an irreparable wrong," leaving him no "honorable way out of it."[37]

For the masses of southern whites, an interest in artistic things and a loose-wristed manner were invitations to mockery and social ostracism. Although somewhat immune because of his family's standing, Will Percy felt the sting of "redneck" comments as he walked to his law office.[38] A brief, typed, undated sketch in the Percy family papers revealed his feelings sometime after Percy had returned from Harvard Law School to join his father's law firm and had taken residence once more in his parents' house. "It was the fifth autumn," he begins. "For the first time there was a definite chill in the air. Snow had begun to fall earlier in the afternoon, but it had soon turned from snow to rain. 'The fifth autumn is upon me,' I said. At that time, five years ago," he continues, "I knew nothing of what was taking place. My father and mother looked at me strangely. My mother gave thanks to God that I was untouched by sin, but she would stop in the midst of her words and weep bitterly. My father said, 'It is in the spring that the seed is eager, is it not?' But my mother would cover his lips with her hands. 'Do not speak,' she would say. 'We do not know what we may be saying.'" He used to walk for hours, Will Percy explains, a solitary figure under the autumnal trees, whose "brown leaves had fallen in slow spirals." He watched "the dark movement of the river" before returning late at night to "hear my mother crying out in her sleep and my father in his room pacing the floor." He would go to his own room, move his chair to the window, pull a bathrobe about his shoulders, "and smoke cigarettes." He confessed, "Sometimes I would sit that way all night. 'The fifth autumn is upon me,' I said. 'And I have not forgotten. It will always be so. When the first snow falls and the first chill creeps into the air my peace will be broken. Spring, that destroys the sleep of others, is to me a release from pain. But always in autumn I shall be stricken and confused with memory.'"[39] Will Percy never published the piece.

For the Adamses, the very opposite outlook prevailed. Exposure of their commonplace books, diaries, and correspondence was a matter of conscience and duty — indeed, of "family honor," as one scholar has called it. As early as 1840, Charles Francis Adams declared that private family letters should be published in order "to transmit to posterity the details for a narration in as complete a form as will in all probability ever be attained by the imperfect faculties of man." The southern habit of reticence was a subtext, it might be said, to the venerable themes of honor and depression to be found at every turn in the Percys' history. In Aeschylus's *Agamemnon*, the Herald asks, "Whence came this gloom of melancholy upon thy spirit?" The Chorus replies, "For a long time I have considered silence a medicine for harm." The ancient mode was far from effective, as the play reveals.[40]

As if to fill the void, the Percys adopted the language and themes of legend with which to invest the family's identity. Will Percy was convinced that Charles Percy was indeed "the lost heir of the earls of Northumberland," although he put the matter in print in the form of a question. Will's uncle "Willie" Armstrong Percy of Memphis tried to prove a connection with Bishop Thomas Percy, a famous collector of folk poetry in the eighteenth century, and with Thomas Percy, leader of the infamous Gunpowder Plot of 1605. With reference to the latter, William Percy conjectured in 1904, "This cheerfully disposed old gentleman was descended from the 4th Earl of Northumberland." In 1907 LeRoy Percy, Will's father, boasted to a cousin, "We claim back to the Northumberland Percys." When in 1917 the Birmingham *News* announced the death of Walker Percy at his own hand, the editor noted that the attorney "came of the old English Hot-spur Percy blood, and there flowed in his veins the finest traditions of the old Virginia gentlemen. He had the truest of pride, and was the embodiment of honor in all his relations." These fancies afforded Walker Percy in his novels the chance to identify the family with the Arthurian legends of Sir

Percival, with the unruly Harry Hotspur, son of the first earl of Northumberland, and, finally, with the early seventeenth-century "Wizard Earl," ninth in the line, noted for his devotion to alchemy and his melancholy temperament.[41]

Ambiguity of lineage was a distinctively southern — particularly southwestern — feature, whereas the Adamses and other New Englanders could ascertain from the meticulous court records who their ancestors were. Partially because of his ambivalent family heritage, Walker Percy could not accept uncritically either the ethic of a smug New South suburban enclave like Covington, where Percy had lived outside New Orleans since the 1950s, or that of the racially bigoted Old South to be found in the hamlets nearby. By contrast, the Adamses never lost faith in the unbroken customs of an austere gentility and, like most Bostonians, assumed the superiority of their city and region, even when they lived far away.[42]

Will Percy found that although he could celebrate the past and its connections with dim and noble times lost in the mists of history, it was also emotionally draining. He idolized his father and made him the centerpiece of *Lanterns on the Levee*. The subtitle is *The Recollections of a Planter's Son*. "It was hard having such a dazzling father," Will Percy said of the senator, "no wonder I longed to be a hermit. . . . He was the fairest thinker and the wisest, he could laugh like the Elizabethans, he could brood and pity till sweat covered his brow and you could feel him bleed inside." In a similar vein, "He stood alone," Henry Adams wrote of his father, Charles Francis Adams. "He had no master — hardly even his father." For Henry Adams, as for Will Percy, the father exhibited "perfect poise" and "intuitive self-adjustment," bravery, honesty. Each was above the ordinary foibles of mankind.[43]

Both sons, who despaired of ever matching their parents' accomplishments, focused their frustration on the political realm and wrote their own jeremiads. The common and central message of *The Education of Henry Adams* and *Lanterns on the Levee* was the moral decline of their respective regions and, by extension, of the United States as a whole.[44] Each work, however, conveyed this message in the idiom of its own sectional culture.

The concept of the southern hero had a social function in a biracial society where order was thought to depend more upon men in full command than upon institutions and law. The moral center of southern culture, thus, lay in the heroic figures of the southern martital romance. For this reason, William Gilmore Simms and even such post–Civil War writers as John Esten Cooke, Thomas Nelson Page, and Thomas Dixon of the cavalier school were not creating artificial melodramas for their own sake. Through fiction, they prescribed a way to judge the world. There was a close connection between southern fiction and the way people actually thought and perceived themselves and their ethical and social aspirations. Walker Percy developed a much more critical

approach to the traditional heroic model than his cousin Will was capable of doing, but he could not entirely escape the combined influence of regional standards and personal longings for a father's praise and acceptance. In *Lancelot*, Walker Percy's most difficult and impressively Dostoevskian novel, the honor-bound hero of the old romantic style becomes a Faustian antihero. Nevertheless, the work conveys the southern traditional scheme of things as an authorial criticism of a soulless modern order. Percy used the half-crazed Father Smith in *The Thanatos Syndrome*, his last novel, to the same purpose. The messenger may be flawed, Percy implies, but the message of American waywardness he wishes the reader to take extremely seriously by seeing it through the lens of a stern moral order — obsolete though it might have become.[45]

Although Walker Percy was eager to assert themes attuned to the general conditions of Western man, the novelist like his guardian Will Percy, was very much involved in the traditions of the Old South, particularly the allegiance to classical Stoicism that Will Percy had taught him to respect if not follow. In his essays and interviews and in his novels *The Moviegoer*, *The Last Gentleman*, and *Lancelot*, Walker Percy stressed the South's long adherence to the models of proper conduct that the Stoics had expounded. "The Southern gentleman," he wrote in *Commonweal*, "did live in a Christian edifice, but he lived there in the strange fashion" of one "who will neither go inside nor put it entirely behind him but stands forever grumbling on the porch. . . . How like him to go into Chancellorsville or the Argonne with Epictetus in his pocket; how unlike him to have had the Psalms."[46]

Actually, from a historical perspective, Walker Percy underestimated the strong Protestant strain that was fast eroding eighteenth-century classicism, a pessimism about the future that mirrored the melancholy felt within the life of the family itself. The Stoic ethic was being kept alive through the love-hate relationship of the modern southern artist — William Faulkner, Allen Tate, Caroline Gordon, and others — and, on a personal level, it was still a vital part of Walker Percy's ongoing dialogue with his guardian. As Jan Gretlund, the literary critic, has noted, "From the start, the novelist defined his fiction in relation to his uncle's [*sic*, Will Percy's] ideas, as if he were having a crucial argument with him and he is still arguing with him."[47] Like Will Percy, Walker could not escape the influence of a father figure, nor could he shake off the family heritage of despair.

A yearning for liberation came to the latter-day Percys and others of the Faulkner generation while the old order collapsed amid the savagery of World War I. Just as depression sometimes led to suicide in this highly gifted family, ambition sometimes killed the spirit and even the body when pursued without respite and perhaps without prudence. The "consuming unsleeping appeaseless thirst for glory" of which William Faulkner wrote and, indeed, personally experienced as an artist was itself a means to gain immortality on earth and conquer the feelings of nothingness that were the consequence of a mordant self-accusatory stance. For centuries in human history, life offered little else but extremities of wealth, vitality, and power on the one hand and penury, helplessness, and marginality on the other. There was seldom much sense of a comfortable middle ground.

Even before Walker Percy gave voice to the emptiness of value and meaning in the modern world, his Percy forebears and numerous others in the upper ranks of southern life had reasons for gloom and even fury. Because so many experienced the multiple burdens of losing the Civil War, loved ones, and wealth, the South's devotion to the Lost Cause legend actually was part of a collective mourning process. The monuments erected in bronze or stone, the Confederate Veterans Day rallies, the poems to banners furled and tattered, the recitation of battle stories that postwar politicians uttered to stir constituents — all were rituals that helped the South deal with the problem of demoralization. How else could one continue to believe in the same God who apparently had forsaken the cause and region? However, the southerners' mourning lacked its natural outcome, that is, the moment when finally grief and anger are purged so that survivors may go on with their lives. Out of such unstable materials sprang the South's need for legends of brooding knights, cavaliers, gentlemen, bloody action, and honorable, defeated aspirations.

These were not factors that the Adamses had to face. They were on the winning side, their wealth undisturbed, their homes unravaged. Moreover, they could live tranquil lives, without the slightest reason to expect a challenge from another member of their social class. At Harvard, observed Adams, New Englanders could slip noiselessly to the floor in their inebriation, but the Virginians "became quarrelsome and dangerous. When a Virginian had brooded a few days over an imaginary grief and substantial whiskey, none of his northern friends could be sure that he might not be waiting, round the corner, with a knife or pistol."[48]

The Percy clan of the Deep South shared and invoked a regional tradition of violence and heroism in which despair and ambition, denial and self-evocation came together with sometimes tragic results. Depression stimulates countermeasures, especially at moments of crisis. Will Percy expressed these feelings when describing his participation as a decorated hero in World War I. Fighting in the trenches of France, Percy wrote in *Lanterns on the Levee*, "had meaning, and daily life hasn't: it was part of a common endeavor, and daily life is lonely and isolated." In the case of the Percys, depression goaded them to make an imprint upon history, to defend community interests as personally conceived, to gain power over men and money, not in the genteel manner of the Adamses in the North but in the frontier mode of the truculent South. For Will Percy, World War I provided an opportunity to reach the heights of military bravery that his ancestors allegedly had attained but his father never had experienced. Nevertheless, for the worshipping son to see his father come home after bird hunting, looking "so heroic and gay, smelling warmish of feathers and corduroy and dogs" was a grander sight than his own homecoming in 1919, wearing a Croix de Guerre with a gold and silver star on his chest. The senator and Camille were filled "with pride and thanksgiving," but for the returning veteran, their pleasure "was embarrassing." Will declared, "I have never before or since felt so incapable of emotion, so dead inside." Other battle-scarred soldiers mourned with him: "It's over, the only great thing you were ever part of. It's over, the only heroic thing we all did together. What can you do now? Nothing, nothing."[49] To survive when so many had fallen was itself a source of anguish, but the longing for lost comradeship would endure.

Walker Percy once reported sarcastically to the critic Wilfred Sheed, "You know, a Southerner never saw a war he didn't like!" including the vicious one in Viet Nam.[50] It was a matter of permanent regret for Walker Percy that as a resident at Bellevue Hospital in New York he had contracted tuberculosis in 1942 and was possibly destined to die in a safe and antiseptic sanatorium rather than in a foxhole. His two brothers served with distinction, returning with decorations as marks of their valor. With respect to the glories of warfare, the southerner was more attuned than other Americans to the rest of the world. The founding New Englanders had not come from the bleak, conservative Borderlands but from the East of England, and John Adams and his descendants reflected the stolid, orderly values of that district. None of the Adamses of the nineteenth century served in uniform. In fact, Henry Adams's wartime depression stemmed in part from a sense of guilt that his assignment was as his father's secretary at the U.S. ministry in London and not a post in the Union forces.

No wartime service was possible for Walker, LeRoy, and William Armstrong Percy, but all three brothers, sons of the Gray Eagle, made political struggle a battlelike affair. During LeRoy's tumultuous campaign to defend his senatorial seat against Vardaman in 1911, they, as well as LeRoy's son Will, carried concealed firearms, which they were more than prepared to use if need arose. In fact, as an aide to his brother's faltering campaign, the novelist Walker Percy's grandfather plotted at a hotel restaurant in Lauderdale Springs, Mississippi, with young Will Percy and his own teenage son to tempt the Vardamanite campaign leader, Theodore Bilbo, into reaching for a gun as an excuse to gun him down. Bilbo, however, refused to respond when called a slimy son of a bitch and other epithets. He continued eating his breakfast cereal as if spooning it down required his undistracted attention.[51] On December 7, 1941, remembering his World War I experiences, Will Percy rejoiced that the United States would have to war against Japan and Germany and envied his adopted sons' chance to fight. In Walker

Percy's *The Moviegoer*, Aunt Emily Cutrer repeats a constant refrain on Will Percy's lips: "In this world goodness is destined to be defeated. But a man must go down fighting. That is the victory. To do anything less is to be less than a man."[52]

Because Walker Percy's father, whom everyone called "Roy," had taken up the dangerous new experiment of flying, he was ordered to serve as an instructor at U.S. bases, and much to his frustration, he never reached the front in World War I. Reportedly, in the 1920s, Roy Percy and another Birmingham attorney, Will Denson, each of them a crack shot, prepared to fight it out over a courtroom dispute before they both realized that neither one of them would survive a shootout. With mutual agreement and a shake of hands, they canceled their private duel.[53] The era of Percy violence came to a close when Roy Percy shot himself in the attic of his house in Birmingham. All the violence thereafter would appear only in fictional form through the pen of his son Walker.

Violence may have occupied one end of the Percys' axis, but a quest for spiritual assurance resided at the other, a pursuit that also engaged the Adamses. Given the mordant temperament of the two clans, a search for an anchor of faith to weather the storms within and outside their minds would seem natural. In this respect, regional culture affected both families. The Percy founder (whom Will Percy liked to call "Don Carlos") had been Roman Catholic. Perhaps it was only a matter of convenience during the Spanish occupation, because Charles Percy boasted of his standing with Governor Gayoso De Lemos of Natchez. Yet, a number of Don Carlos's descendants with a literary cast of mind converted to Catholicism or married Catholic partners. Camille Bourges Percy, Will Percy's mother, who came from French parentage, reared him in her faith. In fact, until he went to Sewanee for college, he was so devout that it worried his parents, who feared he might embrace celibacy and join the priesthood. At the University of the South, an Episcopal school, Will lost his faith completely. For the last time he returned from mass in Winchester, some 12 miles away, "mournful and unregretful, knowing thenceforth I should breathe a starker and a colder air, with no place to go when I was tired."[54] After Will Percy's death but while his memory was still very much alive, Walker picked up the discarded religious standard and carried it to the end of his life.

The loss of Christian belief scarcely meant a lessening of Will Percy's passion for moral certainty. He fastened his hopes upon the austere code of honor that the Emperor Marcus Aurelius had adumbrated in his Stoic "meditations." His father LeRoy had adopted that credo as solace for his own defeats. "I guess a man's job is to make the world a better place to live in, so far as he is able — always remembering the result will be infinitesimal — and to attend to his own soul."[55] That was the Stoic message that the senator conveyed to his son and that Will

Percy then passed along as the ultimate voice of wisdom to his ward, Walker Percy.

Like Henry Adams, who was also an agnostic, but out of the Protestant rather than Catholic tradition, Will Percy was, nevertheless, fascinated with religious issues. Like Adams and so many intellectuals of the Victorian era who had timorously entered the Age of Doubt, Rationalism, and Darwinian science, he was intrigued with the medieval Age of Faith. Will Percy's poems celebrated holy men, notably St. Francis, but also Mary Magdalene and Mary, mother of God.[56] The most impressive and simplest of his verses, written in 1924, was called "His Peace." In it, Percy had dwelt upon a consequence of divine grace that Walker Percy would many years later make a theme in his novels: the solitariness and affliction that the Christian pilgrim experiences even when equipped with the favor of grace. In "His Peace," the poet invokes the story of the ordinary "fisher-folk" whose lives had been reshaped by the peace of God, a benediction that also had destroyed them. The apostles had proclaimed the good news but in their martyrdom discovered, as all Christians would, that "The peace of God, it is no peace, / But strife closed in the sod." Yet, despite the attendant agony, the poet entreats his fellow believers to "pray for but one thing, / The marvelous peace of God."[57]

When Walker Percy contemplated his religious yearnings in the 1940s and converted to Catholicism, he was fulfilling a mission — completing what Will Percy had failed to do, even on his deathbed, by returning to a faith that offered structure, ritual, and doctrine as antidote to anomie and self-dissolution, both of which afflictions the Church considered grievous sins against the Holy Spirit. In Will's opinion, there was no rest in life, no freedom from pain, only temporary moments of companionship and rapture. Such had been his own experience and, indeed, the experience of a family, always striving for perfection, for honor, for justice. That was what mattered — the heroic struggle on behalf of a noble cause. In Will's judgment, redemption ends in a bleak prospect, in the "sod," not in heaven.

These concepts would scarcely have been alien to the thoughts of Henry Adams, as Will Percy discovered. Janet Dana Longcope, a distant cousin from the Royal Navy Lieutenant Robert Percy side of the line, lived near Henry Adams in Washington and often sat by the side of his sickbed. In 1919, as a long and close friend, she advised the returning war veteran Will Percy, whose spirits were especially low at the time, to read Adams's *Mont-St. Michel and Chartres*, a copy of which she forwarded to him. Adams, "an old, old man," she remarked to her cousin, "could have written Ecclesiastes there was such a taste of ashes in his philosophy." Her choice was appropriate. Percy found an affinity with the melancholy Yankee, with Adams's laments for the decline of aristocracy and the rise of modern vulgarity, tastelessness, and shallow materialism — all of which Percy would later echo with a southern accent in *Lanterns on the Levee*.[58]

The two statues whose description opened this chapter not only reveal something of the character of the two families but also the regional cultures in which they were at home. The Saint-Gaudens statue has a peculiarly abstract though evocative character. It is neither Christian nor pagan, neither modern nor ancient. Its statue's donor wisely observed in *The Education of Henry Adams*, "The interest of the figure was not in its meaning, but in the response of the observer." Adams noticed that clergymen visiting the cemetery were outraged and passionately denounced to their companions "the figure of despair, of atheism, of denial." With a certain perversity or bitterness, Adams, however, said it represented "the Peace of God," a phrase that Will Percy would have appreciated.[59] In view of his own and his intellectual wife Clover's agnosticism, there may have been little difference between the one interpretation and the other. Yankee society had turned away from the God of the Puritan forefathers, but as an abstraction, "Grief" exemplified the disembodied, Platonic, and coldly rational disposition of the Unitarian and Transcendental legacy. There is no hint of sexuality, no sign of tension between the glorious past of Adamses and their political impotence in the age of democracy, but its somber beauty is as moving as a Mahler symphony.

In contrast, "Patriot" signified the romantic, honor-obsessed, and patriarchal character of the South. Will Percy meant it to symbolize the martial values to which he had dedicated himself in World War I but also the meaning of his father's life. At the close of *Lanterns on the Levee*, he moves among the graves of his forebears and contemporaries in the Greenville cemetery. The memorialist imagines "the long wall of a rampart sombre with sunset, a dusty road at its base." Above the fortress he sees "the glorious high gods, Death and the rest," while below on the highway move the "tribes of men, tired, bent, hurt, and stumbling, each man alone." With Hoffman's bronze in mind, he then has the statue speak as "the High God" and challenges the traveler with the words, "'Who are you?' The pilgrim I know should be able to straighten his shoulders, to stand his tallest, and to answer defiantly, 'I am your son.'"[60]

NOTES

1. Quoted in *Memphis Commercial Appeal*, 4 November 1933.

2. Interview with Mrs. A. K. Stokes, in William Charles Sallis, "A Study of the Life and Times of LeRoy Percy" (M.S. thesis, Mississippi State College, 1957), 166; LeRoy Percy to Mrs. Anne K. Stokes, 12 August, telegram, to Mrs. LeRoy Pratt Percy, 13 August, to William Alexander Percy, 17 August, telegram, Secretary to William Armstrong Percy (nephew), 19 October 1929, Percy Family MSS (Mississippi Department of Archives and History, Jackson, hereafter MDAH); Carol Malone,

"William Alexander Percy: Knight to His People, Ishmael to Himself, and Poet to the World" (M.A. thesis, University of Mississippi, 1964), 19.

3. Malvina Hoffman, *Yesterday is Tomorrow: A Personal History* (New York, 1965); Jay Tolson, *Pilgrim in the Ruins: A Life of Walker Percy* (New York, 1992), 49.

4. William Alexander Percy, *Lanterns on the Levee: Recollections of a Planter's Son* (1941; reprint ed. Baton Rouge, 1973), 154.

5. Quotations in Ernest Samuels, *Henry Adams* (Cambridge, 1989), 279, 280.

6. Hoffman, *Yesterday is Tomorrow*, 115–29, 376 (probably an inaccurate date); Patricia O'Toole, *The Five of Hearts Club: An Intimate Portrait of Henry Adams and His Friends, 1880–1918* (New York, 1990), 165–66; R. P. Blackmur, *Henry Adams* (New York, 1980), 339–43.

7. *Burke's Genealogical and Heraldic History of the Knightage*, Peter Townsend, ed. (105th ed., London, 1970), 1998; Edward Barrington De Fonblanque, *Annals of the House of Percy, from the Conquest to the Opening of the Nineteenth Century* (2 vol., London, 1887), 1:1ff. *Als Gernon* means "William with the Whiskers," the latter hair style being a Saxon custom and Normans being clean-shaven.

8. The four writers were Catherine Ann Warfield, the most prolific of them all and author of the popular gothic *The Household of Bouverie*; her sister Eleanor Percy Lee, who coauthored with Catherine two books of poetry; Sarah Ann Dorsey, their niece; and Kate Lee Ferguson, daughter of Eleanor Percy Lee.

9. Edward Chalfant, *Both Sides of the Ocean: A Biography of Henry Adams, His First Life, 1838–1862* (Hamden, 1982), 34.

10. See Princeton Alumni Subject Files for Thomas George Percy and Thomas George Ellis (Princeton University Archives); Samuel Brown to John Williams Walker, 29 June 1821, John Williams Walker MSS (Alabama Department of Archives and History, Montgomery); Samuel Brown to Orlando Brown, 19 June 1822, Samuel and Orlando Brown MSS (Filson Club, Louisville); Lucy Leigh Bowie, "Madame Grelaud's French School," *Maryland Historical Magazine* 39 (1944): 141–48.

11. See John Hereford Percy, *The Percys of Louisiana and Mississippi, 1776–1943* (Baton Rouge, 1943), 5; Sargent Prentiss Knut to Mary D. Butler Dana, 14 March 1913, Duncan Longcope and Mellie L. Johansen Family Papers, Cornhill Farm, Lee, Massachusetts (private collection, hereafter Longcope-Johansen Collection).

12. See, for instance, Percy to Percy, 7 May 1792, an undated, unsigned document located in the Longcope-Johansen Collection, and Robert Dow to Robert Percy, 27 July 1804, in the John Hereford Papers owned by Dr. O. M. Thompson and William Wright, Baton Rouge, Louisiana.

13. Percy, *Lanterns on the Levee*, 40; Francis Pousset to Governor Gayoso de Lemos, 31 January 1794, Book C. p. 95, Spanish Records (Office of the Chancery Clerk, Adams County Courthouse, Natchez, Mississippi); Robert Dow to Robert Percy, 12 February 1794, in John Hereford Percy, *The Percy Family of Louisiana and Mississippi, 1776–1943* (Baton Rouge, 1943), 50; Walker Percy, *Love in the Ruins: The Adventures of a Bad Catholic at a Time Near the End of the World* (New York, 1971) and *Lancelot* (New York, 1977).

14. Percy, *Lanterns on the Levee*, 271; Hugh C. Bailey, *John Williams Walker: A Study in the Political, Social and Cultural Life of the Old Southwest* (University, 1964).

15. William Alexander Percy, Alumni Office Records (Princeton University Archives), and *Biographical and Historical Memoirs of Mississippi* (1891; 2 vol., reprint ed., 1978), 2:582; *Jackson Clarion-Ledger* [?], 26 October 1930, newspaper clipping, William Alexander Percy Subject File (MDAH); *Greenville Times*, 12 December 1874 (quotation), 2 January 1875, 17 March 1875; James Wilford Garner, *Reconstruction in Mississippi* (1901; reprint ed., Baton Rouge, 1968), 311.

16. Percy, *Percy Family*, 65, 66; *Nashville Presbyterian Record*, 16 December 1848, and other papers among the genealogical records in the Charles Brown Percy Papers, I-A-5 (Tennessee Historical Society, Tennessee State Archives Building, Nashville, hereafter TSA); see Thomas George Ellis (Charles Percy's grandson), tombstone, Routh Cemetery, Homochitto Street, Natchez.

17. "Death of Col. W. A. Percy," *Greenville Times*, 21 January 1888, clipping in LeRoy Percy Family MSS (MDAH); Nannie Armstrong Percy to Ladie Armstrong, 1 January 1888, Armstrong Family Papers (Southern Historical Collection, University of North Carolina, Chapel Hill). On Northumbrian mortality and ill health, see De Fonblanque, *Annals of the House of Percy*, 2:487.

18. See Lynda Lasswell Crist and Mary Seaton Dix, eds., *The Papers of Jefferson Davis, 1856–1860* (6 vol., Baton Rouge, 1989), 6:196n; William C. Davis, *Jefferson Davis: The Man and His Hour* (New York, 1991); Paul D. Escott, *After Secession: Jefferson Davis and the Failure of Confederate Nationalism* (Baton Rouge, 1978), 260–63, (quotation) 262; see also Clifford Dowdy, *Experiment in Rebellion* (New York, 1946), 32, 70, 143, 205, 304, 346, 359; Thomas E. Schott, *Alexander H. Stephens of Georgia* (Baton Rouge, 1988), 9, 17, 22, 58–59, 134–35, 189–90, 453, 501–3; Stephen B. Oates, *With Malice Toward None: The Life of Abraham Lincoln* (New York, 1977), 31, 462–63; William H. Herndon and Jesse W. Weik, *Abraham Lincoln: The True Story of a Great Life* (2 vol., New York, 1892), 1:130; and Howard I. Kushner, *Self-Destruction in the Promised Land: A Psychocultural Biology of Suicide* (New Brunswick, 1989), 141.

19. Percy, *Lanterns on the Levee*, 345; *Greenville Times* (Miss.), 30 June 1882; *Birmingham News*, 9 February 1917, 9 July 1929; *Birmingham Age-Herald*, 9 February 1917, 9 July 1929.

20. Sarah Percy Ware, tombstone, Routh Cemetery, Homochitto Street, Natchez; Percy, *Percy Family*, 65, 66; *Nashville Presbyterian Record*, 16 December 1848, and other papers among the genealogical records in the Percy Papers, I-A-5 (TSA); Percy, *Lanterns on the Levee*, 272–73; *Greenville Times*, 30 June 1882.

21. Earl N. Herbert, *The Force So Much Closer Home: Henry Adams and the Adams Family* (New York, 1977), 4 (quotation). John Quincy Adams had just vacated the White House when the tragedy took place. Chalfant, *Both Sides of the Ocean*, 35–39. Samuel Flagg Bemis, *John Quincy Adams and the Union* (New York, 1956), 178–81, takes the father's part and condemns the emotionally disturbed young man on purely moral grounds.

22. Paul C. Nagel, *Descent from Glory: Four Generations of the John Adams Family* (New York, 1983), 5; Chalfant, *Both Sides of the Ocean*, 38–39.

23. William Armstrong Percy III, interview with author, 22 July 1989, Boston; Tolson, *Pilgrim in the Ruins*, 44.

24. Nagel, *Descent from Glory*, 3, 5, 18; Page Smith, *John Adams* (2 vol., Garden City, 1962), 2:736, 822, 867, 1006 (quotation).

25. Interview with Mrs. Anne K. Stokes, in Sallis, "A Study of the Life and Times of LeRoy Percy," 166; LeRoy Percy to Mrs. Anne K. Stokes, 12 August (telegram), Percy to Mrs. LeRoy Pratt Percy, 13 August, to William Alexander Percy, 17 August (telegram), Secretary to William Armstrong Percy (nephew), 19 October 1929, Percy Family MSS (MDAH); Lewis Baker, *The Percys of Mississippi: Politics and Literature in the New South* (Baton Rouge, 1982), 148–49.

26. Nagel, *Descent from Glory*, 99, 284; Carl Schurz quoted in Ernest Samuels, *The Young Henry Adams* (Cambridge, 1948), 331n.

27. Entries for 9 August, 23 December 1904, Henry Waring Ball 1885–1935, Diary, p. 57 (MDAH); Walker Percy, "Introduction" to Percy, *Lanterns on the Levee*, vii–viii.

28. Percy, "Introduction" to Percy, *Lanterns on the Levee*, viii (quotation), 57 (quotation).

29. Interview by author with Mrs. Charles (Donie) Allison, Birmingham, 7 August 1988; Tolson, *Pilgrim in the Ruins*, 47, 48, 98; Percy, "Introduction" to Percy, *Lanterns on the Levee*, viii, ix, 333; entries for 7 April 1931 and 3 April 1932, Harry Ball Diary; Malone, "William Alexander Percy," 33; *Greenville Delta Democrat-Times*, 2 April 1932.

30. Eugenia Kaledin, *The Education of Mrs. Henry Adams* (Philadelphia, 1981), 45–50, 225, 239, 240; Charles Francis Adams, Jr., quoted in O'Toole, *The Five of Hearts*, 15, 16; Bertram Wyatt-Brown, *Lewis Tappan and the Evangelical Crusade against Slavery* (Cleveland, 1969), 301; Bertram Wyatt-Brown, *Yankee Saints and Southern Sinners* (Baton Rouge, 1985), 96.

31. Quoted in Ernest Samuels, *Henry Adams: The Middle Years* (Cambridge, 1965), 272; Kaledin, *The Education of Mrs. Henry Adams*, 222; O'Toole, *The Five of Hearts*, 157; Henry Adams to Henry Osborn Taylor, 15 February 1915, in R. P. Blackmur, *Henry Adams*, Veronica A. Makowsky, ed. (New York, 1980), 323–24. On LeRoy Pratt Percy's alleged improvement before his death, see Martha Susan Percy to LeRoy Percy, n.d., (ca. June 1929), Percy Family MSS (MDAH).

32. Janet Dana Longcope to William Alexander Percy, 19, 29 December and n.d. (ca. November–December 1929), Percy Family MSS (MDAH); William Alexander Percy to Sarah Kilpatrick, 2 June 1932, in Billups Phinizy Spalding, "William Alexander Percy: His Philosophy of Life as Reflected in His Poetry" (M.A. thesis, University of Georgia, 1957), 109.

33. Quoted in Samuels, *Henry Adams*, 222; Henry Adams to Elizabeth Cameron, 20 December 1914, in J. C. Levenson, Ernest Samuels et al., eds., *The Letters of Henry Adams* (6 vol., Cambridge, 1988), 6:672; Nagel, *Descent from Glory*, 229, 280, 360.

34. Henry Adams, *The Education of Henry Adams* (New York, 1990), 12; Percy, *Lanterns on the Levee*, 27. See Felix Brown, "Bereavement and Lack of a Parent in Childhood," in E. Miller, ed., *Foundations of Child Psychiatry* (London, 1968), 435–55; Sigmund Freud, "Mourning and Melancholia (1917)," in Ernest Jones, ed., *Collected Papers of Sigmund Freud* (21 vol., London, 1948), 4:152–70.

35. Chalfant, *Both Sides of the Ocean*, 25, 32–33, 53–54, 103–4, 399–400; Adams to Charles Milnes Gaskell, 10 May 1907, in Levenson et al., eds., *Letters of Henry Adams*, 6:63; Adams to Henry James, 6 May 1908, ibid., 6:136.

36. See "Editor's Preface," in Adams, *The Education of Henry Adams*, 5.

37. See *Greenwood Enterprise*, 16 August 1895.

38. Interview by author with Leon Koury, 10 February 1993, Greenville, Mississippi.

39. "The Fifth Autumn," in Percy Family MSS (MDAH).

40. Charles Francis Adams quoted in Herbert, *The Force So Much Closer Home*, 13; Aeschylus, *Agamemnon*, in *Aeschylus*, trans. Herbert Weir Smyth, vol. 2 of *The Loeb Classical Library*, G. P. Goold, ed. (1926; Cambridge, 1983), 2:49 (l. 547–48). I have partially adopted a translation kindly given me by Professor Philip Stadter.

41. William Armstrong Percy to Mrs. William Butler Duncan, 18 December 1904 (quotation), Longcope-Johansen Collection; Percy to William L. Percy, 25 April 1907, Percy Family MSS (MDAH); *Birmingham News*, 9 February 1917 (quotation). See particularly Walker Percy, *Lancelot* (New York, 1977) and *Love in the Ruins*.

42. Samuels, *Henry Adams*, 274–75.

43. See Richard L. King, "Mourning and Melancholia: Will Percy and the Southern Tradition," *Virginia Quarterly Review* 53 (Spring 1977): 260; Percy, *Lanterns on the Levee*, 57 (quotation); William Merrill Decker, *The Literary Vocation of Henry Adams* (Chapel Hill, 1990), 26 (quotation).

44. King, "Mourning and Melancholia," 256.

45. See Michael Kreyling, *Figures of the Hero in Southern Narrative* (Baton Rouge, 1987); Percy, *Lancelot* and *The Thanatos Syndrome* (New York, 1987); William Rodney Allen, "Father Smith's Confession in *The Thanatos Syndrome*," in Jan Nordby Gretlund and Karl Heinz-Westarp, eds., *Walker Percy: Novelist and Philosopher* (Jackson, 1991), 195–96.

46. Walker Percy, "Stoicism in the South," *Commonweal* 64 (6 July 1956): 343.

47. See Jan Gretlund, "On the Porch with Marcus Aurelius: Walker Percy's Stoicism," in Gretlund and Westarp, eds., *Walker Percy*, 74–83; Bertram Wyatt-Brown, "God and Honor in the Old South," *Southern Review* 25 (April 1989): 283.

48. Adams, *The Education of Henry Adams*, 58.

49. Percy, *Lanterns on the Levee*, 58, 223.

50. Quoted in Tolson, *Pilgrim in the Ruins*, 339.

51. Percy, *Lanterns on the Levee*, 149–59.

52. Walker Percy, *The Moviegoer* (New York, 1961), 26, 54.

53. Tolson, *Pilgrim in the Ruins*, 34–35; LeRoy Pratt Percy to LeRoy Percy, 17 February and 18 May 1923, Percy Family MSS (MDAH).

54. Percy, *Lanterns on the Levee*, 78–79, 88, 95 (quotation).

55. Ibid., 75.

56. William Alexander Percy, *Collected Poems* (New York, 1943), 213, 250.

57. The Hymnal of the Protestant Episcopal Church in the United States of America (New York, 1940), No. 437; see also Percy, Collected Poems, 212. (I am indebted to the Rev. Heather Cook of Bedford, New York, for bringing this hymn to my attention.) William Alexander Percy to A. T. Molligen, 21 September 1939, cited in Spalding, "William Alexander Percy," 101.

58. Janet Longcope to Percy, 8 April 1919, Percy Family MSS (MDAH).

59. Henry Adams, *The Education of Henry Adams* (1918; reprinted ed., New York, 1930), 329; Henry Adams to R. W. Gilder, 14 October 1895, in Ward Thoron, ed., *The Letters of Mrs. Henry Adams, 1865–1883* (Boston, 1936), 458.

60. Percy, *Lanterns on the Levee*, 348.

2

Law, Slavery, and Petigru: A Study in Paradox

Jane H. Pease and William H. Pease

James L. Petigru, the Charleston lawyer who chose Union and the federal Constitution over nullification and secession, was for many the quintessential southern dissenter. Born in the Carolina upcountry near Abbeville into a Scots-Irish yeoman farm family on his father's side and a rather more successful clerical French Huguenot family on his mother's side, Petigru, as he ruefully noted on the eve of the Civil War, was almost exactly the same age as the Constitution. Educated at Moses Waddel's Willington academy and at the newly opened South Carolina College in Columbia, he began his law practice in Coosewhatchie but moved to Charleston in 1819. There he spent the rest of his life, engaged in private legal practice broken only by a brief political career as a leader of Unionist opposition to South Carolina's nullification of the 1828 and 1832 tariffs. His two terms in the state legislature and a single one on Charleston's city council all were served in the 1830s. Twenty years later, when no other South Carolina lawyer was willing to accept the post in the aftermath of the Compromise of 1850, Petigru served as U.S. district attorney for South Carolina during the administration of Millard Fillmore. Neither legal theorist nor judge, he was marked in his own day as an accomplished trial lawyer and the acknowledged leader for nearly 40 years of the South Carolina bar.

Well known among politicians, lawyers, and judges both North and South, Petigru's reputation was rooted in his highly successful practice in his own state. Yet, historians have focused on his widely publicized conservative defense of Constitution and Union and his withering commentary on the politics of his state and region. Despite that, in 1859, the state legislature chose him to codify South Carolina's statute law only five years after he had represented black sailors contesting his state's Negro Seamen's Acts and won damages for an alleged abolitionist who had been punished by whipping after a summary and extralegal trial.[1] Yet, Petigru himself was a slaveholder who never directly challenged the peculiar institution, nor did he ever win a decision that would moderate South Carolina's slave code.[2] The part of his legal career that addresses the rights and interests of African Americans defines, therefore, a study in paradox.

Petigru, who came from a slaveholding family, acquired his first slaves on his wedding day, in August 1816, when his marriage settlement with Jane Postell gave him joint use and control of her ten slaves.[3] Thereafter, for the rest of his life, he bought and sold slaves for himself and other family members. As an attorney, too, he guided clients through the thickets of slave ownership, coping with implied warranty for a slave's good health and devising strategies to counter disputed claims of ownership. For one client, Petigru successfully challenged Charleston's special sales tax on out-of-state slaves brought into the city for sale; for another, he defeated a surtax on those slaves of nonresidents hired out in the city. Even when he prepared a petition for the pardon of a convicted slave, he served master as well as servant, because if the slave was saved from the gallows, his owner was spared significant financial loss.[4]

Furthermore, Petigru played no part in defending those charged with insurrection in the Denmark Vesey plot of 1822.[5] Surely he must have been as aware of the trials as the lawyers engaged by slaveowners to defend the accused. He was, after all, the law partner of Charleston's intendant (mayor), James Hamilton. Perhaps because he was only 33 and only two years a resident in the city, he was too little known to such prestigious slaveowners as Governor Thomas Bennett, who doubted that an insurrection had been planned, questioned the procedures of the Magistrates' and Freeholders' courts, and sought the best legal talent to defend those of his own servants who were accused. However, Petigru's election by the legislature as the state's attorney general that same year argues against his invisibility as a lawyer.[6]

In any event, Petigru's absence from the Vesey plot cases set the pattern of his whole career, which produced no cases that either his contemporary John Belton O'Neall or twentieth-century scholars Donald Senese and A. E. Keir Nash could cite as enlarging the rights of Carolina's free blacks or extending new rights to slaves.[7] Nonetheless, Petigru did aid white clients in attempting to circumvent the state's prohibitions against emancipation, and in his state's appeals courts, he more openly argued cases that benefited individual slaves and free blacks. However, even in those cases, his goals were more internally consistent than his means, because although he worked to gain the greatest protection for individual Negroes that the law would permit, he never tried to change the legal system of slavery. This was equally true whether his slaveholding clients were black or white. Never an antislavery reformer, Petigru, in short, took his cases one by one, approached them pragmatically, and sought primarily to be as effective a lawyer as he could for each client. The result was a widely varied practice.

When, as attorney general, he represented the state, Petigru tried to check the power of whites over blacks by prosecuting slaveowners who killed their own slaves. The year after the Vesey affair, for example, Petigru blocked the appeal for a new trial by a master who had captured a runaway, tied his hands behind him, set him adrift in a boat, and then summarily shot him. This, Petigru insisted, was murder. It was the "highest offence which an individual [could] commit against his fellow man," despite the grand jury's contention in another case that Petigru prosecuted that the owner's "sudden heat and passion" made killing a disobedient slave something less. Consequently, the attorney general demanded the full punishment mandated by law — a fine and exclusion from ever holding public office.[8]

A sense of common humanity informed that argument, but it was a common humanity cloven by race. Many years later, Petigru demonstrated the ambivalence that shaped his course in such matters. In a letter intended to bring peace between two black men but written, in fact, to one white slaveowner on behalf of another, he observed that Toney, the slave of his client, had, in addition to his owner's confidence, "a character among people of his degree, that he would not like to lose; and in that I think he is right." Richard, the other slave, should, therefore, be restrained from making false accusations against Toney "and learn that even a Negro's character is of some account."[9] That was a patronizing, if humane, attitude, but granting even so much in a courtroom was likely to alienate a jury. Petigru, therefore, early adopted a contrary style. "The only way to defend a white man who has taken [the] part of a slave," Francis Lieber noted that Petigru had told him, "is to treat the latter like a dog."[10]

Within the double constraints imposed by a society frequently hostile to his sense of justice but a society many of whose values he shared, Petigru crafted his legal arguments touching on slavery. Necessarily, they were often oblique. In 1851, for example, when a hapless sea captain was brought to court for having accepted at face value the North Carolina free papers tendered by a slave to whom the shipping agent had sold passage from Charleston to Philadelphia, the jury imposed damages of over $1,100. Petigru appealed the verdict, contending that the captain had not been negligent when he accepted the validity of the free papers and that trover was an inappropriate action because no evidence had been adduced to show that the captain had "converted" the putative slave property to his own use. However, the prevailing political climate countered this technical argument, largely because Congress only four months before had passed a new fugitive slave law and because, at the very moment of the appeal, Carolinians were choosing delegates to a secessionist convention called to challenge the Compromise of 1850. In such an atmosphere, no appeals judge nor any jury would exonerate a white man who had carried a fugitive slave to a free state.[11]

In another episode enshrined in family lore, Petigru revealed in sharp detail the constant tension between his sense of fair play and justice, on the one hand, and the values of southern white society that he never relinquished, on the other. Happening late one evening upon an illiterate city guardsman who, unable to read a slave's legitimate pass, had seized the poor fellow and was marching him to the guardhouse, Petigru intervened, and the frightened slave fled. The guardsman then tried to arrest Petigru, who, in turn, knocked him down. After he had ignored two summonses for his arrest, Petigru indignantly responded to a third in a letter to the mayor, protesting a violation not of the slave's rights but of his own as a "law abiding citizen."[12]

More often than not, Petigru's actions on behalf of slaves did address the limiting or defending of white action. Thus, a legal fight over the right of a favored slave to choose which heir would inherit him in fact protected the owner's expressed intention.[13] Similarly, whenever Petigru arranged the manumission of slaves, he was overtly following the owners' wishes. To have acted otherwise would have been to ignore — or to challenge — his culture's postulates about race relations and community power.

In such cases, Petigru pressed hard against (when he did not actually overstep) the outer limits of South Carolina manumission law. Although until 1800 there had been virtually no legal restriction against emancipating slaves, the increasing frequency of the practice led the state to require the express approval of a board of magistrates and freeholders for any contemplated manumission. That condition was tightened in 1820 by requiring legislative petition and approval for any such action. Then, amid the increasing tensions of the growing anti-slavery movement in the North and the concomitant unease in the state during the 1830s, South Carolina effectively legislated in 1841 a prohibition upon all emancipation or even "nominal slavery." The single remaining loophole was that a master might personally take a slave out of state and there free him or her, but, as had been the case since 1820, such a free person would be barred from reentering the state.[14]

Nevertheless, within the limited scope of South Carolina's manumission law, Petigru did assist individual slaves. At least twice he circumvented the intent of the law by becoming de jure owner and guardian of slaves whose owners wished them to live as though they were free. On one such occasion, he agreed to assume responsibility for a woman and her 12 children. Later, when he was 73, he undertook a similar but more limited responsibility. Although in the first instance the owner changed his mind before Petigru had actually taken charge and in the latter Petigru asked to be relieved of the obligation, he had in accepting these cases implicitly challenged the law by defying it.[15]

Nor was this the whole of his defiance. His longtime friend and client, Eliza Kohne, who commuted annually between her Charleston and Philadelphia homes, was given to philanthropy and was grateful for faithful service. When, therefore, she wanted to free her coachman Jake, Petigru utilized Maryland's liberal emancipation procedures and arranged to have a Baltimore law firm draw up the necessary manumission documents. On her next trip north, Kohne signed the papers, and Jake became legally free. The secrecy that attended the matter was as much for Kohne's convenience as for Jake's, because the state law that prohibited free blacks' entering South Carolina would have left her without her coachman. Still, in aiding her, Petigru had helped Jake even more.[16]

Even more complex was an emancipation stratagem that challenged the color line as well. In 1859 Petigru began a negotiation among a Charleston doctor, a slave mother, and the would-be guardian of their daughter that ultimately provided that the infant should, in defiance of the law, be brought up as both free and white.[17] Many other of Petigru's cases also tested the permeability of the color line. Even so, there were few legal confrontations like that that ruffled Charleston's sense of racial community in 1831. The South Carolina Medical Society denied Dr. John Schmidt, Jr., a license to practice medicine because, it contended, he was of a "different *Caste* or *Status* from those who are entitled to a License." Not even his father's membership in the society helped him, because, in the eyes of those who had blackballed him, the problem was his mother. Her mother, the young doctor's grandmother and a refugee from the Haitian revolution, was said to be a mulatto. To settle the matter and force the society to issue his son a license, the elder Schmidt retained Petigru to seek a writ of mandamus.[18]

Though it was no easy victory, the trial that resulted vividly illustrated Petigru's humor and courtroom skill. The key witness for the society was another refugee, who testified that young Schmidt's grandmother had always sat in pews reserved for people of color in her Haitian church. Then the wily Petigru began a near-legendary cross-examination. Opening routinely enough, he turned suddenly upon the witness and asked whether he had ever attended that church. Momentarily dumbfounded, the witness, protesting that the question was unfair, refused to answer. Backed by the judge, Petigru pressed the question, and the witness confessed his dilemma. If he said he had attended the church, he would be ostracized in his own community, but if he admitted he never attended church, he would perjure himself. Petigru left it at that.[19] In the end, Schmidt apparently got his license, but soon afterward he left town and the stigma the proceedings had produced.

A variation on the same theme involved James Clark, whose claim that he was free because his mother was white Petigru had established in legal proceedings before 1840. When Clark was again arrested and was convicted in the Magistrates' and Freeholders' Court, where only blacks — free or slave — were tried, he turned once more to Petigru. The Court of General Sessions, which had, in the earlier instance, established his freedom, now proceeded to set aside the decision of the Magistrates' Court. Once again, the key to success lay largely with Petigru's cross-examination. Facing an unfriendly witness, Petigru forced him to admit that Clark, his neighbor, had customarily voted with the witness's party in public elections and had long served in the militia unit that the witness commanded. Clearly, therefore, though common belief held that Clark was a mulatto, the son of a black slave as well as a free white mother, he should never have been tried in Magistrates' Court in the first place, because legally he was white.[20]

In pressing Clark's claim to the legal process guaranteed white persons, Petigru went directly to the central feature of American slavery — that race and status were both intertwined and separable. In South Carolina, civil status and race were determined by the mother. When the mother was a white person, the law prescribed that her child was white as well as free. Thus, Clark, whatever his appearance, was entitled to trial by jury in the Court of General Sessions, and his trial and sentence in the Magistrates' Court defied the law.

Although personal ambiguity sometimes marked Petigru's responses to slavery and matters of caste, his commitment to defending the rights of free blacks was far less complex.[21] He grasped whatever protection state law might afford them, and when there were grounds for a legal or constitutional challenge to oppressive state laws, he was willing to pursue such a challenge even though he doubted its efficacy. This was clearly the case with the Negro Seamen's Acts. First passed in the wake of the abortive slave revolt led by Denmark Vesey, who had come to Charleston as a seaman, the law required that out-of-state black mariners be jailed while their ships remained in South Carolina ports. Maintenance fees were to be paid by their captains. If the ships' masters refused to pay the fees, the sailors, even if they were free, could be sold at auction into involuntary servitude for a five-year period, renewable until they left the state.[22]

Whatever the domestic context of its passage, the law soon became an international issue, contravening, as it did, commercial accords between the United States and Great Britain. The first test was brought in 1823 on behalf of a black British seaman, Henry Elkison, who had been placed in the Charleston jail by Sheriff Francis Deliesseline. Aided by the British consul, Elkison sought a writ of habeas corpus from William Johnson, a South Carolina-born U.S. Supreme Court justice then presiding over the federal circuit court in his native city.[23]

It was, however, not Attorney General James Petigru but, rather, two members of the South Carolina Association, recently organized to strengthen government control of the state's black population, who defended the sheriff and the constitutionality of the state law. Justice Johnson was unmoved by their arguments. In a Marshall-like opinion, he ruled that the Negro Seamen's Acts was unconstitutional because it infringed a treaty that, with federal statutes and the Constitution itself, comprised the supreme law of the land. Nevertheless, he refused to issue the requested writ because, he said, there was no federal law authorizing him to do so.[24]

Even though it lacked practical effect, Johnson's opinion was so at odds with local sentiment that the press refused to print it. When, therefore, he published it at his own expense, he asserted outright that state officials, including Attorney General Petigru, had refused to enforce the law because they, too, believed it was unconstitutional. Quite possibly this refusal to act marked the beginning of Petigru's independent political path, and quite clearly it marked his willingness to challenge the paramount authority assumed by South Carolina.

Petigru's next confrontation with the Negro Seamen's Acts occurred some 20 years later. In November 1844 Governor Edward Everett of Massachusetts sent Judge Samuel Hoar to Charleston to collect evidence for a test case on behalf of black Massachusetts sailors. After Hoar and his daughter had been in town for only four days, they were warned by Sheriff John Irving that they were in personal danger as long as they remained in the city, and before another four days had passed, they were escorted to the wharf by some 70 "gentlemen," including the sheriff, and placed aboard a vessel headed north. The haste in expelling them stemmed in part from South Carolina Governor James Hammond's fear that Hoar, in response to a legislative resolution asking the governor to expel him, would retain Petigru.[25]

In 1850 a new British consul arrived in Charleston. Openly determined to force a modification of South Carolina's laws governing black seamen such as other consuls had obtained from North Carolina, Alabama, and Louisiana, Britain's new commercial representative, William Mathew, asked Petigru for a legal assessment of the South Carolina acts and then began lobbying the legislature and the governor. When Mathew, acerbic and undiplomatic in the extreme, failed to achieve his purpose at once, he vented his frustration by publishing his program in the press and buttressed it with Petigru's logically argued and meticulously prepared opinion.[26]

In this memorandum to Mathew, Petigru presented his clearest exploration of the issue, elaborating the unconstitutionality of the Seamen's Acts. Closely agreeing with Justice Johnson's earlier decision, he wrote that the U.S. Constitution permitted no state to contravene either federal law or national treaty. Relying heavily on the 1815 commercial treaty between Britain and the United States, he quoted its provision for "reciprocal liberty of commerce" whereby the "inhabitants of the two countries . . . shall have liberty freely and securely to come with their ships and cargoes to all such places . . . to which other foreigners are permitted to come." Moreover, he maintained, a treaty was a contract so protected under the federal Constitution that not even one of the contracting parties could unilaterally break it. How then, Petigru asked, could a state, which lacked the power to make such a contract, intervene to break it? Finally, in a masterful political stroke, Petigru denied that internationally recognized rights of quarantine could justify the Carolina law. He pointed out that South Carolina's own John C. Calhoun, as secretary of state, had asserted that it "cannot be pretended that the rights guarantied, [sic] by Treaty between two independent Powers, may be abridged or modified by the municipal regulations of one of the parties, without and against the consent of the other." And that would seem to settle that.[27]

In a private letter, which Mathew never published, Petigru also expressed doubt that the British government could win its point in either federal or state courts. "The Juries," he said, "would not give vindictive damages and the Federal Court has no jurisdiction of suits under 500 dollars." The best hope for a test case, he thought, would lie in a state court, because it would rule that the Seamen's Acts were constitutional and, thus, afford grounds for an appeal to the federal Supreme Court. However, even if the Supreme Court found the acts unconstitutional, the decision would be a "barren victory," because the initial case would necessarily be remanded to a state court, where, again, no jury would award damages of more than a few pennies. Nothing, in short, would be changed. "In the present temper of the people here, the unconstitutionality of the law would not stagger them at all," he concluded ruefully. "They would continue to enforce it, even after the Supreme Court had declared it void, & if it produced a collision the result would only [be] so much the more to their taste."[28]

Petigru, the pragmatist, believed that Mathew's only viable course of action was to treat "with Governor [John] Means as puissance a puissance" and gain his support for legislative change.[29] However, Mathew's "tactless, argumentative, and threatening" style when he had chosen to make his complaints public blocked that route.[30] Thus, Petigru embarked on a path of court action whose outcome he much doubted. In April 1852, acting on the consul's instructions, he went to a state judge for a writ of habeas corpus for Manuel Pereira, who had been jailed under a provision of the Seamen's Acts. The steward aboard a storm-damaged British merchantman that had sought refuge and repairs in Charleston harbor, Pereira, a British subject though a "Portuguese mestizo," fell afoul of the 1835 revision of the law, which had ended the earlier exemption from imprisonment for sailors driven into a South Carolina harbor by shipwreck.

Judge Thomas Withers summarily dismissed Pereira's petition, and Petigru at once appealed. However, the appeals court did not sit in Charleston until the following January, and by that time, Pereira's captain and Mathew had agreed, on humanitarian grounds, to pay the jail fees and free Pereira to sail with his ship. Consequently, Judge John Belton O'Neall, speaking for the court, struck the case from the docket because, with Pereira gone, the court "should do a vain act to hear this appeal."[31]

Despite his sense of its futility, Petigru then sued for damages in the federal circuit court in another action initiated by Mathew. Only six weeks after Judge Withers had rejected Pereira's petition, Reuben Roberts, a Nassau-born cook aboard the British ship *Clyde*, had been jailed for eight days. Nearly a year later, Judge Robert Gilchrist, presiding in the U.S. Circuit Court, heard the case, in which Petigru pressed a $4,000 suit against Sheriff Jeremiah D. Yates for "assault, battery, and false imprisonment."[32] The legal talent assembled for Yates's defense included Attorney General Isaac Hayne, Senator (and former state judge) Andrew P. Butler, and two leading Charleston lawyers, Christopher Memminger and Edward McCrady. They did little to block Petigru's strategy — to move the case and its test of the constitutionality of the Seamen's Acts as swiftly as possible to the Supreme Court. He limited his argument, therefore, to seeking a ruling from Judge Gilchrist "that the laws and statutes of South Carolina, relied on in said plea [of the defendant], being in contravention of the treaty of 1815, and the reciprocity and proclamation of 1830, were unconstitutional, and therefore invalid and of no force." However, as Petigru doubtless anticipated, Gilchrist instructed the jury that the South Carolina laws were indeed constitutional, and the jury accordingly found for Yates.[33]

Nevertheless, the year's delay between Roberts's arrest and the circuit court decision in April 1853 sabotaged the planned appeal. Mathew had been called home and replaced by Robert Bunch, who practiced a low-key style that contrasted sharply with Mathew's abrasive manner. Furthermore, Secretary of State Daniel Webster, who had protested Mathew's lobbying a state government on matters of U.S. foreign policy and had, thus, influenced the British government's shift from legislative to court action, had died, and the administration of Millard Fillmore, who had made Petigru district attorney for South Carolina, had ended in March 1853.

Because the obstacles to seeking legislative modifications of the Negro Seamen's Acts were, thus, removed, the British Foreign Office dropped the Roberts appeal. Instead, Bunch engaged in the effective lobbying that, after three years, achieved at least some modification of the law. The limited changes permitted a ship captain to post bond that black seamen in his employ would remain aboard their ship while it was docked in South Carolina and, thus, prevent their arbitrary imprisonment. The new law was passed in December 1856, immediately after Petigru's brother-in-law Robert F. W. Allston had been elected governor, and Consul Bunch gave the credit for the change to two legislators, one of whom was Petigru's close friend Alfred Huger.[34]

How much Petigru's course in the *Pereira* and *Roberts* cases was a matter of politics rather than law cannot be determined from remaining documents. However, the circumstances surrounding the law's revision, his own position in the Fillmore administration, his political friendship with Daniel Webster, and his willingness to represent the British government against his better judgment point to yet another paradox in his legal representation of black interests.

In defending free Negroes from enslavement or reenslavement, Petigru's course was clearer and more consistent, and here both law and public sentiment were more sympathetic. The 1820 law that severely limited manumission, for example, also mandated penalties for trying to sell free persons into slavery. Those penalties were subsequently stiffened by an 1837 law that permitted fines of $1,000 and a year's imprisonment for attempting to enslave free African Americans. For actually doing so the penalty was 39 lashes — a physical punishment usually inflicted only on Negroes.[35] Thus, there was a legally established and a culturally accepted context within which free blacks had at least minimal protection. It was Petigru's accomplishment to take effective advantage of that environment.

Doubtless the precipitant for arranging the emancipation of Eliza Kohne's coachman Jake in 1842 was the arrest of his fellow servant Emma Farbeaux earlier that year. Farbeaux had lived with Kohne in Philadelphia as a free woman but had been a slave when first taken to the North. Arguably, therefore, she was still a slave when she returned to Charleston in violation of an 1835 law prohibiting an owner's bringing back to South Carolina a slave earlier taken north of the Potomac. A local slaveowner and magistrate, James Simons, reported Farbeaux's return to his fellow magistrate B. C. Pressley, who ordered her arrest and trial in the Magistrates' and Freeholders' Court. If the accused was found to be an illegally returned slave, she could be confiscated and sold, and the proceeds would be divided between the state and Simons, the informer. In addition, the court could fine Eliza Kohne $1,000.

Petigru appeared at once before Judge O'Neall seeking a writ of prohibition. O'Neall granted the writ on the grounds that the confiscation of a citizen's property by a Magistrates' and Freeholders' Court, which had no jury, violated South Carolina's constitutional guarantee that "no free man of this State shall be in any manner deprived of his life, liberty or property, but by the judgment of his peers, or by the law of the land." The constitutional issue, therefore, lay not in the power of the Magistrates' and Freeholders' Court to try black Emma Farbeaux without a jury but in its action to deprive white Eliza Kohne of her slave property without a trial by her peers, and the Court of Errors, reviewing the case, again protected Kohne's rights.

Petigru's subsequent decision to have Kohne's coachman manumitted under Maryland law was a clear attempt to outwit Carolina statutes, because Jake then could show free papers if he were stopped outside of South Carolina while he could suppress them and avoid trouble at home. Furthermore, Petigru made clear what a defiance of Carolina law and custom it was by informing the Maryland attorney who assisted him that Jake, when freed, would return at once to Charleston. It was a tortuous and secretive affair, because if South Carolina authorities learned of the out-of-state manumission, the lawyer who had arranged it might well be open to the charge of having undertaken a fraud against the state. Run that risk, however, Petigru did.[36]

Petigru again and again used the legal rights of white persons in protection of their property to extend and defend the de facto freedom of black persons. Most often this happened when owners tried, either directly or indirectly, to free their slaves in defiance of the 1820 and 1841 laws. In one such case, Joseph Dougherty challenged the 1844 will of his father, John. John had written his own will and, in apparent ignorance of the law, had ordered that seven slaves — a woman not improbably his mistress, her children, and her mother — be freed at once and that the rest, whose use he left to his niece, be freed after her death. The son, bequeathed only an annual income of $700 and better informed than his father about the law, brought action against his parent's executors to void the will's provisions for all the slaves and, thus, to gain possession of them for himself. Petigru and his partner, Henry D. Lesesne, were retained by the executors but could do nothing for the slaves who had been promised immediate freedom, because John Dougherty had defied the law outright. They did, however, convince the equity appeals court to save for the niece her life use of the slaves so specified, which at least delayed Joseph's claim to their ownership.[37]

Murkier situations allowed Petigru more room for maneuver, as in the case of the reenslavement of a Mr. Wigg's children. More than 30 years before the case came to light in 1857, Wigg had sent the children with Amelia, their slave mother, to Cuba, intending that they should all stay there and live in freedom. However, Amelia and two of her sons, Charles and John, had so disliked that place that they had returned home in 1823. Wigg then deeded the three of them to a Robert Habersham, who promised to allow them to live as free. Thus, the "absurd man, in this business," as Petigru lamented about Wigg, "took a course that opened the way to the very thing he meant to prevent."

Had he done nothing, there would have been no record that Amelia, John, and Charles, who had entered the United States from Cuba when federal law prohibited the foreign slave trade, were anything but free persons. Indeed, Amelia, John, and Charles Wigg lived as free in Georgia until the deed to Habersham surfaced. Then Wigg's "pious" white son "laid his hands" on his half-brothers in order to sell them "as lawful spoil." Petigru thought that federal law actually made them free, and he was determined to defend that freedom because, as he wrote to Habersham, "I am not so thoroughly Southern as to encourage the Selling of free negroes."[38] The "brutal son" chose to prosecute his claim in South Carolina courts because, Petigru snorted, he found that it "was too rank for the atmosphere of Georgia."[39] However, because the African-American Wiggs had lived near Savannah, Petigru had to collect affidavits on their behalf from Georgians, and by the time the case came to trial in Charleston, only the Habersham affidavit had arrived. Thus, for lack of adequate evidence, "the trial of the Wiggs for freedom" was lost, and there is no record whether Petigru ever got the new trial he intended to seek.[40]

To insure freedom to the children for whom a white father had so provided was no easy task, even for a lawyer of Petigru's standing and courtroom prowess. Yet, he undertook several such cases pro bono, one of which dragged on for almost 20 years. In this, his task was to uphold the de facto freedom of the slaves of English-born George Broad, who had died in 1836. Broad's will had bequeathed Daphne, her 11 children, and her 2 grandchildren in trust to his executor, John Dangerfield, who was to let them work and live on Broad's farm, keep their earnings, and enjoy the full use of Broad's entire estate. Clearly, Broad had come as close as he could to emancipating his family.

Almost at once Broad's arrangements were challenged. In 1837 Rebecca Rhame, the remarried widow of George Broad's brother-in-law and Broad's nearest white relative, hired John Singletary to seize the slaves, claiming that Dangerfield's trust was illegal. Accompanied by Rhame, her sister Jane De Hay, and Jane's son, Singletary went to Broad's farm, threatened Dangerfield with violence, and attempted to run off the slaves. James Ferguson, a neighboring planter, intervened, and doubtless it was he who had Rhame and her cohort prosecuted and fined for committing a riot.

Even though the appeals court upheld her conviction, Rhame did not give up. Motivated perhaps by a greed rooted in poverty or perhaps by family resentment that a kinswoman's place as Broad's wife had been usurped by Daphne, she brought an action of trover to recover Broad's slaves from Dangerfield. At least by 1839, when her suit named Ferguson as well as Dangerfield, the conflict took on a class aspect, when wealthy planters rallied to the defense of Dangerfield and the slaves he held in trust. Ferguson himself owned a plantation of 1,500 acres and 125 slaves in St. John's Berkeley, and another planter, Dr. Theodore Gaillard, was a key witness against Rhame's charge that Dangerfield let the Broad slaves live without working and allowed them guns with which they shot cows as well as deer. Dr. Gaillard swore that the trustee did indeed supervise the slaves, who supported themselves by growing and selling corn. By the time this case reached the appeals court, the partnership of Petigru and Lesesne represented the defendants and again defeated Rhame's attempt either to work the Broad slaves for her benefit or to sell them.[41]

In 1842 Ferguson and Dangerfield attempted to collect the court costs and counsel fees awarded them in the previous trials by suing Jane De Hay, who, as surety for her sister, was made solely responsible by Rhame's insolvency. Although Petigru won this suit in the lower court, the appeals court ruled that in order to collect, Ferguson and Dangerfield must consent to reopening the decisions handed down in the earlier cases. Such an unattractive option left them to pay their own court costs and very likely left Petigru without a fee for their defense.[42]

Undeterred, however, Petigru continued to follow the Broad slaves' fate. When, in 1854, after John Dangerfield had died, his heirs claimed Broad's estate as their rightful inheritance, Petigru again intervened. Some years earlier, Dangerfield had violated his trust by selling three of the Broad slaves to meet his own financial needs. When Petigru discovered this "foul dishonesty," he extracted Dangerfield's promise, never fulfilled, to deed the remaining slaves to Ferguson. However, "partly from indolency," as Petigru himself admitted, the attorney had not followed through. So now, a dozen years later, he confronted once again the insecurity of the Broad slaves' hold on their relative freedom.[43]

Intent this time on finding a sure guarantee against their reenslavement, Petigru negotiated with the American Colonization Society and raised funds to carry the Broad slaves to Liberia.[44] Before they could leave, however, the claims of the Dangerfield heirs had to be fully and finally extinguished, and it was with the cooperation of South Carolina's attorney general and the support of numerous prosperous residents of St. John's Berkeley, including Theodore Gaillard and John Ferguson, who again bore court costs, that Petigru executed a legal about-face. In another triumph of pragmatism over theoretical consistency, he argued in *F. A. Ford, Escheator ex. rel J. Ferguson* v. *Starling J. Dangerfield* that because the Broad will did indeed violate state law, the Dangerfield trust had never been valid and, thus, any claims by the Dangerfield heirs were without substance. Moreover, voiding Broad's will meant that in effect Broad had died intestate and that, in the absence of legal heirs, his estate must be escheated by the state.[45]

Not until January 1856 did the Court of Appeals in Equity finally agree. Meanwhile, Petigru also had to defend Dr. Gaillard. In his anxiety that the Dangerfields might make off with the Broad slaves, Gaillard had taken them under his protection and, as a result, had been charged by the Dangerfields with "running Negroes." In addition, Petigru had solicited "Gentlemen's" signatures on petitions that convinced the state legislature to emancipate the Broad slaves and to dedicate the proceeds from George Broad's escheated estate to their use. Finally, as the last act in the drama, Petigru located the man to whom Dangerfield had improperly sold Sammy and Simon Broad. Purchasing them with funds appropriated by the legislature, he enabled them to join their Liberia-bound siblings.[46]

That Petigru frequently undertook to defend the disadvantaged bespeaks a genuinely humane spirit, though it in no way portrays an activist as the late twentieth century understands that term. Rather, court records and professional correspondence alike portray a man responding to a variety of social forces. As an attorney who retained his youthful idealism about justice, Petigru often offered legal services to the weak and the poor regardless of color. However, it is equally true that, like most lawyers, he more frequently represented slaveowners than either enslaved or free blacks, just as he more frequently represented creditors than debtors. He dedicated himself to protecting the civil liberties guaranteed in state and federal constitutions, yet he was equally committed to defending the property rights and the sanctity of contracts similarly guaranteed. A politically inclined American whose public career was enshrined in — and stunted by — his devotion to the federal Union, Petigru directly challenged South Carolina laws governing Negroes only when those statutes defied the supreme law of the land. As a courtroom lawyer par excellence, the trial process for him was not a means to legislate but a tool to protect the interests of very specific people.

Because slavery was so pervasively a part of his life and so entrenched in his culture, Petigru could challenge it only obliquely. In that way, he did gain freedom for some slaves as individuals and he managed to protect other African southerners from losing whatever degree of freedom they enjoyed. If in so doing he slightly reshaped the law so that it better protected those with fewest legal rights, he did so most effectively by shielding the rights and prerogatives of the more privileged. It is this confluence of contradictions that best defines the person, the legal practice, and ultimately the paradox of James L. Petigru.

NOTES

1. *Ex Parte Manuel Pereira*, 6 Richardson 149–50 (1853) (16 S. C. Reports 59–60); *Reuben D. Roberts* v. *Jeremiah D. Yates*, 20 Federal Cases (1853), Case No. 11, 919, 937–38 (16 Law Reports 49). For discussion of these cases, see below, 13–19. The case of Reuben Smalle, the alleged Yankee abolitionist, is summarized in the Charleston *Daily Standard*, 4 December 1854.

2. Several reasonably available studies sketch Petigru's career: James Petigru Carson, ed., *Life, Letters and Speeches of James Louis Petigru* (Washington, 1920); Joseph Blyth Allston, "Life and Times of James L. Petigru," a series of articles in the Charleston *Sunday News* in 1899–1900, collected and paged as a scrapbook, Copy

(South Caroliniana Library, University of South Carolina, hereafter SCL); and the memoir by his lifelong friend William J. Grayson, *James Louis Petigru. A Biographical Sketch* (New York, 1866). The authors are currently preparing a book-length study of James L. Petigru.

3. James Louis Petigru and Jane Amelia Postell, Marriage Settlement, 22 August 1816, Marriage Settlements (South Carolina Archives, hereafter SCA).

4. Concerning cases of warranty and disputed sale, see, for example, *Wm Wells* v. *Wm Spears*, 1 McCord 421–25 (1821) (5 S. C. Reports 171–73); *F. Y. Porcher ads Richard Caldwell*, 2 McMillan 329–34 (1842) (11 S. C. Reports 138–40); and *Wm B. Campbell* v. *George Kinloch*, 9 Richardson 300–12 (1856) (17 S. C. Reports 102–6); also considerable correspondence relating to these issues in the R.F.W. Allston Papers (South Carolina Historical Society, hereafter SCHS), passim, and in the Petigru and King Letterbooks (SCL), passim. On slave taxation and hire, see, for example, *The State of S. C. ex relatione James Adger* v. *the Mayor and Aldermen of the City of Charleston*, 2 Speers 719–35 (1844) (12 S. C. Reports 298–305); also correspondence relating to *City* v. *Mordecai* (1856), especially Petigru and King to W. D. Porter, 5 February 1856, to John Belton O'Neall, 18 April 1856, and to Messrs. Capers and Heyward, 30 April 1856, all in Petigru and King Letterbooks (SCL). For cases involving convicted slaves, see Petigru to Governor [Richard Irvine] Manning, 12 February 1825, William Chestnut Manning Family Papers (SCL); B. K. Henagan to Petigru, 2 October 1840, Miscellaneous Manuscripts (SCL); and Laura A. White, "The South in the 1850s, as Seen by British Consuls," *Journal of Southern History* 1 (1935): 33.

5. Singularly frustrating about the Vesey affair is that no evidence has come to light that provides any clues about Petigru's views concerning it or any possible response to it. The record is silent on the issue.

6. It has also been suggested by Professor Paul Finkelman that because Petigru was still a partner of James Hamilton, it would have been at least inappropriate, "if not a violation of ethics," for Petigru to have taken the other side of the case from that that Hamilton, by virtue of his office, represented as "more or less the prosecutor." Paul Finkelman to the authors, 12 October 1991.

7. A. E. Keir Nash, "A More Equitable Past? Southern Supreme Courts and the Protection of the Ante-Bellum Negro," *North Carolina Law Review* 48 (1970): 197–242; and A. E. Keir Nash, "Negro Rights, Unionism, and Greatness on the South Carolina Court of Appeals: The Extraordinary Chief Justice John Belton O'Neall," *South Carolina Law Review* 21 (1969): 141–90; John Belton O'Neall, *The Negro Law of South Carolina* (Columbia, 1848); Donald J. Senese, "The Free Negro and the South Carolina Courts, 1790–1860," *South Carolina Historical Magazine* 68 (1967): 140–53. The trial record of the Vesey case is in Lionel H. Kennedy and Thomas Parker, *An Official Record of the Trial of Sundry Negroes, Charged with an Attempt to Raise an Insurrection in the State of South Carolina* (Charleston, 1822. Reprinted as *The Trial Record of Denmark Vesey* [Boston, 1970] and also reprinted in Paul Finkelman, *Slavery, Race, and the American Legal System* [New York, 1987]).

8. The quotations, in order, from two cases involving the murder of a slave: *The State* v. *William H. Taylor*, 2 McCord 483–92 (1823) (6 S. C. Reports 190–93), 486/191; and *State* v. *Gulden*, 2 McCord 524–26 (1823) (6 S. C. Reports 206–7), 524/206. The position of South Carolina courts is spelled out in Earl M. Maltz, "Fourteenth Amendment Concepts in the Antebellum Era," *American Journal of Legal History* 32 (1988): 305–46. In *State* v. *Harden*, 2 Speers (1832), it was held that "Slaves are chattels and their right of protection belongs to the master and is, therefore, not cast, as far as regards them personally, on society" (quoted in Maltz, "Fourteenth Amendment," 329). For free blacks, however, the case, as Maltz points out, was different. "The rights of life, liberty and property, belong to them, and must be protected by the community in which they are suffered to live. They are regarded, in law, as

persons capable of committing and receiving an injury; and for the one, they are liable to punishment, for the other, they are entitled to redress" (Maltz, "Fourteenth Amendment," 330).

9. Petigru to J. P. Deveaux, 18 July 1853 (Draft), Petigru Correspondence (Library of Congress, hereafter LC).

10. Francis Lieber, Pocket Notebook of Miscellaneous Memoranda, 31 January 1835, Francis Lieber Papers (Huntington Library).

11. *John W. Ellis* v. *S. M. Welsh* (1850), Court of Common Pleas, Pleadings and Judgments, Roll 5157 (SCA); *J. W. Ellis* v. *S. M. Welsh*, 4 Richardson 468–79 (1851) (16 S. C. Reports 189–94).

12. Carson, *Life*, 353.

13. *Daniel E. Huger, and Others* v. *Isabella I. Huger, and Others*, 9 Richardson Equity 217–43 (1857) (28 S. C. Reports 75–85). In rejecting the appeal of the appellants to disallow the sale of certain property while reserving the right of the favored slave to choose his new master, the court held that the executors had been given virtual carte blanche in disposing of the property, that they had done so within the specific terms of the law, and that "as to Jackey [the slave in question], the authority of the executors was unlimited. They had the power of a proprietor, and might indulge their discretion, and even their caprice, in selecting their vendee." The executors were the sons of testator and were upholding their father's wish to allow Jackey his own choice. Petigru, as their attorney, supported that position, though his arguments can only be inferred from the decision of the court.

14. H. M. Henry, *The Police Control of the Slave in South Carolina* (1914; reprint New York, 1968), 168–89.

15. Phillip F. Bessellen to Petigru, 19, 26, 29 April 1839, 15 June 1840, and 26 May 1842, Petigru Letters, Vanderhorst Papers (SCHS); T. J. Bessellen to Petigru, 1 March 1853, Petigru Correspondence (LC); and for the second occasion, Petigru to Emma Starr, 23, 25 April 1861, Petigru and King Letterbooks.

16. Petigru to Hugh S. Legaré, 5 April 1842, Miscellaneous Manuscripts (SCL). Petigru to William G. Read, 27 April 1842, Petigru Family Papers (Duke University).

17. James Moultrie to Petigru, 15 November 1859; Petigru to R. A. Pagan, 17 November 1859; A. V. Wylie to Petigru, 20 January 1860; Petigru to Wylie, 24 January 1860, all in Petigru Letters, Vanderhorst Papers (SCHS).

18. Medical Society of South Carolina, Minutes, 2, 5 May 1831, Waring Historical Library (Medical University of South Carolina), quotation at Vol. II:29.

19. Grayson, *James Louis Petigru*, 157–58; Allston, "Life and Times," 14.

20. *James Clark* v. *Richard H. Jones et al.* (1840), Court of General Sessions, Pleadings and Judgments, Rolls 610 and 611 (SCA). The nature of the charge is not specified in the roll.

21. For Petigru's involvement in three such cases very late in his life, see Petigru to Jane North, 13 November 1899 [*sic*, 1862] and 20 November 1862; Allston, "Life and Times," 46; same to same, 29 November 1862; Carson, *Life*, 461.

22. For the various Negro Seamen's Acts, see *Statutes at Large of South Carolina* (Columbia, 1836–98), 1820: VII:459–60; 1823: VII:463–66; 1835: VII:471–73. On the question of Petigru's relationship to free blacks, Professor Edmund L. Drago observes that antebellum Charleston had, if not quite fully, at least the general character of a three-tiered social structure, in which the elite free black community occupied, de facto, a middle position, acting in times of potential unrest as "a kind of early warning system in case of slave insurrection." Given Petigru's conservative belief in a hierarchical governmental order and social organization, Drago further postulates that it is likely that he identified with the elite free black community as part of such a three-tiered structure. By taking cases defending free blacks, therefore, Petigru not only was acting a humane role or even only the role of a pragmatic attorney but also

was lending conscious support to a three-tiered social structure. Although there is some evidence to support this hypothesis, we have very little evidence pointing directly to Petigru's relationship with the elite free black community. Thus, as Drago wisely cautions, such an hypothesis must remain tentative. Edmund L. Drago to authors, 29 April 1991.

23. *Elkison* v. *Deliesseline*, Case No. 4366, 8 Federal Cases 493–98 (1823). The British had earlier complained that the 1820 law exposed "the vessels of His Majesty's Subjects entering the ports of that State [South Carolina], in prosecution of their lawful commerce, more especially such as are engaged in the Colonial trade, to a treatment of the most grievous and extraordinary description." Stratford Canning to [John Quincy] Adams, 13 February 1823, Copy, Justice Department, Attorney General's Papers, Record Group 60 (National Archives).

24. Donald G. Morgan, *Justice William Johnson, The First Dissenter: The Career and Constitutional Philosophy of a Jeffersonian Judge* (Columbia, 1954), 196; Philip M. Hamer, "Great Britain, the United States, and the Negro Seamen's Acts, 1822–1848," *Journal of Southern History* 1 (1935): 7.

25. Alan F. January, "The First Nullification: The Negro Seamen Acts Controversy in South Carolina, 1822–1860," (Ph.D. diss., University of Iowa, 1976), 284–306, especially 298–99 and 306.

26. Philip M. Hamer, "British Consuls and the Negro Seamen's Acts, 1850–1860," *Journal of Southern History* 1 (1935): 141–56; January, "The First Nullification," 339–50.

27. Charleston *Mercury*, 15 December 1851.

28. Petigru to W[illiam] Mathew, 26 March 1851, Foreign Office, General Correspondence United States of America, Series II, 5/551. Petigru's assertion was perhaps more complex than at first appears. According to the terms of the Judiciary Act of 1789, Section 11, such a suit could be brought in Circuit Court only if the "matter in dispute exceeds . . . the sum or value of five hundred dollars." It might possibly have been brought in District Court, but that is unlikely because it was neither international law nor United States treaty but rather state law that was at issue. Furthermore, as Professor Paul Finkelman has perceptively noted, even were the District Court a viable alternative legally, the issue could not hope to have a sympathetic hearing in a court over which a local judge presided. In short, Petigru's outright assertion that the federal courts lacked jurisdiction also carried the freight of political reality within South Carolina in it. Paul Finkelman to the authors, 12 October 1991.

29. Petigru to W[illiam] Mathew, 26 March 1851, Foreign Office, General Correspondence United States of America, Series II, 5/551.

30. Hamer, "British Consuls," 156–57.

31. F. C. Adams (pseud.), *Manuel Pereira: or the Sovereign Rule of South Carolina with Views of Southern Laws, Life, and Hospitality* (Washington, 1853), 168–69, 272–73; *Ex Parte Manuel Pereira*, 6 Richardson 149–50 (1853) (16 S. C. Reports 59–60), the quotation at 150/60.

32. *Reuben D. Roberts* v. *Jeremiah D. Yates*, 20 Federal Cases (1853), Case No. 11, 919, 937–38 (16 Law Reports 49). The case is summarized in both the Charleston *Courier* and the Charleston *Mercury*, 22 April 1853; also in January, "The First Nullification," 358–59.

33. Charleston *Mercury*, 22 April 1853. Robert B. Gilchrist was a federal district court judge, but in the *Roberts* v. *Yates* case he sat for the circuit court judge, who was unable to attend. In an older form, Edward McCrady was sometimes spelled McCready.

34. On the shift in British tactics and the modification of the seamen's legislation, see the Charleston *Courier*, 20 June 1853; also White, "The South in the 1850s,"

34–35; Hamer, "British Consuls," 166; and January, "The First Nullification," 371–88.

35. *Statutes at Large*, VI: 574.

36. *The State ex relatione Mrs. Kohne* v. *James Simons and B. C. Pressley*, 2 Speers 761–68 (1844) (12 S. C. Reports 316–19), 767/318. The possibility of Petigru's having committed a legal fraud against the state in the case of Jake was called to our attention by Professor Paul Finkelman. Paul Finkelman to the authors, 12 October 1991.

37. *Joseph Dougherty* v. *Executors of John Dougherty et al.*, 2 Strobhard Equity 63–69 (1848) (26 S. C. Reports 34–37). Similarly, John Clarkson's will, despite Petigru's best efforts, did not hold, again for lack of legal sophistication in its drafting. It was clear that Clarkson had left his entire estate to his brother in trust, but the will did not specify the beneficiaries or other purposes of the trust, although a separate addendum, which was added nine years after the will itself was prepared, specified that his brother was to free John's slaves in South Carolina if that was possible, otherwise to send them where they could be freed. Challenged by a nephew because both alternatives were illegal under South Carolina law, the will was completely invalidated, not for its substance, but because the unwitnessed addendum was inadequate. Chancellor Dunkin ordered that the entire estate should be sold and the proceeds divided among the three heirs at law. Then William Clarkson, as executor of John's will, appealed, arguing his right to carry out as much of the will as was legally tenable. However, here the court went against him and Petigru, who was attorney for the legatees, and upheld Dunkin's ruling. *W. C. Johnson by next friend* v. *William Clarkson and T. B. Clarkson*, 3 Richardson Equity 305–18 (1851) (27 S. C. Reports 125–30).

38. All the preceding in Petigru to Robert Habersham, 16 April 1857, Petigru and King Letterbooks.

39. Petigru to Habersham, 8 May 1857, Petigru and King Letterbooks.

40. Petigru to John Postell, 16 November 1857, Petigru and King Letterbooks.

41. The progress of the Broad slaves' case is summarized in *The State* v. *John J. Singletary, Rebecca Rhame, and others*, Dudley 220–23 (1838) (10 S. C. Reports 83–86). The argument claiming the illegality of the trust rests on an 1800 law that required that any emancipated slave had to be young and strong enough to be self-supporting and on an 1840 law that prohibited emancipation altogether.

42. *Jane De Hay ads Ferguson and Dangerfield*, 2 McMillan 228–30 (1842) (11 S. C. Reports 96–97).

43. Petigru to J. J. Browning, 31 October 1855, Petigru and King Letterbooks.

44. Wm. McLain (American Colonization Society) to Petigru, 28 February 1854, Petigru Letters, Vanderhorst Papers; Petigru to Theodore Gaillard, 2 June 1854, Petigru and King Letterbooks.

45. *F. A. Ford escheator ex rel J. Ferguson* v. *Starling J. Dangerfield*, 8 Richardson Equity 95–111 (1856) (28 S. C. Reports 33–39). The development of this final chapter of the case of the Broad slaves is covered in extensive correspondence in the Petigru and King Letterbooks, especially June, July, and November 1854 and October and December 1855.

46. Petigru and King to C. H. Simonton, 14 July 1854, and Petigru and King to Theodore Gaillard, 20 August 1855, both in Petigru and King Letterbooks. "An Act to Vest the Title of the State in Certain Escheated Property in Certain Persons Therein Mentioned," Act No. 4237, *Statutes at Large*, XII: 363–64, awarded the Broad slaves to Theodore Gaillard. James S. Dangerfield was awarded the Broad plantation, Act No. 4313, *Statutes at Large*, XII:495–96. For the final disposition of the Broad slaves to Liberia, Petigru and King to Randolph Mott, 23 February and 19 March 1857, and Petigru to J. S. Mustian, 31 December 1857, all in Petigru and King Letterbooks. In a separate case, but one similar to that of the Broad slaves, Petigru tried to defend a

will and trust arrangement made by a shiftless drunkard in order to prevent the return of a family of racially mixed parentage to very real, rather than merely nominal, slavery: *Carsten Vose Adm of Josiah Dangerfield* v. *R.S.H. Hannahan*, 10 Richardson 465–73 (1857) (17 S. C. Reports 157–60).

3

The Agony of Defeat: Calvin H. Wiley and the Proslavery Argument

John B. Weaver

The South is a Christian, a civilized, and a progressive land, and the owners of slaves are enlightened, civilized, and Christian men. If they are committing errors against their own interests, they will be sure to find them out in time.

—Calvin H. Wiley, *A Sober View of the Slavery Question*

It is surprising, in light of the considerable attention that historians of the United States have given to the study of southern history, that the proslavery argument has been until recently the focus of a relatively limited number of works. Various other factors — racism, economic self-interest, republican ideology, concepts of honor and paternalism — have been taken as the keys to explaining the rise and persistence of a slave society in the South, while historians airily dismissed proslavery thought as mere cover or rationalization for other, more "real" motivation. Today, however, the study of proslavery ideology is part of a highly respected and growing body of scholarship that examines the entire spectrum of the cultural and intellectual interests of the Old South. The encyclopedic survey of William S. Jenkins, which long stood in relative isolation, now has been joined by the work of Drew Gilpin Faust, Larry E. Tise, Eugene Genovese, David Donald, Kenneth S. Greenberg, William Freehling, and others.[1] As a result, proslavery thought finally has been recognized as an essential strand in the web of ideas and interests that characterized the South in the colonial and antebellum periods.

There still is a need to relate proslavery arguments to specific contexts of place, time, and person. The ideas of leading southern intellectuals, theologians, and politicians of a learned bent have been dissected and analyzed, rather thoroughly in some cases.[2] Now, more attention needs to be paid to less prominent individuals and to those for whom a contribution to proslavery thought was secondary to some other professional interest.

Calvin Henderson Wiley (1819–87) of North Carolina is a figure known to students of the Old South for his contributions to public education, but he is not one whose name readily comes to mind in the proslavery context. Having served as his native state's first superintendent of public schools, from 1852 to 1865, Wiley has been called the "Horace Mann of the South." He overcame much public opposition and apathy to build up a system that, although meager by antebellum northern standards, gave the Tar Heel State the largest public school enterprise in the South. As a devout Presbyterian who in the later years of his life turned to full-time work in the Christian ministry, Calvin Wiley approached his crusade for public education out of a wider concern for the moral and social climate of his state and region. This context gives Wiley's thought on slavery its particular value and significance.

The son of a farmer whose Scots-Irish ancestors had emigrated from Pennsylvania to North Carolina in 1752, Wiley was born in Guilford County, near present-day Greensboro, on February 3, 1819. His father had prospered in agriculture and owned both house and field slaves. Young Calvin was sent to the nearby Caldwell Institute, a Presbyterian academy, then on to the University of North Carolina, from which he graduated in 1840. At Chapel Hill he came under the influence of Professor Elisha Mitchell, a mathematician and Congregational-turned-Presbyterian clergyman who taught at the university from 1817 to 1857. The northern-born Mitchell had attended Yale during the presidency of Timothy Dwight and had imbibed Dwight's conservative, Federalist ideology. Mitchell held decidedly proslavery views, which he imparted to a generation and more of Carolina students.[3]

Nothing indicates that the young Wiley struggled with his personal outlook on slavery. He came of age after a time when the ideology of the American Revolutionary era may have inclined slaveowners to harbor reservations or be apologetic about slavery. He may or may not have known, for example, of the secret antislavery views held by the Reverend Eli Washington Caruthers, pastor of the Alamance Presbyterian Church, in which Wiley had grown up. For fear of reprisal, Caruthers did not publish a lengthy, polemical manuscript he wrote setting forth his opposition to slavery as inimical to the values of liberty and equality. However, in 1861 Caruthers was driven out of his pastorate after he publicly disparaged the cause for which the young men of his congregation were marching off to battle.[4]

Wiley spent much of the 1840s in search of a profession. As a lawyer, newspaper editor, and novelist, he was not a total failure, but not until he won appointment as superintendent of common schools in 1852 did he truly find his métier. As a Whig, he firmly believed that the state had a proper role in guiding the social and economic development of society, a view he shared with most of the first generation of American professional public educators. For the remainder of the 1850s, Wiley engaged in nothing less than a crusade for public schools in the Tar Heel State. To overcome apathy, indifference, and even positive hostility, he cultivated the support of both political parties by arguing for the practical utility of education and its benefits to the state. Although the schools themselves were largely locally financed and locally controlled, Wiley inspected schools, encouraged parents to take an active interest in their children's education, urged promising young people to become teachers, and created professional standards for teachers to emulate.[5]

Somehow, Wiley managed to keep a semblance of common school activity alive during the Civil War, but Union victory in 1865 brought his educational career to a sudden end. Wiley could not get the state's wartime political elite interested in reestablishing the antebellum system during the period of presidential Reconstruction from 1865 to 1867. When the Radical Republicans, many of whom did favor extensive public education, came to power in the wake of congressional Reconstruction, Wiley the southern patriot was informed that his services were no longer desired.[6]

The issue was race. Wiley and his supporters had never labored for the cause of educating North Carolina's black children. The very idea of doing so, in the antebellum years, was beyond the realm of imagination. Yet the concepts of white and black, of education and slavery, were never completely divorced in Wiley's thought.

Antebellum North Carolina shared certain political, economic, and social characteristics with the South as a whole. A seemingly vigorous two-party system, "democratized" to permit the inclusion of almost all adult white males, in fact produced a state government firmly in the control of the slaveholding elites in both parties, who guided the process of "reform." Black slavery was the essential element in uniting all whites across an otherwise wide economic chasm. "Humble" North Carolina was hardly less devoted to slavery or more "democratic" than its immediate neighbors north and south.[7]

The Piedmont, the central section of North Carolina, was Wiley's native region and had fewer slaves and large plantations than did the eastern part of the state, and the setting of his lifelong home influenced Wiley's thinking on slavery and race to a degree. Residents of the Piedmont and the mountain areas farther west frequently struggled with eastern planters over issues of internal improvement, taxation, and legislative apportionment, but geographical location was not a major determinant of their thought. In the final analysis, they were from a slaveholding region of a slaveholding state.[8]

For Wiley and other southerners, time was more significant than local geography. Not until the 1830s was Wiley old enough to begin formulating his own outlook on the South's "peculiar institution." Southerners, of course, did not suddenly change from antislavery to proslavery after 1830, but the Nat Turner revolt in 1831 and the emergence of a more radical abolitionist movement in the North in the early 1830s did change the tone and atmosphere of the debate. Nat Turner and his followers in Virginia were close enough to the Tar Heel State to have a profound effect on white North Carolinians. Conditions for slaves became harsher and more repressive, and support for, or even toleration of, arguments for colonization and gradual emancipation withered, while the volume and sophistication of proslavery writings steadily increased.[9]

Calvin Wiley was part of the last full generation of southerners who grew to adulthood before the Civil War. By then, all that remained for southern intellectuals was to defend their way of life in the face of northern hostility and to idealize slavery as part of a magnificent, divinely ordained social order. At most, they could exhort the slaveholders to do more to realize the ideals being preached. Wiley did not live in a time when the morality of slavery itself was questioned, and there is no evidence that he felt any guilt or even any youthful doubt concerning his part in the life of a slave society. It is, thus, virtually impossible to see Wiley's defense of slavery as the expression of an alienated man at odds with his own society, as one historian has characterized the proslavery argument.[10]

Wiley was the kind of conservative elitist who favored the modernization, such as railroad building, that would bring greater order, prosperity, and opportunity to southern society without changing basic social relations. More humane, "enlightened" treatment of black slaves and greater provision for the education of poor white children also were parts of his conservative quest. A staunch Whig in the antebellum years, Wiley criticized certain Democrats for espousing a dangerous social egalitarianism and, instead, compromised with the wealthy planter Democrats who dominated his state's politics in the 1850s. As a result, the North Carolina public school system remained less fully developed than it might have been. Having permitted local elites to exercise much control over schools in their areas in order to mold public opinion along conservative, deferential lines, after the Civil War Wiley was harshly critical of the Radicals who tried to build on the system of public education that he had worked to advance.[11]

Wiley's life and career closely paralleled those of his contemporary, Robert J. Breckinridge of Kentucky. Born in 1800, Breckinridge received a careful education under Presbyterian influences, spent some time as a lawyer, and entered the Presbyterian ministry in 1832. As superintendent of Kentucky's public schools from 1847 to 1853, Breckinridge tried to rouse that state from its lethargy and hostility toward public education. However, the two superintendents clearly differed on the question of slavery. Breckinridge tried several times, without success, to put Kentucky on the road to gradual emancipation, then remained a Unionist during the Civil War, and became a close adviser to President Abraham Lincoln on border state matters. Within his own state, however, Wiley had greater success than his Kentucky counterpart in advancing public education, at least in part because his views on slavery were compatible with those of the elite.[12]

There had been some antislavery sentiment among southern Presbyterians in the late eighteenth and early nineteenth centuries, but with the increasing growth of a slave economy in the region, such views became less common. Instead, conscious defense of slavery powerfully influenced the course of Presbyterianism in the South after 1830. In the Old School–New School schism of 1837, although issues of theology and ecclesiastical polity also were at stake, the Old School side was clearly far less interested in attacking slavery as a social and moral evil. The vast majority of Presbyterians in the South chose sides accordingly, and until 1861 they could remain comfortably in a national denomination that refused to condemn slaveholders. Only after the Old School General Assembly came to a clear defense of the Union in May 1861 did its southern members feel the need to break with their northern brethren.[13]

In his study of the 1837 schism, Elwyn A. Smith concluded that, for the Old School, "the agreement to be silent on slavery meant that majority Presbyterianism had affirmed that this overarching issue of national and private morals was unrelated to the corporate custom and teaching of the church." The calls for "slavery reform" that Wiley and other southern Presbyterians would later issue show that such a sweeping assertion is too unqualified, but there is a degree of truth in it. A doctrine that came to be known as the "spirituality of the church" was widespread among antebellum southern Presbyterians. In the hands of one of its principal advocates, James Henley Thornwell of South Carolina, theologian and college president, this doctrine became a powerful check against antislavery dissent within the church.[14]

Thornwell argued that Christianity's earthly mission was primarily, if not entirely, spiritual, to convert the individual to belief in Christ. In political and social matters, the churches should do nothing that God had not specifically commanded through the revelation of scripture. If the Bible did not declare a practice to be sinful, it was wrong for Christians to do so on their own. Because Thornwell could find no specific condemnation of slavery in Holy Scripture, he concluded that antislavery agitation, whether in or out of the church, was an affront against God and nature. Yet, Thornwell's attitude toward slavery itself was a complex and somewhat tortured one, as James Oscar Farmer, Jr., Theodore Dwight Bozeman, and William W. Freehling have made clear.[15] Opposed to the unlimited power of slaveholders and the resistance of many of them to the protection of the bonds of marriage and family among the slaves, in the late 1840s, Thornwell recommended state legislation to recognize slave marriages and to repeal the prohibition against teaching slaves to read.[16]

Like Thornwell, Calvin Wiley adhered to the Old School in the Presbyterian schism of 1837 and stayed with the southern wing of the Old School when northern and southern Presbyterians went their separate ways at the start of the Civil War. The resemblance between the writings of the two men is strong and may reflect either a larger climate of opinion in which they both shared very deeply or the North Carolina educator's familiarity with the specific ways that Thornwell was articulating that more general outlook. In any case, Wiley was much closer in his thinking to Thornwell than, for example, he was to Eli Caruthers, the pastor of the congregation to which Wiley had belonged since his youth.

Wiley's perspective on race relations and the role of blacks in southern society began to develop in the 1840s. Some of his earliest ideas were expressed in two rather unsuccessful novels he published before becoming an educator. In *Alamance*, set in North Carolina during the time of the Revolutionary War, a loyal and trusted slave becomes one of the heroes. In *Roanoke*, by contrast, a slave named "Wild Bill" utters inflammatory insurrectionist rhetoric. Responding to hostile critics of *Roanoke*, Wiley claimed "Wild Bill" was a character type that simply did not exist to the extent that fearful whites imagined.[17]

Wiley's first publication to address racial issues directly was a pamphlet, *A Sober View of the Slavery Question, by a Citizen of the South*, that appeared in 1849. Wiley argued there that the slaves' welfare would be enhanced if their high concentration in some areas could be reduced by diffusing the black population over a larger geographical region, including the new territories acquired from Mexico in the late 1840s. In relatively unsettled areas, the slaves would advance more rapidly as they developed skills useful in meeting the demands of frontier life. Here, Wiley's views fit into the larger notion of slavery as a "school" for blacks, rather than slavery as an end in itself.[18]

Wiley rejected both immediate emancipation and the colonization of U.S. blacks to Africa as dangerous and impractical. He predicted that if slaves were immediately freed, whites would "tyranize [*sic*] over them, out-wit them, and oppress them without remorse."[19] Yet, African colonization was no alternative because blacks would be better off in the "higher form of Christian civilization" that the United States had to offer. Unlike some other southern evangelicals, Wiley never evinced sympathy for groups such as the American Colonization Society.[20]

Wiley had no use for northerners who lectured southern whites about their moral responsibilities. The South already had an educated class, fully capable of guiding society to its true destiny through the enlightenment of the people. For this enlightenment, common schools were necessary because the moral guardians of society were to be patient and use the arts of persuasion, not coercion. Change would be gradual but inevitable if, as Wiley planned, his ideas for developing public education were never to get too far ahead of the voluntary consent of the people.[21]

So it was with slavery. Emancipation might be the goal, but only when slaveholders were ready for it:

If slavery is to be abolished, directly or indirectly, immediately or gradually, it must be the voluntary act of those that own the slaves; they must be allowed to manage their own burdens, and to discover and repent of their own sins. Public opinion is free. It is a Christian, a civilized, and a progressive land, and the owners of slaves are enlightened, civilized, and Christian men. If they are committing errors against their own interests, they will be sure to find them out in time. . . . *Let them alone*; leave them to the . . . lessons of their own teachers and preachers.[22]

Wiley's longest treatise on slavery, his unpublished manuscript "The Duties of Christian Masters," probably was written during the middle and late 1850s.[23] In it, Wiley presented his views on the origins of slavery, the qualities that should characterize slavery in a civilized land, the particular responsibilities of the Christian master, and the future destiny of the slaves. He deplored the fact that since slavery had become such a political issue, its truly religious character as a field of missionary enterprise had been neglected. Unlike some other religious defenses of slavery, Wiley's contribution would completely avoid "political considerations."[24] Because church and state moved in different spheres, each had its own legitimate interests with regard to slavery. Reforming slavery was as much the work of the church as it was of the state.

For Wiley, the origin of slavery was sin. All social imperfections (and slavery was one of them) were rooted in human depravity. If there had been no fall from an original state of perfection, each person would have been content to occupy the station in life for which he or she was best suited. When divine will had been disregarded, however, ambition and avarice had crept in. As a result of sin, men "trample each other in mad pursuit for the wrong things." The earth, thus, became a place of discipline and probation, where the more righteous controlled and restrained their weaker brethren for the common good.[25]

Wiley wanted to avoid any implication that blacks were not fully human, that they had not also been created in God's image, on the other hand, the more vividly he portrayed the African past as utterly savage, the more beneficent did the Africans' enslavement in a Christian, progressive United States become. Wiley, thus, attributed the low state of the Africans to their lack of contact with the Judeo-Christian tradition whose influence had elevated the caucasians over the centuries. He claimed that because Africans had had no sense of personal dignity or national loyalty whatsoever, uprooting them from their native land could not have destroyed any culture worth preserving. Rather, enslavement had been the working of divine providence to place the Negro under the moral and social restraint that both justice and mercy required.[26]

In the United States, and especially in the southern states, the two races, united in one humanity but far, far apart in all other respects, were to live side by side. The presence of a superior and an inferior race, with the temptation of the former to oppress the latter, was but an example of the distinctions among people that threatened the stability of any heterogeneous society. Against these disparities, religion provided the key to social harmony, Wiley believed, because the knowledge that all men had sinned created a "bond of union and sympathy between all ranks and classes of a state."[27] Wiley seemed unable to separate worldly status and perceptions of rank from the judgment of an impartial God. He equated the black slave with ignorance and sin and the white master with enlightenment and Christianity. What really concerned him at this point was to find a rationale for social inequality. Religion, he wrote, "enables the inferior classes to understand the origins of authority, and the causes of distinctions and subordinations, and vindicates to their hearts and consciences the existence of society whatever its apparent inequalities."[28]

As Wiley saw it, those who had taken up antislavery had forgotten that the rule of one person over another was a universal phenomenon. The existence of government itself reflected the fact that the world, for the benefit of sinful man, had become a place of discipline — "an intermediate state between heaven and hell." Fortunately, the U.S. government, influenced by the Christian character of its people, was enlightened and humane, resorting to coercion and force only when necessary, but all political power, no matter how oppressive, was divinely ordained for the discipline of the people.[29]

Having explained the role of government in an imperfect world, Wiley acknowledged that men often were rebellious. This tendency, however, could be overcome by spiritual regeneration and could be mediated by the family. If strong and pure family relations were established, it would be "comparatively easy" to induce men to accept government. In the well-ordered family, the husband had authority over the wife, the parent over the child, the elder over the younger, and the master over the slave.[30]

According to Wiley, the Christian master had to establish standards of conduct for his slaves and punish them when these standards were violated. Wiley stressed the Ten Commandments as the basis for teaching the slaves religion and compared the mid-nineteenth-century slaveholder with Moses on Mt. Sinai. There was no reason why "truly pious" slaves could not conduct prayer meetings, but the slaves could not be given complete freedom to shape their own forms of religious expression in which they would be led by their love of the visual and the sensual to construct "graven images" of the deity. Whites also would have to guard against the use of vivid imagery in trying to focus the slaves' attention upon God.[31]

In following the Commandments, Wiley believed that the slaves should have a day of rest on the Sabbath but that it was wrong to use the day to teach any secular knowledge to the slaves. Wiley also was quite firm in his conviction that the master must safeguard and enhance the stability of slave marriages and do the utmost to avoid separating slave parents and children by sale or trade.[32] Yet, because the ultimate authority of the master had to remain intact, slave children were to *honor* their parents but *obey* them only if it involved no conflict with the master's will.[33]

Wiley thought that it was inevitable that the slaves would advance with the passage of time. Tremendous progress had, in fact, already been made, even for slaves whose masters were not Christians.[34] Slavery was a prime example of how God could use human choices for divine ends. As Wiley put it:

Perhaps the first authors of slavery did not anticipate such (beneficial) results — perhaps at least very few of them were influenced, in fact, by religious motives — but whatever be the proper estimate of their conduct, it has nothing to do with the consequences which the goodness and mercy of God have extracted from it.[35]

In a rare moment, Wiley pondered that for some blacks, the time already might have come when slavery was of no more benefit to them.[36] More often, however, Wiley claimed that, because the whites also were advancing along with the slaves, the gap between them would never quite disappear. It, therefore, was best that blacks remain as rural slaves, doing simple tasks under the master's watchful eye.[37] It even was up to the master how far and how fast the slaves should advance. Those who taught their slaves to read and write had Wiley's full approval, but he was not about to condemn others who cited the law as their reason for letting the slaves remain illiterate. Wiley would be reasonably content as long as the slaves heard the gospel preached to them, adding that "where the laws of the state forbid the teaching of slaves to read, we have nothing to say."[38]

In Wiley's view of the slaves' progress over the generations, to bring in more Africans in the 1850s would only threaten to undo all the gains. Wiley, thus, disagreed with some southern nationalists and condemned all talk of reopening the slave trade as a way of bolstering the South's economic and political position in the nation.[39] He took seriously the view that slavery was good because it had cut the slaves off from their African past: "The slave trade was permanently arrested before the country became deluged with these savages — the tide of inflowing barbarism was cut off, and Africa, and all its soul-destroying influences forever shut from view."[40] With each new generation, the civilizing process had become easier.

The busy life of a public official limited the degree to which Calvin Wiley could participate in larger southern worlds of intellect, piety, and power. Yet, Wiley's ideas on slavery were broadly resonant with prevailing currents of thought in the Old South. His positive appreciation for the benefits of dispersing slavery over a wider area, for example, echoed sentiments that Thomas Jefferson had expressed at the time of the Missouri Controversy in the early 1820s, although ridding Virginia of its "excess" slave population figured more centrally in Jefferson's analysis.[41]

In Wiley's quest for the "moral reform" of slavery, one can see the strongest parallels with a large number of like-minded individuals. The degree to which proslavery southern clergy voiced a zealous concern for the moral dilemmas of slaveholding suggests a certain latent tension between these "reformers" and southern slaveholders.[42] Neither an active clergyman nor an owner of many slaves, in the antebellum years, Wiley was not directly involved in either the development of theological positions on slavery in the denominational press or in plantation missions to slaves. Nonetheless, the themes of James Henley Thornwell and Charles Colcock Jones, who were active in such religious matters, correspond with those enumerated by Wiley.

The leading Presbyterian advocate of the religious instruction of slaves, Charles Colcock Jones also wanted a higher standard of conduct between master and slave. Like Wiley, Jones had little or no appreciation for the indigenous culture of African Americans and thought that whites alone should guide and control the slaves' Christian experience. He defended his program as essential for the conservative order of society, in the best self-interest of the slaveholder, but simultaneously projected a vision of the future that required great change on the part of the masters. As Wiley would eventually have to admit as well, Jones knew that the churches' real impact on masters and slaves was largely ineffectual. The African Americans' own appropriation of Christian motifs and symbols to their actual experience far outran the scattered efforts of the white evangelicals.[43]

The question remains, however, why Wiley, who was engaged in a professional task that he found absorbing, even took time to write his unpublished manuscript. One clue lies in the exceptional vehemence with which he attacked the advocates of reopening the African slave trade in the 1850s. Was he concerned that southern-rights extremists and slaveowners who did not share his religious sensibilities were threatening to gain the upper hand in southern politics and culture? Did he sense a reckless spirit of defiance in a South embittered by northern resistance to slavery expansion? If so, he ultimately chose not to publish the manuscript. Perhaps he realized that southern nationalism also could have its uses for an educator who couched in terms of resistance to the North the quest for modernization and the tacit acceptance of Yankee values it entailed.[44]

It was the economic, cultural, and moral imperative of "enlightening the governing race" that gripped Wiley's imagination. For him, the defense of slavery was important but secondary to the educational crusade he had launched. One could speculate on the future of slavery, but only God really knew what the future would bring.[45]

The Civil War and its aftermath were extraordinarily cruel to Wiley's vision of a South of common schools and Christian masters. At first, the war seemed to be a necessary price southerners must pay to protect their institutions.[46] As the Confederacy went down to defeat, however, it became clear that something had gone wrong. Believing God had become angry with the South's reluctance to practice slavery on a truly biblical basis and feeling remorse for not publishing his own warning earlier, Wiley was at last moved to take a realistic view of the failures of southern society.[47] He was too late. It was a bitter blow to become a reform activist and then find that there was nothing left to reform.

Before the war, Wiley was a most unlikely secessionist, regarding proponents of such a course as obstacles to the path of moral improvement that the South needed to take. As late as December 1860, he lamented that the proposed Confederacy, "looking only to the Cotton interest . . . would grind . . . North Carolina into the earth."[48] However, two months later, he had changed his mind.[49] He approved North Carolina's decision to join the Confederacy after the attack on Fort Sumter and Lincoln's call to arms, proclaiming that the South now remained the only truly moral nation left on earth.[50]

Wiley's major concern during the first years of the war was not slavery but the fate of the common schools.[51] To keep them open, female teachers would have to be found and textbooks would have to be produced at home. Wiley reminded North Carolinians that the North would be delighted to find the South's leading public educational system unable to survive in wartime and argued that closing the schools would hurt civilian morale and lead to moral decline in the next generation.[52] The state's Literary Fund, chief source of school revenue, was not diverted to military use. At least a few schools were operating throughout the war period, but, in some localities, it became difficult to continue even the limited provisions that had been made before the war.[53]

Wiley's buoyant optimism faded after the Confederate forces had been turned back at Gettysburg.[54] His conclusion that God was punishing the South found its way into a book Wiley published late in 1863 under the title *Scriptural Views of National Trials*. Like the heathen nations that in Old Testament history had taken Israel into captivity, the North, "this wicked enemy whom we abhor," was being used by God to chastise the South.[55] It was a painful but necessary admission that the "Christian element" in the South had not done all that the Lord required, "and as its strength in numbers, learning, wealth and position gave it a predominant influence the deplorable state of things proves that it could not have been true to this obligation." Southern churchmen had not done enough to impress upon masters the seriousness of their duties. They had not been firm enough in demands that slave marriage be encouraged and respected, that slaves be given opportunities for religious worship and instruction, and that slaves be treated kindly and justly.[56]

Wiley pointed out what he believed were the reasons the churches failed. Church leaders had wasted their time *defending* from outside attack an institution that needed no elaborate defense at all.[57] God had ordained slavery, and that was that. Fear that the free-soilers would be encouraged by any admission that slavery as practiced was not always just also had distracted the South from reform.[58] Even now, there still was a danger that the South would overlook its own sins while "filled with just indignation at the injustice and cruelties of those whom God had made instruments for our chastisement."[59] The Confederacy's only hope as an independent nation was to reform slavery immediately. Although a bitter war was raging, Wiley saw it as an unmatched opportunity: "We are cut off from intercourse with all foreign influences; and never again can we legislate or labor in society with such perfect exemption from the outside pressure exerted on all states of the world."[60]

Scriptural Views of National Trials included no concrete legislative proposals. Wiley has been mentioned as a leading spokesman for "slavery reform" in the Confederacy, but his practical efforts hardly matched those of other Presbyterian clergymen who shared similar concerns.[61] A reticent man when it came to politics, Wiley preferred to persuade rather than confront. He privately advised a friend in the state legislature that "discreet commissioners" could be appointed to revise the slave code and that laws could be passed forbidding the separation of slave families, legalizing slave marriages, requiring masters to give slaves a day of rest on the Sabbath, and making emancipation easier.[62]

As the Confederacy's position became truly desperate in late 1864 and early 1865, President Jefferson Davis and other high officials advocated conscription of slaves for military service, with the possibility of emancipation to follow.[63] Interest in the move came too late to affect the military situation, but Wiley, along with most other North Carolina leaders, abhorred the very thought of armed slaves defending the Confederacy.[64] He predicted that "if we put the negro even in the army, we will be compelled to free their families and give the race political equality; and there is nothing any earthly power can do for us worse than this."[65] The result would "Africanize the country," and to that outcome, Wiley admitted, a Yankee victory would be preferable.[66]

Wiley remained convinced that only slavery reform could deliver the South from its enemies. To wait any longer was to invite national suicide.[67] He appealed to Governor Zebulon Vance for action, and in reply, Vance intimated that he also had long believed that slavery had to be reformed. At the same time, Vance revealed the great distance separating Wiley from even those politicians sympathetic to reform by resisting *immediate* action and limiting his promises for action to a time when the military threat should ease.[68]

At first, Wiley had a very hard time realizing that the end of the war also meant the end of slavery. He explained to John Gilmer, "I am sure our people are ready to modify the institution and to agree to abolish it by degrees, say in twenty years, or even less time, and what more can reasonably be asked?" Gilmer was going to Washington as part of a North Carolina delegation to seek as favorable a set of terms as possible from the new president, Andrew Johnson. Wiley urged Gilmer to press for a scheme whereby emancipation would be delayed for five years while the blacks, in preparation for freedom, would remain bound to their present masters as apprentices.[69]

Eventually, Wiley came to accept the simple truth that slavery as he had known it was over. In retrospect he concluded that the institution had been deteriorating even before secession. Laws had become harsher and more rigid, the freedom to emancipate a slave had been restricted, slave "marriages" had been increasingly degraded, and no significant number of slaves were being taught to read and write. A slave insurrection would have destroyed or radically modified slavery even without the war.[70] The secessionists, the "greatest madmen of the human race,"[71] had sealed the fate of slavery, because a Confederate victory could have been secured only at the expense of a social revolution, the arming of the slaves. Fortunately, God saw fit, before the slaves were conscripted, to bring on a northern victory and sudden abolition — which in the long run was the lesser of two evils.[72]

Wiley did not modify his views too drastically, however, even though the old order would never return. Although God was no longer using slavery to carry out His purposes, God had left the freedmen in the South so that southerners could redeem themselves for their past sins by educating and guiding former slaves to maturity.[73] Yet another reason Wiley cited for watching over the freedmen's welfare was to protect social order and, thus, minimize the pernicious influence of northern teachers who already were flocking to the South.[74]

Fear of the new society taking shape in the postwar South led Wiley back to his old zeal in urging a resumption of the common schools and in calling for active white interest in the social and spiritual welfare of blacks. Yet, similar fears prompted different reactions from others. Politicians who once had actively supported Wiley's educational crusade scuttled the common schools, citing potential dangers of integration and Yankee influence. Many of Wiley's fellow Presbyterians saw the black exodus from their churches as justification for benign neglect. Only a few ministers who felt compelled to do something for their black brethren withdrew from the North Carolina presbyteries after the war and helped blacks form their own Catawba Presbytery, which affiliated with the Old School Presbyterian church in the North.[75] Wiley was not among those clergymen.

Wiley could not fully accept either of the alternatives in race relations open before him — to ignore and neglect the blacks, thereby hoping to keep them subordinate, or to accept and work with them on a basis approaching racial equality. His outlook was the most enlightened to be found among white conservatives, but he could never completely free himself from the forces of tradition and fear that prevented a thorough change in thought and behavior.[76]

Having so heavily invested in the proslavery ideology as the key to the social and moral progress of the South, Wiley could not envision a new basis for progress in the "New South" and became fundamentally pessimistic on the prospects for society. As Jack P. Maddex, Jr., points out, many antebellum southern Presbyterians held to a postmillennial view of biblical prophecy in which the reform of slavery would help to usher in a "golden age" of righteousness. Wiley was a disillusioned postmillennialist who decided after the war that the only proper interpretation of eschatology was the amillennial one. The future would bring a continuing conflict between the forces of good and evil that would not be resolved in the secular realm.[77]

The religious defense of slavery was not the robust, unrestrained creed that would have encouraged the slaveholder to exercise unlimited selfish power and sanctioned endless greed. Yet, the argument largely failed to change southern society despite the case of a slaveowner here and there who did seek to conform his ways to the standards set forth by religious leaders. A look at Calvin Wiley suggests that a religious perspective on slavery could encourage a posture of passivity and complacency as much as one of action and anguish.

Intellectually and temperamentally, Wiley was committed to voluntarism and persuasion and disliked any approach that seemed unnecessarily coercive. In addition, he was not entirely free from racial fears and wanted to avoid change that damaged the delicate structure of racial control. Then there also was the influence upon Wiley of southern Presbyterian doctrine, which tended to separate the mission of the church from that of the state. Wiley's ultimate reliance upon God, and not men, to guide the South out of its moral dilemma made the need for immediate action seem less urgent. Indeed, he took the Confederacy's successful beginning as a sure sign that God was satisfied with the progress the South already had made in solving its racial problem.

It was Wiley's trust in God that finally enabled him to accept the Confederacy's tragic end. He had been complacent about reform because he had trusted God to "work out" the dilemmas that southerners were unable or unwilling to face themselves. Now, events left Calvin Wiley with only one possible conclusion: God's method for dealing with slavery had been neither peaceful nor gradual. His will had been done. Slavery and the Old South were destroyed.

NOTES

1. William S. Jenkins, *Pro-Slavery Thought in the Old South* (Chapel Hill, 1935); Drew Gilpin Faust, *A Sacred Circle: The Dilemma of the Intellectual in the Old South, 1840–1860* (Baltimore, 1977); Larry E. Tise, *Proslavery: A History of the Defense of Slavery in America, 1701–1840* (Athens, 1987); Eugene Genovese, *The World the Slaveholders Made: Two Essays in Interpretation* (New York, 1969); Eugene Genovese, *Roll, Jordan, Roll: The World the Slaves Made* (New York, 1974); David Donald, "The Proslavery Argument Reconsidered," *Journal of Southern History* 37 (1971): 3–18; Kenneth S. Greenberg, *Masters and Slaves: The Political Culture of American Slavery* (Baltimore, 1985); William W. Freehling, *The Road to Disunion: Secessionists at Bay, 1776–1854* (New York, 1990). A useful, if now slightly dated, bibliography on proslavery thought is found in Drew Gilpin Faust, ed., *The Ideology of Slavery: Proslavery Thought in the Antebellum South, 1830–1860* (Baton Rouge, 1981), 301–6.

2. A convenient summary of many of these studies is Drew Gilpin Faust, "The Peculiar South Revisited: White Society, Culture, and Politics in the Antebellum Period, 1800–1860," in John B. Boles and Evelyn T. Nolen, eds., *Interpreting Southern History: Historiographical Essays in Honor of Sanford W. Higginbotham* (Baton Rouge, 1987), 99–119.

3. For biographical information on Wiley's early life, see Howard Braverman, "Calvin Henderson Wiley, North Carolina Educator and Writer" (Ph.D. diss., Duke University, 1951), 1–21. For Elisha Mitchell's career at the University of North Carolina, see Tise, *Proslavery*, 396–97.

4. Calvin H. Wiley, *Alamance Church: A Historical Address Delivered at the Dedication of its Fourth House of Worship, on October 18th, 1879* (Raleigh, 1880), 7; George Troxler, "Eli Caruthers: A Silent Dissenter in the Old South," *Journal of Presbyterian History* 45 (1967): 95–111.

5. M. C. Noble, *A History of the Public Schools of North Carolina* (Chapel Hill, 1930), 220–32; Braverman, "Wiley," 163–97; Frederick M. Binder, *The Age of the Common School, 1830–1865* (New York, 1974), 140–41.

6. Paul M. Ford, "Calvin H. Wiley and the Common Schools of North Carolina, 1850–1869" (Ph.D. diss., Harvard University, 1960), 258–79, has an excellent account of the events of 1865 and 1866 that affected the school system and Wiley's place in it. Conservative politicians such as Zebulon B. Vance and Jonathan Worth preferred no system of public education rather than one that would educate both black and white children. A letter from Provisional Governor William W. Holden, dated 18 September 1865, informing Wiley that he has been relieved of his duties as school superintendent, is in the Calvin H. Wiley Papers (North Carolina State Department of Archives and History, Raleigh).

7. Thomas E. Jeffrey, *State Parties and National Politics: North Carolina, 1815–1861* (Athens, 1989), 7–11; Paul D. Escott, *Many Excellent People: Power and Privilege in North Carolina, 1850–1900* (Chapel Hill, 1985), 3–59; Paul D. Escott, "Yeoman Independence and the Market: Social Status and Economic

Development in Antebellum North Carolina," *North Carolina Historical Review* 66 (1989): 275–300.

8. William E. Farrison, "The Negro Population of Guilford County, North Carolina before the Civil War," *North Carolina Historical Review* 21 (1944): 319–29.

9. Charles E. Morris, "Panic and Reprisal: Reaction in North Carolina to the Nat Turner Insurrection, 1831," *North Carolina Historical Review* 62 (1985): 29–53.

10. Donald, "The Proslavery Argument Reconsidered." On the question of guilt over slavery, see also Gaines M. Foster, "Guilt over Slavery: A Historiographical Analysis," *Journal of Southern History* 56 (1990): 665–94.

11. Thomas E. Jeffrey, "'Our Remarkable Friendship': The Secret Collaboration of Calvin H. Wiley and John W. Cuningham," *North Carolina Historical Review* 67 (1990): 28–58. Cuningham was a long-time Democratic member of the North Carolina General Assembly with close ties to the wealthy planter elite. For his criticism of egalitarianism, see Calvin H. Wiley, *Address Delivered before the Two Literary Societies of Wake Forest College* (Raleigh, 1845).

12. On Breckinridge, see Charles W. Dabney, *Universal Education in the South* (2 vol., Chapel Hill, 1936), 1:274–77; and Andrew E. Murray, *Presbyterians and the Negro — A History* (Philadelphia, 1966), 77–80.

13. Murray, *Presbyterians and the Negro,* 3–28, 63–75, 106–12; Ernest Trice Thompson, *Presbyterians in the South* (3 vol., Richmond, 1963–73), 1:377–94, 530–50, 563–66; C. Bruce Staiger, "Abolitionism and the Presbyterian Schism of 1837–1838," *Mississippi Valley Historical Review* 36 (1949): 391–414; Elwyn A. Smith, "The Role of the South in the Presbyterian Schism of 1837–38," *Church History* 29 (1960): 44–63.

14. Smith, "Role of the South," 61; Ernest Trice Thompson, *The Spirituality of the Church: A Distinctive Doctrine of the Presbyterian Church in the United States* (Richmond, 1961), 24–26.

15. James Oscar Farmer, Jr., *The Metaphysical Confederacy: James Henley Thornwell and the Synthesis of Southern Values* (Macon, 1986); Theodore Dwight Bozeman, "Science, Nature and Society: A New Approach to James Henley Thornwell," *Journal of Presbyterian History* 50 (1972): 307–25; William W. Freehling, "James Henley Thornwell's Mysterious Antislavery Moment," *Journal of Southern History* 57 (1991): 383–406.

16. Freehling, "Thornwell," 397, 401–2; Haskell Monroe, "Southern Presbyterians and the Secession Crisis," *Civil War History* 6 (1960): 351–60; Thompson, *Presbyterians in the South,* 2:63–86.

17. Ford, "Wiley," 60–98, discusses these novels and their importance in the development of Wiley's thought.

18. Calvin H. Wiley, *A Sober View of the Slavery Question, by a Citizen of the South* (Washington, 1849), 5–6.

19. Ibid., 3.

20. Southern evangelicals' support for colonization is discussed in Anne C. Loveland, *Southern Evangelicals and the Social Order, 1800–1860* (Baton Rouge, 1980), 213–14, 261.

21. Calvin H. Wiley to David S. Reid, 24 May 1853, Calvin H. Wiley Papers (Duke University Library); Calvin H. Wiley, "Common School Department," *North Carolina Journal of Education* 2 (May 1859): 150.

22. Wiley, *A Sober View,* 3–4.

23. The manuscript of "The Duties of Christian Masters" is in the Calvin H. Wiley Papers (Southern Historical Collection, University of North Carolina at Chapel Hill). An accompanying note by his daughter, Mary C. Wiley, states that Wiley wrote it between 1854 and 1860. Stephen B. Weeks, *The Beginnings of the Common School System in the South* (Washington, 1898), 1474, says that Wiley worked on the

manuscript in 1858. There is a passing reference in the manuscript to John Brown's raid on Harpers Ferry in October 1859. Most of the work is in sections of 10 to 40 pages each, with the pages consecutively numbered throughout. Evidently, these were to have been separate chapters for a published version. For purpose of citation, each section has been assigned a number, based on the order in which they were found in the Wiley Papers. Citations that include no section number refer to loose pages, numbered consecutively from 67 to 292, that have been grouped together to form the concluding portion of the manuscript.

24. Wiley, "The Duties of Christian Masters," section 9, 1.

25. Ibid., section 10, 1–3; section 11, 25–28; section 12, 1–5.

26. Ibid., section 11, 29–32.

27. Ibid., section 3, 11.

28. Ibid., section 3, 12.

29. Ibid., section 2, 1–12; section 3, 5–9; section 4, 2; section 10, 50; Calvin H. Wiley, "The Origins of National Troubles," unpublished MS, Wiley Papers (Southern Historical Collection).

30. Wiley, "The Duties of Christian Masters," section 2, 3; section 3, 5–12.

31. Ibid., 104–11, 156, 160.

32. Ibid., 176–77, 277.

33. Ibid., 159, 166.

34. Ibid., section 11, 31–36; section 19, 23.

35. Ibid., 88.

36. Calvin H. Wiley, MS fragment on slavery, undated, Wiley Papers (Southern Historical Collection) (not part of "The Duties of Christian Masters").

37. Wiley, "The Duties of Christian Masters," section 11, 39–42; section 16, 19–24.

38. Ibid., 111–12.

39. The campaign to reopen the African slave trade is examined in Ronald Takaki, *A Pro-Slavery Crusade* (New York, 1971).

40. Wiley, "The Duties of Christian Masters," 93.

41. John C. Miller, *The Wolf by the Ears: Thomas Jefferson and Slavery* (New York, 1977), 234–42.

42. Farmer, *Metaphysical Confederacy*, 214–16; Loveland, *Southern Evangelicals*, 206–18; Freehling, "Thornwell," 389–99.

43. On Charles C. Jones and the matter of religious instruction of the slaves, see Albert J. Raboteau, *Slave Religion: The "Invisible Institution" in the Antebellum South* (New York, 1978), 151–210; Erskine Clarke, *Wrestlin' Jacob: A Portrait of Religion in the Old South* (Atlanta, 1979), 9–37.

44. Jeffrey, "'Our Remarkable Friendship,'" 36–37. Wiley frequently defended public education in terms of its contributions to the interests of the South against the North. See, for example, *Report of the Superintendent of Common Schools for 1860*, 11; "Common School Department: The Best Defence," *North Carolina Journal of Education* 3 (February 1860): 57–59.

45. Calvin H. Wiley, MS fragment on slavery, undated, Wiley Papers (Southern Historical Collection).

46. Calvin H. Wiley, "Address to the People of North Carolina," *North Carolina Journal of Education* 4 (July 1861): 194–97.

47. Calvin H. Wiley to Zebulon B. Vance, 31 July 1863, Zebulon Baird Vance Papers (North Carolina State Department of Archives and History).

48. Quoted in Jeffrey, "'Our Remarkable Friendship,'" 48.

49. Calvin H. Wiley, "Thoughts [on his birthday, 3 February 1861]," Wiley Papers (Southern Historical Collection).

50. Wiley, "Address to the People," 204.

51.   Calvin H. Wiley, "Letter of Instructions and Suggestions," *North Carolina Journal of Education* 4 (May 1861): 150–58.

52.   Calvin H. Wiley to Zebulon B. Vance, 26 September 1862, in Frontis Johnston, ed., *The Papers of Zebulon Baird Vance* (Raleigh, 1963–), 1:231–34.

53.   Local tax funds for schools were diverted to other purposes in at least two counties, Lenoir and Mecklenburg. Matt Whitaker, Jr., to Calvin H. Wiley, 24 April 1862, and W. J. Gates to Calvin H. Wiley, 30 January 1862, Wiley Papers (North Carolina State Department of Archives and History).

54.   Calvin H. Wiley to John W. Cuningham, 8 July 1863, John W. Cuningham Papers (Southern Historical Collection); Calvin H. Wiley to Zebulon B. Vance, 13 October 1864, Vance Papers.

55.   Calvin H. Wiley, *Scriptural Views of National Trials; or, The True Road to the Independence and Peace of the Confederate States of America* (Greensboro, 1863), 115.

56.   Ibid., 131; see also Drew Gilpin Faust, *The Creation of Confederate Nationalism* (Baton Rouge, 1988), 76.

57.   Calvin H. Wiley to James Henley Thornwell, n.d. (1862?), Folder 140, Wiley Papers (Southern Historical Collection).

58.   Wiley, *Scriptural Views of National Trials*, 189.

59.   Wiley to Thornwell.

60.   Wiley, *Scriptural Views of National Trials*, 162.

61.   Thompson, *Presbyterians in the South*, 2:25–26, 61–62; Bell I. Wiley, "The Movement to Humanize the Institution of Slavery during the Confederacy," *Emory University Quarterly* 5 (1949): 207–20.

62.   Wiley to John W. Cuningham, n.d. (1864–65?), Cuningham Papers. Wiley may have signed a petition presented to the North Carolina General Assembly in 1855 proposing similar changes in the laws relating to slavery, including permission for slaves to learn to read. Nothing specific came of the proposal. To the contrary, one scholar found that just before the Civil War, slaves and free blacks in North Carolina were subject to increasing restrictions and tighter controls. See Raleigh *Register*, 18 April 1855; B. H. Nelson, "Some Aspects of Negro Life in North Carolina during the Civil War," *North Carolina Historical Review* 25 (1948): 166.

63.   See Robert F. Durden, *The Gray and the Black: The Confederate Debate on Emancipation* (Baton Rouge, 1972).

64.   Ibid., 95, 173–76, 240–41, 252–53.

65.   David L. Corbitt, ed., "Calvin H. Wiley on the Evils of Slavery and the Causes of the Civil War," *North Carolina Historical Review* 3 (1926): 646.

66.   Wiley to Cuningham.

67.   Corbitt, "Wiley," 643.

68.   Zebulon B. Vance to Calvin H. Wiley, 3 February 1865, Wiley Papers (Southern Historical Collection). Vance's interest in slavery "reform" may have been genuine, but before the Civil War, he was more certain that slavery would be a permanent institution, guided by men, rather than subject to the dictates of God. See Zebulon B. Vance, *Speech . . . on the Slavery Question . . . March 16th, 1860* (Washington, 1860).

69.   Calvin H. Wiley to John A. Gilmer, 27 April 1865, and Calvin H. Wiley to John A. Gilmer, 5 May 1865, Wiley Papers (Southern Historical Collection).

70.   Calvin H. Wiley, "The Institution of Slavery," unpublished MS, n.d. (1865–66?), Wiley Papers (Southern Historical Collection).

71.   Corbitt, "Wiley," 644.

72.   Wiley, "The Institution of Slavery."

73.   Calvin H. Wiley to S. S. Murkland, 30 June 1865, quoted in Raleigh *Observer*, 15 February 1878.

74. Ibid.; North Carolina Department of Public Instruction, *Report of the Superintendent of Common Schools for 1865* (Raleigh, 1865), 27–32.

75. Murray, *Presbyterians and the Negro*, 139–51; John L. Bell, Jr., "The Presbyterian Church and the Negro during Reconstruction," *North Carolina Historical Review* 40 (1963): 15–36.

76. The contrast between Wiley and a contemporary of his is instructive on this point. The Reverend S. S. Murkland, a native of Scotland, was forced to leave his pastorate at the Bethany, North Carolina, Presbyterian Church in late 1865 because he had accepted a commission from the northern Presbyterians to serve as a missionary to the freedmen in North Carolina. Later, he helped to organize the predominantly black Catawba Presbytery. Murkland was skeptical of the good intentions of former slaveholders and identified strongly with black Presbyterians in their struggle to organize their own churches. Wiley could not accept these manifestations of black independence and self-reliance. For information on Murkland, see Murray, *Presbyterians and the Negro*, 143–44, and Bell, "The Presbyterian Church and the Negro," 24. See also S. S. Murkland to Calvin H. Wiley, 9 September 1865, Wiley Papers (Southern Historical Collection).

77. Jack P. Maddex, Jr., "Proslavery Millennialism: Social Eschatology in Antebellum Southern Calvinism," *American Quarterly* 31 (1979): 46–62.

4

John Tyler as President: An Old School Republican in Search of Vindication

Sylvan H. Kesilman

In September 1841, John Tyler, tenth president of the United States, arrived at a decision that would shape his political destiny and place in history. Less than a year before, in the celebrated "log cabin and hard cider" campaign of 1840, the Whig party had won a great victory, electing William H. Harrison president and Tyler vice-president and gaining control of both houses of Congress. Then, in April 1841, only a month after being inaugurated, Harrison died in office, making Tyler the first vice-president ever to rise to the presidency under such circumstances. Still buoyed by their victory, the Whigs, in an extra session of Congress called for that summer, proceeded to enact a legislative program of their own. Led by Senator Henry Clay of Kentucky, himself a perennial presidential aspirant, the agenda included an attempt to recharter a national bank, which Tyler for three decades had been known to oppose. When Tyler vetoed a first bank bill sent to him in August and outlined his objections, a second bill was prepared in a form he supposedly would approve, but he found this measure similarly unacceptable. Its drafting frequently has been viewed as a maneuver by Clay and his friends in Congress to embarrass the president.[1]

Tyler now faced the critical moment of his political career, involving what appeared to be a winless decision.[2] If he signed the bill, he would violate his long-standing opposition to this type of bank but would emerge, to Clay's detriment, as the Whig party's presidential leader. If he disapproved it, he would be true to his principles but incur the Whigs' wrath, leaving himself a president without a party and clearing the way for Clay's nomination in 1844. Tyler did not hesitate long before vetoing this bill on September 9, opening the door for the Whigs to read him formally out of the party, abuse him thereafter in speeches and the press, and oppose his measures in Congress for the remainder of his term.

Following his succession to office, Tyler had retained all the members of Harrison's cabinet, most of whom were Clay supporters. Two days after the second veto, these secretaries staged a scenario without parallel in U.S. history to discomfit the president and possibly force his resignation. Following a conference at one of their homes, they sent in their letters of resignation throughout the afternoon of September 11. John Tyler, Jr., the president's private secretary, stood by his father's desk with his watch in hand and observed that the letters all arrived at intervals between noon and 5:30 P.M. Only one cabinet member did not follow that course. Secretary of State Daniel Webster, long a rival of Clay for Whig party leadership and then involved in important negotiations with Great Britain, entered the president's office while the resignation letters were arriving and in the following dialogue helped set the tone for Tyler's future course: "Where am I to go, Mr. President?" "You must decide that yourself, Mr. Webster." "If you leave it to me, Mr. President, I will stay where I am." Tyler then rose from his chair, extended his arm, and exclaimed: "Give me your hand on that, and now I will say to you that Henry Clay is a doomed man from this hour!"[3]

In the months that followed, Tyler further defined the mood for the independent course that he would pursue. The light of burning effigies, he told a supportive audience in his home state of Virginia, only illuminated his duty to carry on, placing confidence "in the patriotism, discernment, and intelligence of the American people, whose interests are always best sustained by a firm observance of constitutional requirements."[4] On a similar note, he wrote to Webster, "Our course is too plainly before us to be mistaken. We must look to the whole country and the whole people."[5]

As Tyler's moment of decision defined the political setting and challenges of his presidency, it can be used as a point of departure for assessing his performance in office and examining where his independent course might lead him among the existing array of factions. To understand the basic motivation for his decisions and actions, it must be stressed that Tyler was an "Old School Republican," part of a small philosophical group devoted to Thomas Jefferson's original teachings of states' rights and strict construction of the Constitution. By the 1830s those principles no longer were the concern of most Americans or the basis of partisan division. Consequently, the advocates of those doctrines struggled to preserve them by shifting their allegiance to whichever major party seemed more compatible at the moment.

Tyler's lifelong devotion to states' rights and strict construction was demonstrated throughout his early career and has been acknowledged by many historians.[6] It, therefore, cannot be charged that he invented or invoked these views at a later time just to resolve his personal dilemmas. Furthermore, his record shows that, unlike some of his southern colleagues who used states' rights to weave Old Republican dogma or promote southern sectionalism, he was very much a nationalist, willing, within constitutional limits, to use federal power to meet the whole country's needs.

In the late nineteenth and early twentieth centuries, most American histories were written by northerners who continued to flay the Old South and its representatives for generations after the Civil War. Influenced by the continuous attacks on Tyler as president by both Clay Whigs and those Democrats who resisted his return to their party, these historians were especially harsh on Tyler, who not only was a Virginia planter and slaveowner but also ended his career as a member of the Confederate Congress.[7] In those postwar years, the only effort to cast Tyler in a more favorable light came from his son, the noted southern historian Lyon G. Tyler, through such works as his three-volume collection, *The Letters and Times of the Tylers*.[8]

During the twentieth century, historians have tended to favor presidents who fit into the so-called progressive or liberal reform tradition represented by Jefferson, Jackson, Wilson, Roosevelt, and Truman. As a result, even Democratic chief executives such as James K. Polk and Grover Cleveland, who did not gain lofty regard in their own times, have been construed by recent scholars to have been great presidents.[9] Although from that same perspective Tyler ranks below average, Thomas A. Bailey and Norma Peterson maintained that his accomplishments warranted higher ratings. Clinton Rossiter ranked Tyler among the second highest group of presidents, and Victor Laski placed him among the highest.[10]

Because Tyler frequently is dismissed or misrepresented as a weak president and stubborn sectionalist who surrounded himself with only southern states' rights advisers, it is common to find careless or downright erroneous statements about him in many otherwise sound historical writings.[11] Some authors, imbued by their abhorrence of slavery, are quick to assail a president strongly identified with the South and some of its more outspoken advocates.[12] Other historians have written syntheses of politics in the period when Tyler rose to and occupied the White House without even mentioning him at all.[13]

During the past quarter century, the "new political history" of the antebellum period has rejected the traditional emphasis on slavery and sectionalism and has stressed instead the national orientation of both political parties. Although not much concerned with Tyler (indeed, as noted previously, sometimes without even mentioning him), these new histories provide a basis for contending, as this chapter does, that Tyler conducted his office with predominantly national, rather than sectional, concerns.[14] Despite those works, many recent scholars have perpetuated the view that parties became irrevocably sectionalized by the Texas annexation issue in 1844, that slavery was the driving force behind the Tyler administration's Texas policy, and that Tyler was an active practitioner of sectional politics. Still, some of these writers provide broader perspectives for viewing southern leaders such as Tyler by noting that slavery was not the only force that motivated them.[15]

Thorough investigation reveals that Tyler was a moderate on the bipartisan spectrum of his time and an able administrator who included men from all sections of the country in his councils. He fit the southern ideal of career public servant devoted to his constituents and meriting their trust.[16] This chapter will demonstrate how Tyler's early career as a southerner concerned with strict construction of the Constitution led him to his "moment of decision." It then will discuss his political position after breaking with the Whigs, including his shift toward the Democrats, their response to the prospect of his return, and the influence of the independent Tyler movement, propagated by newspapers and popular meetings, on the election of 1844 and the annexation of Texas.[17]

John Tyler came from a prominent Virginia tidewater family with a tradition of public service. His father, also named John Tyler (1747–1813), had a long career as state legislator, governor, and state and federal judge. An associate of Jefferson, Edmund Randolph, Patrick Henry, and other eminent Virginians, he was an early advocate of American independence and later an antifederalist opponent of the new U.S. Constitution, which he felt created too strong a central government. Future supporters of President Tyler would attribute to this paternal background the son's strict commitment to Jeffersonian Republican principles.[18]

The future president was born on March 29, 1790, at Greenway, the family estate in Charles City County. He was educated at a private country school and at the College of William and Mary, graduating in 1807. After a legal apprenticeship with Edmund Randolph and serving as an aide to his father, the governor, he practiced law privately for two years. In 1811, at the age of 21, he began his public career, serving five years as a member of the Virginia House of Delegates, followed by five as a U.S. Representative. This early period evinces his lifelong dedication to the Jeffersonian Republican faith, including opposition to a national bank. As state legislator, he went on record against the attempt in Congress in 1811 to recharter the first national bank, which he called "the original sin against the Constitution."[19] As congressman, he participated on a committee that recommended in 1819 that the Second Bank of the United States have its charter revoked and opposed other strong federal measures such as a national bankruptcy act and John C. Calhoun's "Bonus Bill" to finance internal improvements.[20]

During the Missouri debates in 1820, Tyler voiced his views on slavery and its expansion. A lifelong slaveowner, like many of his contemporaries, he opposed the overseas slave trade and favored plans for gradual emancipation and African colonization. He believed that the best way to achieve slow liberation was by allowing slavery to disperse freely over the western territories, where its "paucity" would lead incoming states to enact emancipation just as the northeastern states had done. Tyler, thus, argued the case for the "diffusion" of slavery and voted against the Missouri Compromise, believing Congress should not deny new states the right to make their own choice on slavery.[21]

In the years following 1816, the basic political positions of the next three decades began to take shape. The old Hamiltonian Federalist party had died out, and for the first several years, its descendants, as well as those of Jefferson, went by the name "Republican." As a new spirit of nationalism characterized these years, Henry Clay proposed his famous "American system," combining Hamilton's old program of a national bank and a protective tariff with Clay's plan for federally financed internal improvements. Among other prominent leaders of the time, John Quincy Adams shared Clay's favor for strong central government. Although Andrew Jackson and John C. Calhoun later would modify their views, Jackson initially supported protection and internal improvements, and Calhoun also advocated both of them as well as the bank.[22] When those four all became presidential candidates in 1824, none was acceptable to that dwindling number of persons, including Tyler, endeavoring to carry on Jefferson's original principles of strict construction and limited government. This group of "Old School Republicans" supported William H. Crawford of Georgia for president in 1824. None other than the octogenarian Jefferson himself stated in 1823 that Crawford's candidacy embodied the resistance of "Old School . . . Republicanism" to the evils of "Federalism."[23]

Tyler's supporters in the 1840s would maintain that only they — and he — had upheld Jeffersonian principles throughout the years when others, including Jackson and Calhoun, had strayed from the faith. They would argue further that a "Republican" party existed independently of the regular Whig and Democratic organizations, its members descended from the Crawford supporters of 1824, who in 1828 allied with the Jacksonian Democrats and later combined with the Whigs.[24] Tyler himself would recall in 1860, "I belonged, in short, to the old Jeffersonian party, from whose principles of constitutional construction I have never, in one single instance, departed."[25] In the early 1820s, Tyler resigned from Congress because of illness but later served two more terms in the Virginia House of Delegates, followed by two years as governor (1825–27). As governor, he delivered at the capitol in Richmond the official eulogy upon Jefferson's death in 1826, an appropriate honor considering his identification with the deceased leader.[26]

In 1827 Tyler was elected U.S. senator, defeating incumbent archRepublican John Randolph of Roanoke thanks to backing in Virginia's legislature from National Republican supporters of the Adams administration, who found Tyler a less undesirable choice than Randolph.[27]

The new senator, however, did not consider himself bound to the administration by their support, as Adams's apparent federalism caused him to favor the opposition headed by Jackson. Although Tyler had favored Crawford over Jackson in 1824, as senator he saw that Old Hickory more recently had abandoned his advocacy of tariff protection and internal improvements. Tyler, therefore, was confident that a Jackson administration would be characterized by "republican simplicity" and "a limited construction of the Constitution."[28] From Old Hickory's election in 1828 until the mid-1830s, Senator Tyler and the Old Republicans were allied with the Jacksonian Democrats. Tyler backed Jackson in the elections of 1828 and 1832 and applauded his vetoes of the Maysville Road Bill and national bank recharter. On the other hand, he opposed the president's use of the "spoils system" for not appointing enough states' rights Republicans to office.[29]

The tariff and nullification crisis of 1832–33, however, drove Tyler much farther from Jackson. Tyler was not a nullifier but did oppose the high tariff rates of 1828 and 1832 as well as the president's threat to use force against South Carolina when it nullified those laws. Now as a senator and later as president, Tyler believed that the Constitution allowed import duties solely to raise revenue for the government, not to protect industry; "incidental protection" could accrue only as the side effect of a revenue tariff.[30] Participating in Senate discussions with Clay, Calhoun, and other leaders, Tyler endorsed a plan to reduce tariff rates by gradual steps. His involvement prompted some of his later admirers to insist that he had been the true originator of Clay's famous Compromise Tariff of 1833.[31] In any case, Tyler was drawn closer to the Kentuckian, admiring him thereafter as a conciliator.[32] Tyler's lasting commitment to the bill's principles would shape his future tariff policy as president, when he would clash with the legions of Clay.

By 1834, the opposition to Jackson taking shape in Congress included National Republicans such as Webster, Clay, and Adams; southern nullifiers such as Calhoun; and states' rights strict constructionists such as Tyler. Allied in their feeling that "King Andrew" was usurping too much executive power, they began to be known as Whigs. For the time, their differences over bank and tariff questions receded from the limelight, not to reappear until Tyler was in the White House. Many southern planters and strict constructionists defected from the Democracy in the mid 1830s, maintaining their self-awareness by calling themselves "States' Rights Whigs." Backed by the new coalition, Tyler in 1835 was elected president pro tempore of the Senate.[33]

Although Tyler had welcomed the president's veto of a new charter for the Bank of the United States and supported his reelection in 1832, he considered Jackson's effort to cripple the bank in its remaining years by transferring the government's deposits to his "pet" state banks as an abuse of executive power.[34] Tyler, therefore, supported Clay's March 1834 Senate resolution censuring Jackson for his action. Two years later, when Virginia's legislature instructed its two senators to support a motion to expunge the censure from the Senate journal, Tyler faced what could be viewed as another great moment of decision in his career. Regarding it as unconstitutional to alter the journal, yet feeling bound by duty to obey his state's instructions, he resigned from the Senate on February 29, 1836.[35]

In the election of 1836, Whigs of the different sections backed various candidates. Tyler was vice-presidential nominee in the southern states, as running mate to Judge Hugh Lawson White of Tennessee. He also was placed on the ballot in Maryland, running with General William Henry Harrison. With the Whigs not yet united, the Democrats won the contest, electing Martin Van Buren. The new president, however, soon encountered problems with the Panic of 1837, during which his reliance on "pet" state banks and the newly created Independent Treasury did not resolve the nation's financial ills.[36] He was further weakened by his personal lack of popular appeal and his image as a political manager. His support of the Independent Treasury and opposition to any type of federal banking agency associated him in the public mind with the radical, hard-money "Locofoco" Democrats of New York.[37] This perception drove many conservative Democrats in the late 1830s to join the opposition, completing the Whig coalition.

Much optimism, therefore, surrounded the Whig party's first national convention, held in Harrisburg, Pennsylvania, in December 1839. Passing over Clay, the delegates nominated General Harrison of Ohio for president and, to balance the ticket with a southerner, named Tyler as his running mate. The Whigs' unity in opposing the policies of Jackson and Van Buren far overshadowed the variety of viewpoints found among their partisans on many major issues.[38] They proceeded to wage their colorful campaign, portraying Harrison as a simple frontiersman opposing an aristocratic Van Buren and employing such engaging slogans as "Tippecanoe and Tyler too," "Van, Van is a used-up man," and "We will vote for Tyler therefore, without a why or wherefore."[39] Although specific issues were generally avoided, Harrison at one massive rally in Dayton, Ohio, on September 10, 1840, proclaimed that although the Constitution did not specifically authorize the creation of a national bank, one might be chartered should there be no other way for the government to perform its fiscal operations.[40] Tyler, in his own campaigning, concurred with Harrison's Dayton speech, pledged commitment to preserving the Compromise Tariff, and reiterated his Old Republicanism.[41] It remained open to later controversy whether either candidate during the campaign had implied support for a bank. When the Whigs elected Harrison and Tyler and gained control of both houses of Congress, Senator Clay stepped forth in a self-styled role as "premier," like a parliamentary prime minister in the Whig model of legislative superiority, attempting to dictate cabinet appointments, presidential policies, and the party agenda. Harrison finally expelled him from the White House, and Tyler, not long after succeeding Harrison, did likewise.[42]

During the special session of Congress, previously called by Harrison at Clay's urging to deal with the fiscal crisis plaguing the nation, Whig majorities passed and Tyler signed into law a repeal of the Independent Treasury, a bankruptcy act, a preemption bill for cheap public land sale, and an act to distribute the land sale revenues as long as it should not become necessary to raise import duties above the level of the Compromise Tariff.[43] On the bank question, Tyler demonstrated flexibility and amenability to working out an appropriate financial program. He let Congress know that he was willing to approve an agency to expedite the government's handling of funds and the exchange of monetary notes among the states. His basic stipulation, stemming from strict constructionist thinking, was that the agency could not establish in *nonconsenting* states branches that would issue currency to local banks at a discount rate of interest. Two prominent southern States' Rights Whigs, Hugh L. White and N. B. Tucker, had sent proposals for such an agency to Tyler and Clay, but the Senate leader had rejected them. When Congress passed instead the two objectionable bills, the president faced his moment of decision.[44]

Braving the consequences, Tyler vetoed each bill in turn. Because Democrats and States' Rights Whigs in Congress had enough combined votes to sustain the vetoes, the extra session adjourned without producing a fiscal measure. The cabinet members, except Webster, then resigned; the pro-Clay majority of Congress issued a proclamation reading the president out of the party; and the Whig war on Tyler commenced, to continue unabated for the rest of his term. Whig publications resounded with denunciations of the executive and his vetoes.[45] Some charged him with treachery, while others branded him indecisive, doing so with enough persuasiveness to influence modern historians.[46] Conversely, the most eminent Democratic leaders and editors brimmed with praise, overlooking, for the time being, the danger of building up a recent adversary who might become a force in their own party. Jackson, Van Buren, Calhoun, Thomas Hart Benton, Francis P. Blair, Franklin Pierce, and Amos Kendall were among the many who then lauded Tyler's action.[47]

The president perceived a "well-planned conspiracy" on the part of Clay and the Whigs. He wrote in October 1841 that his bank opinion had been "all along known . . . and that no power on earth could induce me to approve such a Bank bill as would alone satisfy the ultra-federalists. This fact was thoroughly known to Clay [but still Clay had] seized upon this as a favorable opportunity to press me to the veto — and by forcing me into a position of great awkwardness to raise the cry of Treason — to set all his presses upon me." Three years later, Tyler would ask in retrospect: "Did the federal portion of the Whig party indulge a dream that when we went into union with them [in 1840] that thereby we had covenanted to lay at their feet our principles, our judgments and all our thoughts and emotions?"[48]

The breach with the Whigs in the fall of 1841 ushered in a new phase of Tyler's administration that has not received as much attention as the bank war — namely, the period in which he proceeded to govern without a party and build whatever support he could among independents, moderate Whigs, and Democrats. His new cabinet was not a homogeneous body of states' rights southerners, as some writers have carelessly implied; there were at that time only two such members — Abel P. Upshur of Virginia and Hugh S. Legaré of South Carolina. Among the northern Whigs who did not bow to Clay were Webster and John C. Spencer of New York. Conspicuously overlooked by historians who stress sectionalism, Spencer would serve until May 1844, first as secretary of war and then of the treasury, defending his chief, drafting legislation, and managing the federal patronage.[49]

Webster's stay in the cabinet until May 1843 suggested that he and Tyler might try to build a "middle of the road" party, prompted by their mutual rivalry with Clay. Despite their vastly different backgrounds, the two maintained a warm working relationship and common commitment to service. They hoped their enterprise might attract moderates from both parties, operating between the two extremes of Clay Whigs and Locofoco Democrats and, thereby, possibly defusing sectional tensions in the country and laying a base for Webster later to succeed Tyler as president. In fact, some extreme states' righters behind Tyler were dismayed by his apparent moderation and collaboration with Webster. Still, the prospect of success for such a "middle party" was limited. Most Whigs then favored Clay, and most Democrats had loyalties to Van Buren or other candidates. As Arthur M. Schlesinger, Jr., wrote, "Tyler lingered affably in the middle, a President with a policy but without a party."[50]

To Tyler's credit, he devoted his efforts to governing despite the resistance he faced. In 1842 the Whig-controlled Congress twice attempted to provide needed revenues by raising the tariff without discontinuing distribution of the proceeds from land sales. Tyler's persistence in vetoing both bills finally impelled the legislators to pass a tariff without distribution, which he signed into law.[51] To resolve the financial situation, he sent Congress a recommendation for an agency called the Exchequer, which would provide control of monetary affairs while avoiding the objectionable features of a national bank. Reflecting the proposal sent in 1841 by Hugh L. White and supported by Webster, Spencer, and other moderate Whigs in the cabinet, this middle-road plan was defeated by a coalition of probank Whigs and antibank Democrats in Congress.[52] After this, there would be no true national fiscal agency until 1913, when the Federal Reserve was created, bearing similarities to Tyler's Exchequer plan.

In the area of foreign affairs, the Tyler administration's accomplishments were outstanding. Most notable was the Webster-Ashburton Treaty of 1842, which defused a threat of war between the United States and Great Britain over the Canadian boundary and policing against the slave trade. Tyler's proposal that the U.S. and British navies guard jointly against slave-trading vessels shaped the content of the treaty. Both Webster and the British minister, Lord Ashburton, acknowledged that the president's congeniality and personal supervision of their talks facilitated the settlement.[53] Tyler's government also concluded agreements to settle claims of U.S. citizens against Mexico and to expand U.S. trade with China (the Treaty of Wanghia) and the Germanic states (Zollverein Treaty, disapproved by the Whig Senate). His administration ended the eight-year-old Seminole War, opening the door to statehood for Florida in 1845, and extended the Monroe Doctrine to the Hawaiian Islands in a proclamation sometimes called the "Tyler Doctrine."[54]

By the midpoint of Tyler's presidency in 1843, it was not yet clear whether in the next campaign he would be heading an independent movement or combining with the Democrats. His own states' rights faction no longer was included in the Whig party, and only some moderate Whigs and independents still stood by him. In the fall elections of 1842, the Democrats had won control of the House of Representatives and the New York and Ohio governorships. His followers, having worked with the Democrats, claimed some credit for the results and saw them as popular approval of his policies against the Whigs.[55] This suggested a possible return to his old party, which was divided over accepting him.

Martin Van Buren, as the former Democratic president and heir of Jackson, was backed by most of the party's established managers and organizations, but Calhoun, James Buchanan, Lewis Cass, and Richard M. Johnson were Democratic leaders who stood as alternative choices, just as it appeared that Tyler also might join the fray. Clearly, it was in the Van Burenites' interest to keep the president out, because there was already enough potential rivalry in the field. Thus, Tyler and the other Democratic candidates had a mutual adversary in the Van Buren forces, who hoped to produce a "packed" national nominating convention in 1844. The other candidates' supporters wanted to establish an "open" convention of delegates freely chosen in the various congressional districts. Tylerites, in mid-1843, joined with those forces in a crusade to establish the district system as a vehicle for popular influence against political dictation.

An outstanding example of these interests in conflict was the New York state Democratic convention held at Syracuse on September 5, 1843. Led by Van Buren's managers, it rejected a proposal for the district system and appointed to the national convention a slate of 34 delegates committed to the "Little Magician." The Syracuse convention subsequently became a symbol of boss domination to friends of Tyler and other candidates. It especially helped to combine the New York followers of Tyler and Calhoun, who both had hoped to gain influence from the convention.[56]

Although all Democrats commonly opposed the national banks that Jackson and Tyler had vetoed, their differences on other fiscal matters determined how close an individual or faction might be to Tyler. A familiar feature of this era was the conflict in many states between the "radical" or "locofoco" Democrats, who disliked all types of banks and paper money, even at the state level, and moderate or conservative Democrats, who frequently had ties to state banks and commercial activity.[57] Locofocos, being generally tied to Van Buren and the extreme antibank position of the Independent Treasury, found it harder than moderates to accept Tyler's Whig interlude and willingness to create the Exchequer, a limited form of national fiscal agency.[58] Moderates, including supporters of Cass and Calhoun, were more likely to work with Tyler and accept him back in the party.

In 1843, Tyler first appointed to his cabinet Democrats who had not been part of the 1840 Whig coalition. Two of these nominees were particularly controversial, being enemies of Van Buren and the radicals in their states, namely, James Madison Porter of Pennsylvania, who was appointed secretary of war, and David Henshaw of Massachusetts, as secretary of the navy. Tyler gained ties from these appointments with Porter's brother, Governor David R. Porter of Pennsylvania,[59] and with the Massachusetts Calhounites, who supported Henshaw.[60] Because Congress was out of session for most of 1843, Porter and Henshaw served in the cabinet for several months without Senate confirmation, but when the legislature reconvened at the end of the year, an alliance of Whigs and Van Burenite Democrats rejected the nominations. Some moderate Democrats, who were less inclined to thwart the president, supported the appointments.[61]

Several prominent Democrats in 1843 expressed approval of Tyler's acts and stated that he should be allowed to enter the party if he wished.[62] Amos Kendall, who still supported Van Buren, advised the Little Magician that attacks on the president would only drive Tyler and Calhoun closer together and enable them to defeat Van Buren's renomination bid. In his paper, the *Expositor*, Kendall repeatedly proclaimed that the party should accept the president.[63] Wilson Shannon, two-term governor of Ohio (1838–40 and 1842–44), publicly defended the president, recalling Jackson's praise of Tyler's bank vetoes.[64] Isaac Hill of New Hampshire, another distinguished old Jacksonian leader, also allied with Tyler.[65]

The leading Democratic paper in the nation was *The Globe*, published in Washington by Francis Preston Blair, Sr., who had been the official printer of Democratic presidents and Congresses and chief journalistic spokesman for Jackson and Van Buren.[66] His editorials generally were followed nationwide by a network of party presses. Blair had praised Tyler's bank and tariff vetoes but had attacked the more Whig-like Exchequer plan, Distribution Act of 1841, Tariff of 1842, and treaty with Britain, attributing them to the federalistic influence of such advisers as Webster and Spencer.[67] When Tyler's friends interpreted the 1842 election results as popular endorsement of his policies and began to proclaim that they and the Democrats had become "indivisible," it was more than Blair and some Democrats could take.[68] Blair began attacking Tyler personally, and the other papers that followed *The Globe*'s line took up his position, proclaiming that Tyler must repent for his past "heresies" in order to become a Democrat.[69] This caused Tyler's papers to charge that *The Globe* was acting as dictator of the party by setting forth terms for the president's atonement.

It soon became clear that there was hardly a way for Tyler to satisfy these writers' conditions for his becoming a Democrat. Whereas Blair had first complained that there was not "a single known Democrat" in the cabinet, he did not change his tone when Webster resigned in 1843 or when Tyler began appointing Democrats. Instead, he lashed out at such established party members as the Porters, Henshaw, and Hill, branding them panderers to federalism and reading them out of the ranks.[70] No longer did Tyler have to appoint Democrats in order to gain acceptance in the party; rather, individuals ceased to be Democrats when they came to his side. He could not even find favor with these writers by recommending that Congress refund the $1,000 fine imposed on General Jackson in 1815 by a federal judge in New Orleans.[71]

It was between such attacks by Democrats and Whigs that the Tyler movement proceeded. The president had been thinking of building a third party from the time of his break from the Whigs in the fall of 1841. He believed that by pursuing a "middle course, avoiding ultraism on both sides," he could gain support from the general public and moderates in both parties. He added, late in 1842, that "I am still destined . . . to navigate the barque of State amid all the convulsions and agitations of factions. The *Ultrae* of both the prevailing factions will not consent to ground their arms, even though the signal defeat which one [the Whig] has encountered should teach wisdom to both. Is there any other course for me to pursue than to look to the public good irrespective of either faction?" He reaffirmed, "My strong determination is therefore to hold, as I have heretofore done, the politicians of both parties and of all parties at defiance, and continue to act . . . on patriotic motives and broad principles of public good."[72]

In later years, Tyler and two of his sons each stated that he had never really expected to gain reelection. By waging a third-party effort, they explained, he might better serve the public interest, prevent Van Buren's renomination, secure the annexation of Texas, and insure that his followers would receive fair treatment from the Democrats. Lyon G. Tyler pointed out that his father's third-party effort in 1844 was no more unrealistic than that of James G. Birney, the historically respected Liberty party candidate, who, like Tyler, had a limited following.[73]

By 1843, the Whigs were solidifying behind Clay, while the forces of Cass, Calhoun, and other Democrats were battling at the state level against Van Buren. Standing aloof, Tyler remarked that he would readily allow his opponents a portion of each day for attacking him "if the residue of their time could be given to the public good."[74] He advised his chief spokesman, John B. Jones, editor of the Washington *Madisonian*, to "preserve a dignified reserve," "let them fight it out," be prudent, "use my name as little as possible," "hold off as much as possible [from attacking any Democratic factions] and let your fire be directed against Clay. He broke up the Whig party for his own selfish ends." Tyler suggested that the Democratic groups were expecting the election to go to the House of Representatives and implied that he himself might be selected in the final outcome.[75]

Using patronage more than before, in 1843 Tyler authorized Secretary of the Treasury Spencer to make widespread replacements. Although his foes frequently charged that the so-called Tyler movement consisted exclusively of federal appointees and editors bought with government printing contracts, he replaced only one-tenth of all federal officeholders and left many unfriendly persons in their posts. In contrast, Jackson had turned out one-tenth to one-fifth of all officeholders, and Lincoln would replace nearly all of them.[76] Moreover, most supportive journals, including the patronized ones, had either been Republican Whig, Conservative Democratic, or moderate independents before formally becoming "Tyler papers" as a natural continuation of their previous positions, rather than the result of receiving favors.

Networks of partisan newspapers played an important role in promoting Tyler's cause, just as they did for the major party candidates. The Washington *Madisonian* was their flagship. It was founded in 1837 as part of the Democratic opposition to Van Buren, supported the Whig ticket in 1840, and took up Tyler's cause in 1841. John B. Jones, who purchased the paper from its founder late in 1841, served as the president's spokesman for the rest of his term, defending him against Whig charges of treachery, attacking *The Globe* faction for attempting to dominate the democracy, publicizing the nationwide proliferation of Tyler sentiment, and promoting Tyler's candidacy as either a Democrat or an independent.[77]

Popular favor for Tyler was expressed at meetings across the country, the earliest of which occurred in the fall of 1841, just after the bank vetoes. On July 11, 1843, the *Madisonian* issued a call for the president's friends throughout the states to organize and hold local meetings, "having as their main object the presentation of Mr. Tyler's name to the consideration of the country" and the Democratic party. Accounts of the resulting activity appeared in nearly every issue of the supportive papers in late 1843 and early 1844. Unless the journals were directly fictionalizing, there was more popular support for Tyler than historical works have recognized. Tyler's critics, of course, enjoyed disparaging his rallies as involving only the local officeholders. Nevertheless, many meetings were well-attended, for Tyler's papers frequently listed the names of participants, sometimes numbering in the hundreds. This evidence calls for reconsideration of the many uninformed accounts that belittle the Tyler movement and shows the growing popular base for the president's influence on the 1844 election. Well-attended rallies, including some city and state Tyler conventions, were held in Baltimore; Portsmouth and Norfolk, Virginia; Columbus, Ohio; Norwich, Connecticut; Philadelphia; and New York City. In the latter two cities the president drew particular enthusiasm from Irish Americans because of his support for Irish independence.[78]

Study of Tyler meetings held throughout the country shows the greatest centers of activity to have been in New York City, Philadelphia, several parts of Ohio, and southeastern Virginia. As foes charged, officeholders were present, but in fact, they were outnumbered by those not on the federal payroll. City directories and county histories reveal that participants named in the newspapers came from every walk of life. Furthermore, the number of northern newspapers involved and the many popular meetings held in the North should dispel any perception that this was exclusively a southern movement. In fact, there was much more Tylerite activity in the North than in the South, where the president's cause was overshadowed among Democrats by the Van Buren-Calhoun rivalry, until Calhoun withdrew as a candidate in December 1843.[79]

The winter and spring of 1844 was a time of great anticipation, as Americans looked ahead to the national nominating conventions. The president and the Tyler Central Committee, established at the *Madisonian* office on February 26, decided to hold their own separate convention in Baltimore in May, when the Whigs and Democrats also would be meeting in that city. Because many state organizations by then had planned to send slates of pledged Van Buren delegates to the Democratic convention, Tyler did not want to be bound to support the nominee, although Van Buren's selection was not yet a certainty. The president's supporters met throughout the country and within a short period chose 1,000 delegates for Tyler's national convention.[80]

It was at this point that the president thrust into the campaign an entirely new element that would eclipse candidates' personalities and fiscal views as an issue. In late 1843, Secretary of State Abel P. Upshur discretely had begun negotiating a treaty to annex the independent Republic of Texas to the United States. When Upshur, along with five others, was killed on February 27, 1844, by an accidental cannon explosion aboard the U.S.S. *Princeton*, Tyler named Calhoun, who by then had withdrawn as a presidential candidate, as Upshur's successor to complete the negotiations.[81] The treaty was signed on April 12 and sent for ratification to the Senate on April 22.

Many prominent Americans, especially in the South and West, endorsed the treaty. Tyler saw annexation as his greatest undertaking, which would bring luster to his much-maligned administration. His message that accompanied the treaty to the Senate stressed the economic and strategic benefits of annexation to the entire nation and contained not a word about slavery or any sectional interest.[82] Still, the appointment of Calhoun, long identified with promoting slavery's interest, and the activities of other southerners associated with the administration gave annexation a sectional overtone. Indeed, Upshur had long been known as a defender of slavery, having authored articles on the subject. Duff Green, Tyler's special agent in Europe, had inflamed fear in 1843 with reports that the British were secretly attempting to influence Texas to abolish slavery.[83] Then, after Upshur's negotiations were underway, in February 1844, Tyler's friend Senator Robert J. Walker of Mississippi wrote in an open letter reminiscent of Tyler's own diffusion speech of 1820 that slaves could be drawn from the older southern states to the fresh lands of an annexed Texas, from whence they could ultimately pass off into Mexico.[84] In April, Secretary of State Calhoun wrote to the British envoy at Washington, Sir Richard Pakenham, an in-depth exposition on the merits of slavery.[85]

Such actions have prompted historians to analyze intently the degree to which annexation may have been inspired by slavery. Those preoccupied with sectionalism, particularly Frederick Merk in two books on the subject, have viewed the effort as driven by the forces of slavery expansion, involving Upshur, Green, Walker, Calhoun, and others, whom Merk called the "Tyler junto." Merk and other writers have suggested that Green's anti-British reports were inaccurate and designed to play on southern fears of abolitionism.[86] An alternative viewpoint sees Texas as a national partisan issue, indicating that the purpose of Walker's letter was simply to rejuvenate the Democrats by stopping Van Buren, while northern and southern Whigs united behind Clay in opposing annexation.[87] Most historians, however, including those who accentuate the slavery motives of Tyler's lieutenants, concede that the president himself supported annexation as a popular national concern or a fresh way to bring credit to his administration.[88] In fact, after leaving office, Tyler expressed regret that Upshur and Calhoun had brought slavery ideas into the proceedings.[89]

Tyler's introduction of the treaty required leading figures to take a stance on it in the midst of the political season. Jackson, influenced by Green's reports, declared annexation necessary for national security against the alleged British threat. Thomas Hart Benton and Francis P. Blair also spoke out in favor of annexation.[90] On April 27, the most eagerly awaited statements from the front-running Clay and

Van Buren were published in their respective party organs. Both contenders opposed annexation for the time, largely on grounds that it could lead to war with Mexico.[91] Van Buren's pronouncement was especially awkward for his party because Jackson and *The Globe* had already spoken in favor of the treaty. The pact was awaiting Senate action when the nominating conventions met.[92]

On May 1 the Whigs in Baltimore nominated Clay and opposed annexation in a show of unity that would strongly contrast with the divisions among the Democrats, who met in that same city on May 27. All of Van Buren's Democratic rivals supported annexation. After nearly three days of voting, in which neither Van Buren nor Cass could gain the required two-thirds majority, the convention finally nominated the "dark horse" candidate, James K. Polk of Tennessee, who favored annexation.[93]

Tyler's convention also opened on May 27, right across the street from the Democrats'. This timing was consistent with the president's later confession that his actual goal had been to influence the Democrats to select a pro-Texas candidate. The *Madisonian* reported more than 1,000 persons present, although the number has been disputed.[94] In a hall draped with banners proclaiming "Tyler and Texas," and following a series of laudatory speeches by delegates from various parts of the country, the president's supporters nominated him for another term. On May 28, the convention left the choice of a vice-presidential candidate for a committee to decide later, suggesting the possibility of reconciliation with the Democrats. Still, follow-up meetings to nominate full slates of candidates for presidential electors, Congress, and state and local offices would be held in various cities in July.[95]

In his message to his followers accepting their nomination, Tyler stated that he had vetoed the Whig bills rather than yield his "cherished" principles and constitutional duty in the name of political expediency. Yet, the Democratic leaders and papers, "for motives altogether too obvious," had joined "with the rabid Whig press" in attacking him. He stated that his present motive was to annex Texas for the good of the country, not "the poor and contemptible desire to be in office for the mere sake of office." He also hinted he might withdraw should the present Congress come to support annexation, but on June 8, the Whig-controlled Senate rejected the Texas treaty by a partisan-line vote of 35 to 16.[96]

Four presidential candidates were then in the fray, including Polk and Tyler on the pro-Texas side and, on the opposite, Clay and James G. Birney, the Liberty party candidate. Tyler told Senator Walker that he did not really expect to be reelected and would gladly withdraw in favor of Polk and Texas if "assured on reliable authority" that his friends, whom he estimated to number 150,000, would be welcomed back in the Democracy "as brethren and equals."[97] On July 26, Old

Hickory, in a publicized letter, spoke kindly of the president and stressed that Tyler's withdrawal from the race would unite him and his friends in a common Democratic fold. Similar feelings were expressed by Democratic papers and meetings, and the president's new brother-in-law, Alexander Gardiner, arranged for the New York City Democratic organization to share patronage with Tyler's followers if Tyler gave up his candidacy. On August 6, a deputation of New York Democrats visited Tyler at the White House, praising his policies and calling for all Republicans to unite against "the federal candidate, Henry Clay."[98]

A few weeks later, Tyler informed Jackson that he planned to withdraw his candidacy, claiming that his action would insure Polk's election by bringing in the necessary votes to carry Ohio (where he counted 40,000 supporters), Pennsylvania, New Jersey, and Virginia. Only one concern remained. "The Republican Whigs of 1840," he said, would be pleased to return but were disturbed by the long-abusive policy of The Globe toward them. Shortly thereafter, Blair received and concurred with a request from the old general to discontinue his attacks and treat the Tylerites "as brethren in democracy."[99] On August 20, Tyler officially withdrew his candidacy in favor of Polk, who was elected in the fall by a close margin. Early in 1845, the two houses of Congress annexed Texas by joint resolution, and Tyler, with much satisfaction, put the measure into effect on March 3, his last day in office.[100]

Study of the Tyler movement shows that had he not withdrawn his candidacy, he may well have sapped enough of Polk's votes in New York to favor Clay, who then would have won the election. A similar scenario could be constructed for Pennsylvania. If Clay had been elected, the mandate would not have existed for Congress to annex Texas in the final months of Tyler's term. Because Clay and the Whigs also would not have gone to war with Mexico, the United States would not have acquired new southwestern territory in the late 1840s. The whole course of sectional conflict thereafter may well have been different. The sectionalist historians have maintained that Tyler's annexing Texas divided the parties along regional lines and set the nation on an inexorable course toward disunion.[101] The nonsectionalist political historians hold that although Tyler's independence seriously threatened the new two-party system that had just coalesced in 1840, it managed to spring back and survive through the 1850s.[102] Indisputably, Tyler brought about the downfall of his most formidable rivals, Clay and Van Buren.

By any of these perspectives, Tyler's influence, constructed with the support of popular meetings and journalistic arguments, significantly affected the course of events. It is important not to let biases held against him since his lifetime obscure what actually occurred and inject misinformation into historical writings. His administration accomplished remarkably much, given the resistance it faced. Had it not been for his estrangement from the major parties, his programs and dedication to national service could have brought him more political success in his own time and a brighter place in history. Tyler, however, did not get to govern under more favorable circumstances. He made his critical decision on the bank bill and was prepared to live with the results.

NOTES

1. *John Tyler — His History, Character, and Position, with a Portrait* (pamphlet, New York, 1843), 27–31; Lyon G. Tyler, *The Letters and Times of the Tylers* (hereafter *LTT*) (3 vol., Richmond and Williamsburg, 1884, 1896), 2:81; Oliver P. Chitwood, *John Tyler: Champion of the Old South* (New York, 1939), 210–11, 258–64; Robert Seager II, *And Tyler Too* (Boston, 1963), 151–53; Glyndon G. Van Deusen, *The Jacksonian Era, 1828–1848* (New York, 1959), 154–55, 158; Frederick J. Turner, *The United States, 1830–1850* (1935, reprint ed., New York, 1965), 496–98; Robert V. Remini, *Henry Clay, Statesman for the Union* (New York, 1991), 593–94; George R. Poage, *Henry Clay and the Whig Party* (Chapel Hill, 1936), 47; Clement Eaton, *Henry Clay and the Art of American Politics* (Boston, 1957), 147; Hugh R. Fraser, *Democracy in the Making: The Jackson-Tyler Era* (Indianapolis, 1938), 248.

2. William Freehling, *The Road to Disunion* (New York, 1990), 363.

3. Tyler to Alexander Gardiner, 6 May 1845, *LTT*, 2:97; John Tyler, Jr., to Lyon G. Tyler, 29 January 1883, *LTT*, 2:121–22; Frank G. Carpenter, "A Talk with a President's Son," *Lippincott's Monthly Magazine* 41 (May 1888): 417–18; Webster to Hiram Ketcham, 10 September 1841, in Fletcher Webster, ed., *The Correspondence of Daniel Webster* (2 vol., Boston, 1855), 2:109. The five secretaries who resigned were Thomas Ewing, George E. Badger, John Bell, John J. Crittenden, and Francis Granger.

4. Washington *Madisonian*, 11 November 1841.

5. Tyler to Webster, 11 October 1841, *LTT*, 2:126.

6. *LTT*, passim; John Fiske, "Harrison, Tyler, and the Whig Coalition," in *Essays Historical and Literary* (2 vol., New York, 1902), 1:327–60; William R. Brock, *Parties and Political Conscience: American Dilemmas, 1840–1850* (New York, 1979), 88–89; William J. Cooper, *The South and the Politics of Slavery, 1828–1856* (Baton Rouge, 1978), 150; William J. Cooper, *Liberty and Slavery: Southern Politics to 1860* (New York, 1983), 194, 203; Norma L. Peterson, *The Presidencies of William Henry Harrison and John Tyler* (Lawrence, 1989), 263.

7. Tyler's ultimate support of the Confederacy does not belie the fact that before the Civil War he was never a spokesman for sectionalism. In February 1861, he presided over the Virginia Peace Convention, which attempted by compromise to avert disunion. He only followed his state in secession when that effort failed. See James Ford Rhodes, "The Failure of the Peace Convention," in Philip Van Doren Stern, ed., *Prologue to Sumter* (New York, 1961), 293–95; Thomas H. O'Connor, *The Disunited States: The Era of Civil War and Reconstruction* (New York, 1972), 122–23. The modern persistence of sectional bias against Tyler was displayed in a recent conversation with one northern historian of the presidency who remarked, "I can't forgive him for becoming a rebel."

8. Tyler had two marriages, each of which produced seven children. His first wife, Letitia, who was his own age, died in 1842; two years later, he married Julia Gardiner, 30 years his junior, and continued fathering into later life. John Tyler, Jr., his presidential secretary, was from the first marriage and Lyon from the second.

9. Such views appear in the familiar scholars' rankings of presidents compiled by Arthur M. Schlesinger, Sr., for *Life* 25 (1 November 1948): 65–66, and later for the *New York Times Magazine*, 29 July 1962; in Morton Borden, ed., *America's Eleven Greatest Presidents* (2nd ed., Chicago, 1971); and in Robert M. Murray and Tim H. Blessing, "The Presidential Performance Study: A Progress Report," *Journal of American History* 70 (1983): 535–55.

10. Thomas A. Bailey, *Presidential Greatness* (New York, 1966), 23–25, 280–81; Peterson, *Harrison and Tyler*, 263–65.

11. A most blatant example is Norman K. Risjord, *The Old Republicans: Southern Conservatism in the Age of Jefferson* (New York, 1965), which concludes that Old Republicanism ended in the mid-1830s with the deaths of several of its spokesmen, overlooking the fact that Tyler, whom the author names as an Old Republican, became president in the 1840s and based his administration on the movement's principles. Other examples will be given throughout this chapter.

12. William Freehling, in *The Road to Disunion*, 369, states that Tyler, after breaking with the Whigs, could attract to his service only "southerners on the fringes" and supports this by focusing on Abel P. Upshur of Virginia, ignoring the roles of Webster, John C. Spencer, and other northerners in the cabinet. Elbert B. Smith, in *The Death of Slavery, 1837–65* (Chicago, 1967), 59, denied the legitimacy of opposing a bank by stating that Tyler as president "promptly reverted to the principles of a states' rights Virginia planter. . . . The Whig party was in chaos, its splendid victory of 1840 turned to ashes by the obstinacy of John Tyler." William Cooper similarly blamed Tyler for turning the Whig victory into disorder and overlooked the non-southerners in his cabinet. See Cooper, *Liberty and Slavery*, 203; Cooper, *South and Politics of Slavery*, 178.

13. Examples of this are Robert Kelley, *The Cultural Pattern in American Politics, The First Century* (New York, 1979); Richard L. McCormick, *The Party Period and Public Policy: American Politics from the Age of Jackson to the Progressive Era* (New York, 1986); and Lawrence F. Kohl, *The Politics of Individualism: Parties and the American Character in the Jacksonian Era* (New York, 1989). Kohl mentions Peggy Eaton but not President Tyler.

14. This interpretation, including writers who either espouse the "new political history" or in some way reflect its nonsectionalist approach, appears in the pioneer work, Lee Benson, *The Concept of Jacksonian Democracy: New York as a Test Case* (Princeton, 1961); Richard P. McCormick, *The Second American Party System: Party Formation in the Jacksonian Era* (1966, reprint ed., New York, 1973); Richard P. McCormick, *The Presidential Game: The Origins of American Presidential Politics* (New York, 1982); Joel H. Silbey, *The Shrine of Party: Congressional Voting Behavior, 1841–1852* (Pittsburgh, 1967); Joel H. Silbey, *The Partisan Imperative: The Dynamics of American Politics before the Civil War* (New York, 1985), a collection of essays that reflect the debate over the years; Kelley, *Cultural Pattern*; McCormick, *Party Period*; Michael F. Holt, *Forging a Majority: The Formation of the Republican Party in Pittsburgh, 1848–60* (New Haven, 1969); and Michael F. Holt, *The Political Crisis of the 1850s* (New York, 1978).

15. Frederick Merk, *Slavery and the Annexation of Texas* (New York, 1972), passim. Cooper, *South and Politics of Slavery*, 148, 163, 178, 181; Cooper, *Liberty and Slavery*, 177, 181, 191, 195–96; Cooper maintains that the uniting of southern Whigs behind Clay's fiscal policies during Tyler's presidency was the one time that slavery took a back seat to economics. Kenneth S. Greenberg, *Masters and Statesmen: The Political Culture of American Slavery* (Baltimore, 1985), vii, ix. The foremost adversary of the "new" political historians for their denying the importance of sectionalism is Eric Foner, *Politics and Ideology in the Age of Civil War* (New York, 1980) and other works. Further studies that maintained an emphasis on sectionalism after

the emergence of the "new" political history are David Potter, *The Impending Crisis, 1841–1861* (New York, 1976); Kenneth M. Stampp, *The Imperiled Union: Essays on the Background of the Civil War* (New York, 1980); Don S. Fehrenbacher, *The South and Three Sectional Crises* (Baton Rouge, 1980); Freehling, *Road to Disunion*; Brock, *Parties and Political Conscience*, 151; and Smith, *Death of Slavery*, chap. 5.

16. Tyler's representation of this southern "ideal" is portrayed in Greenberg, *Masters and Statesmen*, 4–7.

17. This chapter is adapted from the doctoral dissertation I wrote under Merton Dillon's mentorship at The Ohio State University in 1973, entitled "John Tyler and the Presidency: Old School Republicanism, Partisan Realignment, and Support for His Administration."

18. *A Brief Sketch of the Life of John Tyler, Compiled from Authentic Sources* (pamphlet, Philadelphia, 1842), 3. Biographical accounts of the father appear in *LTT*, 1:56–270, 3:1–7, and in Chitwood, *Tyler*, chap. 1, which is entitled "A Republican Judge." Ongoing sources for the present account of Tyler's early life, in addition to those later cited, are the *Brief Sketch* and *Tyler, His History* pamphlets and the much more detailed information found throughout vol. 1 of *LTT*.

19. Fiske, "Harrison, Tyler," 336.

20. *Annals of Congress*, 15th Cong., 2nd sess., 1310–27; *Brief Sketch*, 4; *Tyler, His History*, 16–19.

21. *Annals of Congress*, 16th Cong., 1st sess., 1382–94; *LTT*, 1:313–24, 3: 26–27.

22. Thomas P. Abernathy, *From Frontier to Plantation in Tennessee: A Study in Frontier Democracy* (Chapel Hill, 1932), 229–30, 242–45; Gerald M. Capers, *John C. Calhoun: Opportunist* (Chicago, 1969), 81–88; Margaret L. Coit, *John C. Calhoun: American Portrait* (Boston, 1950), 111–16; Robert V. Remini, *Andrew Jackson* (New York, 1969), 93; George Dangerfield, *The Awakening of American Nationalism, 1815–1828* (New York, 1965), 212–13, 218.

23. *LTT*, 1:477–78n. It is important to note that in contemporary usage, words such as "federalist," "democrat," and "republican" were sometimes spelled with capital first letters and sometimes with lower case. With the small initials, the terms denote ideologies existing independently of formal political parties. When capitalized, they refer to official names of parties or ideas commonly associated with a party at a particular time. In order to be able to make that distinction, that variation will be continued in use here.

24. For later assertions of the Old Republican heritage, see Dayton (Ohio) *Miamian*, 20 January, 18 May 1844; Richmond *Republican Sentinel*, 16 March 1844; Henry A. Wise, *Seven Decades of the Union* (Philadelphia, 1881), 180–82; and *LTT*, 1:283–85. For comparisons of Tyler to Jefferson, see accounts in the Washington *Madisonian* of Tyler rallies that were held throughout the early months of 1844.

25. *LTT*, 1:467.

26. The entire speech is printed in *LTT*, 1:345–54.

27. *Brief Sketch*, 8; *LTT*, 1:363–65; Fiske, "Harrison, Tyler," 332–33.

28. Tyler to John Rutherford, 8 December 1827; Tyler to Dr. Henry Curtis, 16 December 1827; *LTT*, 1:376–80; Dangerfield, *Awakening*, 231–41.

29. *LTT*, 1:397–401, 405–11, 417–26.

30. *Tyler, His History*, 20; *LTT*, 1:449–53, 463; Van Deusen, *Jacksonian Era*, 71–75; Fiske, "Harrison, Tyler," 327; Eaton, *Clay*, 104–6.

31. *Tyler, His History*, 20–23; *LTT*, 1:456–57; Fiske, "Harrison, Tyler," 335; Van Deusen, *Jacksonian Era*, 76–78.

32. Tyler expressed this admiration in speaking at the dedication of a Clay statue in Richmond in April 1860.

33. Cooper, *Liberty and Slavery*, 175; Fiske, "Harrison, Tyler," 327, 336, 338; Fiske cited Tyler as the individual who most embodied States' Rights Whiggery.

Arthur C. Cole, *The Whig Party in the South* (Washington, 1913), 16–30, 65–72; Eaton, *Clay*, 113. Calhoun in the late 1830s would return to the Democrats.

34. Tyler to Littleton Tazewell, 25 December 1833, *LTT*, 1:481–82; Capers, *Calhoun*, 172–74.

35. *Brief Sketch*, 10. Tyler's explanation to the Virginia legislature of his resignation appears in *LTT*, 1:536. The state's other senator, Benjamin W. Leigh, disobeyed the instructions without resigning but was not reelected at the end of his term.

36. Van Deusen, *Jacksonian Era*, 116–29; Reginald C. McGrane, *The Panic of 1837: Some Financial Problems of the Jacksonian Era* (1924, reprint ed., Chicago, 1965), especially chap. 4.

37. On Locofocoism, see Van Deusen, *Jacksonian Era*, 95, 103; Turner, *The United States, 1830–1850*, 108–9; Edward Pessen, *Jacksonian America* (Homewood, 1967), 293–97; McGrane, *Panic of 1837*, 149–55; Arthur M. Schlesinger, Jr., *The Age of Jackson* (Boston, 1945), 397–98.

38. Notable comments on the unique diversity of the 1840 Whig coalition are found in Wise, *Seven Decades*, 167, 178–81; Fiske, "Harrison, Tyler," 339; Robert J. Morgan, *A Whig Embattled: The Presidency under John Tyler* (Lincoln, 1954), 149; and Cooper, *Liberty and Slavery*, 194.

39. See Robert G. Gunderson, *The Log Cabin Campaign* (Lexington, 1957), 173; Chitwood, *Tyler*, 177–78; Van Deusen, *Jacksonian Era*, 145–48; Fiske, "Harrison, Tyler," 349–50.

40. *Brief Sketch*, 12–14; *LTT*, 1:620; Wise, *Seven Decades*, 176; Chitwood, *Tyler*, 183–84; Gunderson, *Log Cabin Campaign*, 170; Washington *Madisonian*, 29 September 1840.

41. *Brief Sketch*, 14; *Tyler, His History*, 25; *LTT*, 1:623; Wise, *Seven Decades*, 176–77; Chitwood, *Tyler*, 185–91; Gunderson, *Log Cabin Campaign*, 193.

42. Clay's styling himself as legislative chieftain in 1841 and attempts to dominate both Harrison and Tyler are noted in many contemporary writings and later histories: *LTT*, 2:10–11, 33–34; Clay to Harrison, 15 March 1841, in Calvin Colton, ed., *The Private Correspondence of Henry Clay* (Cincinnati, 1856), 452; Clay to N. B. Tucker, 15 April 1841, *LTT*, 2:30–31; Tyler to Clay, 30 April 1841, *LTT*, 3:92–93; Wise, *Seven Decades*, 180; Washington *Madisonian*, 8 July 1842; Carl Schurz, *Henry Clay* (2 vol., 1899, reprint ed., New York, 1980), 2:219–20; Poage, *Clay and Whig Party*, 36–37; Eaton, *Clay*, 143–45; Remini, *Clay*, 571–76, 581–84; Van Deusen, *Jacksonian Era*, 153; Fraser, *Democracy*, 171; Brock, *Parties and Political Conscience*, 81, 86; Cooper, *South and Politics of Slavery*, 151; Freehling, *Road to Disunion*, 363; Peterson, *Harrison and Tyler*, 263–64.

43. Fraser, *Democracy*, 173; Van Deusen, *Jacksonian Era*, 160–62.

44. Edwin S. Williams, ed., *Presidents' Messages from 1787 to 1846* (New York, 1846), 2:1229–32, 1232–42, 1244–48; *LTT*, 2:15–17, 29, 54–56, 65, 73–88, 99–100; Clay to Tucker, 15 April 1841, *LTT*, 2:30–31; Tyler to Clay, 30 April 1841, *LTT*, 3:92–93; Webster to Tyler, 20 August 1841, *LTT*, 2:85–86; *National Intelligencer*, 13 September 1841; "The Diary of Thomas Ewing," *American Historical Review* 18 (October 1912): 111–12; Wise, *Seven Decades*, 187–90; Chitwood, *Tyler*, 215, 220–23, 239–42, 258–64, and 469–70, which analyzes differences in text between early and final versions of the second bank bill, revealing that the one enacted by Congress was unlike what Tyler had indicated to intermediaries that he could approve; Poage, *Clay and Whig Party*, 40; Fraser, *Democracy*, 169; Brock, *Parties and Political Conscience*, 89–98; Peterson, *Harrison and Tyler*, 263; Turner, *The United States, 1830–1850*, 534.

45. *Congressional Globe*, 27th Cong., 1st sess., 1841, 391–92; Philadelphia *Public Ledger*, 14, 16 September 1841; *Ohio State Journal*, 21, 24, 28 September 1841; *LTT*, 2:95, 101; Oscar D. Lambert, *Presidential Politics in the United States*,

1841–1844 (Durham, 1936), 43, 45; Fraser, *Democracy*, 219, 229–30; Morgan, *A Whig Embattled*, 45.

46. William Brock in *Parties and Political Conscience*, 100–101, wrote that Tyler "deserved to fail" in his subsequent attempts to build a national following, because he had not made it clear to the Whigs what type of bank bill he would approve. Brock's source for this was John P. Kennedy's campaign tract, *Defense of the Whigs* (New York, 1844), 91, 94, although other evidence as cited above shows that Tyler had made his requirements clear.

47. Washington *Madisonian*, 21 August 1841; Columbus *Old School Republican* (hereafter *OSR*), 16, 30 August, 6 September 1843; Richmond *Enquirer*, 16 April 1844; Washington *Globe*, 9, 16, 17 August, 9, 10, 14 September 1841; Fraser, *Democracy*, 190.

48. Tyler to Thomas A. Cooper, 8 October 1841; Tyler to Littleton Tazewell, 11 October 1841; and Tyler to M. S. Sprigg, 20 August 1844, Tyler Papers (Library of Congress [hereafter TPLC]).

49. Spencer had formerly been associated in his home state with the Clinton faction, which had once been Van Buren's foes, and the Antimasons, who had opposed Clay's becoming the Whig nominee in 1840. In October 1842, his lengthy written defense of Tyler's vetoes and accomplishments appeared in most major papers. See Washington *Globe*, 26 October 1842; Robert V. Remini, *Martin Van Buren and the Making of the Democratic Party* (New York, 1970), 5–6.

50. Upshur to Tucker, 7 September 1841, TPLC; Wise, *Seven Decades*, 192, 195–96; Chitwood, *Tyler*, 279–80; Peterson, *Harrison and Tyler*, xiii, 147, 167–68, 174, 177–78; Schlesinger, *Age of Jackson*, 395.

51. U.S. Senate, *Veto Messages of the Presidents of the United States, with the Action of Congress Thereon* (Washington, 1886), 169–79; *Brief Sketch*, 19–23; Wise, *Seven Decades*, 206–7; Chitwood, *Tyler*, 293–99; Van Deusen, *Jacksonian Era*, 164–65.

52. Tyler to Tazewell, 2 November 1841, *LTT*, 2:129; Tyler to unnamed correspondent, 14 June 1842, TPLC; Williams, *Presidents' Messages*, 2:1260–63; *LTT*, 2:129–32; Wise, *Seven Decades*, 205; Fraser, *Democracy*, 258–60; Chitwood, *Tyler*, 293.

53. *Niles' Register*, 64:79; *LTT*, 2:217, 219, 238, 240, 3:205–7; Williams, *Presidents' Messages*, 2:1253–55, 1290–96, 1301–2; George Curtis, *The Life of Daniel Webster* (2 vol., Boston, 1859), 2:104–7; Chitwood, *Tyler*, 311–15; Van Deusen, *Jacksonian Era*, 173–75. Contrary to the statements of both Webster and Ashburton, William Brock, in *Parties and Political Conscience*, 108, stated that the treaty "owed little to Tyler."

54. Williams, *Presidents' Messages*, 2:1303, 1339, 1387–88; Claude M. Fuess, *The Life of Caleb Cushing* (2 vol., Boston, 1923), chap. 10; Peterson, *Harrison and Tyler*, 143; Current, *Webster*, 131–33.

55. *OSR*, 9 August 1843; Washington *Globe*, 7 November 1842; *LTT*, 2:249.

56. Dayton *Miamian*, 2 September, 3 December 1843; New York *Aurora*, 17–19, 22–25, 29 August, 4, 6–9, 14 September 1843; *OSR*, 20, 27 September 1843; Philadelphia *Mercury*, 11 October 1843. Although Van Buren's rivals viewed their enterprise as a democratic crusade, one historian has dismissed Calhoun's bid as a "disruptive influence . . . on the makeup and procedures of the national convention." McCormick, *The Presidential Game*, 179.

57. See note 37, above; also, McGrane, *Panic of 1837*, 154–64, on the divisions between radical and conservative Democrats in various states.

58. This viewpoint frequently appeared in the editorials of the Washington *Globe* and kindred Democratic papers in November and December of 1842.

59. See J. E. Friedman and W. G. Shade, "James M. Porter, A Conservative Democrat in the Jacksonian Era," *Pennsylvania History* 42 (July 1975): 189–204; W. A. Porter, *Life of David Rittenhouse Porter* (n.d., privately published pamphlet at Historical Society of Pennsylvania); Washington *Madisonian*, 6 April, 8, 14, 15 May 1843; Washington *Globe*, 5, 16 April, 10 July 1843.

60. Turner, *The United States, 1830–1850*, 70; Pessen, *Jacksonian America*, 239–40, 284; Washington *Globe*, 10, 14, 17, 18, 21, 24, 26 July, 8 August 1843; *OSR*, 2, 16 August 1843.

61. Washington *Globe*, 30 January 1844; Washington *Madisonian*, 17 January, 20 February 1844.

62. Dayton *Miamian*, 17 February 1843, 20 March 1844; *OSR*, 2 August, 9 October 1843.

63. *OSR*, 23 August, 6 September 1843; Washington *Globe*, 14 August 1843; Kendall to Tyler, 20 October 1843, TPLC; Kendall to Jackson, 28 August 1844, in John S. Bassett, ed., *The Correspondence of Andrew Jackson* (7 vol., Washington, 1926–35), 6:315; William E. Smith, *The Francis Preston Blair Family in Politics* (2 vol., New York, 1933), 1:159–61; Schlesinger, *Age of Jackson*, 392–93.

64. Ohio Historical Society, *The Governors of Ohio* (Columbus, 1954), 42–45; John O. Marsh, "Wilson Shannon," sketch in Shannon Papers (Ohio Historical Society); Henry Holt, *Party Politics in Ohio, 1840–1850* (Columbus, 1930), 186 ff.; Francis P. Weisenburger, *The Passing of the Frontier* (Columbus, 1941), 407–12, 415–17; Dayton *Miamian*, 17 February, 2 December 1843.

65. Donald B. Cole, *Jacksonian Democracy in New Hampshire* (Cambridge, 1970), 187–207; Washington *Globe*, 28, 30, 31 March 1843.

66. See Smith, *Blair Family*, which covers Blair's career from the 1820s through the Civil War era. Blair's newspaper hereafter is cited by its actual title, *The Globe*, which, unlike most papers, did not include the name of the city.

67. *The Globe* 9, 16, 17 August, 9, 10, 14 September 1841, 3 January, 6, 10, 13,14 June, 2 August, 9 September, 14 October 1842; *OSR*, 30 August, 6 September 1843; Smith, *Blair Family*, 1:152–61.

68. *The Globe*, 31 October, 2, 7, 11, 23 November 1842; Peterson, *Harrison and Tyler*, 167–68. Webster blamed the Whigs' losses on the policy of Clay's followers toward the president. Some of Webster's statements at this time, as cited by Peterson, suggested that he still may have been entertaining the prospect of forming a "middle party" with Tyler, but he finally resigned in May 1843 to remain a Whig, as Tyler leaned increasingly toward the Democrats.

69. Among those Democratic papers that followed *The Globe*'s direction in attacking Tyler (derisively called "little Globules" by the Tyler press) were the *Bay State Democrat* (Boston), New York *Evening Post* and *Plebeian*, Philadelphia *Pennsylvanian*, *Ohio Statesman* (Columbus), Belfast (Me.) *Journal*, Cincinnati *Enquirer*, Harrisburg *Democratic Union*, and New Orleans *Morning Herald*.

70. *The Globe*, 7, 8, 21, 29 November, 2, 10, 20 December 1842, 26 April 1843.

71. *The Globe*, 6, 12 April, 23 May, 19, 28, 30 June, 21 September 1843. Tyler proposed refunding Jackson's fine in his opening message to the new Democratic Congress in December 1843. His signing of the bill that was quickly passed endeared him to Jackson and many moderate Democrats, but the Van Burenites could not afford to express any praise.

72. A. P. Upshur to N. B. Tucker, 12 December 1841, *LTT*, 2:247; Tyler to Littleton Tazewell, 24 October 1842, TPLC; Tyler to Alexander Gardiner, 11 July 1846, *LTT*, 2:341; also see statements cited in note 3.

73. *LTT*, 2:341, 374, 3:124; Carpenter, "An Interview with a President's Son," 420–21.

74. *Niles' Register*, 20 May 1843, quoted in Brock, *Parties and Political Conscience*, 107.

75. Tyler to J. B. Jones, 13 September 1843, TPLC; Morgan, *A Whig Embattled*, 170.

76. Tyler to Spencer, 12 May and 2 September 1843, TPLC; Tyler to Spencer, 22 May 1843 and 17 February 1844, Gratz Collection (Historical Society of Pennsylvania); Beb Poore, *Perley's Reminiscences* (2 vol., Philadelphia, 1886), 1:289; *LTT*, 3:310–13; Van Deusen, *Jacksonian Era*, 35; Schlesinger, *Age of Jackson*, 47; H. J. Carman and R. H. Luthin, *Lincoln and the Patronage* (1943, reprint ed., Gloucester, 1964), 331; Brock, *Parties and Political Conscience*, 107; Cooper, *South and Politics of Slavery*, 177; Cooper, *Liberty and Slavery*, 207; Peterson, *Harrison and Tyler*, 146–47; Seager, *And Tyler Too*, 224–27.

77. Washington *Madisonian*, 13 April, 6 November 1841. Among the papers that followed the *Madisonian* in supporting Tyler were the Columbus *Old School Republican*, Dayton *Miamian*, New York *Aurora*, Philadelphia *Mercury*, St. Louis *Old School Democrat*, Portsmouth (Va.) *Old Dominion*, and Chicago *Republican*. Because they stayed in business throughout the party battles of 1843 and 1844, there were apparently enough readers who favored their position to those of other factions' journals. For extensive listing, by affiliation, of partisan presses throughout the nation, see tables 4 and 5 in Kesilman, "John Tyler and the Presidency."

78. *OSR*, 16 August, 20 September 1843; *Madisonian*, 12, 16 January, 6, 9, 13, 22, 24, 26 February, 1, 2, 6, 22, 23, 24 April 1844; Dayton *Miamian*, 13 January 1844; New York *Aurora*, 21 March 1844; Tyler to group of Irish Philadelphians, 15 March 1844, TPLC; Tyler to New York committee, 23 March 1844, TPLC.

79. Cooper, *South and Politics of Slavery*, 166.

80. *LTT*, 2:314, 317; Poore, *Perley's Reminiscences*, 1:319–20; *Madisonian*, 28 May 1844; *The Globe*, 28 May 1844.

81. Calhoun had withdrawn as a candidate on 21 December 1843 after realizing that the Democratic convention would be packed in favor of Van Buren. He could not bind himself to support that body when it might, under northern control, adopt a tariff policy unfavorable to the South. Calhoun's withdrawal letter reprinted in *Madisonian*, 2 February 1844; Charles M. Wiltse, *John C. Calhoun: Sectionalist* (Indianapolis, 1951), 147; Cooper, *South and Politics of Slavery*, 171.

82. Williams, *Presidents' Messages*, 2:1384–87.

83. See Frederick Merk, *Fruits of Propaganda in the Tyler Administration* (Cambridge, 1971), 17, 21–23, and the appendix to Merk's *Slavery and the Annexation of Texas*, which reproduces Green's letters and related documents; Greenberg, *Masters and Statesmen*, 118; Peterson, *Harrison and Tyler*, 178–79, 185–86.

84. Merk, *Fruits*, 221–47. For elaboration on the "diffusion" theory, see William L. Barney, *The Road to Secession: A New Perspective on the Old South* (New York, 1972), chap. 2.

85. John C. Calhoun, *Works*, R. K. Cralle, ed. (6 vol., New York, 1853–56), 6:44–45; Van Deusen, *Jacksonian Era*, 183; Peterson, *Harrison and Tyler*, 213–15.

86. Merk, *Fruits*, and Merk, *Slavery and Texas*, passim; Cooper, *South and Politics of Slavery*, 184–86; Freehling, *Road to Disunion*, 447; Foner, *Politics and Ideology*, 42.

87. Holt, *Political Crisis*, 41–42.

88. Brock, *Parties and Political Conscience*, 117; Cooper, *South and Politics of Slavery*, 187–88; Cooper, *Liberty and Slavery*, 208; Holt, *Political Crisis*, 40; Peterson, *Harrison and Tyler*, xiii, 215. Merk, in *Slavery and Texas*, 50–51, 98, acknowledges Tyler's nationalist reasons for submitting the treaty while still reproving him for leading a band of southern extremists.

89. Tyler to Alexander Gardiner, 18 June 1847, *LTT*, 2:426; Tyler to Webster, 17 April 1850, TPLC.

90. *The Globe*, 15 April 1844; Jackson to Blair, 7 May 1844, *Jackson Correspondence*, 6:283–85.

91. *National Intelligencer*, 27 April 1844; *The Globe*, 27 April 1844.

92. For additional material on Texas and the 1844 campaign, see Chitwood, *Tyler*, 348–57; Lambert, *Presidential Politics*, 122ff.; Van Deusen, *Jacksonian Era*, 178–86.

93. *The Globe*, 27, 28, 29 May 1844. The *Madisonian* on 29 May printed a chart showing the number of votes cast for each Democratic candidate on all of the ballots. There were no votes for the president, because the Democratic delegates were already pledged to various candidates and his supporters all would be attending the separate Tyler convention.

94. The *Madisonian* of 28 and 29 May 1844 reported 1,000 delegates present on the first day and 2,000 in a full house on the second. A contrary account in *Niles' Register* caused Norma Peterson in *Harrison and Tyler*, 224–25, to call the convention "a small affair" in an uncrowded room. Merk, *Slavery and Texas*, 95, and Schurz, *Clay*, 2:253, state, without citing a source, that most of the delegates were officeholders. Short of checking out the identity and occupation of each person present, the amount of preconvention Tylerite activity, as described above, suggests that a larger number than the current federal workforce could have been involved.

95. *Madisonian*, 28–30 May 1844; *LTT*, 2:317–21, 337, 341; Chitwood, *Tyler*, 375–78.

96. *Madisonian*, 30 May 1844; *The Globe*, 9 June 1844.

97. Walker to Polk, 10 July 1844, *LTT*, 3:139–41.

98. *Madisonian*, 26 July 1844; *LTT*, 2:338–40, 3:143–46; Chitwood, *Tyler*, 379–82.

99. Tyler to Jackson, 18 August 1844, *Jackson Correspondence*, 6:315; Jackson to Blair, 29 August 1844, *Jackson Correspondence*, 317.

100. The joint resolution actually contained an option, proposed by Benton, to allow postponement of executive action to the new president, but Tyler and Calhoun chose not to delay, and Polk afterward let their action stand. *LTT*, 2:364–65; Van Deusen, *Jacksonian Era*, 190–91; Turner, *The United States, 1830–1850*, 531–32; Merk, *Slavery and Texas*, 160–61; Freehling, *Road to Disunion*, 447.

101. Brock, *Parties and Political Conscience*, 151; Cooper, *Liberty and Slavery*, 210–11; Foner, *Politics and Ideology*, 42–43; Merk, *Slavery and Texas*, ix, 181; Smith, *Death of Slavery*, 74.

102. Kelley, *Cultural Pattern*, 180; McCormick, *Presidential Game*, 179; Silbey, *Shrine of Party*, chap. 4.

5

"There Is a Great Work for You to Do": The Evangelical Strategy of David Walker's *Appeal* and His Early Years in the Carolina Low Country

Peter P. Hinks

"Everything must be transacted through the medium of negroes," complained the Scottish naturalist Alexander Wilson in 1809 upon visiting a tavern in Washington, North Carolina, a town near the center of the state's coast. Later in the same year, while describing Charleston in a letter, Wilson characterized this dependence much more graphically: "Everything must be done through the agency of these slovenly blacks and a gentleman here can hardly perform the services of Cloacina without half a dozen negroes to assist him." Wilson's ridicule, however, was not far off the mark. In the same letter, he observed more soberly that the "superabundance of negroes in the Southern States has destroyed the activity of the whites. The carpenter, bricklayer, and even the blacksmith, stand with their hands in their pockets, over looking their negroes."[1] In evincing his concern for the enervation of free white labor, Wilson also made clear that while the white craftsmen loitered, their black charges actually performed the skilled trades. Wherever he looked along the southeastern coast of the United States, Wilson found blacks overwhelming whites demographically and performing virtually every task required to keep the region alive and growing.[2]

Similar dynamics prevailed in Wilmington, North Carolina. Lying near the southern corner of the North Carolina coast in New Hanover County and equidistant from Washington and Charleston, Wilmington had a black demographic majority from the first federal census in 1790 through at least 1820.[3] The town and the surrounding Lower Cape Fear District — named for the large southern branch of the Cape Fear River that passed through the region — relied heavily on black labor and artisanry. The production of naval stores, rice cultivation, river and coastal pilotage, cooperage, metal working, and vending at the marketplace were just some of the essential local enterprises largely dependent on black workers. No industry in the town of Wilmington so clearly depended on skilled black labor as did the building trades. White contractors often assembled whole teams of black masons, carpenters, plasterers, and other craftsmen to work on large projects, and these artisans were not uncommonly supervised by a black foreman. Many of the town's elegant antebellum houses were the product of slave and free black labor.[4] Wilmington's most famous mansion from that age — the Bellamy Mansion on Market Street — was built exclusively by black labor in 1860.

Fifty years after Alexander Wilson made his observations in Charleston, Rufus Bunnell of Vermont, architect of Bellamy Mansion, was reiterating the same theme in Wilmington, albeit with a more sympathetic outlook toward African Americans. The black artisans so readily grasped the instructions in his sophisticated drawings that they soon required almost no supervision from him. Yet, Bunnell could not help but be uncomfortably puzzled by the fact "strange to ever keep in mind, that almost to a man these mechanics (however seemingly intelligent), *were nothing but slaves.*"[5]

David Walker, a free black born in late-eighteenth-century Wilmington, came of age surrounded by all this painful evidence of black power amid powerlessness. That memory would deeply color the work for which he is best remembered, *Appeal to the Coloured Citizens of the World*, one of the most influential black political documents of the nineteenth century.[6] Written in 1829 in Boston, where Walker had moved four years earlier, the *Appeal* decried in vivid and personal terms the savage, unchristian treatment blacks suffered in the United States, especially as slaves. Walker challenged African Americans to organize themselves and cast off this oppression that, he proclaimed, God found an intolerable provocation and sinful for them to endure any longer. Walker's innovative efforts to circulate his pamphlet in the South in late 1829 and throughout 1830 terrified white southern authorities, because it bespoke probably the boldest and most extensive plan of slave empowerment and rebellion ever conceived in the antebellum United States.[7] Although he died in 1830 as officials in the South detected and quashed his plot, his work remained a rallying point for many young blacks who, by the early 1830s, were becoming much more assertive in their calls for an end to slavery and racial discrimination.[8]

Little, however, is known about David Walker's life. Although numerous historians acknowledge his significance, only a handful have investigated and treated him at any length, and their focus has been overwhelmingly on his more accessible Boston years and on exegeses of the *Appeal*.[9] The character of Walker's critical early years in the South and their impact upon him have remained a mystery.

Yet, Walker has provided us with a few fertile clues. In two places in the *Appeal* he refers to having travelled extensively in the United States and observed most of what he described in his work.[10] At another point, he mentions time passed in Charleston.[11] In 1842 his widow made the important contribution of identifying Wilmington as his birthplace to a biographer.[12] Through a close investigation of these various clues and a careful reconstruction of the world in which he probably travelled, we can begin to determine the details of Walker's early life and assess its impact upon him.

Walker's southern experience almost certainly created in him a profound sense of paradox about the capacities of African Americans and left him struggling with the gnawing question of how to unshackle so powerful a people from their deep sense of powerlessness. Walker often fretted in his text that the sufferings of the blacks might have crushed their personal integrity and led them to believe that they were slavish by nature. "Oh! coloured people of these United States, I ask you, in the name of that God who made us, have we, in consequence of oppression, nearly lost the spirit of man, and, in no very trifling degree, adopted that of brutes?"[13] Elsewhere he exclaimed:

I aver, that when I look over these United States of America, and the world, and see the ignorant deceptions and consequent wretchedness of my brethren, I am brought oftimes solemnly to a stand, and in the midst of my reflections I exclaim to my God, "Lord didst thou make us to be slaves to our brethren, the whites?"[14]

At another point, he all but abandoned the slaves to a cowering complicity in their own subordination.

Here now, in the Southern and Western sections of this country, there are at least three coloured persons for one white, why is it, that those few weak, good-for-nothing whites, are able to keep so many able men, one of whom, can put to flight a dozen whites, in wretchedness and misery?[15]

Despite his numerous proclamations that African-American courage would be fueled by the wrath of God, Walker's *Appeal* belied his deep anxieties about the slaves' capacities to strike for themselves.

While forcing the conundrum upon him, David Walker's southern years also brought him to recognize its solution. He believed the key to elevating blacks to their full entitlement of strength and meaning was through the preaching of a gospel that reflected African-American experience and promoted God's promise of their empowerment. For Walker, this would most likely occur through black-controlled churches. Walker was probably exposed to a black-dominated Methodist church during his early years in Wilmington. He also might have been in Charleston for at least some of the time between 1817 and 1822 when Morris

Brown and numerous other African Americans labored to build an African Methodist Episcopal (AME) church in this unlikely environment. The tribulations the Charleston church and its leaders endured so infuriated a member named Denmark Vesey that he and a circle of his associates began to plot an insurrection and recruited conspirators with the argument that God reviled slavery and any black submission to it. Although the Vesey conspiracy was uncovered and suppressed in June 1822, David Walker was very possibly exposed to Vesey and his teachings. If so, he no doubt was impressed with how Vesey's yoking of religion with black empowerment and resistance rallied many local blacks to take the difficult step to challenge their enslavement. Indeed, Walker's likely southern experiences might have shaped his *Appeal* and his northern actions much more deeply than previously has been suspected.

David Walker was born, probably in the 1790s, in or around Wilmington, North Carolina. Unfortunately, no free black David Walker is to be found in official records anywhere in the South prior to the arrival of his pamphlet there. A thorough search through tax lists, censuses, county court minutes, wills, deeds, and assorted miscellaneous records related to slaves and free people of color in Wilmington's county of New Hanover, in the neighboring counties of Brunswick and Duplin, as well as in Charleston and Savannah and their surrounding districts yielded no David Walker.[16] Instead, the sole biographical data we have on Walker's years in the South come from the fleeting references he made in the *Appeal* to time passed there and from a short biography of him by the black Presbyterian minister and abolitionist Henry Highland Garnet, contained in Garnet's 1848 reprint of the third edition of the *Appeal*.[17] In his brief but very important sketch, Garnet wrote that "Mr. Walker was born in Wilmington, North Carolina, Sept. 28, 1785. His mother was a free woman, and his father was a slave." Yet, even the source of this information is not completely clear. Despite the assistance of Walker's widow, Garnet cautioned that "in regard to his life, but a few materials can be gathered." They are, however, probably correct on something so basic as his birthplace, especially because many Walkers — both white and black — inhabited the Lower Cape Fear District.

Although historians and commentators have always listed Walker's birth date as 1785, drawing on Garnet's work, we can actually place little confidence in that date. First, within the Garnet sketch itself, Walker is said to have died at the age of 34. Perhaps a typographical error reversed the numbers of the age of 43, but neither figure squares with a birth in 1785 and a death in 1830. The possibility that the younger age was correct and the birth date wrong is increased by the fact that Walker's death record in Boston lists his age in 1830 as 33, although it does not offer a birth date or birthplace.[18] The age at death of 34 in Garnet's work seems much more viable than the birth date

Garnet cites because Walker's widow might have misremembered his age slightly from a distance of 18 years.

Pinpointing Walker's birth date is of more than mere antiquarian interest. It can help explain his absence from official records in North Carolina as well as indicate at about what age he went to Charleston. If he was born in 1796 or 1797 and left Wilmington in the latter years of the 1810s, he would have been too young to appear on all but a few North Carolina tax or census lists. However, if he was born in 1785, the gap in the records becomes comparatively more difficult to explain, because the probability that he would appear on official records increases significantly. The chances that Walker could elude state reckoning for over 30 years are small, given that all free black males and females of 16 years and older were subject to annual poll taxes. Walker's absence from these lists and others tends to support a later birth date, around 1796 or 1797.[19]

Walker's Wilmington years probably also helped forge the intense commitment to autonomous black Methodism that he had developed by the 1820s. It is likely he was acquainted with an independent black congregation in Wilmington. In the Piedmont and western parts of the state, the white yeomanry early embraced Methodism, but in eastern and coastal North Carolina, blacks were the first to accept the faith. This was especially true in Wilmington. Although the town had been nominally part of a circuit after the Revolution, Francis Asbury, the church's first bishop, all but abandoned it as hopelessly unregenerate after a visit in 1785.[20] There were no stationed preachers there or even visits from circuit riders for a number of years after 1785.

Yet, a core group of African Americans carried on the faith in the town. Almost ten years later, when an itinerant white preacher named William Meredith stopped to preach in Wilmington, this core group asked him to stay there and be their pastor. Meredith was a disaffected former adherent of William Hammett and his Primitive Methodist church in Charleston, which itself had broken with Asbury's episcopacy. Despite intense persecution from local whites, in the few years before his death in 1799 Meredith helped to build two meeting houses, restored ties with Asbury, and placed Methodism among the town's blacks on a stable foundation. A white ministerial presence, however, would remain negligible until 1806. Nevertheless, the church continued to grow among local blacks — having almost 900 black members in 1803 and only a few white members — and was shepherded by a number of African-American stewards and elders who reported to Asbury. Not until 1813 did the day-to-day administration of the church fully shift to whites with the appointment of the energetic William Capers as pastor. Capers, who would soon become controversial for his effort to Christianize the slaves, looked back on that time several years later and remarked with dramatic candor that then "the negro meeting-house was become the Methodist church."[21]

The likelihood that David Walker was exposed to Wilmington's black Methodist church in his childhood is very high. Wilmington had only the Methodist church and an Episcopal one until a Presbyterian congregation was created in 1818.[22] Moreover, the Methodists directly solicited blacks, unlike the Episcopalians, who only later would open their facilities for some form of limited black participation. The intensity of Walker's adult commitment to the AME might well have had roots in his participation in this Methodist church. Equally probable was that this childhood experience might have led him as well to Charleston's African church.

Sometime between 1815 and 1820, David Walker apparently chose to leave Wilmington and make the short journey south to Charleston. One reason for an ambitious young African American to make that decision was demographic. In 1800 the 1,125 blacks in Wilmington constituted 68 percent of the total population, but only 19 of them were free. As a result, almost all skilled and unskilled labor performed by blacks in Wilmington was reserved exclusively for slaves.[23]

The situation could not have been more different in Charleston. Between 1790 and 1820 the free black population in Charleston District nearly quadrupled, from 950 in 1790 to 3,615 by 1820.[24] In the South, only Baltimore and New Orleans could boast a larger figure. The most spectacular increase in this population, however, occurred between 1810 and 1820, when over 1,800 new free blacks came to reside in the Charleston District, more than doubling the inhabitants, from 1,783 to 3,615. Natural increase contributed to a portion of this rise, and a wave of refugee free blacks from St. Domingue accounted for much growth in the 1790s. However, after 1800 — and particularly from 1810 to 1820 — most of the African-American newcomers were migrants from surrounding southern states.[25]

The prospect of employment was one of the principal reasons free blacks came to Charleston.[26] No city on the eastern seaboard south of Baltimore could compare with Charleston for such opportunity. A sampling of some of the skilled occupations followed by free blacks in Charleston in 1823 lists no less than 35 trades, ranging from carpenter and tailor to fisherman, hairdresser, and bricklayer. There also was a good deal of tolerance among local whites for the existence of a broad class of free black artisans and laborers. Free blacks were also, at all levels, less expensive to hire than were whites. The petitions of white mechanics seeking to restrict black artisans were regularly denied by the cost-conscious Charleston city council, who, despite the racial ethos, refused to abandon the benefits of cheap free black labor. The city's economy offered options for a free black that were inconceivable in the slave-dominated environment of Wilmington.[27] In turn, the large number of free blacks who flocked to the city were able to create numerous mutual aid associations that further secured their place in local society.

By 1817 Charleston offered African Americans another attraction: an AME congregation that was free of any control by local white churches and drew heavily, although not exclusively, on the support of free blacks. Prior to 1815, black Methodists in Charleston had administered their affairs with a good deal of autonomy. Although formally under the control of the stationed preacher, black stewards, exhorters, and class leaders actually preached, taught classes, oversaw love feasts, and collected and disbursed funds.[28] In 1815 a newly stationed preacher, the Reverend Anthony Senter, sought to remove this independence and bring the blacks more directly under white supervision. He abolished separate black Quarterly Conferences, required all trials of black members to be before a white minister, and placed black collections under white stewardship because he feared their subversive use.[29] Over the next two years, Morris Brown and other prominent leaders of the black Methodists secretly began to organize support among their followers for a break with the white Methodist church. In 1816 Brown slipped away to Philadelphia and met with Bishop Richard Allen of the AME denomination, received ordination from him, and planned for the creation of an AME congregation in Charleston. Soon after his return from the North in the next year, Brown and over 4,000 black Methodists made a dramatic departure from Senter's church and began to build a wholly separate AME church in Charleston. Although they were vigorously challenged every step of the way, the congregants struggled successfully for seven years to prevent a much more powerful opponent from wresting control of their church from them.

There is no question that David Walker was in Charleston for at least part of the time that the dramatic events around the establishment of the AME church unfolded. In Article 3 of the *Appeal* he stated:

I remember a Camp Meeting in South Carolina, for which I embarked in a Steam Boat at Charleston, and having been five or six hours on the water, we at last arrived at the place of hearing, where was a very great concourse of people, who were no doubt, collected together to hear the word of God.[30]

This event could not have occurred any earlier than 1816 because steamboats were not employed on any regional river or waterway before then.[31] Rather, this particular meeting likely was held in 1821 when on 17 and 21 April a number of advertisements in the Charleston *City Gazette* announced passage, for the first time ever, by packet, schooner, or steamboat to two sites where camp meetings were currently ongoing, Sullivan's Island and Goose Creek.[32] Goose Creek was probably the site Walker visited, because the first Methodist camp meetings in Charleston were initiated there in 1814. Moreover, the steamboat would have required five hours to travel the 17–18 miles upriver from Charleston to Goose Creek, and these boats often only made four miles per hour or less going against the current, especially with the number of hazards that then still cluttered the Cooper River. Transport to Sullivan's Island, which was in the bay, would not have requirednearly so long a journey.[33]

Walker referred elsewhere in the *Appeal* to time passed in South Carolina: "I saw a paragraph, a few years since, in a South Carolina paper, which, speaking of the barbarity of the Turks, it said: 'The Turks are the most barbarous people in the world — they treat the Greeks more like *brutes* than human beings.'"[34] A thorough search through the Charleston *Courier* and the Charleston *City Gazette* for the years 1817 through 1823 did not yield this exact quotation, but it produced nearly every approximation of this quotation from the middle of 1821 onward. In early 1821 a 29-year-old Greek rebel, Alexander Ypsilanti, led a band of followers out of Russia into Rumania with the intention of rallying Greeks and pro-Greek elements in the Turkish empire to revolt. Although his particular maneuver failed, it touched off rebellion among Greeks in the Ottoman realm that flared through 1829. These revolts were heavily covered in American newspapers, especially in the early years, and highly colored commentary on Turkish barbarity was frequent.[35] The fact that Walker specifically cited a South Carolina newspaper strongly argues for his having seen the paper in that state and retained the portion of it from which he quoted.[36] This quotation and the reference to the camp meeting both make it highly likely that David Walker was in Charleston at least through 1821.

David Walker's later impassioned commitment to the AME church and Bishop Richard Allen suggests he was exposed to the church in Charleston.[37] In the *Appeal*, he wrote with familiarity about events surrounding the tumultuous early history of the denomination in the South:

Tyrants and false Christians however, would not allow him [Richard Allen] to penetrate far into the South, for fear that he would awaken some of his ignorant brethren, whom they held in wretchedness and misery — for fear, I say it, that he would awaken and bring them to a knowledge of their maker.[38]

His probable relationship with the AME church in Charleston was of immense importance for Walker's later career because that church already was the center of discontent and plotting among blacks that culminated in Denmark Vesey's conspiracy of 1822. Many of the people who had spearheaded the church's creation and become its leading laity — men like Vesey, Peter Poyas, "Gullah Jack" Pritchard, Ned Bennett, and Jack Glenn — also were the principals in the 1822 plot. They were prominent advocates for black religious autonomy in Charleston, and Walker's exposure to them would not be surprising. He could only have perceived them admirably for their struggle against the "tyrants and false Christians." All five conspirators had believed that the integrity and the continuing elevation of the black community absolutely hinged upon a strong and independent black church in which biblical doctrine established the value of African Americans in the eyes of God and decried the injustice of slavery. When the viability of the church was threatened by white authorities, black leaders quickly counteracted.

Historians often have overlooked the critical fact that Denmark Vesey's conspiracy began to coalesce as early as 1818, when local officials first attacked the church. "Gullah Jack" Pritchard, an African-born conjurer who was a leading conspirator, proposed rebellion in the year "when the Negroes of the African Church were taken up" for congregating against city ordinance, and Peter Poyas traced the planning for the 1822 revolt back four years to the time of the arrests Pritchard cited. Indeed, according to Vesey, the fact "that our Church was shut up so that we could not use it" necessitated resistance and revolt as much as did the more pervasive ways whites deprived the blacks of their rights and dignity.[39]

Planning for the revolt and preparing the minds of numerous blacks for justifying it certainly occurred in one form or another within the several African congregations and their associated classes. The best-informed whites all concluded that the existence of the African Church was essential to the development of the plot, both ideologically and organizationally. One observer remarked that the blacks

Had been allowed to assemble for *religious* instruction. — The designing leaders in the scheme of villainy, availed themselves of these occasions to instill sentiments of ferocity, by *falsifying the Bible*. All the severe penal laws of the Israelites were quoted to mislead them, and the denunciations in the prophecies, which were intended to deter men *from* evil, were declared to be divine commands which they were to *execute*.[40]

The magistrates of the conspirators' trial likewise concluded that "inflammatory and insurrectionary doctrines, without any direct proposal for such an attempt, were inculcated" at class meetings that were also "to be used as places of rendezvous and rallying points for communicating to all, the exact night and hour, on which the first blow was to be struck." Three of the five men identified as principal conspirators — Denmark Vesey, Peter Poyas, and Ned Bennett — were class leaders in the church. Likewise, Richard Furman, a local white Baptist minister, described a fourth leader, Jack Glenn, as "a Preacher among them, & for one of his Oportunities [*sic*], of extraordinary Talents." Of the 35 men found guilty and executed for being the most heavily involved in the affair, 21 (60 percent) of them definitely belonged to the church, and many of the others possibly did as well.[41] Although the black revolt uncovered in Charleston in 1822 would have remained a possibility without the AME church, its organizational potential would have been severely curtailed.[42]

David Walker's thinking on black empowerment and resistance bears an uncanny resemblance to Vesey's stratagems and suggests some level of familiarity with the plotting. In Charleston, Walker may have concluded that an independent black church with its own system of biblical interpretation could be the single greatest threat to white authority because of the degree to which it upheld a vision of black autonomy, solidarity, and mission. This empowering institution might well be the key to resolving the painful paradox of vigorous independence and degrading submission that he observed in African-American society. Those testifying about Vesey at his trial often noted that he placed religion at the very heart of his strategy for black regeneration and empowerment.

His general conversation was about religion which he would apply to slavery, as for instance, he would speak of the creation of the world, in which he would say all men had equal rights, blacks as well as whites, — all his religious remarks were mingled with slavery. . . . He studied the Bible a great deal and tried to prove from it that slavery and bondage is against the Bible.[43]

Walker was equally convinced that the Bible and right Christianity were antislavery and that they justified racial solidarity and aggressive actions against enslavement and oppression.

Your full glory and happiness, as well as [those of] all other coloured people under Heaven, shall never be fully consummated, but with the *entire emancipation of your enslaved brethren all over the world.* . . . For I believe it is the will of the Lord that our greatest happiness shall consist in working for the salvation of our whole body. When this is accomplished a burst of glory will shine upon you, which will indeed astonish you and the world. . . . There is a great work for you to do, as trifling as some of you may think of it.[44]

Walker shared with Vesey and the Charleston conspirators a form of argumentation that did not exist — at least publicly — before 1827 among northern free black political and religious leaders. Walker played a critical role among these leaders in gaining currency for this line of thought, which the impress of events in Charleston may have brought him to embrace for the first time.

Walker's plan for disseminating his pamphlet and its ideas resembled Vesey's organizational strategy minutely. Vesey strove to build a small, tightly knit cadre of coconspirators who alone knew all the details of the planned revolt and worked aggressively against informants. Networks of mobile agents extending out from the port exhorted large numbers of blacks in the Charleston region to increase their sense of personal worth and power as well as their anger against their enslavement. Walker's method was identical except that it sought to create a grid of overlapping networks emanating from various ports along the southern seaboard that would ideally unite blacks throughout the South, not just in the area of one port.

Walker intended to speak directly, through the *Appeal*, to the very select group of educated, evangelical, and politically conscious blacks who he believed lived in ports throughout the South. He directed them to take exclusive charge of both organizing strategic details in their region and empowering the mass of local blacks by introducing them to the essential ideas and aspirations of the *Appeal*.

Some of my brethren, who are sensible, do not take an interest in enlightening the minds of our more ignorant brethren respecting this BOOK, and in reading it to them, just as though they will not have either to stand or fall by what is written in this book. Do they believe that I would be so foolish as to put out a book of this kind without strict — ah! very strict commandments of the Lord? . . . He will show you and the world, in due time, whether this book is for his glory, or written by me through envy to the whites, as some have represented.[45]

The remarkable breadth with which the *Appeal* spread in Virginia, North Carolina, and Georgia attests to the fact that Walker did find the local distributional systems he expected to use. His confidence that these individuals and structures existed may well have come from his knowledge of the details of Vesey's conspiracy.

David Walker's *Appeal to the Coloured Citizens of the World* was an anguished recounting of the brutalities African Americans had endured in the United States juxtaposed with an impassioned promise of the personal and social salvation available to blacks confused and demoralized by this treatment. Although Walker did worry that "it is just the way with black men — eight white men can frighten fifty of them," he immediately followed with a clarion of hope for blacks' ultimate recognition of their strength, worth, and purpose:

If you can only get courage into the blacks, I do declare it, that one good black man can put to death six white men; and I give it as a fact, let twelve black men get well armed for battle, and they will kill and put to flight fifty whites. — The reason is, the blacks, once you get them started, they glory in death. . . . There is an unconquerable disposition in the breasts of the blacks, which, when it is fully awakened and put in motion, will be subdued, only with the destruction of the animal existence.[46]

The key to breaking blacks' identification with the slavishness imposed upon them and awakening this "unconquerable disposition" was to help them realize that God offered each of them a special love and mission that would uplift them to freedom and personal integrity and respect.

A direct and personal encounter with the true Word of God and its revulsion with the enslavement and brutalization of God's people would overcome the paradox of the powerlessness of the powerful, would regenerate and transform African Americans into a nation ready to undertake a great mission of social liberation. The 50 shuffling men intimidated by eight white men would then become a phalanx putting the eight and hundreds more slaveholders to flight. The way out was through a biblical message and a church that empowered and organized African Americans. Although surrounded by the vibrant black church throughout his first years in Wilmington, David Walker likely did not fully embrace this strategy of religion and black action until Denmark Vesey and the African church led the way in Charleston. At that decisive moment in Walker's history, he started forging his own fiery *Appeal*.

NOTES

1. Clark Hunter, ed., *The Life and Letters of Alexander Wilson* (Philadelphia, 1983), 299, 310–11.

2. For an excellent description of the various tasks and skills performed by black labor in late-eighteenth-century Charleston as well as an analysis of the significant economic influence slave laborers wielded in the town, see Philip Morgan, "Black Life in Eighteenth-Century Charleston," *Perspectives in American History*, New Series 1 (1984): 185–222.

3. In 1790 blacks comprised 56 percent of the population of New Hanover County, which had Wilmington as its seat: 3,026 whites to 3,738 black slaves and 67 free blacks. By 1800, blacks' percentage of the total population in New Hanover had actually increased to 59 percent: 2,908 whites to 4,058 slaves and 94 free blacks. In the town of Wilmington itself, blacks had an even greater presence, with 68 percent of the inhabitants: 545 whites to 1,125 slaves and 19 free blacks. The census of 1810 witnessed only a small decrease in the black share of the population (57 percent), although their actual number continued to increase dramatically: whites were 4,891 of the inhabitants of the county and blacks accounted for 6,574, 132 of whom were free blacks. Unfortunately, census figures for Wilmington alone are not available for 1810, but the town had a significant fraction of this county figure. *Heads of Families at the First Census, 1790: North Carolina* (Washington, 1908); 1800, 1810, 1820 Federal Census, North Carolina, New Hanover County.

4. Catherine W. Bishir, "Black Builders in Antebellum North Carolina," *North Carolina Historical Review* 61 (1984): 422–61.

5. "Autobiography of Rufus Wiliam Bunnell," (typescript) in Box #20, file 360, Bunnell Family Papers (Yale University Archives).

6. David Walker, *Appeal to the Coloured Citizens of the World, but in Particular, and Very Expressly, to Those of the United States of America*, Charles M. Wiltse, ed. (New York, 1965).

7. For a fuller discussion of this covert circulation and Walker's strategy, see Clement Eaton, "A Dangerous Pamphlet in the Old South," *Journal of Southern History* 2 (1936): 323–34; Peter P. Hinks, "'We Must and Shall Be Free': David Walker, Evangelicalism, and the Problem of Antebellum Black Resistance" (Ph.D. diss., Yale University, 1993), 193–279.

8. For example, Amos G. Beman, a black Congregationalist minister in New

Haven, Connecticut, from the late 1830s until the Civil War and a prominent Garrisonian abolitionist, remembered in one of his scrapbooks how Walker's *Appeal* along with the *Liberator* and other writings by William Lloyd Garrison gave him and other African Americans in Middletown, Connecticut, the courage in the early 1830s to take a public stand against the American Colonization Society. Scrapbook, II, 87, Amos G. Beman Papers in James Weldon Johnson Collection, Beinecke Rare Book Library (Yale University).

9. See Herbert Aptheker, *"One Continual Cry": David Walker's Appeal to the Colored Citizens of the World (1829–1830) — Its Setting and Its Meaning* (New York, 1965); Merton Dillon, *Slavery Attacked: Southern Slaves and Their Allies, 1619–1865* (Baton Rouge, 1990), 145–50; Vincent Harding, *There Is a River: The Black Struggle for Freedom in America* (New York, 1981), 75–100; Donald Jacobs, "A History of the Boston Negro from the Revolution to the Civil War" (Ph.D. diss., Boston University, 1968), 55–79; Donald Jacobs, "David Walker: Boston Race Leader, 1825–1830," *Essex Institute Historical Collections* 107 (1971): 94–107; Sterling Stuckey, *Slave Culture: Nationalist Theory and the Foundations of Black America* (New York, 1987), 98–137; Wilson Jeremiah Moses, *Black Messiahs and Uncle Toms: Social and Literary Manipulations of a Religious Myth* (University Park, 1982), 38–46.

10. Walker, *Appeal*, 1, 76.

11. Ibid., 39.

12. *Walker's Appeal, with a Brief Sketch of His Life. By Henry Highland Garnet. And Also Garnet's Address to the Slaves of the United States of America* (New York, 1848), v–vii.

13. Walker, *Appeal*, 26.

14. Ibid., 28.

15. Ibid., 62.

16. It is important to mention here that the critical census schedule for 1810 — listing heads of households and numbers and age groupings of household members — is missing for North Carolina for that year, presumably either lost or destroyed. Thus, this source, which might have listed David Walker, cannot be checked. Tax records for antebellum New Hanover County also are very spotty, with the years 1815–19 being the most reliably documented. See New Hanover County Tax List, 1815–1819; New Hanover County Tax List, 1816, 1836, 1838; New Hanover County Tax Records, 1779–1869 (broken series), all in North Carolina State Archives, Raleigh.

17. *Walker's Appeal*, v–vii.

18. *Index of Deaths, 1801–1848*, 300, in Registry of Births, Marriages, and Deaths, City of Boston.

19. One further possibility that cannot be dismissed is that Walker and his parent(s) may have lived on the land of a white person as laboring tenants and, thus, were listed in census records as members of that white person's household. There are numerous examples of such unnamed free blacks in North Carolina census schedules. It would not be unlikely for free black tenants to make arrangements with planters to cover their poll taxes; in fact, such a relationship became formalized in state law in 1827. John Hope Franklin, *The Free Negro in North Carolina, 1790–1860* (Chapel Hill, 1943), 104. Yet, the names of taxables still should have appeared on the appropriate lists, at least up until 1827.

20. After visiting Wilmington in 1785, Bishop Francis Asbury observed, "I felt the power of the devil here," and left the town to its own devices. Elmer T. Clark, ed., *The Journal and Letters of Francis Asbury* (3 vol., London, 1958), 1:486.

21. William M. Wightman, *Life of William Capers, . . . Including an Autobiography* (Nashville, 1858), 174. This was quite literally true: the church building that Meredith and local blacks built had become by Capers's time the seat of

the established Methodist church in Wilmington and had been named the Front Street Methodist Episcopal Church. Blacks had been moved from the lower floor to the galleries, the construction of which Asbury's African-American stewards paradoxically had largely overseen.

22. An interesting section entitled "Wilmington Churches" appears in James Sprunt, *Chronicles of the Cape Fear River, 1660–1916* (2nd ed., Raleigh, 1916), 603–47.

23. For further data on the relative population of free blacks and slaves in Wilmington, see note 3 above.

24. Charleston District comprised not only the city of Charleston but also both Charleston Neck, a long, thin stretch of land commencing immediately west of the city boundary and running between the Ashley and Cooper Rivers, and several parishes to the north and west. The Neck was famous for its very high concentrations of free blacks and self-employed slaves.

25. Marina Wikramanayake, *A World in Shadow: The Free Black in Antebellum South Carolina* (Columbia, 1973), 17–22. For an example of white Charlestonians' complaints against the influx of free black immigrants from neighboring states, see their very interesting petition, 16 October 1820, in General Assembly, Petitions, 1820 #143 (South Carolina Department of Archives and History, Columbia).

26. For instance, Bishop Capers, writing of the itinerant, free black shoemaker Henry Evans, who came from Virginia and brought Methodism to Fayetteville, North Carolina, remarked that "while yet a young man, he determined to remove to Charleston, S.C., thinking he might succeed best there at his trade." Wightman, *Life of William Capers*, 125.

27. Wikramanayake, *A World in Shadow*, 100–5; Ulrich B. Phillips, "The Slave Labor Problem in the Charleston District," *Political Science Quarterly* 22 (1907): 427–28. The Phillips article contains the excerpted "Memorial of the Citizens of Charleston . . ." (1822), which states "Every winter, considerable number of Germans, Swiss, and Scotch arrive in Charleston, with the avowed intention of settling amongst us, but are soon induced to emigrate towards the West by perceiving most of the mechanical arts performed by free persons of color" (431). In Leonard P. Curry, *The Free Black in Urban America, 1800–1850: The Shadow of the Dreams* (Chicago, 1981), Curry argues in Chapter 2 that within the antebellum United States, occupational opportunity for free blacks was greatest in the lower South, especially in Charleston and New Orleans. As one progressed northward, possibilities were increasingly curtailed.

28. Bishop Capers gives a very interesting description of his overseeing of the black wing of his Methodist church in Charleston in 1811. "Men of intelligence and piety, who read the Scriptures and understood them, and were zealous for religion among the negroes, . . . were permitted to hold meetings with the negroes pretty freely" and did so not only in Charleston proper but also in such widely scattered places as Goose Creek, Cooper River, Wando, Wadmalaw Islands, Pon-Pon River, and the parishes of St. Paul, St. James, and St. John. Capers goes on to discuss the powers granted these men.

> Our plan was to recognize them as our agents. We authorized them to admit and exclude members; kept regular lists of their classes as belonging to our charge in Charleston; (for there was no other to which they could belong;) and they reported to us minutely on Monday what had been done on Sunday. They were the only persons who for Christ's sake were zealous enough to undertake such a service, and who, at the same time, could get access to the people that that service might be rendered.

It is of central importance that Capers stressed the degree of their allegiance to the church and Christ's cause. These men, almost all of whom were skilled artisans, were fervent evangelicals. When actions were taken to curtail their independence, no less than three of the eight mentioned men — Smart Simpson, Harry Bull, and Alek Harlston — would put their names on the petition requesting the right to form an AME church. Wightman, *Life of William Capers*, 138–40.

29. Some suspicion existed that Senter wanted to wrest control of finances from the black stewards because, along with using these funds for charitable purposes, they were also secretly purchasing the freedom of some slaves with them. Albert Deems Betts, *History of South Carolina Methodism* (Columbia, 1952), 237.

30. Walker, *Appeal*, 39.

31. A reference to the launching of a new steamboat in Charleston, in the Charleston *Courier*, 3 March 1817, seems to suggest that this was the first such launching. By 1818–19, talk of steamboats is incessant in the *Courier*. Steamboats also had just appeared in Savannah, a town that was developing this mode of transportation in close conjunction with Charleston. See Ulrich Bonnell Phillips, *The History of Transportation in the Eastern Cotton Belt to 1860* (New York, 1908).

32. Similar advertisements in earlier issues of the Charleston *Courier* were never noted.

33. Charleston *City Gazette & Commercial Daily Advertiser*, 17 and 21 April 1821; Rev. F. A. Mood, *Methodism in Charleston* (Nashville, 1856), 125–30. The site of Goose Creek Campground appears on a map in John B. Irving, *A Day on the Cooper River*, reprinted with notes by Samuel Gaillard Stoney (3rd ed., Columbia, 1969).

34. Walker, *Appeal*, 12.

35. For example, the Charleston *Courier* for 20 September 1821 exclaimed that "the Turks were prominent in giving proofs of the most inhuman barbarity." Such characterizations were very common.

36. Otherwise, why not have used much more readily obtainable newspapers — both past and current — in Boston?

37. In the *Appeal*, Walker exclaimed:

[Richard Allen] has under God planted a Church among us which will be as durable as the foundation of the earth on which it stands. Richard Allen! O my God!! The bare recollection of the labours of this man, and his ministers among his deplorably wretched brethren, (rendered so by the whites) to bring them to a knowledge of the God of Heaven, fills my soul with all those very high emotions which would take the pen of an Addison to portray. . . . Suffice it for me to say, that the name of this very man (Richard Allen) though now in obscurity and degradation, will notwithstanding, stand on the pages of history among the greatest divines who have lived since the apostolic age, and among the Africans, Bishop Allen's will be entirely pre-eminent. (58–59)

Walker was certain that Allen's church or one like it would be the key to smashing blacks' slavishness and ignorance. See 59–60.

38. Walker, *Appeal*, 59.

39. John Oliver Killens, ed., *The Trial Record of Denmark Vesey* (Boston, 1970), 52, 85–89.

40. [Edwin Clifford Holland], *A Refutation of the Calumnies Circulated against the Southern & Western States, Respecting the Institution and Existence of Slavery among Them . . .* (Charleston, 1822), 79.

41. Killens, *The Trial Record of Denmark Vesey*, 15–16, 140–41; Wikramanayake, *A World in Shadow*, 60, 125; Richard Furman to Governor Thomas Bennett, ca. 1822 (incomplete), Richard Furman Papers (South Caroliniana Library, University of South Carolina, Columbia).

42. Preaching and organizing in the outlying regions around Charleston among blacks who also were drawn into Vesey's conspiratorial network could have been performed by the black Methodists serving the parishes of St. Paul, St. James, and

St. John and other churches at least since 1811. Several of these preachers became closely affiliated with the African church. Their noted zeal suggests that they would not have easily abandoned their missions to the slaves in the countryside.

43. Killens, *The Trial Record of Denmark Vesey*, 61, 64. It is important to note that all statements attributed to Vesey issue from witnesses who heard him directly. None come from Vesey, because he remained silent throughout the trial. Yet, numerous statements linked to him are repeated by various witnesses in essentially the same form, pointing to the overall accuracy of the attributions. The court also attests to leaving evidence "as it was originally taken, without even changing the phraseology, which was generally in the very words used by the witnesses" (Killens, 1). Although some overstatement probably exists here, the court's claims on evidence suggest the relative accuracy of the transcriptions.

44. Walker, *Appeal*, 29–30.

45. Ibid., 71n.

46. Ibid., 25.

II

VARIETIES OF ANTISLAVERY AND REFORM IN A NORTHERN CONTEXT

6

Garrison, Phillips, and the Symmetry of Autobiography: Charisma and the Character of Abolitionist Leadership

James Brewer Stewart

When explaining the motivations of America's white abolitionists, many historians emphasize the importance of "grass roots" approaches. Yet, the problem of motivation can also be fruitfully investigated by considering the movement "from the top down," in this instance by comparing the biographies of William Lloyd Garrison and Wendell Phillips. By examining the lives of these two preeminent abolitionists and then by suggesting their impact on their less well-known associates, it becomes possible to understand the leadership of Garrisonian abolitionism as well as the sources of the movement's collective motivation.

In the following analysis, qualities of leadership and the biographical elements that nourished them will be of central importance, particularly the roles in the lives of Phillips and Garrison of absent fathers, of dominant single mothers, of climactic moments of self-definition, and of the long-term influences of wives, marriages, and families.[1] The longevity of the Garrisonians' collective commitment to their cause must be attributed in some measure to the powerful inspiration contributed by these visible men. The sources of their personal magnetism, in turn, can be found in Garrison's and Phillips's lifelong responses to these intimate circumstances and influences.

No two individuals can seem to have had less in common than did Phillips and Garrison — the Beacon Hill "aristocrat" versus the nondescript commoner, the Harvard graduate versus the self-taught printer's devil, the cosmopolitan orator versus provincial scribbler, the Calvinist intellectual versus the Christian utopian. Contemporaries puzzled over how these two could tolerate each other, let alone share so close a friendship.[2] Yet, the friendship itself suggests that these two leaders sensed their less apparent commonalities of temperament, wrought by similarities of background and experience. These shared characteristics endowed both men with qualities that continuously deepened their own commitments to leadership in abolitionism while allowing them to nurture the long-term participation of their colleagues. Lawrence Friedman has demonstrated that groups of abolitionists found refuge from a hostile world in family-like communities that clustered around dominating personalities. Some found a supportive leader in the congenial Gerrit Smith, while others were attracted to the steady evangelicalism of Lewis Tappan. Garrisonians, by contrast, responded to the charisma of Garrison and Phillips, leaders whose very natures seemed to radiate spiritual inspiration and spontaneous insight.[3]

As both Max Weber and Anthony F. C. Wallace have employed the term, charisma is a quality imputed to visionary moral leaders by their followers, especially in times of great social uncertainty, when traditional institutions and venerable moral categories seem to have lost their public support. According to both of these scholars, charismatic leaders derive their power from ambiguous historical contexts and from the perceptions of crisis on the part of their followers, not just from the innate qualities possessed by leaders themselves. If ever there was a period when traditional institutions and received wisdom no longer seemed capable of supplying direction to human affairs, the early 1830s seemed just such a time. However, as Weber and Wallace also explain, charismatic leaders articulate their own intense opposition to society's perceived loss of moral anchor, not just the anxieties of their fervent supporters. They regard themselves as standing at dramatic turning points in history, empowered to articulate fundamental insights that can reverse society's plunge into chaos and inaugurate a new era of harmony based on universal truth. To express the truth with the power they feel it deserves, such leaders invent new words, ideas, and symbols in a style that is often highly personalized and contemptuous of established institutions. All this, of course, roughly parallels general characteristics that historians attribute to the rhetoric of the abolitionists. At the same time, charisma also reshapes the private lives of the leaders themselves, sending them on lifelong quests to secure moral unity between their understandings of their private worlds and their ongoing senses of public mission.[4]

In Jacksonian America, personifications of charismatic leadership seem to have multiplied, starting with "Old Hickory" himself. The "Age of Jackson" was also the age of Joseph Smith, Frances Wright, John Humphrey Noyes, and Charles G. Finney, as well as of Garrison and Phillips — whose anointees believed that their leaders evoked a heavenly new order for a nation mired in blasphemy. In this broad sense, Weber's concept of charisma and the Jacksonian world that spawned so many social visionaries seem to explain each other uncommonly well.

The same observation also obtains as we consider specifics of Garrison's and Phillips's biographies.[5]

Phillips spent his Boston childhood studying at the fashionable Latin school, while Garrison, on the streets of nearby Newburyport, sold apples and homemade candy to fend off family impoverishment. As Phillips prepared for Harvard in his parents' Beacon Hill mansion, Garrison wandered with his family to Lynn, Massachusetts, and then to Baltimore, apprenticing to first a shoemaker and next a cabinet-maker. Finally, at age 12, he left his mother and sister in Baltimore and returned alone to Newburyport, where for the next seven years he learned the printer's trade. While the handsome Phillips — athletic, popular, and eloquent — flourished at Harvard and stayed on in Boston to begin his legal practice, the self-conscious Garrison taught himself the rudiments of literacy and published occasional articles as he served out his apprenticeship at the *Newburyport Herald*. Soon after, Garrison went on to fail in several attempts to establish himself as a political moralist and newspaper editor. Until he and Phillips finally met in 1835 or 1836, no two lives could have seemed less connected. Yet, their remarkable similarities are actually not hard to find.[6]

Garrison and Phillips both spent their formative years struggling with the legacies of vanished fathers, the exacting expectations of extraordinary single mothers, and the dreams of futures that would allow them to rest secure with their disrupted pasts. Phillips's father died suddenly when his youngest son was 12, and Garrison's father abandoned his family when his William was three. The elder Phillips had achieved a distinguished career in business, politics, and philanthropy that built on the formidable traditions of his Puritan ancestors; the elder Garrison was given to sloth and strong drink. Nevertheless, their absent fathers and the powerful, pious mothers who brought them up unaided created comparable emotional challenges for the two young boys.

For young Garrison, paternal abdication drove the remaining family into poverty and his older brother to alcoholism, sexual abusiveness, and self-exile. This shameful legacy Garrison strove both to suppress with unbending moral self-control and to transcend by frantically seeking an extraordinary measure of the world's attention. He began in adolescence to dream of a future when the American public, morally redeemed by his courageous example, would unite to honor him with power and respect. Meanwhile, Garrison's mother complicated her son's yearnings with a regime of unremitting evangelical discipline and guilt-provoking warnings against the "snares and temptations" hidden in his vaulting ambitions.[7]

As Phillips struggled with the implications of his father's death, he, like Garrison, dreamed of transforming the future. However, instead of confronting a legacy of failure, Phillips faced his family's extraordinary heritage of public service (two governorships of Massachusetts, the founding of Phillips Exeter and Andover Academies, and the first mayorship of incorporated Boston, just to mention some of the highlights) that extended unbroken to earliest Puritan days. While Garrison dreamed of gaining fame for his devotion to morality, Phillips absorbed himself in Puritanism's revolutionary history and directed his fantasies into the past. He identified strongly with Cromwell, Burke, Sam Adams, and other men who seemed to Phillips to share his ancestors' ability to twist the direction of history in liberty's favor. Once installed in his law office, he remained immersed in his studies, linking his investigations quite explicitly to familial expectations by developing an elaborate genealogy of his forebears. All the while, like Garrison, he also remained quickly responsive to his dominating, pious mother. She frequently had summoned him home from Harvard to account for himself, and after he opened his law office, she continued her demands while pushing him to slough off his seeming disinterest in advancing his worldly position.[8]

Apart from these similar patterns of uncertainty, the stories of Garrison's and Phillips's entries into abolitionism are textbook fare. Garrison, in 1829, became the editorial partner of the Quaker abolitionist Benjamin Lundy, was soon after jailed in Baltimore for libeling a slavetrader, and by 1831 had returned to Boston to launch his famous *Liberator*. Phillips, six years later, had already impulsively married the militantly emancipationist Ann Terry Greene when he learned of the murder of abolitionist editor Elijah Lovejoy by a proslavery mob in Alton, Illinois. At the meeting called in Faneuil Hall to protest this event in November 1837, Phillips suddenly rose and electrified the audience as he eulogized Lovejoy and announced his own conversion to "the cause."[9] Buried in the details of these familiar narratives were some of the dynamics that transformed dreamers into leaders and unsure young men into the charismatic builders of a revolutionary crusade. A brief contrast between the personal outlooks of America's eighteenth-century's founding fathers and those of Garrison and Phillips suggests how such dynamics might be identified.

As Douglass Adair has suggested, the men of the Revolutionary era conducted their lives with eyes fixed on posterity. Vindication, they believed, could be achieved only through the favorable verdicts of their future biographers, whom they set out to influence with elaborate displays of virtue. Garrison and Phillips, by contrast, embarked on lifelong searches to establish through their abolitionism the moral unity between their private worlds and their public missions. In place of the founding fathers' preoccupations with history, Garrison and Phillips substituted a charismatic drive to confirm for themselves that their lives cohered in dramatic moral symmetries. Vindication would come not from posthumous historical judgments but from first-hand experiences that documented to their own satisfaction their lives' moral wholeness.[10]

For an aging Garrison, in the summer of 1864, Baltimore was the most logical place to reconfirm the symmetry of his life as an abolitionist. Truly, the city was replete for Garrison with memories of his beginnings. Also, because the Republicans had invited him to the city as an honorary delegate to attend their presidential nominating convention, Baltimore offered Garrison a unique opportunity to fuse his sense of his past with the present in one grand design. Here, 40 years earlier, he had prayed with his mother for the last time as she lay on her deathbed, racked by tuberculosis and by fears that her son was succumbing to godless ambition. Here, earlier still, he had assisted his mother in her work as a domestic servant by carrying slop jars while his older brother struggled with bouts of violent drunkenness. Here, finally, had been the site of Garrison's most climactic moment in the odyssey that led to his abolitionist destiny — his 49-day incarceration after his conviction for libeling the Newburyport slavetrader. Baltimore, to Garrison, documented a lifetime of triumphant coherence between public achievement and private morality.[11]

When wildly applauded by the assembly that renominated Abraham Lincoln, Garrison sensed vividly his moment of vindication, informing his wife, Helen, that the tumultuous reception "gives a full endorsement of all the abolitionist 'fanaticism' with which I stood branded for all these years." After the convention adjourned, he lingered in the city, connecting his sense of fulfillment with memories of his abolitionist beginnings. He searched in vain for the old city jail in which he had served his sentence, but after being told that it had been torn down, Garrison prevailed on the city clerk to check for surviving jurors. When the clerk, who identified eight, asked Garrison if he would like to reempanel the jury in the hope of securing a more favorable verdict, Garrison replied that he was happy with their original finding. Although deprived of the chance to read an ode to emancipation that he had inscribed on the wall of his now-demolished cell, Garrison felt satisfied that he had shaped his life with transcendent moral exactitude. As he revealed to Helen, his retrospections "have been such to gladden my heart and almost make me fear that I am at home dreaming, not in the state of Maryland."[12]

Phillips, like Garrison, set out at the end of the Civil War to confirm his sense of his lifetime's completeness, touring the North in mid-1867 and speaking to enormous audiences on the necessity of radical Reconstruction. In every city, as he reported to his wife, Ann, "mayors, congressmen, and all the leading men" eagerly sought private audiences with him. Much as had Garrison in Baltimore, the orator clearly sensed his life, and his lifetime's cause, achieving a common fulfillment. "The day dawns," he exulted. "May we be worthy to rejoice at it's [sic] noon."[13]

Remote Alton, Illinois, however, was not a place for attracting huge audiences and bevies of "leading men." Instead, his visit there inspired in Phillips a retrospection that took him back to Faneuil Hall in 1837, when the murder of Elijah Lovejoy had first ignited his passion for emancipation. Though this was to be his only visit there, Alton was just as freighted with symbols of moral symmetry for Phillips as was Baltimore for Garrison. Visiting Alton prompted Phillips to recall how, decades before, the terrible news of Lovejoy's murder had "scattered" his "world of dreams" by revealing so vividly the moral terrorism of slavery. Ever since, Phillips explained, the mention of Alton's name had always filled him with "an involuntary shudder," but now this visit had "broken that spell." On this "beautiful spring day," as Phillips stood high on a wooded bluff above the broad Mississippi contemplating the destruction of slavery, he finally achieved reconciliation between his sense of the present and his abolitionist past. Now, as he explained, he preferred "to think of Alton as the home of brave and true men," inspired by Lovejoy, who, in resisting mob tyranny, had "consecrated this great valley to liberty." For Phillips as for Garrison, memory and a sense of the present came together to capture the essence of a lifelong commitment. Assessing his own life as he wrote of Lovejoy's, Phillips exclaimed: "What world-wide benefactors these 'imprudent' men are — the [John] Browns, the Lovejoys, the saints and the martyrs. How prudently most men creep into nameless graves while now and then a few forget themselves into immortality!"[14]

Nearly all abolitionists indulged in self-congratulation as Union military victory finally led to slave emancipation.[15] However, in the midst of the general jubilation, Phillips's and Garrison's vivid attempts to relive their abolitionist origins remain illuminating. Above all, their actions document the enduring influences of their initial moments of commitment in prompting them to structure their lives as unfolding dramas of moral unity.

Although neither Phillips's nor Garrison's climactic moment represented a first encounter with "the cause of the slave," the events of Faneuil Hall and the Baltimore jail marked culminations of struggles by both to address their youthful dilemmas through the medium of abolitionism. Garrison had moved back to Baltimore in 1829 to coedit *The Genius of Universal Emancipation* with Benjamin Lundy. Earlier, in Boston, Garrison had spoken strongly against slavery and had endorsed immediate emancipation. Phillips, too, was no stranger to abolitionism prior to his address in Faneuil Hall. Like Garrison, he had defied a dominating mother, specifically by suddenly proposing marriage to the abolitionist Ann Terry Greene, even as his mother lay on what all believed was her deathbed. Both men, in short, already were involving themselves in abolitionism as they attempted to address their inner turmoil.

Neither, however, seemed to be making much progress. Garrison already had bankrupted three newspapers with his editorial vehemence. Phillips, no less stymied, had lingered around the fringes of abolitionism. After his wedding to Ann, where guests gossiped that Sarah Phillips behaved "like a perfect dragon," he found his situation increasingly complicated by conflicting loyalties to mother and wife. For Phillips no less than for Garrison, abolitionism now provided a promising means for self-assertion in response to parental influences. However, for precisely this reason, it also added deeply to each man's personal tensions. Elijah Lovejoy's death and Garrison's guilty verdict suddenly impelled these impasses toward resolution.[16]

Alton and Baltimore provoked remarkably similar responses in Garrison and Phillips, because both locations embodied the nation's middle ground, the contested borderland shared by slavery and freedom that Barbara Fields, William Freehling, and other historians have described. Although Garrison experienced Baltimore first-hand while Phillips confronted Alton only in his vivid imagination, the middle ground, for both, epitomized terrifying moral opposites operating in disturbing proximity. The close interaction of slavery with freedom provoked all-encompassing responses from Garrison and Phillips that transformed dreams into visions and confusion into clarity.[17]

For Garrison, the provincial Yankee, Baltimore meant immersion not only in memories of family tragedy but also in jarring experiences with races and sectional cultures. He and Lundy boarded with two free African Americans, and for the first time, Garrison began sensing the precariousness of the distinction between enslavement and freedom. Moreover, day after day, he visited the local slave auction, mingled with masters, and then composed editorials condemning all that he had seen. In this manner the middle ground emphasized the gulf Garrison already sensed between his personal values and the conduct of daily life, prompting his attempt to knit his life together through a comprehensive series of actions.[18]

Francis Todd, a respected merchant from Garrison's old hometown of Newburyport, inadvertently provided the precipitating moment. In July 1829, when Todd transshipped 80 slaves from Baltimore to New Orleans, Garrison condemned Todd in a vitriolic editorial as a "MURDERER" who "should be sentenced to solitary confinement for life." He then posted a copy of this bitter attack to Ephraim Allen, the editor in Newburyport to whom Garrison had been apprenticed. Hoping to demonstrate to all in his hometown who remembered him that he had risen to unassailable moral ground, Garrison instructed Allen to publish the attack at once.

Todd aided Garrison unintentionally by filing and winning a criminal libel suit against the young editor. For 49 days of benign incarceration, Garrison continued to pull past and present into a tight moral focus by acting out his self-proclaimed martyrdom. To fuel the controversy in Baltimore, he wrote barbed letters to Francis Todd and the prosecuting attorney. Meanwhile, to advance his reputation in Newburyport, he goaded Ephraim Allen into commenting on the case in the *Herald*. Also, instead of paying his fine, Garrison used the last of his funds to print and mail hundreds of copies of a pamphlet in which he trumpeted his innocence. He claimed that he feared himself "in danger of being lifted up beyond measure, even in prison by excess panagyric and extraordinary sympathy," but that was exactly what Garrison sought to achieve.[19]

By attracting such notoriety, Garrison believed he was now proving false his mother's warning that his search for fame would lead him one day to "starve in some garrett [*sic*] or some place that no one inhabits."[20] Confinement, instead, was winning him popular recognition for his uncompromising embrace of abolitionist principle. Self-respect and moral certitude finally had become his:

I pay no rent and am bound to make no repairs — and enjoy all the luxury of independence. I strut like the lions of the day, and of course attract a great number of visitors. . . . How do I bear up under my adversities? I answer — like the oak — like the Alps — unshakeable — storm proof. Opposition, and abuse, and slander, and prejudice and judicial tyranny are like oil to the flame of my zeal. . . . Am I to be frightened by dungeons and chains? Can they humble my spirit? . . . If need be, who would not die a martyr to such a cause?[21]

It is not surprising that 35 years later, Garrison felt drawn back to Baltimore to reflect on his lifelong fidelity to this moment of illumination.

While Garrison experienced the middle ground first-hand, Phillips, in Boston, confronted it no less comprehensively in his highly developed imagination. Mob-ridden Alton, for Phillips, connoted a society debased by southern influences, driven to bloodlust and murder, a denial of all morality that suddenly demanded his adamant opposition. For Phillips as for Garrison, the moral provocation of the middle ground stimulated a dramatic transformation from personal uncertainty to a lifetime molded around abolitionist truths. Also like Garrison, Phillips was moved to action by the behavior of one of his own prominent townsmen, the attorney general of Massachusetts, James T. Austin. For both abolitionists, self-transformation began with vehement attacks on respected local custodians of traditional authority.[22]

At the Faneuil Hall meeting, Austin delivered an impassioned defense of the Alton mob. After castigating the murdered editor as a "firebrand," he equated the mob's actions to the resistance of the patriots of 1776, arguing that violence was justified in both instances to protect popular liberties. As Phillips listened, Austin seemed to be perverting the precious familial legacies of service and patriotism with which Phillips had always so deeply identified. To believe Austin, Phillips was soon to protest, "you must read our revolutionary history upside down." Even worse, from Phillips's perspective, Austin was daring to utter these falsehoods in Boston's shrine of patriotic resistance,

Faneuil Hall, on whose wall hung huge portraits of Sam Adams, James Otis, and John Hancock, the leaders whom Phillips had so long yearned to emulate. As Phillips reacted to Austin's provocation, present and past began to synthesize with one another, much as they had for Garrison in Baltimore.

Phillips's rebuttal pictured Alton as a political culture run amok, cut off from New England's heritage of liberty and overrun by corruption from the nearby South. "The people there seem to have forgotten the blood-tried principles of their fathers the moment they lost sight of our New England hills," he exclaimed, acting instead like "a community, staggering like a drunken man, indifferent to their rights and confused in their feelings." The town had been reduced by a pack of "drunken murderers" into "the tyranny of this many-headed monster, the mob," which only the valiant Lovejoy had found courage to resist. "The crisis had come," Phillips insisted. "It was time to assert the laws," to reassert boldly "the priceless value of the freedom of the press," just as had the patriots whose memories Austin had just impugned. "The men of the revolution went for right as secured by law," Phillips exclaimed. "The rioters of today go for their own wills, right or wrong."

Gesturing toward the portraits of Adams, Otis, and Hancock, Phillips next described his own reaction upon hearing Austin equate Lovejoy's killers with his beloved patriots. Suddenly, it became clear how completely Phillips was fusing his dramatic embrace of patriotic abolitionism with the legacies of family and his inspirational view of his own destiny. "I thought," Phillips exclaimed, "those pictured lips would have broken into voice to rebuke the recreant American — the slanderer of the dead. . . . In the sentiments he has uttered, on the soil consecrated by the prayers of Puritans and the blood of patriots, the earth should have yawned and swallowed him up." Afterward, Phillips always insisted that it had been the portraits, not the audience, to whom he had spoken.[23]

The Lovejoy of Phillips's imagination, like the imprisoned Garrison, embodied moral supremacy in the middle ground by defying slavery's licentiousness. Phillips himself, by attributing charismatic qualities to Lovejoy, likewise transformed his own self-understanding into that of the heroic leader, the role he had so associated with the obligations of his lineage and had so long dreamed of assuming. At the same time, he also claimed Ann Phillips's abolitionist vision as his own, putting to rest his conflicting loyalties to mother and wife. Now he could feel himself an extension of the heroic history with which he so strongly identified and the worthy heir of the legacies left him by his father. Phillips had begun to construct an inspiring design for living. At Lovejoy's gravesite three decades later, he would remember vividly how the news of his hero's murder had "shattered" his "world of dreams."[24]

Once personal history and public leadership finally had begun to cohere for Garrison and Phillips, the synthesis grew to encompass their most intimate levels of daily living. Their parents had influenced Garrison and Phillips to think of themselves as heroic individuals, acting with solitary force to conform the world to their wills. Their wives, by contrast, influenced them to expand their qualities of leadership around their understandings of themselves as husbands and as men. Helen Benson Garrison and Ann Greene Phillips, in completely contrasting manners, taught their husbands to foster nurturing relationships and to value collective effort.

Because the differences between Garrison's and Phillips's spouses were so striking, such assertions might at first seem impossible. Ann Greene Phillips possessed a force of personality that certainly matched that of her mother-in-law, Sarah, but Helen Benson Garrison was remarkably passive, judged against any standard. Wendell and Ann Phillips, sexually repressed and childless, lived as recluses while he nursed her through a lifetime of rheumatoid arthritis. The Garrison household, teeming with children and relatives, meanwhile became famous as "the abolitionist hotel," always open to out-of-town guests. Wendell and Ann Phillips grew intellectually as peers and became inseparable collaborators in abolitionism. Helen Garrison, by contrast, played no active role in the workings of the crusade. During four decades of confidential philanthropy, Wendell and Ann Phillips slowly divested themselves of two enormous inheritances. The Garrisons, always in need, openly relied on friends such as the Phillipses to help meet rent and tuition payments.[25]

Yet, these obvious contrasts obscure more important similarities. Ann Phillips and Helen Garrison both led their husbands to discover comprehensive connections between their private family affairs and their leadership within abolitionism. Their relationships with their spouses enabled both men to transform indelible memories of their mothers into new symmetries between their senses of domestic fulfillment and their leadership roles in abolitionism.

Ann Phillips matched genealogies and fortunes with all the Beacon Hill aristocrats, Sarah Phillips included. She also commanded the strength and sophistication necessary to overcome her prepossessing mother-in-law, who hated her abolitionism and resented her hold on Wendell. Their choice to live reclusively, far from Beacon Hill, announced that Wendell had freed himself from his mother's day-to-day dominion and the conventions of "brahmin" society. Yet, Phillips testified to his mother's enduring influence by marrying someone so like her in temperament. Indeed, he felt no hesitation in acknowledging to Ann the power of his memories of his mother. "If there be any truth in spiritualism," he told his wife, "I think my mother may be my guardian angel — the thought of her comes to me so often and at such singular times. It ought to make me [a] better [person]. Perhaps it will." Ann, for her part, always acknowledged, apparently without resentment, that Sarah "was everything to Wendell."[26]

Soon after marrying, Wendell Phillips had to confront the terrible afflictions that suddenly overcame his spouse. Usually bedridden in a semidark room, Ann relied on Wendell as her lifelong nurse, as well as her sole intellectual and social reference. As a result, Wendell Phillips developed a deeply nurturing side to his personality and suppressed all hint of aggression while he and Ann framed their relationship around her moment-to-moment medical and emotional needs. By turning himself into her caregiver and their home into what both jokingly termed "the hospital," the Phillipses reversed conventional gender roles with results that became apparent to colleagues in the abolitionist movement. The self-styled hero who dominated podiums and enforced Garrisonian orthodoxy was also able to develop close and enriching collaborations with some of the nation's most powerful and self-expressive activists, his own wife foremost among them.[27] Phillips soon declared woman's rights a central tenet of his abolitionism. He now explained that it was not only Elijah Lovejoy but also Ann and her feminist friends who had first "annointed" him in the cause and thanked them "for all that they have taught me." In the same vein, he attested that he drew special inspiration from female abolitionists and feminists, declaring that he had "never seen a more intelligent or cultivated audience [or] more ability guided by better taste on a [speaker's] platform" than at their meetings.[28]

Wendell Phillips, in short, ultimately interpreted his own abolitionism through powerful women such as Ann Phillips as well as through powerful male symbols such as Elijah Lovejoy. Of Ann, he was given to say to others, "A sick wife though she may be, I owe the little I am and do to her guardian spirit." To Ann herself he once wrote, slipping into the third person, "I am not worthy to button her old black shoes. She is my motive and inspiration. He owes her everything."[29] Again, in Phillips's outlook, past and present, public and private had merged into a symmetrical pattern of motivation and style of leadership. The solitary postures of Phillips the dominating orator now began to mesh with powerful collaborative instincts that Ann brought out in him during the course of their marriage.

Marriage also led Garrison to discover new and powerful connections between family life and abolitionism. Soon after their wedding, Garrison wrote to his "Dearest Helen": "Am I not a strange compound? In battling with the whole nation, I am as daring, as impetuous as unconquerable as a lion, but in your presence I am as gentle and as submissive as a dove." The spiritual inspiration of their wedded love, he assured her, would only lead him to battle all the more fiercely for slavery's overthrow because he could now "realize how dreadful a thing it is for lover to be torn away from lover, the husband from the wife, parents from children."[30]

Finding himself at last in the center of a loving family, Garrison began to flourish emotionally. With patient Helen he could, for the first time, let down his defenses, relax, and unguardedly respond to what he described as his "womanish" self, that is, his feelings of vulnerability and desires to give and receive emotional nurturing. His children knew him as a deeply involved, expressive father with a playful sense of humor and a genuine love for the routines of domestic life such as baking pastry and putting up jam. He so fully absorbed his in-laws into his own family that distinctions between the two groups became close to irrelevant. Further still, Garrison used the security of his new family to ease some of the pain left over from the old. When his brother James suddenly reappeared, terminally ill after more than 20 years of suffering and abusive living, Garrison took him in, lovingly nursed him through his final months, and assisted him in making his peace by helping him compose a confessional history of his life. Garrison, the solitary prophet, had become Garrison the empathetic spouse, brother, father, and colleague. As in Phillips's development, marriage and mission became fully enjoined. Of Helen, Garrison once remarked, "I did not marry her expecting that she would assume a prominent station in the anti-slavery cause, but for domestic quiet and happiness."[31] Yet, that very "quiet and happiness" enabled the defiant, prophetic Garrison to exert the appealing collaborative influence that inspired so many for so many years. Garrison, like Phillips, found in his marriage some of his deepest sources of motivation and leadership.

Absent fathers, dominating mothers, dreams of heroic transcendence, provocations from the middle ground, moments of self-liberation, and emotionally nurturing marriages — syntheses of dominance with collaboration — all combined to make Garrison and Phillips embrace as life's purpose securing moral symmetry through abolitionism. The public and private experiences of both men thus generated the aura of charisma. What remains to explore is the impact over the years of such powerful styles of leadership within the Garrisonian movement as a whole.

As several historians have observed recently, the Boston-based Garrisonian wing of abolitionism, by contrast to the groups that coalesced around Gerrit Smith and Lewis Tappan, upheld the overriding value of individual self-expression. These particular Garrisonians viewed with deepest suspicion all "godless" hierarchies that suppressed the individual, not only by spawning enslavement in the outside world but also by threatening their movement's liberating inner purity. Rooting out such impious distinctions led first to immediatism, then to endorsements of woman's rights, and finally to comprehensive changes in established conventions of gender. Some men within this branch of abolitionism developed androgynous expressions of "fraternal love," involved themselves in fund-raising bazaars, and interested themselves in childrearing. Some women, meantime, joined executive committees, edited newspapers, gave speeches, and invented new modes of expression in material culture, popular literature, and public address. Distinctions, thus, blurred between the traditional "male" world of power politics and the "female sphere" of "domestic influence."[32] Boston Garrisonianism, in short, thrived as a spontaneous fellowship of anti-authoritarians that required charismatic leadership to give it both inspiration *and* order. By embodying in equal measure unflinching heroism and collaborative benevolence, Garrison and Phillips met these two requirements perfectly.

Phillips and Garrison never hesitated when unilaterally defining the essential beliefs of the movement as a whole. Garrison took the lead when he decreed a powerful theology of woman's rights, abstention from voting, and disunionism. Phillips soon joined Garrison in zealously guarding the movement's borders by purging those who embraced communitarianism, tried to lead others to the ballot box, or confused the problem of poverty with the sin of slavery. Naturally, the two developed a division of responsibility consistent with their public roles. Although Garrison promulgated the movement's religion with perfectionist formulations, Phillips embellished its politics with "golden eloquence" and articulated theories of agitation and justifications for overthrowing the federal union.[33] Charisma, according to Weber, marks leaders in the eyes of their followers as inspired and unquestionable lawgivers, roles that Garrison's and Phillips's most fervid supporters happily ascribed to them.

While acting as lawgivers, however, Garrison and Phillips simultaneously began to extend to their friends and coworkers their experiences of marriage, fostering an environment of openness that freed participants to follow their private visions far into public life. Strict divisions of labor began to blur, along with distinctions of race and class. As Lawrence Friedman has suggested, Garrisonians did, indeed, come to comprise a family that conducted its relationships through self-expressiveness rather than by precedent.[34] Garrison and Phillips remained intensely involved in the process, insisting upon the frank exchange of differing ideas and offering warm support to all parties. "I think Garrison has done his work wisely and well," Ann Warren Weston once confided to Phillips, so that "there might be honest differences of opinion."[35]

Garrison and Phillips reciprocated their colleagues' loyalty and attraction with intensely emotional warmth. Coworkers began referring to "father Garrison," because, indeed, he did embody both authority and affectionate nurturing. Garrison eagerly multiplied the bonds between himself and his coworkers by constantly addressing them as his "dearest brothers and sisters." He freely opened his home to them all, wept over their griefs, laughed over their moments of happiness. Carrying these impulses further still, Garrison named all of his children after his dearest abolitionist friends and happily accepted gifts of his colleagues' money to meet his domestic expenses. For Garrison, the public and private had meshed in a synthesis sufficiently powerful to be felt by others as charisma.[36]

Although Garrison extended his actual family to encompass his friends, Phillips offered them instead all that his forebears had left in his care. The Phillips's home remained closed to outsiders. He and Ann had no children to name after his abolitionist comrades, and no one ever dared to call this aristocrat "father Phillips." Yet, like Garrison, Phillips equated the abolitionist movement with "family." By sharing his extraordinary wealth, his education, his indisputably privileged position with his fellow abolitionists, Phillips incorporated them into the paternal heritage of responsibility he so deeply revered.[37]

Although Phillips technically refused to practice law under a proslavery constitution, he spent countless uncompensated hours as the Garrisonians' personal attorney, managing the family affairs of his closest colleagues and friends. Among his clients, besides the Garrisons, were Abby and Steven Foster, Lydia Maria Child, Henry C. Wright, and Parker and Sarah Pillsbury, all prominent but financially strapped abolitionists. When legal assistance proved insufficient, Phillips opened his bank account, creating yet another level of synthesis between the domestic affairs of the family of abolitionism and the legacies of his own.[38]

In the final analysis, however, it was Garrison, not Phillips, whose presence and leadership most fully embodied the movement throughout the decades. In the Garrison family, as Phillips freely admitted, there could be but one father. For Phillips, the dictates of moral symmetry ultimately moved him to exalt Garrison, not compete with him, through the formidable power the orator exercised as the movement's patriot-hero. Phillips understood that Garrison was a truly charismatic figure whose inspired vision had opened vistas of freedom for African Americans while endowing abolitionists like himself with lifetimes of transcendent purpose. "How can we ever thank him?" Phillips once asked an audience of coworkers. Because of Garrison's fearless insights, abolitionists now found it possible to defy injustice and expose hypocrisy while seeking life's most fulfilling meanings. "Life, what weariness it is," Phillips exclaimed, "with its drudgeries of education, its little cares of today, all to be lived over again, its rising, eating, lying down, only to continue the monotonous routine!" Then, describing the precious gift that he believed Garrison offered to all who followed him, Phillips concluded:

Thank God that He has inspired any one of us to awaken from wearing these dull and rotting weeds — revealed to us the joy of self-devotion — taught us how we intensify life by laying it on the altar of some great cause. . . . My friends, if we never free a slave, at least we have freed ourselves in our efforts to free our brother man.[39]

It is hard to imagine a more concentrated explanation of the sources and consequences of charisma for these abolitionists, or why, for all committed Garrisonians, the "personal" was always so inextricable from the "political." It also becomes clearer why they were so tenacious in their lifetime quests to destroy slavery and discrimination. For all of them, not just for Phillips and Garrison, lifetimes inspired by visions of moral symmetry seemed always within their grasps.

NOTES

1. For the latest survey of the historiography of abolitionist motivation, see Richard O. Curry and Lawrence Goodheart, "'Knives in Their Heads': Passionate Self-Analysis and the Search for Identity in Recent Abolitionist Historiography," *Canadian Journal of American Studies* 13 (1983): 401–14. Among the best recent examinations of the dynamics of abolitionism from the "bottom up," see Nancy A. Hewitt, *Women's Activism and Social Change: Rochester, New York, 1822–1872* (Ithaca, 1984); and Christopher Padgett, "Hearing the Abolitionist Rank and File: The Wesleyan Methodist Schism of 1843," *Journal of the Early Republic* 12 (1992): 63–84.

2. The most recent treatments of both of these figures have been written by the author of this chapter, but subsequent documentation on both, wherever possible, will refer the reader to primary documentation. Generally, see James B. Stewart, *William Lloyd Garrison and the Challenge of Emancipation* (Arlington Heights, 1991); James B. Stewart, *Wendell Phillips: Liberty's Hero* (Baton Rouge, 1986).

3. Lawrence J. Friedman, *Gregarious Saints: Self and Community in American Abolitionism* (New York, 1982).

4. For an extended discussion of the concept of charisma, as Weber and other political theorists have developed it, see Reinhard Benedix, *Max Weber: An Intellectual Portrait* (New York and London, 1960); Ruth Willner, *Charismatic Leadership* (New York, 1990); Ruth Willner, *The Spellbinders: Charismatic Political Leadership* (New York, 1984); Max Weber, *Economy and Society: An Outline of Interpretive Sociology* (2 vol., Cambridge, 1950), 1:215–45; Anthony F. C. Wallace, "Revitalization Movements," *American Anthropologist* 58 (1956): 264–81. I am deeply indebted to Calvin Roetzel, Department of Religious Studies, and Jeff Nash, Department of Sociology, Macalester College, for their clear and patient guidance on the points discussed above regarding charisma. Three evaluations of abolitionism in terms compatible with the concept of charisma are Lewis Perry, *Radical Abolitionism: Anarchy and the Government of God in Antislavery Thought* (Ithaca, 1973); Robert M. Abzug, *Passionate Liberator: The Life of Thedore Dwight Weld* (New York, 1978); Stanley Elkins, *Slavery: A Problem in American Institutional and Intellectual Life* (Chicago, 1959).

5. A stimulating exploration of this point that also furnished a starting point for this inquiry is Thomas Brown, "From Old Hickory to Sly Fox: The Routinization of Charisma in the Early Democratic Party," *Journal of the Early Republic* 11 (1991): 339–70.

6. Stewart, *Garrison*, 1–40; Stewart, *Phillips*, 1–35.

7. Frances Lloyd Garrison to William Lloyd Garrison, 29 August 1817, in Wendell Phillips Garrison and Francis Jackson Garrison, *The Life of William Lloyd Garrison as Told by His Children, 1805–1879* (4 vol., Boston, 1889), 1:33 (quotation). Stewart, *Garrison*, 1–40; R. Jackson Wilson, *Figures of Speech: American Writers and the Literary Marketplace from Benjamin Franklin to Emily Dickinson* (Cambridge, Mass., 1989), 117–60.

8. Stewart, *Phillips*, 1–53.

9. Ibid., 36–63; Stewart, *Garrison*, 41–55.

10. Douglass Adair, "Fame and the Founding Fathers," in Trevor Colbourn, ed., *Fame and the Founding Fathers: Essays in Honor of Douglass Adair* (Chapel Hill, 1974), 3–26.

11. Stewart, *Garrison*, passim.

12. Ibid., 187–89; William Lloyd Garrison to Helen Benson Garrison, 8 June 1864, Garrison Papers, Antislavery Collection (Boston Public Library).

13. Stewart, *Phillips*, 270–83; Wendell Phillips to Ann Phillips, 19 April 1867, Crawford Blagden Collection (Houghton Library, Harvard University); *National Anti-Slavery Standard*, 29 April 1867.

14. *National Anti-Slavery Standard*, 29 April 1867.

15. See James M. McPherson, *The Struggle for Equality: The Abolitionists and the Negro during the Civil War and Reconstruction* (Princeton, 1964), 135ff.

16. Stewart, *Garrison*, 28–55; Stewart, *Phillips*, 36–63; Caroline Weston to Ann Warren Weston, 17 October 1837, Weston Family Papers, Antislavery Collection.

17. Barbara Fields, *Slavery and Freedom in the Middle Ground: Maryland in the Nineteenth Century* (New Haven, 1985); William W. Freehling, *The Road to Disunion, Volume I: Secessionists at Bay* (New York, 1990).

18. Stewart, *Garrison*, chap. 4.

19. Ibid.

20. Frances Lloyd Garrison to William Lloyd Garrison, 3 June 1823, reprinted in Garrison and Garrison, *Life of Garrison*, 1:31.

21. For extensive documentation on Garrison's trial and imprisonment, including all of the quotations above, see Garrison and Garrison, *Life of Garrison*, 1:179ff.

22. For evidence of these images of Alton, see Wendell Phillips, "The Murder of Lovejoy," in *Speeches, Lectures and Letters* (Boston, 1863), 2–10.

23. Stewart, *Phillips*, 58–63.

24. *National Anti-Slavery Standard*, 25 May 1867.

25. Stewart, *Phillips*, 84–96; Stewart, *Garrison*, 75–81.

26. Wendell and Ann Phillips to Elizabeth Pease, 31 January 1846, Garrison Papers, Antislavery Collection; Phillips to Ann Phillips, 10 December 1867, Crawford Blagden Collection.

27. Perusal of the files containing the correspondence between Phillips and Lydia Maria Child, Stephen S. and Abby K. Foster, Mary and George Luther Stearns, Caroline Dall, Parker and Sarah Pillsbury, Sidney and Elizabeth Neale Gay, Edmund Quincy, Lucretia and James Mott, Samuel J. May, Samuel May, Jr., and two of William Lloyd Garrison's sons — Francis Jackson Garrison and Wendell Phillips Garrison — document this statement.

28. Wendell Phillips, "The Boston Mob," in *Speeches*, 226–27; Wendell Phillips, "Woman's Rights and Woman's Duties," in *Speeches, Lectures and Letters*, second series (New York, 1891), 110–27.

29. Wendell Phillips to Richard D. Webb, 29 June 1842, Garrison Papers, Antislavery Collection; Wendell Phillips to Ann Phillips, 24 March 1867, Crawford Blagden Collection.

30. William Lloyd Garrison to Helen Benson Garrison, 24 April 1834, Oswald Garrison Villard Papers (Houghton Library, Harvard University). See also Walter Merrill, "A Passionate Attachment: William Lloyd Garrison's Courtship of Helen Eliza Benson," *New England Quarterly* 29 (1956): 116–34.

31. William Lloyd Garrison to Anna E. Benson, 14 April 1834, Garrison Papers, Antislavery Collection, contains a statement to his sister-in-law on this matter that is worth quoting at length. "I feel more and more child-like as time hurries me on to the maturity of manhood. My mind is as succeptable [sic] as it was in my infancy — it is a fountain of tenderness. It is not unusual for men to indulge in tears; yet how fre-

quently do I weep! Not that I am unhappy when I weep . . . exactly the reverse is true. . . . I *know* that I possess an Indian fortitude, which the fires of persecution can never subdue — a hostile world cannot move me from the path of duty — yet I am a very woman in the gentleness of my disposition." The quotation referring to Garrison's expectations in marrying Helen is found in William Lloyd Garrison to George Benson, 5 October 1838, Garrison Papers, Antislavery Collection.

A number of scholars have depicted Garrison as an emotionally repressive father, citing as evidence a tragedy that occurred when he fatally scalded his young son, Charles Follen Garrison. An instinctive follower of faddish "cures," Garrison attempted to treat his son with hot sitz-baths for what was feared to be rheumatic fever. Overriding the boy's cries of great pain, Garrison forced the boy to remain in the bath until he received terrible burns from which he soon died. John L. Thomas, *The Liberator: William Lloyd Garrison, A Biography* (Boston, 1965), 133–35, was the first to use this tragedy to document Garrison's repressive instincts and the general repressiveness inherent in abolitionist motivation. Another account that repeats this view is Ronald Walters, *The Antislavery Appeal: American Abolitionism after 1830* (Baltimore, 1976). By contrast, Aileen Kraditor, *Means and Ends in American Abolitionism: Garrison and His Critics on Strategy and Tactics* (New York, 1969), documents a more flexible and relaxed Garrison, a view that comports with my own impression of his temperament. A wise commentary on the problem of repressiveness is Lewis Perry, "'We Have Had Conversation with the World': The Abolitionists and Spontaneity," *Canadian Journal of American Studies* 8 (1980): 116–33.

32.   For some of the more recent studies bearing on these matters, see Donald Yacovone, *Samuel Joseph May and the Dilemma of Liberal Reform* (Philadelphia, 1991), chap. 4; Lewis Perry, *Childhood, Marriage and Reform: Henry C. Wright* (Chicago, 1980); Hewitt, *Women's Activism and Social Change*; Lori Ginsburg, *Women and the Work of Benevolence: Morality, Politics and Class in the Nineteenth-Century United States* (New Haven, 1991), 11–132; Jean Fagin Yellin, *Women and Sisters: The Antislavery Feminists in American Culture* (New Haven, 1990), chap. 1–4; Friedman, *Gregarious Saints*, 129–59.

33.   On these points, see John L. Thomas, "Antislavery and Utopia," in Martin Duberman, ed., *The Antislavery Vanguard: New Essays on the Abolitionists* (Princeton, 1965), 240–70; Jonathan Glickstein, "'Poverty Is Not Slavery': The Abolitionists and the Labor Market," in Lewis Perry and Michael Fellman, eds., *Antislavery Reconsidered: New Perspectives on the Abolitionists* (Baton Rouge, 1979), 195–218.

34.   Friedman, *Gregarious Saints*, 43–67.

35.   Ann Warren Weston to Wendell Phillips, 16 May 1846, Garrison Papers, Antislavery Collection.

36.   Friedman, *Gregarious Saints*, 49–57.

37.   See note 25.

38.   Stewart, *Phillips*, 127–32.

39.   *The Liberator*, 24 January 1851.

7

At the Crossroads: Leonard Bacon, Antislavery Colonization, and the Abolitionists in the 1830s

Hugh Davis

In 1845 Joshua Leavitt, an abolitionist editor, charged that an important group of religious leaders in the United States had "put forth their anti-slavery sentiments as an apology for acting against abolition." Among this group, he stated, "no one has from the beginning come nearer to abolition without hitting it" than had Leonard Bacon.[1]

Historians have long sought to explain why some opponents of slavery came to embrace the doctrine of immediate emancipation while others did not. Especially during the early and mid-1830s, the abolitionists waged a bitter struggle for northern public opinion with the colonizationists, who hoped that the removal of slaves and free blacks to Africa would eventually end slavery. In addition to Leonard Bacon, the leading proponents of colonization included Ralph R. Gurley, Lyman Beecher, Joseph Tracy, Theodore Frelinghuysen, and Robert Finley. Bacon, whom J. Earl Thompson, in his study of Lyman Beecher and the slavery question, has termed "the most astute, persuasive proponent of colonization in New England" by the late 1820s,[2] stood at the eye of the storm, engaging in an often bitter debate with William Lloyd Garrison, Gerrit Smith, James G. Birney, Elizur Wright, Simeon Jocelyn, and other immediatists. In the course of this debate he presented a wide-ranging critique of the abolitionists' ideology and tactics. Indeed, he remained one of their harshest, most persistent, and most influential critics throughout the antebellum era.

The differences between Bacon and the immediatists should not be exaggerated, however. James R. Stirn believes that northern antislavery thought in the 1830s was not divided sharply between immediate emancipation and colonization but, instead, moved along a "complex, frail, and often overlapping attitudinal continuum."[3] An examination of

Bacon's views on the race issue, and particularly his efforts to carve out a moderate antislavery position while continuing to espouse colonization, may well confirm Stirn's assertion.

Bacon first expressed opposition to slavery while an undergraduate at Yale in 1818 and 1819, when he and other members of the Brothers in Unity, a student organization, resolved that slavery should be abolished. For Bacon and many other New Englanders, the Missouri debates intensified concerns about slavery just as the American Colonization Society, founded in 1816, was making its initial appeal for public support. When he was a student at Andover Theological Seminary in 1823, Bacon embraced the colonization cause. The movement had received a warm reception at Andover, because the seminary's leading professors, Moses Stuart and Leonard Woods, were active in the cause and because the spirit of Samuel J. Mills, who had recently died while serving as a missionary in Africa, permeated the institution.[4]

As a member of Andover's Student Society of Inquiry Respecting Missions and later in the 1820s as pastor of Center Church in New Haven, as editor of the evangelical *Christian Spectator*, and as a prominent member of the Connecticut General Association of Congregational Ministers, the Connecticut and the American Colonization Societies, and the African Education Society, Bacon articulated his reasons for supporting the colonization movement's diverse agenda. Throughout the decade, he called for the repatriation of free blacks on the grounds that they could never rise from their degraded condition in the United States. Free blacks, he informed Ralph R. Gurley, secretary of the American Colonization Society, "must always remain a separate *caste*, distinguished by all that is wretched in ignorance and degradation." Their removal, he argued, would preserve order and morality in American society.[5]

Bacon and many other northern colonizationists also insisted that repatriation would benefit both slaves and free blacks. They subscribed to what George Fredrickson has termed an "environmental racism," which posited that blacks were not innately inferior but, rather, were unable to improve their lives in the United States because of an implacable white prejudice. Emigration, Bacon asserted, would permit the colonists to "show themselves capable of becoming industrious and enterprising and useful citizens" of Africa.[6]

Bacon further believed colonization would extend Christianity and civilization to Africa. A son of missionaries to the Indians on the Michigan frontier who was prepared to follow his parents' suit when he graduated from Andover in 1824, he naturally was attracted to this aspect of the colonization movement. Indeed, throughout the 1820s, he was a driving force behind efforts to establish an African seminary, which would train blacks in the United States to serve as ministers and teachers in Africa, and in 1829 he helped to found the African

Education Society as a means of implementing this plan.[7] As he put it, colonization would "cover Africa with the institutions of civilized freedom and religion, and the whole Negro race is raised in a moment, from its hopeless degradation."[8]

At the same time, Bacon frequently condemned slavery. In the early 1820s, he branded the system "an immense moral and political evil" that diminished the wealth of the South, raised the specter of slave insurrection, and degraded the slave. In perhaps his harshest attack on slavery prior to the inception of the abolitionist movement, he charged in a sermon he preached on July 4, 1826, that because slavery was "a criminal invasion of the rights of man," every Christian was obligated "to promote, by all means in his power, the gradual and legal abolition of slavery."[9]

Yet, during the 1820s, Bacon and many other opponents of slavery were uncertain how the system could be abolished. For them, congressional measures were unthinkable because slavery was a local institution, but widespread southern opposition to emancipation precluded any immediate antislavery action within that region. Moreover, they feared that extreme northern attacks on slavery would reignite the passions and threats that had surfaced in the Missouri Controversy.[10] These considerations prompted Bacon to conclude, as early as 1823, that colonization was the only reasonable means of ending slavery while preserving sectional peace. For young idealists such as Bacon, who wished to do something about slavery but who also valued ideological moderation, the cause was appealing. If anything, he became increasingly confident during the 1820s that, by removing free blacks from the United States, colonization would ultimately persuade masters to free their slaves.[11]

Bacon counseled both northerners and southerners to avoid "indignant invective," and he was especially critical of the "friends of universal liberty," such as Benjamin Lundy. He agreed with them on the goal of abolition but heartily dissented from what he considered their desire to "fan the flame of excitement."[12] He stated only months before William Lloyd Garrison established the *Liberator* that men of "sound judgment, sterling minds, and acknowledged weight of character" must provide leadership if slavery was to be abolished.[13]

Many of the men and women who launched the abolitionist crusade in the early 1830s certainly did not meet Bacon's standards of moderation and respectability. Reflecting the emerging aspirations for the liberation of the individual from historical and institutional limitations, they articulated a message of redemption of the sin of slavery that necessitated its immediate abolition. The colonizationists, they charged, served to deepen racial prejudice by seeking to rid the United States of all blacks and to protect slavery by refusing to condemn it openly. Further, they ridiculed the colonization scheme as impractical and deceptive, arguing that few blacks had been repatriated by the American Colonization Society, because nearly all free blacks rejected emigration. The colonizationists, they charged, had no real desire to elevate blacks.[14]

Historians have pointed to a variety of life experiences and beliefs that led some opponents of slavery — a number of whom had supported the colonization cause during the 1820s and early 1830s — to embrace the doctrine of immediate emancipation. The converts to abolitionism, historians argue, tended to have parents who emphasized moral uprightness and the ability to improve the world, to be driven by a youthful idealism, to have experienced crises related to career choices during the 1820s, and to adhere to evangelical doctrines that called upon converts, as free moral agents, to act immediately to eradicate sin in the world.[15]

There is, however, a danger of exaggerating the differences that set the pioneer abolitionists apart from critics of slavery such as Bacon who never became immediatists. Bacon and the immediate abolitionists shared, in varying degrees, important experiences and beliefs. His parents were missionaries who emphasized a strict morality and good works. He was an idealistic youth of 21 when he became active in the colonization movement, believing that it would uplift American blacks, eventually end slavery, and civilize and Christianize Africa. Moreover, soon after accepting the pastorate of Center Church in New Haven, Bacon experienced a crisis in his ministry when leading members of his congregation, feeling that his preaching was not sufficiently directed toward sparking a revival in the church, seriously considered removing him from his post. Finally, he was an outspoken defender of the New Haven theology, which emphasized the individual as a free moral agent, and he believed that opposition to slavery should become part of the evangelical witness.[16]

Bacon's views on race and slavery were similar to those enunciated by many abolitionists. Although he vigorously espoused the repatriation of free blacks, in the mid- and late 1820s he also helped to found the New Haven African Improvement Society and worked through it to assist free blacks in establishing schools, churches, and libraries.[17] During the 1830s, the abolitionists' assaults on colonization combined with Bacon's regular contact with free blacks who rejected repatriation to move him away from his tendency to depict African Americans as degraded. He became especially critical of those colonizationists who considered free blacks to be threats to a moral and orderly society.[18]

Bacon concurred with the abolitionists on aspects of the race issue. He agreed, for instance, that state laws oppressing blacks were "repugnant to the spirit" and would someday be declared contrary to the U.S. Constitution. In an 1832 article, he also emphatically endorsed Garrison's contention that blacks "can be improved in the United States and *ought to be.*" He reiterated this view in the *Exposition* that he wrote for the American Union for the Relief and Improvement of the Colored Race when it was established in 1835. Bacon even sent his children to an integrated school in New Haven and urged other whites to do the same. In 1834 he stated, "It has long been a settled principle with me that a colored man should be treated with the same kindness and consideration which would be due to him, if he were a white man."[19]

Bacon also shared with the abolitionists a deep and abiding hatred for the institution of slavery, and he expressed this view more vigorously following the inception of the immediatist crusade than he had during the 1820s. Nevertheless, Gerrit Smith, an old friend in the colonization cause who sought to bring him into the abolitionist camp in the mid-1830s, erred when he argued that Bacon's letters on slavery, antislavery, and colonization, which appeared in the *Journal of Freedom*, edited by Bacon in 1834 and 1835, "show that you do not know yourself, and that you are in fact an immediatist."[20] Bacon agreed with the abolitionists that slavery had no basis either in nature or in the Bible and that it was a "barbarous system" that was "simply and utterly sinful." The entire institution, he believed, must be abolished, but not immediately.[21]

Furthermore, Bacon defended the right of all critics of slavery to speak their minds freely and openly. "My right, and that of every other northern man, to discuss the subject of slavery; to pronounce an opinion on its economy, its policy, its morality; and to use all the power of moral suasion with my fellow citizens to its abolition," he informed Gerrit Smith, "is to me self-evident." He was especially contemptuous of those who participated in, or condoned the actions of, the antiabolitionist mobs, whom he termed "the self-constituted guardians of peace and liberty." Their "hushing rebukes," he asserted, were "too preposterous to need an answer in this country."[22]

Given Bacon's desire to improve the lives of blacks in the United States, as well as his hatred of slavery and his repeated calls for its abolition, why did he not abandon colonization? To be sure, growing opposition to the cause in both the North and South and the small number of blacks repatriated to Africa led him in the mid-1830s progressively to lose faith in the movement's ability to effect complete emancipation. Still, despite appeals by Smith, Elizur Wright, and other converts to the abolitionist cause, he not only refused to cross the line to immediatism but also stood forth as one of its most vocal critics. In order to understand why Bacon made these decisions, it is necessary to consider the personal and professional milieu in which he moved as well as his temperament and his belief system.

Bacon developed close emotional and organizational loyalties to the colonization cause at a formative stage of his life. Both his professors and his fellow students praised the 21-year-old's report to the Society of Inquiry endorsing colonization, and his peers selected him to represent them at the 1823 annual meeting of the American Colonization Society in Washington. His report on that meeting was then printed in the *Christian Spectator* and other evangelical publications. Thus, rather suddenly, Bacon was thrust into the inner circle of the movement, where he was courted by such luminaries in the cause as Ralph R. Gurley, Edward D. Griffith, Theodore Frelinghuysen, Henry Clay, and John Hartwell Cocke, who wished to recruit Andover students as a means of developing a strong base of support for the cause in New England. He even was offered the position of secretary of the American Colonization Society in 1824 while Gurley was in Africa, and during the 1820s and early 1830s, he received several other offers of various positions in the movement.[23]

By the time Garrison threw down the gauntlet against colonization in 1831, Bacon was a highly respected spokesman for the movement he had belonged to for eight years. He was, among other things, a close confidant of Gurley and other members of the national society's executive committee, and he served as secretary of the Colonization Society of Connecticut. As Elizur Wright noted, Bacon had both a professional and a personal stake in defending the cause against its critics. Bacon especially resented those who had recently embraced immediatism and now considered that to be the only legitimate stance on the slavery issue. His resentment was grounded in part in his conviction that many abolitionists were not sufficiently respectful of those who had long spoken out against slavery and urged the elevation of blacks. As Samuel M. Worcester, a colonizationist and old Andover classmate of Bacon, complained in 1834, "upstart youngsters . . . aided by a batch of older novices" now ridiculed and condemned those who "were earliest in the field to storm the citadel of slavery." Bacon himself had caustically reminded Garrison in 1832 that he had favored a "complete education" for blacks, without condition of sending graduates to Africa, "long before Mr. Garrison was an enemy — nay, before he was a friend of the American Colonization Society."[24]

Bacon was a proud, sensitive, and, at times, arrogant man who did not easily brook criticism. As pastor of perhaps the most prestigious church in Connecticut and as a writer whose pamphlets and articles reached a broad evangelical audience, his opinions on a wide range of issues were respected in benevolent and ecclesiastical circles. As a spokesman for the colonization cause, he believed that he stood in the vanguard of efforts to prepare the world for the coming of the millennium. Consequently, the abolitionists' accusations shocked and angered him, especially because the attacks often were quite pointed and personal. For example, Garrison, his harshest critic, charged in 1833 that "no writer in the United States, no slaveholder in the South, has uttered or published more excusatory, corrupt, and blasphemous sentiments as regard slavery" than had Bacon. Bacon genuinely detested Garrison and seemed to place little credence in his barbs. He was deeply hurt and offended, however, by a personal rebuke from the acerbic Elizur Wright, a childhood friend from his early days in Tallmadge, Ohio, where Bacon's father had sought, with little success, to recruit emigré Connecticut families. Wright angrily exhorted Bacon to "take my advice and come out like a man — like a true Christian and confess your sin . . . with up and down honesty, against everlasting hairsplitting and equivocation."[25]

Stung to the quick by Wright's assault on his character, Bacon responded that he was "sorry to see that you have so bad an opinion of me." He was generally inclined to act as a mediator and conciliator. He indicted the abolitionists' use of intemperate language and asserted to Simeon Jocelyn, a fellow New Haven Congregational minister with whom he often had come into conflict following Jocelyn's conversion to abolitionism in 1831, that "it is not my practice as a writer, to call any man or body of men, by *names* which they disavow."[26] Yet, Bacon could, at times, hurl epithets with the best of them. For example, he labeled Garrison a "willful incendiary who would smile to see conflagration, rapine, and extermination sweeping with tornado fury over half the land" and accused James Birney of having defended slavery while a colonizationist in Alabama. Indeed, Bacon acknowledged to Jocelyn that at times he became "unduly excited" by the immediatists' attacks.[27] The emotion invested in these and other charges and countercharges goes far to explain why it was so difficult for Bacon even to consider seriously the invitations by various abolitionists to join their ranks.

Bacon's repudiation of immediatism also was grounded in his social and ecclesiastical milieu. Center Church, the city of New Haven, the Congregational church, and the state of Connecticut all provided an atmosphere friendly to colonization and hostile to abolitionism. Antiabolitionist and antiblack sentiment reached a boiling point in New Haven and other Connecticut communities in the early 1830s. Garrison, Jocelyn, Arthur Tappan, and northern black leaders proposed founding a college for black males in New Haven in 1831. Frightened by the involvement of immediatists in the scheme, concerned about the reaction by southern students at Yale and by southern consumers of New Haven products, and simply opposed to providing college education for blacks, white residents at a mass meeting condemned the proposal by a vote of 700 to 4. An angry mob then shouted obscenities at blacks and stoned Tappan's home.[28]

Bacon was, in some degree, intimidated by New Haven's outpouring of anger. Although he protested that he had long favored a "complete education" for blacks and expressed "mortification and sorrow" with "the *spirit*" of the public meeting, he neither attended the mass meeting nor directly endorsed the proposed college. Rather, he acknowledged that the college's opponents had a right to bar it from the city. He would support such an institution, he noted in 1832, "whenever it shall be proposed in a form which will give us reason to believe that the control of it shall be entrusted with discreet men, and that the course of instruction shall not be calculated to exasperate the pupils and their colored brethren against the institutions and the population of the country, and to fill them with the spirit of wrath and insurrection."[29] In the final analysis, because Bacon was not prepared to confront the pervasive racist sentiment in the community, he could not support an institution that counted abolitionists among its active supporters. Similarly, if he had been at all tempted to join the incipient abolitionist crusade, the sound and fury that erupted in the city certainly helped to change his mind.

The Congregational clergy and the press in Connecticut were instrumental in mobilizing public opinion against the immediatists. A few Congregational ministers joined the abolitionist crusade — including Joel Hawes, a Hartford pastor who had presented the sermon at Bacon's ordination in 1825, and E. L. Cleaveland, a New Haven minister. Overwhelmingly, the Congregational clergy in the state were attracted by the promise of creating a racially pure United States and a Christianized Africa to support colonization. Although periodically condemning slavery, the Connecticut General Association, in which Bacon played a prominent role, heartily endorsed colonization from 1825 on, and Congregational clergymen occupied important positions in the Colonization Society of Connecticut.[30]

In addition, many of Bacon's closest associates and friends in New Haven were dedicated colonizationists. Especially active were those from Yale — Nathaniel Taylor, Jeremiah Day, and Benjamin Silliman — with whom Bacon served in numerous benevolent causes and interacted on an almost daily basis.[31] Procolonization sentiment was also widespread among the pillars of Bacon's church, such as Henry White, a deacon for many years and a leading light in the state colonization society, as well as among members of the Hotchkiss, Wilcox, Whittlesey, Rice, Trowbridge, Sheffield, Treadway, Peck, Bradley, and other mercantile and manufacturing families that depended, in some degree, on the southern market. With their blessing, Bacon regularly appealed to his congregation for contributions to the American Colonization Society, and following his ordination in 1825, Center Church was consistently one of the major contributors to the cause among Connecticut Congregational churches. Although his tenure at the church was relatively secure by the 1830s, his near dismissal a few years earlier was still fresh in his mind. The fact that Bacon was settled in a career he loved at a church where he wished to stay may well have reinforced his tendency to pursue a cautious course on the slavery issue. To have rejected colonization for the highly controversial abolitionist cause could have seriously jeopardized his position in both the church and the community.[32]

Beyond practical and personal considerations, Bacon's differences with the immediatists on both the race and slavery issues were substantial. Historians have noted that white abolitionists often depicted blacks in abstract terms, expected them to adopt middle-class values and to be meek in the face of persecution, and sometimes were blatantly racist in their assumptions and behavior.[33] Many abolitionists, however, expressed a commitment to racial equality and, particularly during the 1830s, strongly condemned racial discrimination and prejudice as extensions of slavery. Neither racism nor slavery, they argued, could be eradicated unless both were destroyed. Bacon was, on the whole, less overtly racist in his pronouncements than were such antislavery colonizationists as Robert J. Breckinridge and Isaac Orr and was less inclined to emphasize the need for a racially homogeneous United States than was Lyman Beecher. Nevertheless, he was far less willing than were many abolitionists to challenge aggressively and directly the pervasive racism in the United States. Historian Timothy Sehr simply errs when he asserts that Bacon considered blacks and whites to be "brothers and inherently equal."[34]

Stung by the abolitionists' charge that the northern clergy, and Christians in general, were thoroughly racist toward blacks, Bacon, in fact, became increasingly defensive, tending to minimize both the extent of white racism and its impact on free blacks. In response to James Birney's contention that colonizationists were responsible for closing many occupations to free blacks, Bacon even claimed, "So far as our observation has extended, colored men are judged each one by his own merits, as truly as white men."[35] He also differed with the abolitionists on how discriminatory laws should be countered. Unlike the immediatists, he believed that laws could not be changed until the prejudice that shaped them was diminished, and he had grave doubts that this would occur for many years. Convinced that prejudice could be eradicated if exposed and attacked, the abolitionists urged agitation and confrontation. Bacon, lacking a sense of urgency, counseled patience and Christian meekness. "Blacks," he maintained, "must vanquish prejudice, not by contention, but by their merits" and by adherence to the "law of love."[36]

Bacon's response to African Americans' aspirations and to agitation on their behalf by white abolitionists was shaped by a blend of racism and paternalism. When he speculated that the difference between whites and blacks in the United States was due in part to blacks' "barbarous lineage," he was blatantly racist. Convinced that the station in society occupied by free blacks would remain below that of the white middle class far into the future, Bacon referred to it as "the sphere in which Providence has placed" them. Bacon said abolitionists who urged blacks to challenge existing racial taboos were seeking to "forbid them to take a lowly station, or to acknowledge the superiority of whites."[37]

Like many other middle-class Americans of the time, Bacon was elitist in his attitudes toward both the white working class and free blacks. He blamed much of the racial conflict in society not on the white middle class but on "low-bred" white workers, whose "vulgar prejudice" was inflamed by fears of competition for jobs and status. At the same time, he assumed that free blacks were unwitting pawns in the hands of the immediatists because the African Americans did not know what their own best interests were. White Christians, Bacon wrote in 1834, should employ their superior wisdom to design and execute schemes of benevolence for uplifting blacks, who should know their place and avoid "an arrogant, assuming, disrespectful behavior."[38]

Indeed, though Bacon came to acknowledge in the early 1830s that some, perhaps many, blacks would choose not to emigrate to Africa, he naively clung to the hope that they would ultimately embrace colonization. That cause, he stated defensively in 1832, "has done, and is doing, more to rescue the African character from degradation, than could be done by a thousand volumes of reproaches against prejudice."[39] He even suggested in 1833 that although he and many other colonizationists desired emancipation, the American Colonization Society could be an effective organization only if it focused upon the sole objective of repatriating blacks to Africa. Thus, it is not surprising that abolitionists bitterly accused him of favoring removal over emancipation.[40]

On one level, Bacon's prolonged debate with the abolitionists appears to have been little more than the petty quibbling over semantics that Elizur Wright termed "everlasting hairsplitting." For example, Bacon quarreled with naming organizations "antislavery societies," claiming that it would have displayed a less "pugnacious, denunciatory attitude" to have termed them "societies for promoting freedom" or "for the emancipation of the enslaved" or even "for the abolition of slavery."[41] In addition, historians have shown that abolitionists themselves disagreed over the precise meaning of "immediate emancipation." Many probably did not interpret it literally to mean the immediate liberation of slaves.[42] Indeed, Bacon acknowledged that Garrison and Amos A. Phelps, among others, were willing to consider a form of temporary guardianship for freedmen. At the same time, he admitted that the process leading to total abolition must begin immediately. "As for the thing, which, when they attempt to speak accurately, they call emancipation," he stated, "we hold it to be the plainest and first duty of every master. As for the thing, which they describe as the meaning of immediate abolition, we hold it to be not only practicable and safe, but the very first thing to be done, for the safety of a slaveholding country."[43]

Bacon believed, however, that the dispute over words was extremely important. The problem, as he saw it, was that the abolitionists' use of terms involved "a certain logical sleight-of-hand, which perplexes, irritates and inflames the public." The immediatists, he insisted to Gerrit Smith in 1834, had one meaning in their definitions and another in their denunciations and popular harangues:

Immediate emancipation, however it may be defined in argument and in order to evade objections, will always be understood to mean in declamation, an immediate and instantaneous conversion of the slave, not merely into a "person," but into a person who is his own master invested like every other adult citizen with the power of self control. . . . The *immediate duty* of emancipation is one thing; the duty of *immediate emancipation* is another thing. I go for the former, but not the latter.[44]

Bacon and many other opponents of slavery, including Albert Barnes, John and Charles Tappan, and Joseph Tracy, agreed with the immediatists that the system was inherently sinful, but they denied the abolitionists' claim that slaveholding was prima facie evidence of sin and, therefore, should exclude all masters from Christian communion. Bacon and his associates clung to the belief that slavery would not survive the cessation of evil practices associated with the system, while the abolitionists feared that piecemeal improvement in the slaves' condition would put the slaveholders' consciences to sleep. The antislavery moderates, Timothy Sehr has noted, drew distinctions between sinful and innocent slaveholders, faithful and unfaithful churches, and the southern law and the southern people.[45]

According to Bacon, a master who bred slaves for profit, treated them like animals, sold off family members, or did not take care of his slaves' physical and spiritual needs should be ostracized as a "heathen and a publican." Meanwhile, he set forth numerous conditions that absolved "good slaveholders" of guilt for participating in the sinful system — inheritance, the need to do what was necessary for the slaves' welfare under existing circumstances, the establishment of an apprenticeship leading eventually to emancipation, and state laws that often rendered it difficult to manumit slaves. Even the purchase of a slave should not always be considered a crime without taking into account "the purposes and views with which the purchase is made."[46]

Bacon also disagreed with the abolitionists who said that to compensate masters for freeing their slaves would reward a sinful practice. In an 1826 sermon, Bacon had asserted that the slave's interests must take precedence over those of the master. However, in the face of the abolitionists' onslaught and the South's mounting intransigence, he retreated from that position in the 1830s, warning that emancipation might well impoverish masters and lead to the economic collapse of the South. At the same time, he rejected arguments by Simeon Jocelyn and William Lloyd Garrison that freedmen deserved to be compensated for the labor they had performed as slaves. Instead of money, Bacon maintained that whites owed blacks a debt of love in the form of efforts to uplift them.[47]

During the 1830s, both Bacon and the abolitionists placed their faith in moral suasion as a means of effecting total abolition. The immediatists thought that masters could be convinced to free their slaves only if confronted with the sin of slaveholding, but Bacon called for gentle persuasion and Christian forbearance toward southerners. He declared that the abolitionists' single-minded fervor and harsh accusations alienated southern Christians, particularly the "good slaveholders" who must lead the way to abolition. In a generally favorable review of William Ellery Channing's book on slavery in 1835, Bacon charged that the immediatists "have silenced, they have annihilated for the time, that party in the southern States, which was opposed to slavery, at least in theory, and which was inclined to promote enquiry respecting a safe and righteous abolition."[48] Bacon certainly engaged in wishful thinking when he contended that an indeterminate number of slaveholders wished to end slavery.

The abolitionists' agitation, according to Bacon, not only stiffened southern resistance to the abolition, or even the amelioration, of slavery but also threatened social order and endangered the general welfare. The mounting violence and social discord — manifested most starkly in Nat Turner's revolt, the Nullification Controversy, and the escalating antiabolitionist and antiblack riots in New Haven and numerous other northern towns and cities in the 1830s — would destroy the delicate equilibrium of a society already experiencing far-reaching social and economic changes. At times, Bacon came close to expressing an apocalyptic vision of America's future. No matter how much the abolitionists explained and declaimed their doctrines, he warned Gerrit Smith in 1834, immediate emancipation would necessarily lead to "misapprehension, misrepresentation, confusion, wrath, denunciation, hatred, violence, tumults," and, quite possibly, "convulsion, bloodshed, and revolution."[49]

Like many of his fellow antislavery moderates, Bacon respected order and propriety. He was a pioneer temperance activist, although he generally drew back from declaring all drinking to be sinful, much as he declined to condemn all slaveholding. Also an outspoken supporter of the American Education Society and other benevolent organizations,[50] Bacon was ever mindful of the limits of reform in all of his endeavors. To him, the abolitionists resembled the drunkard or the sinner in that they appeared to lack internal controls and to be impervious to external restraints. Bacon and other evangelicals, Donald M. Scott points out, believed the clergy must labor to safeguard the order, morality, and self-restraint so necessary for the enjoyment of true freedom.[51] Suspecting that the abolitionists were trying to create a third party, Bacon charged in 1834 that abolitionism was "a low-minded, quarrelsome spirit of faction, the same that has already made the name of politics so infamous — born of self-conceit and nourished by jealousy and envy."[52]

Above all, Bacon and other northern clergymen were concerned that the abolitionists' agitation would divide and disrupt the churches. In 1836 he pushed through the General Association of Connecticut resolutions affirming the right of ministers and their churches to determine whether itinerants and lecturers should be provided access to Congregational pulpits in the state. The resolutions, he informed Simeon Jocelyn, "only insist that the freedom of hearing and not hearing, is as sacred as the freedom of speech." Citing what he termed "unauthorized interference with the rights, duties, and discretion of the pastoral office," which he feared would be "fatal to the peace and good order of the churches," Bacon put himself forth as a defender of ecclesiastical order.[53] In fact, Bacon's resolutions contradicted his earlier defense of the right of opponents of slavery to condemn it publicly, and the abolitionists justifiably branded it "Connecticut's gag law." In an angry debate with Bacon, William Goodell, a New York abolitionist, accused the Congregationalists of undermining their stated belief in religious liberty and branded Bacon "the Nucleus, the Center, and the Spokesman" of "the Grand Ecclesiastical Combination throughout the Country."[54]

Bacon and the abolitionists approached the matter of means and ends from very different directions. On the one hand, the immediatists maintained that the need to prick the conscience of Americans was so urgent that it more than justified any short-term social disorder that might ensue. On the other hand, Bacon was so disturbed by the conflict and division generated by the abolitionists' demands that he was even prepared to abridge their fundamental rights. "Nothing is justice which does more harm than good," he declared in 1835. Much later in his life, in a eulogy to Joshua Leavitt, an abolitionist adversary during the 1830s and 1840s, Bacon charitably conceded that "While my judgment was swayed by the certainty of proximate effects, he looked to the ultimate result and was sure that, whatever might be the reaction and whatever disasters might come, there would be victory at last for justice and liberty."[55]

Bacon, however, was not a social conservative determined to maintain an orderly society at all costs. He condemned in scathing language the "self-constituted guardians of peace and liberty" in both sections. He often despaired of ever persuading southerners to take meaningful steps toward abolition, and his relationship with southerners within the colonization movement deteriorated significantly in the early and mid-1830s. At the same time, he had nothing but contempt for northerners, such as James Watson Webb, editor of the New York Courier and Enquirer, whose "reckless" attempts to arouse popular passions against the abolitionists "all good men of every party must deprecate."[56]

Bacon considered himself an enlightened and benevolent man who stood in the vanguard of efforts to create a moral, Christian republic and to usher in the millennium. Yet, the moral fervor and intensity of the abolitionists seemed alien and frightening to him. He could never bring himself to view immediatism as a personal quest for piety and, in

the words of Elizur Wright, a great struggle between "religious sinceri-
ty and hypocrisy." William Lloyd Garrison was not far from the mark
when he said of men such as Bacon and Channing: "They are polite men
— they are cautious men — they are accommodating men; and they
cherish a sacred horror of fanaticism, and do not like irritation, and
love to sail beneath a cloudless sky upon an unruffled stream."[57]
However, Bacon's efforts to tack a middle course between the conservatives and the abolitionists on the slavery issue did not bring clear sail-
ing. He complained to Simeon Jocelyn in 1836:

I am so unfortunate as to put myself between the opposing fires of two furi-
ously contending parties, and to make myself fully obnoxious to both.
Southern lovers of oppression hate me, and if they had me in their power,
would hang me, as an abolitionist. Anti-Slavery agitators pour out their wrath
upon me as an "ecclesiastical defender of slavery."

Jocelyn, however, replied coldly that southerners probably would not
hang Bacon because he never acted on his principles.[58]

In 1834 Bacon established the *Journal of Freedom*, for which
Garrison suggested the title *Journal of Despotism*,[59] to espouse "moderate anti-slavery" and "rational colonization." He hoped that the paper
would appeal to opponents of slavery who were not identified closely
with either the American Colonization Society or the American Anti-
Slavery Society.[60] One year later, Bacon and other antislavery moderates who favored what James Stirn has termed "urgent gradualism"
founded the American Union for the Relief and Improvement of
the Colored Race. Most of the founders were New England Congregationalists who feared that many moderate opponents of slavery had
joined the abolitionist movement because they desired some action
against slavery. Believing that many other moderates were disgusted
with the bitter struggle between the colonizationists and the immediatists, Bacon insisted that there was "no essential repugnance"
between the goals of the abolitionists and the colonizationists. When he
then professed to share the immediatists' belief that the elevation of
blacks in the United States was an important means to the end of abolition, he took a rather significant step away from colonization. Yet, the
Union's primary objective was the improvement of blacks, not their
emancipation. To Bacon's consternation, neither the immediatists nor
the southern moderates, whose support he counted on, were willing to
consider the Union's ideology and vague proposals, and by 1836 it
ceased to exist.[61]

In the preface to *Slavery Discussed*, a collection of earlier essays
that he published in 1846, Bacon recalled that "Ten years ago, I thought
I had done all that it was my duty to do in this way." Following the
demise of the American Union in 1836, he never again would show
much inclination to associate with organizations devoted to ending

slavery or assisting blacks. He remained a "warm friend" of colonization into the 1860s but was not active in the movement after the 1830s.[62]

Although Bacon seemed unable to articulate a clear-cut ideology, many northerners who also wrestled with the difficult issues of race and slavery identified with his efforts to carve out a middle ground on these matters. During the 1840s and 1850s, Bacon remained an important spokesman for the moderate antislavery forces. He was the leading Congregational clergyman in New England and senior editor from 1848 to 1861 of the *Independent*, one of the most influential northern religious newspapers. In addition, as a frequent contributor to the New York *Evangelist*, a New School Presbyterian newspaper, and to the *New Englander*, a journal he helped to establish in 1843, Bacon influenced the thinking of large numbers of northern middle-class Protestants.[63]

Nevertheless, throughout the two decades, Bacon continued to be criticized by both abolitionists and conservatives.[64] In numerous debates with the immediatists at annual meetings of the American Board of Commissioners for Foreign Missions and the American Home Missionary Society, as well as at Congregational church conventions, he, in concert with Edward and Henry Ward Beecher, Joseph P. Thompson, and other antislavery moderates, warned that for these organizations to withhold Christian fellowship from all slaveholders would hinder abolition by closing lines of communication with those "good slaveholders" who must ultimately end slavery.[65] At the same time, at the annual meetings of the American Tract Society, Bacon joined with the abolitionists in an unsuccessful attempt to force the society's executive committee to incorporate material on slavery in its publications.[66] From 1845 on he also insisted that northern Christians were obligated to judge the southern churches on their relationship with slavery.[67]

Following the annexation of Texas, Bacon argued repeatedly that Congress must use its authority to prevent the spread of slavery into the West and that it was necessary to arouse a moral citizenry to resist the aggressive designs of the slave interests. He believed that an antiextension policy would gradually end slavery in the South and so supported the Wilmot Proviso, the Free Soil party, and, most enthusiastically, the Republican party.[68] Likewise, as the sectional crisis deepened, Bacon was instrumental in mobilizing northern public opinion against the Compromise of 1850 and the Kansas-Nebraska Act. Although he cautioned against violent resistance to the Fugitive Slave Act, he was one of the leading proponents of the belief that, because it violated the higher law of God, Christians were not bound to obey the law.[69] He also actively raised funds to assist Connecticut settlers in Kansas.[70] Moreover, he condemned the Dred Scott decision as "a great outrage of judicial despotism" because it opened the territories to slavery and prevented the states from protecting the rights of blacks.[71]

Whether espousing antislavery colonization prior to the mid-1830s or defending northern antislavery interests as the sectional crisis intensified during the 1840s and 1850s, Bacon always sought to occupy a middle ground on the slavery question. In doing so, he and like-minded Americans both articulated and influenced northern public opinion throughout the antebellum period far more effectively than historians previously have appreciated.

NOTES

1. *Emancipator*, 24 October 1845.
2. J. Earl Thompson, Jr., "Lyman Beecher's Long Road to Conservative Abolitionism," *Church History* 42 (1973): 91.
3. James R. Stirn, "Urgent Gradualism: The Case of the American Union for the Relief and Improvement of the Colored Race," *Civil War History* 25 (1979): 327.
4. Entries for 11 November 1818 and 9 July 1819, Book IV, Records of the Society of Brothers in Unity (Yale University); P. J. Staudenraus, *The African Colonization Movement, 1816–1865* (New York, 1961), 16–19; Leonard Bacon, *Slavery Discussed in Occasional Essays, From 1833 to 1846* (New York, 1846), iii–iv; J. Earl Thompson, Jr., "Abolitionism and Theological Education at Andover," *New England Quarterly* 47 (1974): 250–51.
5. Bacon to Ralph R. Gurley, 28 February 1823, Records of the Society of Inquiry Respecting Missions (Andover Newton Theological Seminary); see also Bacon, "Reports of the Colonization Society," *Christian Spectator* 2, new series (July 1828): 368. David M. Streifford, "The American Colonization Society: An Application of Republican Ideology to Early Antebellum Reform," *Journal of Southern History* 45 (1979): 201–20, emphasizes the connection that many colonizationists made between the repatriation of free blacks and the preservation of republican principles in the United States.
6. Bacon to Ralph R. Gurley, 22 July 1823, Records of the Society of Inquiry Respecting Missions; see also Leonard Bacon, *A Plea for Africa* (New Haven, 1825), 15; George M. Fredrickson, *The Black Image in the White Mind: The Debate on Afro-American Character and Destiny, 1817–1914* (New York, 1971), 6–30.
7. Bacon to Ralph R. Gurley, 28 February 1823, Bacon to Edward D. Griffith, 22 July 1824, Records of the Society of Inquiry Respecting Missions; Ralph R. Gurley to Bacon, 12 July 1826, Bacon Family Papers (Yale University); *Freedom's Journal*, 28 February 1828, 7 March 1829; *Report of the Proceedings at the Formation of the African Education Society: Instituted at Washington, December 28, 1829. With an Address to the Public, by the Board of Managers* (Washington, D.C., 1830), 7–8, 13–16.
8. Bacon, *A Plea for Africa*, 15.
9. Vol. 16 of Dissertations, 7–11, Records of the Society of Inquiry Respecting Missions; sermon of 4 July 1826, 7, 15–16, Bacon Family Papers; see also Bacon, "Review on American Colonization," *Quarterly Christian Spectator* 2, 3rd series (September 1830): 474–75.
10. Bacon was deeply influenced by Joshua Leavitt's articles on slavery that appeared in the *Christian Spectator* in 1825. See Bacon, *Slavery Discussed*, ivn; Joshua Leavitt, "People of Colour," *Christian Spectator* 7 (March and May 1825): 130–38, 239–46.
11. Bacon to Ralph R. Gurley, 22 July 1823, Records of the Society of Inquiry Respecting Missions; Bacon, "Review on African Colonization," 461, 479; "Reports of the Colonization Society," 358; Bacon to Ralph R. Gurley, 6 July 1830, American Colonization Society Papers (Library of Congress).

12. Vol. 16 of Dissertations, 11–13, Records of the Society of Inquiry Respecting Missions; Bacon, "Review on African Colonization," 473.

13. Bacon, "Review on African Colonization," 479.

14. See Leonard I. Sweet, *Black Images of America, 1784–1870* (New York, 1976), 35–68; John L. Thomas, *The Liberator: William Lloyd Garrison* (Boston, 1963), 114–54; Merton L. Dillon, *The Abolitionists: The Growth of a Dissenting Minority* (DeKalb, 1974), 35–46; Lawrence J. Friedman, *Gregarious Saints: Self and Community in American Abolitionism, 1830–1870* (Cambridge, England, 1982), 21–28; Donald G. Mathews, *Slavery and Methodism: A Chapter in American Morality, 1780–1845* (Princeton, 1965), 100–101; William Lloyd Garrison, *Thoughts on Colonization* (Boston, 1832).

15. See, for example, Bertram Wyatt-Brown, "Conscience and Career: Young Abolitionists and Missionaries," in Christine Bolt and Seymour Drescher, eds., *Anti-Slavery, Religion, and Reform: Essays in Memory of Roger Anstey* (Folkestone, England, 1980), 185–90, 194–95; Lawrence B. Goodheart, *Abolitionist, Actuary, Atheist: Elizur Wright and the Reform Impulse* (Kent, 1990), 4–15, 41; Victor B. Howard, *Conscience and Slavery: The Evangelistic Calvinist Domestic Missions, 1837–1861* (Kent, 1990), 6–7; Friedman, *Gregarious Saints,* 18–19, 35–36; Donald M. Scott, "Abolition as a Sacred Vocation," in Lewis Perry and Michael Fellman, eds., *Antislavery Reconsidered: New Perspectives on the Abolitionists* (Baton Rouge, 1979), 62–67.

16. Evidence of these experiences and beliefs is found in David Bacon to Leonard Bacon, 7 August 1800, 26 June 1801, 26 June 1803, Alice Parks Bacon to Leonard Bacon, 1 July 1802, Alice Parks Bacon to Bacon, 28 November 1817, 20 April, 23 August, 1 November 1818, Bacon to Alice Parks Bacon, 30 September 1824, W. Shedd to Bacon, 30 September 1826, Giles Mansfield to Bacon, 3 March 1828, Bacon to B. B. Wisner, 31 March 1831, Bacon to Charles G. Finney, 12 April, 30 May 1831; Bacon to Alice Parks Bacon, 19 March 1833, Bacon to Asahel Nettleton, 29 July 1835. Bacon Family Papers. Wyatt-Brown, "Conscience and Career," 183–200, argues that historians have made too much effort to single out abolitionists, noting that many missionaries shared with the immediatists, among other things, an evangelical conscience, a desire to serve others, and similar patterns of childrearing.

17. See *Third Annual Report of the African Improvement Society of New Haven* (New Haven, 1829), 3, 5, 10, 13–14.

18. Bacon, "The Free People of Color," *Quarterly Christian Spectator* 4, 3rd series (June 1832): 334; "Slavery and Colonization," *Quarterly Christian Spectator* 5, 3rd series (March 1833): 167; *Journal of Freedom,* 17 May, 22 October 1834; *African Repository and Colonial Journal* 8 (August 1832): 174–75. Despite the efforts of Bacon and other colonizationists to improve the lives of blacks, the New Haven Peace and Benevolent Society of African Americans spoke for nearly all northern blacks when it denounced the colonizationists in 1831 as "inhuman in their proceedings, defective in their principles, and unworthy of our confidence." *Liberator,* 31 August 1831.

19. See Bacon, "The Free People of Color," 316, 318, 322, 327; *Journal of Freedom,* 24 September 1834; *Exposition of the Objects and Plans of the American Union for the Relief and Improvement of the Colored Race* (Boston, 1835), 3–15.

20. Gerrit Smith to Bacon, 27 August 1835, Bacon Family Papers.

21. See, for example, Bacon, "Review on American Colonization," 474–75; *Slavery Discussed,* 23–32, 101–5; *Journal of Freedom,* 17 May, 8 December 1834; William Jay to Bacon, 18 April 1834, Bacon Family Papers. Many antislavery colonizationists expressed similar views on slavery. See New York *Observer,* 27 February 1830, 20 September 1834; Boston *Recorder and Religious Herald,* 17 July 1833.

22. *Journal of Freedom,* 8, 15 December, 17 May 1834.

23. See Thompson, "Abolitionism and Theological Education at Andover," 250–51; Solomon Peck to Bacon, 1 May 1823, Bacon to Alice Parks Bacon, 30 June 1823, Moses Stuart to Bacon, 6 January 1834, Bacon Family Papers; Bacon to Edward D. Griffith, 1823, Bacon to Ralph R. Gurley, 22 July 1823, Records of the Society of Inquiry Respecting Missions; Bacon, "The Reports of the American Society for Colonizing the Free People of Colour in the United States, 1818, 19, 20, 21, 22, 23," *Christian Spectator* 5 (September and October 1823): 485–94, 540–51. For offers extended to Bacon by leaders of the colonization cause, see Ralph R. Gurley to Bacon, 24 June 1824, 21 April 1825, 7 September 1828, 13 June 1834, J. Gales to Bacon, 23 August 1834, Elliott Cresson to Bacon, 20 December 1834, Bacon to Ralph R. Gurley, 12 August 1834, John Breckinridge to Bacon, 17 June 1835, Bacon Family Papers.

24. *Liberator*, 27 April 1833; Samuel M. Worcester to Bacon, 20 June 1834, Bacon Family Papers; Bacon, "The Free People of Color," 320. Among the active officers of the American Colonization Society, Gerrit Smith appears to have been alone in defecting to the abolitionists' ranks during the 1830s.

25. Walter M. Merrill, ed., *The Letters of William Lloyd Garrison. Vol. I: I Will Be Heard, 1822–1835* (Cambridge, Mass., 1971), 256; Elizur Wright to Bacon, 27 April 1837, Bacon Family Papers.

26. Bacon to Elizur Wright, 1 May 1837, Bacon Family Papers; *Religious Intelligencer*, 15 October 1836; see also Bacon, "Slavery and Colonization," 153; *Journal of Freedom*, 20 August 1834. Jocelyn accused Bacon of being "very particular in the use of epithets" and noted his "remarkable tact at sarcasm." *Religious Intelligencer*, 8, 22 October 1836.

27. Bacon, "The Free People of Color," 333; *Journal of Freedom*, 8 October 1834; Bacon, *Slavery Discussed*, 58.

28. *Liberator*, 18 June, 17 September 1831; *Religious Intelligencer*, 17 September 1831; Lewis Tappan, *The Life of Arthur Tappan* (reprint; New York, 1970), 148–50; see also Leonard L. Richards, *"Gentlemen of Property and Standing": Anti-Abolition Mobs in Jacksonian America* (New York, 1970), 40.

29. Bacon, "The Free People of Color," 320; *Religious Intelligencer*, 17 September 1831.

30. Lucy Bacon to Bacon, 20 January 1834, Bacon to Joel Hawes, 22 March 1836, Bacon Family Papers; Robert Cholerton Senior, "New England Congregationalists and the Anti-Slavery Movement, 1830–1860" (Ph.D. diss., Yale University, 1954), 27–28, 44–45, 73–74, 158, 160; *African Repository and Colonial Journal* 3 (April 1827): 92; *Third Annual Report of the Colonization Society of Connecticut* (New Haven, 1930), 3–4; *Proceedings of the General Association of Connecticut* (Hartford, 1825), 7 (Hartford, 1832), 5; see also John R. McKivigan, *The War against Proslavery Religion: Abolitionism and the Northern Churches, 1830–1865* (Ithaca, 1984), 48, 174–75.

31. New York *Observer*, 18 July 1833; Sidney E. Mead, *Nathaniel William Taylor, 1786–1858: A Connecticut Liberal* (Chicago, 1942), 236; George P. Fisher, *Life of Benjamin Silliman* (2 vol., London, 1866), 2:47–48, 238–39.

32. New York *Observer*, 18 July 1833; *Fifth Annual Report of the Colonization Society of Connecticut* (New Haven, 1832), 8; *Sixth Annual Report of the Colonization Society of Connecticut* (New Haven, 1833), 15; *Patten's New Haven Directory, For the Years 1841–42* (New Haven, 1841), 18, 25, 56–57, 77, 82, 86, 96, 101; Bacon to Ralph R. Gurley, 13 September 1828, Bacon to executive committee of the American Union for the Relief and Improvement of the Colored Race, 20 March 1835, Bacon Family Papers.

33. See Leon Litwack, "The Abolitionist Dilemma: The Antislavery Movement and the Negro," *New England Quarterly* 34 (1961): 50–73; Friedman, *Gregarious*

Saints, 160–95; William H. and Jane H. Pease, "Antislavery Ambivalence: Immediatism, Expediency, Race," *American Quarterly* 17 (1965): 689–92, 695.

34. *African Repository and Colonial Journal* 9 (January 1834): 310; *American Spectator and Washington City Chronicle*, 12 February, 2 April 1831; Thompson, "Lyman Beecher's Long Road to Conservative Abolitionism," 104; Timothy J. Sehr, "Leonard Bacon and the Myth of the Good Slaveholder," *New England Quarterly* 49 (1976): 206. On the abolitionists' views on racial prejudice, see Dillon, *The Abolitionists*, 66–69, 72; James Brewer Stewart, *Holy Warriors: The Abolitionists and American Slavery* (New York, 1976), 45–47, 53–54.

35. Bacon, "Mrs. Child's Appeal in Favor of the Africans," *Quarterly Christian Spectator* 6, 3rd series (September 1834): 446–47, 449; "The Free People of Color," 318, 321; *Journal of Freedom*, 22 October 1834.

36. Bacon, "The Free People of Color," 322–24. For similar sentiments by northern colonizationists, see Catherine E. Beecher, *An Essay on Slavery and Abolitionism, With Reference to the Duty of American Females* (Philadelphia, 1837), 29–31; Boston *Recorder and Religious Herald*, 24 May 1834; *American Spectator and Washington City Chronicle*, 2 April 1831.

37. *Journal of Freedom*, 22 October 1834; Bacon, "The Free People of Color," 323–24.

38. *Journal of Freedom*, 15 December, 22 October 1834. This view was also expressed by the *American Spectator and Washington City Chronicle*, 2 April 1831; Boston *Recorder and Religious Herald*, 24 May 1834.

39. Bacon, "The Free People of Color," 336; see also *Journal of Freedom*, 17, 24 September 1834; *African Repository and Colonial Journal* 9 (January 1834): 309–10.

40. *African Repository and Colonial Journal* 9 (January 1834): 309–10.

41. Elizur Wright to Bacon, 27 April 1837, Bacon Family Papers; *Journal of Freedom*, 5 December 1834.

42. See Anne C. Loveland, "Evangelicalism and 'Immediate Emancipation' in American Antislavery Thought," *Journal of Southern History* 32 (1966): 172–88; David B. Davis, "The Emergence of Immediatism in British and American Antislavery Thought," *Mississippi Valley Historical Review* 49 (1962): 209–30.

43. Bacon, *Slavery Discussed*, 71–72. However, Joshua Leavitt spoke for most abolitionists when he insisted that emancipation must precede any debate on such a transitional stage. See Hugh Davis, *Joshua Leavitt, Evangelical Abolitionist* (Baton Rouge, 1990), 102.

44. Bacon to Gerrit Smith, 24 October 1834, Bacon Family Papers; *Journal of Freedom*, 8 December 1834.

45. Albert Barnes, *An Inquiry into the Scriptural Views of Slavery* (Philadelphia, 1846), 260–72, 340–75; Bertram Wyatt-Brown, *Lewis Tappan and the Evangelical War against Slavery* (Cleveland, 1969), 134–37; Boston *Recorder and Religious Herald*, 26 December 1834, 30 October 1835, 1 July 1836; Sehr, "Leonard Bacon and the Myth of the Good Slaveholder," 196–97. McKivigan, *The War against Proslavery Religion*, 20–24, 29–35, contends that this was the crucial issue that divided the immediatists and the more moderate opponents of slavery.

46. See Bacon, *Slavery Discussed*, 50, 53.

47. Sermon of 4 July 1826, 7, Bacon Family Papers; *Journal of Freedom*, 8 December 1834; *Religious Intelligencer*, 10 September, 8, 15 October 1836.

48. Bacon, *Slavery Discussed*, 86–87. Bacon discussed his concept of the "good slaveholder" in *Journal of Freedom*, 20 August, 17 September 1834; Bacon, *Slavery Discussed*, 76–79.

49. *Journal of Freedom*, 8 December 1834.

50. See, for example, Bacon, *Total Abstinence from Ardent Spirits; An Address Delivered, by Request of the Young Men's Temperance Society of New Haven, in the*

North Church, June 24, 1829 (New Haven, 1829), 2–10, 16–17; "Discourses on Intemperance," *Christian Spectator* 1, new series (November and December 1827): 587–604, 645–55; *A Discourse on the Traffic in Spiritous Liquors, Delivered in the Center Church, New Haven, February 6, 1838* (New Haven, 1838); "Brief View of the American Education Society," *Christian Spectator* 1, new series (February 1827): 92–98.

51. Donald M. Scott, *From Office to Profession: The New England Ministry, 1750–1850* (Philadelphia, 1978), 97–98, 101–3; see also Mathews, *Slavery and Methodism*, 105–6; Streifford, "The American Colonization Society," 204–6; Fredrickson, *The Black Image in the White Mind*, 33; John L. Thomas, "Romantic Reform in America, 1815–1865," *American Quarterly* 17 (1965): 656–81.

52. See *Journal of Freedom*, 20 August 1834.

53. *Proceedings of the General Association of Connecticut* (Hartford, 1836), 8; *Religious Intelligencer*, 10 July, 18 March 1837; also 10 December 1836.

54. *Religious Intelligencer*, 29 April, 6 May, 3 June 1837; William Goodell to Amos A. Phelps, 24 April 1837, Amos A. Phelps Papers (Boston Public Library).

55. *Journal of Freedom*, 29 January 1835; *Independent*, 6 February 1873.

56. *Journal of Freedom*, 17 May, 17 September 1834; Bacon, *Slavery Discussed*, 85. On the growing breach between Bacon and southern colonizationists, see Bacon, "Gurley's Life of Ashmun," *Quarterly Christian Spectator* 7, 3rd series (June 1835): 332; Stirn, "Urgent Gradualism," 311–14; *Journal of Freedom*, 22 October 1834; Ralph R. Gurley to Bacon, 13, 23 April 1835, Bacon Family Papers.

57. Goodheart, *Abolitionist, Actuary, Atheist*, 37; *Liberator*, 17 January 1835.

58. *Religious Intelligencer*, 10 September, 15 October 1836.

59. *Liberator*, 20 April 1834.

60. See *Journal of Freedom*, 17 May 1834; Bacon to Gerrit Smith, 20 March 1834, Ralph R. Gurley to Bacon, 13 June 1834, Elliott Cresson to Bacon, 20 December 1834, Robert Finley to Bacon, 20 February 1834, Bacon Family Papers; *Colonizationist and Journal of Freedom*, April 1834.

61. *Exposition of the Objects and Plans of the American Union for the Relief and Improvement of the Colored Race*, 3–5, 7, 11, 13, 14, passim; see also Stirn, "Urgent Gradualism," 317, 327.

62. See Bacon, *Slavery Discussed*, viii; "Valedictory Remarks," *Quarterly Christian Spectator*, 10, 3rd series (December 1838): 682; Arthur Granger to Bacon, 1 December 1837, Bacon Family Papers; *Congregationalist*, 8 May 1863; Bacon to Samuel Wilkerson, 28 June 1839, American Colonization Society Papers; *Annual Report of the Connecticut State Colonization Society* (Hartford, 1844), 2.

63. For Bacon's influence on the slavery issue during these years, see *Independent*, 3 January 1861; William Bradford to Bacon, 30 June 1848, Bacon Family Papers; *Leonard Bacon: Pastor of the First Church in New Haven* (New Haven, 1882), 95–96.

64. *Independent*, 21 October 1852.

65. For Bacon's views on "good slaveholders," see, for example, New York *Evangelist*, 23 October 1845, 5 February, 19 March 1846; Bacon to Amos A. Phelps, 29 August 1845, Amos A. Phelps Papers; Bacon, "Thornwell on Slavery," *New Englander* 12 (February 1854): 110–11, 121; *Independent*, 12 April 1849, 23 June 1853, 13 September 1860; *Proceedings of the General Convention of Congregational Ministers and Delegates in the United States, Held at Albany, New York, on the 5th, 6th, 7th and 8th of October 1852, Together with the Sermon Preached on the Occasion, by Rev. Joel Hawes, D.D.* (New York, 1852), 69–70, 77–90. For similar views, see C. C. Goen, *Broken Churches, Broken Nation: Denominational Schisms and the Coming of the American Civil War* (Macon, 1985), 158–62; Clifford E. Clark, Jr., *Henry Ward Beecher: Spokesman for a Middle-Class America* (Urbana, 1978), 97–98.

66. See *Independent*, 5 August 1852, 24 August 1854, 8, 22 February 1855, 8, 15 May 1856, 13 May 1858, 5, 19, 26 May 1859; McKivigan, *The War against Proslavery Religion*, 119–23; Theodore Dwight Bacon, *Leonard Bacon: A Statesman in the Church*, Benjamin W. Bacon, ed. (New Haven, 1931), 406–49.

67. See, for example, New York *Evangelist*, 23 October 1845; Bacon, "The Pulpit and the Crisis," *New Englander* 19 (January 1861): 142–44; *Independent*, 1 January 1852, 29 September 1853, 23 March 1854, 5 April 1855, 11 September 1856, 8 March 1860; Chester F. Dunham, *The Attitude of the Northern Clergy toward the South, 1860–1865* (Toledo, 1942), 3–6, 10–11, 27–44.

68. See New York *Evangelist*, 4 March, 23 September, 21 October 1847; Bacon, "The War with Mexico," *New Englander* 5 (October 1847): 604–13; "Peace — And What Next?" *New Englander* 6 (April 1848): 29–99; *Independent*, 7 December 1848, 12, 26 June, 23 October, 13 November 1856, 15 March, 12 July, 30 August 1860; McKivigan, *The War against Proslavery Religion*, 150–53.

69. For Bacon's views on the Fugitive Slave Act, see *Independent*, 24 May 1849, 14 February 1850, 26 February, 1, 15 April 1852; Bacon, "Conscience and the Constitution," *New Englander* 8 (August 1850): 472–75; "The Question! Are You Ready for the Question?" *New Englander* 8 (May 1850): 300–308.

70. See sermon of March 1854, 5, Henry Ward Beecher to Bacon, 18 February 1854, Bacon Family Papers; Bacon, "Buchanan on Kansas," *New Englander* 15 (November 1857): 682–89; *Independent*, 16 February 1854.

71. See 1857 sermon, 23–24, Bacon Family Papers; *Independent*, 12, 19, 26 March, 9 April, 7 May 1857.

8

A True Woman's Duty "To Do Good": Sarah Josepha Hale and Benevolence in Antebellum America

Angela Howard Zophy

The briefest sketch of the life and career of Sarah Josepha Buell Hale (1788–1879) illustrates the truth of the twentieth-century feminist axiom "the personal is political," while the story of Hale's career shows the impact of the personal upon the professional as well. Because Hale used every advantage as a daughter, sister, and wife to increase her education, she was prepared to secure access to adequate education and employment for future generations of women who had to support themselves and their dependents. In both her specific efforts to increase women's educational and employment opportunities and in her participation in antebellum benevolence generally, personal experience informed Hale's definition of appropriately "womanly" responses to social and civic issues. Neither radical reformer nor feminist, Hale nonetheless employed her influence over a general readership of mainstream women and men to expand the public's definition of woman's sphere and woman's work. She, thus, validated her own public and professional career at the same time that she realized her editorial intent to create a publication "expressly designed to mark the progress of female improvement."[1]

The 1830s witnessed a transition in women's involvement in charitable organizations in northeastern urban centers. In the "manly" world of Jacksonian America, women developed a sense of their own proper sphere within the larger context of American national identity and civic duty. Although a woman's sphere seemingly circumscribed women's roles and duties to the domestic realm, it also could compel women to public action, for example, on the behalf of women and children among the "deserving poor." According to Anne M. Boylan, at the turn of the nineteenth century, benevolent groups typically had pursued a limited and restrictive agenda, but the organizations of the 1830s were more inclusive in their selection of needy women recipients and more practical in their programs, though still clearly conservative in their concern, approach, and membership. Later groups, by contrast, supported more sweeping feminist programs that targeted patriarchy itself as the basis of women's social, economic, and political distress.[2] Hale's leadership and participation in Boston women's organizations during the 1830s and 1840s exemplified those of the conservative women of the transitional period and reflected the events in her life before she moved to the city in 1828.

Hale's public presence was the product of her middle-class New England origins. Her father, Captain Gordon Buell, a wounded veteran of the American Revolution who failed to prosper at farming and tavern-keeping in New Hampshire, encouraged his daughters as well as his sons to read and learn in their home. His marriage to a capable and literate Connecticut woman in her early thirties had proved a shrewd selection of a "help-meet." The embodiment of the post-Revolutionary concept of "Republican Motherhood," Martha Whittlesey Buell reared two patriotic sons and two dutiful daughters, all of whom she bore between 1784 and 1792.[3] Young Sarah was educated at home by her mother and in the local common school. She was inspired by reading Anne Radcliffe's *The Mysteries of Udolpho* (1794), her first exposure to a woman author. She kept pace with her slightly older brother, Horatio, until he was sent to Dartmouth, which, like all such institutions of the era, did not admit women. Before he graduated in 1809, Horatio Gates Buell attempted to share his advanced education with his sister, tutoring her whenever he returned home. In this way, Sarah garnered the contemporary equivalent of an undergraduate education and, at the age of 18, began teaching younger girls in a well-regarded private school. She, thus, was able to support herself and assist her ailing father in Newport after the deaths of her mother and sister in 1811.[4]

Two years later, the 25-year-old Sarah married an aspiring lawyer, David Hale. She might have assumed that her years of financial struggle to support herself and her family were past. Her pursuit of education continued, however, as the newly wedded Hales initiated a rigorous course of self-improvement through study of the liberal arts. Sarah's husband took her brother's role of tutor and mentor in their evening study sessions, which continued even as she bore four children in seven years.[5] Her health almost failed during her third pregnancy, but she recovered and delivered her first daughter, Frances Ann, in 1819.[6] Then, when David Hale suddenly died four days before the birth of their third son, George Emerson, in 1822, 34-year-old Sarah Josepha Hale found herself the sole supporter of five children under the age of seven.[7] Her brief but idyllic marriage followed by the challenges she faced as a widow shaped her opinions on womanhood and on the need of middle-class women for educational and employment opportunities.

From bitter experience she described the plight of "the fatherless and widow, who, when left without support, are the most forlorn and destitute of any class of people in the world, especially those, who, from their place in society, have no affluent friends to whom they can look for assistance."[8]

Hale herself, however, was a widow with both an education and literary ambition, and she was determined to rear her children in a manner worthy of the memory of her beloved husband. A quarter of a century after she began her long editorial career, Hale stated with formal third-person detachment "that she engaged in the literary profession" solely in "the hope of gaining the means of their support and education."[9] Hale would not have chosen a public career over her continued home life with David, but she pursued a public life of accomplishment to fulfill her private duty as a mother and to realize the potential that her husband David had nurtured in her. Her practice of dressing in black, an expression of her own mourning that she continued for the rest of her life, engendered professional benefits, reminding potential critics that she had to support her children and reinforcing her noble and dignified presence. Without any apparent artifice, Hale, thus, was able to link symbolically an unimpeachable personal choice and an unconventional public career.[10]

Hale's first attempts to support her family through the typical early nineteenth-century women's occupations of milliner and teacher contrasted sharply with the success of her publications. As a tribute to David, who had been a member, the Free Masons of Newport published Sarah's *The Genius of Oblivion; and Other Original Poems* in 1823. Four years later, *Northwood: A Tale of New England* (1827), her first novel, received sufficient acclaim to precipitate an invitation from the Reverend John Blake to become editor of his Boston *Ladies' Magazine*. The 50-year editorial career that began when Hale accepted Blake's offer placed her professionally and geographically at the center of the young nation's literary and cultural life. In the antebellum era, few U.S. cities could equal the cultural and reform ferment within Boston, to which Hale moved from Newport in 1828. Reflecting the impact on middle-class women of the city's climate of reform, she campaigned editorially for abolition and temperance, as well as for women's education, employment, and benevolence. In 1837 Hale agreed to Louis A. Godey's invitation to merge her magazine with *Godey's Lady's Book*, and five years later, she moved to Philadelphia, the city of its publication and another major center of antebellum reform.[11]

Before the Civil War, the middle-class urban home became, in theory at least, a refuge and sanctuary for men whose appointed activities comprised the public sphere, while women became the guardians of the home and family as well as the educators of the race within the domestic sphere. After 1820, as industrialization removed the manufacture of clothing and food from the home, middle-class women began to shift their economic role from the production of household commodities to the management of the family's consumption of mass-produced goods. At the same time, they began to transform motherhood into a profession, home care into the science of domestic economy, and the preindustrial practice of individual charity into the group activities that became known as benevolence. As an author and as the editor of the most prominent women's magazine of the mid-nineteenth century, Sarah Josepha Hale played a major role in both the promotion and the ratification of these significant changes in the conception of the role of women.[12]

A dutiful daughter, loving wife, loyal widow, dedicated mother, and displaced homemaker, Hale became a mentor to her ordinary but aspiring women readers. Because her life extended from the early Federalist era to the end of Reconstruction, she confronted the full range of changes experienced by other nineteenth-century women in the northeastern states. Hale was, therefore, the ideal publicist for the response to those changes that has become known as the antebellum "Cult of True Womanhood," and she was a leader among the "scribbling women" who catered to the women's audience within the antebellum popular literature.[13] As the editor of her own *Ladies' Magazine* from 1828 to 1836 and then when she controlled the contents of *Godey's Lady's Book* for four decades from 1837 to 1877, Hale exerted her influence on the public perception of the role of American women. Yet, despite this momentous change through which she was guiding herself and her readers, Hale must be characterized as a mainstream-to-conservative propagandist. Because she had, after all, during her formative years, been influenced by her mother's practice of the concept of Republican Motherhood, Hale often portrayed benevolence as merely womanly nurturing and caretaking on an urban and national scale.[14]

As a result, Hale's public crusades usually were rooted in her personal or family experience. Her determination to see the Bunker Hill Monument completed, for example, reflected not only her patriotism but also her family pride in her father's service during the Revolution. Similarly, her participation in founding the Boston Seaman's Aid Society stemmed from Hale's loss of her brother Charles, a seaman, and from her own identification with other nearly destitute widows. Finally, the editor's campaign to establish Thanksgiving as an annual national holiday expressed both Hale's Yankee pride in New England tradition and her conviction that the celebration would place womanly domestic values on a par with the manly political ones that pervaded the Fourth of July.

Hale's half-century as an editor spanned the period when advances in printing allowed for increased production of books, periodicals, and newspapers that promoted commercialized mass culture to the expanding ranks of literate Americans, including women. As literature became big business in the nineteenth-century United States, it offered middle-class women the possibility of employment as well as education and entertainment, so that Hale was among a growing number of women to succeed in a literary career. Paradoxically, however, constricting roles drove most of the middle-class readers to whom Hale and other literary career women catered into private life and servitude to the family. Hale accepted and even emphasized the obligation of women to serve their families as the very essence of women's sphere, but she expanded her own definition of this core role to allow women to enter into public life either to support their families when necessary or to work without pay for worthy and respectable reform.[15]

Hale was skilled in merging the ideas of others with the concepts of conventional wisdom to craft practical measures for the improvement of women and, through them, the nation. Although the notion of woman's sphere seemed to restrict women to home and the family circle, Hale converted a potential prison into a fortress that protected women's esteem and allowed them to sally forth with respectability to impose "domestic" values on certain situations in the public sphere.

Hale consistently employed a two-fold strategy. First, she demonstrated absolutely no radical intent to alter the gender system, carefully portraying women's "new" activities as traditional and properly complementary of men's role. Describing her first year of editorship in the customary third person, Hale explained:

Whether there is, between the sexes, a perfect equality of intellect, is, in the editor's opinion, a question of small importance, while it must be so obvious to every person of reflection, that the duties of men and women are different. One motive that influenced her to endeavor to add somewhat to the knowledge of her sex, was to make females better acquainted with their duties and privileges as women.[16]

In her nine years as editor of the *Ladies' Magazine*, Hale formulated a doctrine of "Woman's Influence" that empowered women to rule men and children by pious example and moral suasion in *both* the private and the public sphere.[17] Later, at *Godey's*, Hale continued to transform woman's exile from the real world into an opportunity for a "domestic" hegemony over all social and spiritual values.[18]

The second part of Hale's strategy was to support the primacy of maternal influence upon the education of children, which naturally included teaching children in school as well as in the home. Hale's concept of woman's influence then extended woman's maternal role as educator to empower women to guide adult men in the public sphere:

The influence of woman on public sentiment . . . to be truly salutary, must be exerted with a womanly delicacy and in an unobtrusive manner. . . . Women certainly, have, in our country, a great influence over public opinion but — *sub rosa* — let us be cautious of making too much display about it.[19]

Although the always circumspect Hale believed that the boundaries of woman's sphere were finite, by elevating the esteem for woman's traditional domestic role and woman's nonmonetary contributions to the community, she did, indeed, challenge both the decline of women's economic status within the family and the rise of a masculine culture that increasingly venerated the ability to acquire material wealth.[20]

In addition to her editorials and the fiction, poetry, and feature articles she selected for her magazine, Hale provided her readers with the example of her own civic participation. She was active in local women's benevolent organizations that aided the deserving poor, promoted women's education, and offered community service. She had arrived in Boston to edit the *Ladies' Magazine* five years after a Monument Association was incorporated to establish a memorial to the Battle of Bunker Hill. By then, the unfinished monument was an eyesore and a disgrace to Boston and the nation, as well as to the tidy domestic values of American womanhood. Hale was incited to womanly outrage and action to complete the project. Hale's efforts took over ten years, however, and drew upon tactics she honed and networks of associates she developed through her participation in the Seaman's Aid Society and other benevolent groups.[21]

Early in her tenure at the *Ladies' Magazine*, Hale envisioned a program to assist working-class women, but she did not begin an editorial campaign for the Boston Seaman's Aid Society until 1833. Building on a proposal that emerged during a social meeting of the editor's friends, Hale developed a program to assist the wives and children of seamen in cooperation with the Boston Port Society. She then served as president of the Seaman's Aid Society's board and wrote its annual reports through 1840.[22] Her first fund-raising attempt for the society was a craft fair that added over $900 to the treasury. Hale's influence also was evident in the conservative but practical nature of the society's goals. To bring adequate employment to the mothers who could not seek paid employment outside the home but were either the permanent or the temporary heads of their families, instead of supplying donated food and clothing, the society used $300 from its treasury to establish a clothing shop to employ deserving women as seamstresses. The shop, which paid the women a fair wage to work in their homes and set reasonable rates for the clothes, by 1834 employed 50 women and had earned $2000. At the same time, its competitive prices deliberately threatened the trade of shops that exploited the seamstresses and their dependent children.[23]

Encouraged by the success of its clothing shop, the society branched out to found sabbath and infant schools, a vocational school to teach the daughters of seamen to support themselves as seamstresses, and a library for the seamen and their families. In addition, its nonprofit boardinghouse for transient seamen threatened the business of the less respectable and less fastidious waterfront boardinghouses.[24]

By 1841, when Hale had settled in Philadelphia, she had successfully reared and educated all her children. In the new city, increased responsibilities as editor of the merged publication and her advancing age diminished her opportunity to enjoy the kind of active social life she had in Boston. She keenly grieved the loss of her brother Horatio in 1833 and of her eldest son, David Emerson, in 1839 but found satisfaction in the accomplishments of her surviving offspring. Until her elder daughter, Frances Ann, married Philadelphia doctor Lewis Hunter in 1844, Hale and Frances Ann "boarded out." She then moved in with her younger, unmarried daughter, Sarah Josepha, who had returned from teaching in the South to establish a day school in Philadelphia in 1856. After Sarah Josepha died at the age of 43 in 1863, the 75-year-old Hale joined Frances Ann's household.[25]

Both daughters were examples of Hale's vision of the True Woman: the younger, unmarried one devoted herself to her career as a teacher; the older became a respectable society matron and mother of six. Hale's three sons similarly might have been deemed True Men: a West Point graduate and army officer, an explorer and author, and a lawyer who emigrated in 1846 to newly annexed Texas.[26]

Separated from her Boston-based network of friends and associates in benevolence, Hale entered another phase of her career. In Philadelphia, she became a practitioner of "woman's influence" and a formidable lobbyist for national reforms rather than an active participant in "doing good" in her new local community. Hale now edited a major national magazine that was solvent and managed by a seasoned publisher, instead of a regional publication supported only by the limited resources of its editor and the proceeds from subscriptions. From the pages of *Godey's*, Hale passed the torch of activism and participation to her expanded readership:

Woman must do the work, or must begin it, at least. She must cherish a strong hope of the elevation of her sex, and a deep feeling of commisseration [*sic*] for the poor and oppressed. She must devote her thoughts to the means of improvement.... When the moral powers, which women possess in a greater and purer degree, naturally, than men, shall be enlightened by intellectual knowledge, and she shall understand how to use her influence rightly on the domestic and social circle, then the moral powers of men will be incited to an improvement and perfection which has never yet been reached.[27]

During the 1850s and 1860s, Sarah Josepha Hale's womanly discretion combined with Louis Godey's obsession with avoiding any references that might offend his subscribers in the South to produce issue after issue of *Godey's* that focused on the ideals and practices of domesticity and utterly excluded even the slightest acknowledgment of political or social turmoil. Hale confined her editorial remarks to her now-standard causes of women's education, employment, health, and apolitical benevolence. Because the reissue of *Northwood* in 1852 appeared to be a response to the publication that same year of *Uncle Tom's Cabin*, Louis Godey specifically disavowed any such intent. Despite this denial, Hale not only had augmented her original text to reflect the advances in women's education since 1827, but she also had added a suggestion that Thanksgiving Day donations from all religious congregations in the nation should be used to fund the colonization of Liberia by freed American slaves. The next year, Hale edited *Liberia; or, Mr. Peyton's Experiment*, a promotional tract apparently inspired by her colonization proposal in the 1852 version of *Northwood*.[28]

Throughout her tenure as *Godey's* editor, Hale consolidated her reputation as an unimpeachable authority on woman's sphere and on the duties of middle-class, mid-Victorian American womanhood. In 1853 she published *Woman's Record; or, Sketches of All Distinguished Women*, a prodigious biographical collection that spanned all of Western history. Even after 1860, Hale still continued to be a publicist for the conservative mainstream of reformist women's activism, eschewing comment on any aspect of either the abolitionist movement or the woman's movement. Nevertheless, Hale remained constant in her support of women's education and employment issues and effective (if highly selective) in her advocacy of their national benevolent efforts.[29]

Although properly apolitical, Hale was closest to the Whigs in her personal beliefs. She shared the commitment to preserve the Union of Daniel Webster, Henry Clay, and John C. Calhoun. As the editor of *Godey's*, she endorsed general policies at the federal level, rather than specific local reforms. Her major editorial campaigns of the late 1850s and 1860s were the effort of the Mount Vernon Ladies' Memorial Association of the Union (founded in 1853) to purchase Mount Vernon as a national shrine for George Washington and her own one-woman campaign to secure the presidential proclamation of an annual Thanksgiving Day.[30]

During the 1850s, Hale joined with Ann Pamela Cunningham, a South Carolinian and leader of the Mount Vernon Memorial Association of the Union, to organize northern and southern women to purchase the George Washington property after Congress failed to exercise its option to secure the site for the nation in 1853. Hale enthusiastically informed her national readership that the Ladies' Memorial Association, incorporated by the Virginia Legislature in 1856, had appointed *Godey's* one of two "national organs" of its Central Committee of the Union. The editor seemed gratified to have an occasion to endorse a national project for women that transcended the contentious sectionalism of the era. Here was a straightforward task for American women, one for which "no permanent obstacle" existed. To secure funds for purchase of the Washingto estate, *Godey's* printed monthly listings of contributors and urged readers to honor their country by preserving the patriotic site. Hale triumphantly announced the completed purchase in 1860, and even civil war did not diminish the significance of the women's intersectional cooperation to preserve a national site as a means to build a common American identity.[31]

Hale's leadership in the campaign to establish a national Thanksgiving holiday predated the sectional crisis of the 1850s and, indeed, any of her endorsements of women's benevolent activities. Its roots can even be seen in *Northwood* (1827), which described in detail the ideal New England harvest celebration. Hale began her crusade in earnest when she became the editor of the *Ladies' Magazine* in 1828, and by the mid-1840s, she was using *Godey's* as a national forum for the cause. Each October or November issue included fiction and poetry extolling the patriotism and domesticity of the seasonal New England gatherings as "part of the noble patrimony of our Puritan Fathers." Pleased to record the adoption of the custom in southern and western states throughout the 1850s, Hale offered a variety of tempting recipes for the dishes traditionally served at these feasts.[32] Although her aim no doubt was to familiarize distant readers with the preparation of New England cuisine, she also managed to create the only U.S. holiday with a standardized menu and to demonstrate vividly the growing power of mass media to influence mass consumption.

More directly, between 1846 and 1863, Hale exercised her right to petition the governors of both states and territories as well as the successive presidents to have the last Thursday in November declared Thanksgiving Day. Periodically, she reported the number of states won to the cause, but in 1860 Hale challenged her "brother Editors" to divine and implement the proper political procedure to secure the permanent establishment of the annual national holiday. In doing so, she revealed her opinion about the role of women and Thanksgiving in what was, by then, the crisis of the Union.

God had given to man authority, to woman influence; she inspires and persuades, he convinces and compels. For the last twelve years, the editress [*sic*] of the Lady's Book had been endeavoring to bring about this agreement in popular feeling. We have used our influence always, we trust, in a womanly way, and now we would render deep gratitude to God who has blessed our humble prayers and efforts, and express thus publicly our thanks to those generous men who have encouraged and accomplished our plan. We now leave the perpetuation of this good work, by the enactment of a statute in each state, to good and patriotic men everywhere to be found, who love the Constitution and the Union. . . . This American festival adds the third strand to the cord that binds American hearts in nationality. *The twenty-second of February, the Fourth of July, the last Thursday in November* — these three days observed, will keep us American citizens.[33]

Hale never had the chance to test the thesis; the southern states seceded before the national holiday was declared. Only after meeting with President Abraham Lincoln in 1863 was the editor able to prepare *Godey's* readers for a presidential proclamation that, in October of that year, invited all Americans to "set aside and observe the last Thursday of November next as a day of Thanksgiving." By convincing both Andrew Johnson and Ulysses S. Grant to follow Lincoln's precedent, Hale finally secured as customary an annual executive order for the nationwide celebration of Thanksgiving on the same Thursday each November.[34]

The successful campaigns for the preservation of Mount Vernon and the annual presidential proclamation of Thanksgiving Day constituted what might be termed Hale's swan song as an effective propagandist for good works by women on a national scale. By the end of 1865, Hale was 78 years old, and her editorial vigor waned along with her physical stamina and the prestige and popularity of *Godey's*. Before the war, southerners always had been a significant portion of *Godey's* most loyal readership, and many now could not afford to subscribe. The magazine's contents followed the prewar pattern, but its cast of popular and well-loved authors had died or retired by 1870. While Hale and Godey failed to recruit comparable writers to replace them, newer women's magazines gradually drew postwar readers. Hale's response to the rapid changes occurring in American society generally and women's lives specifically no longer seemed direct or effective.[35]

Hale utilized each December issue for an annual and cumulative assessment of the progress of *Godey's* and American womanhood. In 1871 the octogenarian Hale dismissed her extraordinary longevity as merely a benefit of True Womanhood. She believed the hospitable habitat of woman's sphere extended women's life spans as nature's compensation for their eternal care for others: "Men often die for their country; women can *live* for theirs." The editor expressed her gratitude "that I yet retain my desire and my ability to work" and reaffirmed her commitment to women's progress. "For my own part, I hope to spend the remnant of my long life in doing all I can with my pen, in work which I hope will benefit my countrywomen," Hale wrote. She proposed that her readers undertake a new benevolent effort to set up residential institutions for young girls "destitute of that best of educations which comes from the home." "In Germany they burn candles on the birthday of a friend, one for each year of her life. Will not my young friends light up mine with a bright deed, whose radiance will illumine their own hearts, should they count even more summers than mine?"[36] Nearing her ninetieth birthday, Hale informed her readers of her retirement in the December 1877 issue. She devoted her final monthly column to a retrospective of her career, in which she indulged her "strong desire to give to my faithful readers some short account of my efforts for the elevation of my countrywomen during the last half-century." In this synopsis, Hale connected the personal and the professional. Tracing "with gratitude" her development as a literary figure, she recalled her reluctance to accept the "not only unsolicited, but entirely unexpected" invitation in 1827 to "take charge of the Ladies' Magazine" following the success of *Northwood*. "A magazine edited by a woman for women had never been conducted, so far as I know." The editor reiterated her reluctance to engage this "sudden change" in her secluded life as a recent widow who was endeavoring "by my own pen to support my young family of five children, and educate them as their father would have done." Reaffirming her abiding allegiance to woman's domestic sphere, Hale emphasized the sacrifices that her circumstances compelled her to confront when she entered the public sphere.

I must give up this precious home [once shared with David], separate from all my children save one, and go out into the world which I so much dreaded. Yet my faith in God was so strong, that this change seemed to me to be the ordering of Divine Providence, and I accepted these new duties and responsibilities as appointed by His Will.[37]

Hale then listed her accomplishments by priority and chronological sequence. She first cited her efforts on behalf of the education of women and women's entry into the teaching profession. She next submitted her contribution to securing the completion of the Bunker Hill Monument and the development of "an American national thanksgiving." Equally important as her publication of *Woman's Record*, she deemed her successful campaign to substitute "The True Title of Woman" for the use of "female," especially in the titles of women's institutions of higher education, such as Vassar College. She concluded her summary *vita* with her service as the president from its founding in 1860 until 1869 of the Woman's Union Missionary Society to Heathen Lands, a group whose name, as that of the Mount Vernon Ladies' Memorial Association of the Union, represented Hale's attempt to overcome, within woman's proper sphere, the divisiveness that raged in the public sphere during and after the Civil War. The editor combined discussion of her role in the medical missionary movement with her equally productive endorsement from the 1850s onward of women's medical colleges and of pediatrics, obstetrics, and nursing as rightful woman's work.[38]

As Sarah Josepha Hale's own retrospective revealed, her participation in women's benevolence activities during her 50-year literary career charted a moderate course of reform that tried to avoid even the appearance of threatening the gender system of nineteenth-century U.S. society. For the most part, she pursued a pragmatic agenda to educate and train women for paid employments that she considered within woman's sphere and advocated a program of reform that allowed women to contribute to the improvement of their society.

Hale was a woman whose life experience paralleled the lives of her readers and of women in the next century. The activism and advocacy of her career highlight the obstacles and the opportunities that confronted middle-class women in the nineteenth century. For her own and succeeding generations, Hale served as a role model for women who entered professions yet remained anchored in their domestic identification; she set the standard of presenting a facade of nonthreatening accomplishment in the public realm while privately and uncomplainingly struggling to balance the demands of womanly duties with the requirements of a career. Beginning her career in her late thirties, she lacked the time or the incentive to contemplate organizing or executing a full-scale revolution. Hale preferred to pursue immediate and achievable goals to improve women's situation, rather than to challenge the established social order. Her involvement in "doing good" was informed and inspired by her personal experience; the closer an issue was to that experience, the more direct was her participation. This pattern was typical for the women whom Hale represented as well as influenced. Hale contributed to the rise of ordinary women who shared the limitations of comfortable, middle-class status and were unlikely to challenge the gender system.

However, Hale did undermine the arbitrary inequality of the sexes by fortifying women's esteem and crafting an ever-expanding women's sphere. She never anticipated that the spiritual superiority of women that she endorsed to justify their hegemony in the domestic sphere would prove no longer susceptible to circumscription as women applied their tidy values and domestic duty to the chaotic political, economic, and social conditions of the public sphere. Nevertheless, it did, as thousands upon thousands of American women followed the example of Hale herself and made the personal, political.

NOTES

1. "Introduction," *Ladies' Magazine* 1 (January 1828): 3.

2. See Anne M. Boylan, "Women in Groups: An Analysis of Women's Benevolent Organizing in New York and Boston, 1797–1840," *Journal of American History* 71 (1984): 497–523; Anne M. Boylan, "Timid Girls, Venerable Widows and Dignified Matrons: Life Cycle Patterns among Organized Women in New York and Boston, 1797–1840," *American Quarterly* 39 (1986): 779–97.

3. The concept of "Republican Motherhood" resulted from the national imperative to patriotism that followed the American Revolution; American women were to display their patriotism by rearing patriotic sons and dutiful daughters. Patriotic American men supported increased women's education to assure that American mothers were adequately informed to rear and teach the proper (gender-specific) requirements to the next generation of the new nation's citizenry. Mary Beth Norton, *Liberty's Daughters: The Revolutionary Experience of American Women, 1750–1800* (New York, 1980), 242–44.

4. Hale compiled two works that included introductory remarks with autobiographical information: *The Ladies' Wreath; A Selection from the Female Poetic Writers of England and America* (Boston, 1837), and *Woman's Record; or, Sketches of all Distinguished Women* (New York, 1853). More complete biographical information is offered in Isabelle Webb Entrikin, *Sarah Josepha Hale and Godey's*

Lady's Book (Philadelphia, 1946); and Ruth E. Finley, *The Lady of Godey's* (Philadelphia, 1931).

5. Hale, *Ladies' Wreath*, 385.

6. Finley, *The Lady*, 31–33.

7. Entrikin, *Sarah Josepha Hale*, 8.

8. "Fatherless and Widows' Society," *Ladies' Magazine* 1 (January 1828): 48.

9. Hale, *Woman's Record*, 686. See also "Editors' Table," *Godey's* 95 (December 1877): 522.

10. Entrikin, *Sarah Josepha Hale*, 16.

11. Ibid., 10–14; Angela Howard Zophy, "'For the Improvement of My Sex': Sarah Josepha Hale's Editorship of *Godey's Lady's Book*, 1837–1877" (Ph.D. diss., Ohio State University, 1978), 24. For a summary of Hale's support of advances in women's education and employment opportunities during her editorial career in Boston and Philadelphia, see also Angela Howard Zophy, "Sarah Josepha Hale, Matron of Victorian Womanhood," in Frank Annunziata, Patrick Reagan, and Roy Wortman, eds., *For the General Welfare: Essays in Honor of Robert H. Bremner* (New York, 1989), 61–89.

Hale held the position of editor of the *Ladies' Magazine* from 1828 to 1836; she became part owner of the periodical and changed its title in 1834 to the *American Ladies' Magazine* to distinguish her publication from such magazines in other nations. There was no mention in the 1834 volume of the *Ladies' Magazine* of the details of Blake's departure from the partnership. When she merged her magazine with that of Louis A. Godey in 1837, the full title of the new publication became *Godey's Lady's Book and American Ladies' Magazine*. The title *Ladies' Magazine* will be used in this article to refer to Hale's earlier publication; *Godey's Lady's Book*, or simply *Godey's*, will be used to refer to their joint effort after 1837. Hale and Godey, as editor and publisher, respectively, constituted a harmonious and productive team until Godey retired four months before Hale, in 1877.

12. Early examples of these endorsements by Hale are *Ladies' Magazine* 1 (January 1828): 48; (February 1828): 96; (October 1828): 478; 2 (January 1829): 40 [benevolence]; 3 (February 1830): 88–89 [Bunker Hill Monument]; 4 (November 1831): 519–522 [Thanksgiving]; 5 (March 1832): 136; (April 1832): 182 [infant schools].

Hale's life and career have been cited as examples of trends in antebellum women's experience in Glenda Riley, *Inventing the American Woman: A Perspective on Women's History* (Arlington Heights, 1987), 88–148; and Nancy Woloch, *Women and the American Experience* (New York, 1984), 97–147, 170–71.

Godey's circulation rose from 10,000 in 1837 to a peak of 150,000 in 1860. Louis Godey claimed 500,000 subscribers in 1869, but only 50,000 subscribers were estimated in 1885. See Zophy, "Editorship," 49–50.

13. Barbara Welter, "The Cult of True Womanhood," *American Quarterly* 18 (1966): 151–74; Ann Douglas Wood, "The 'Scribbling Women' and Fanny Fern: Why Women Wrote," *American Quarterly* 23 (1971): 3–24.

14. Norton, *Liberty's Daughters*, 242–44. Early examples of Hale's pronouncements on motherhood are "Letters from a Mother," *Ladies' Magazine* 1 (April 1828): 166–69; 1 (May 1828): 211–23; 1 (June 1828): 324–26. As the editor of *Godey's*, Hale became a proponent of the concept of "Woman as the Mother of the Race," from which she and other advocates of woman derived the concept of "Woman as the Teacher of the Race." Hale and her peers fell into the category of activists who were advocates for woman without challenging the patriarchal gender system. Nancy Cott, "What's in a Name? The Limits of 'Social Feminism': or, Expanding the Vocabulary of Women's History," *Journal of American History* 76 (1989): 820, 827; Temma Kaplan,

"Female Consciousness and Collective Action: The Case of Barcelona, 1910–1918," *Signs* 7 (1982): 545–66.

15. Frank Luther Mott, *A History of American Magazines* (2 vol., New York, 1930), vol. 1; Helen Woodward, *The Lady Persuaders* (New York, 1960), chap. 2; James P. Wood, *Magazines in the United States* (3rd ed., New York, 1971); Lawrence Martin, "The Genius of Godey's 'Lady's Book,'" *New England Quarterly* 1 (1928): 41–70; Zophy, "Editorship," 15, 25; Zophy, "Sarah Josepha Hale, Matron of Victorian Womanhood," 63–65, 79–81.

16. "The Beginning," *Ladies' Magazine* 2 (January 1829): 3.

17. *Ladies' Magazine* 2 (March 1829): 137; Finley, *The Lady*, 70.

18. "An Appeal to the Ladies of the United States," *Ladies' Magazine* 2 (November 1829): 516; see also "The Influence of Woman on Society," *Ladies' Magazine* 4 (June 1831): 256–69; Zophy, "Editorship," 28–30; Ann Douglas, *The Feminization of American Culture* (New York, 1977), 353.

19. "An Appeal to the Ladies of the United States," *Ladies' Magazine* 2 (November 1829): 516.

20. See Glenda Riley, "The Cult of True Womanhood: Industrial and Westward Expansion, 1816–1837," in *Inventing the American Woman*, 63–87.

21. "Editors' Table," *Godey's* 95 (December 1877): 522; Entrikin, *Sarah Josepha Hale*, 71.

22. [Boston Seaman's Aid Society], *Annual Reports* (Boston, 1833–40); Boylan, "Women in Groups," 505–6.

23. Sarah Josepha Hale to Mathew Carey, 26 November 1833, Mathew Carey Papers (Historical Society of Pennsylvania); Finley, *The Lady*, 75–79; Nancy A. Hewitt, "Beyond the Search for Sisterhood: American Women's History in the 1980s," *Social History* 10 (1985): 311; Boylan, "Women in Groups," 497, 504; Entrikin, *Sarah Josepha Hale*, 39–40.

24. Entrikin, *Sarah Josepha Hale*, 40–41; Finley, *The Lady*, 76–79. For context and comparison of the Boston Seaman's Aid Society activities, see Boylan, "Women in Groups."

25. Finley, *The Lady*, 88–92.

26. "In Memoriam [*sic*]," [Hale's obituary for her daughter, Sarah Josepha], *Godey's* 67 (August 1863): 148–49; Entrikin, *Sarah Josepha Hale*, 41, 69, 120, 123.

27. "The Ladies' Mentor," *Godey's* 15 (August 1837): 93. Hale's acclimation to Philadelphia included abandoning her New England Congregationalist affiliation to join Holy Trinity, the Episcopal parish of Louis A. Godey; many of her new associates as well as a significant portion of *Godey's* readers in the South were Episcopalian. See Entrikin, *Sarah Josepha Hale*, 73.

28. Harriet Beecher Stowe, *Uncle Tom's Cabin; or, Life Among the Lowly* (Boston, 1852); Sarah Josepha Hale, ed., *Liberia: or, Mr. Peyton's Experiment* (New York, 1853); *Godey's* 65 (December 1852): 579; 37 (September 1848): 179; Entrikin, *Sarah Josepha Hale*, 109–10.

Hale did endorse conservative reforms for women's legal rights that fell within the issues of the woman's movement: Editor, "Rights of Married Women," *Godey's* 14 (May 1837): 213–14; see also 32 (January 1846): 44–45; 45 (December 1852): 524–48; 52 (January 1856): 79–82; 70 (March 1865): 278; 81 (July 1870): 86; 82 (May 1871): 477.

29. Entrikin, *Sarah Josepha Hale*, 101; Zophy, "Editorship," 183, 185–86.

30. Zophy, "Editorship," 183–84; *Godey's* 51 (August 1855): 177–78; (September 1855): 277; 52 (January 1856): 468; (June 1856): 558–59; 60 (January 1860): 80–81. See also Entrikin, *Sarah Josepha Hale*, 116; Marion Tinling, *Women Remembered: A Guide to Landmarks of Women's History in the United States* (Westport, 1986), 243–44. Tinling implies that the title of the association dropped the reference to the

Union after the Civil War. The Ladies' Memorial Association retained its control of the site, despite the disruption of the war and resistance to the efforts of Cunningham's association as a woman's organization; Cunningham did not move to the site as resident director until 1867.

31. *Godey's* 51 (August 1855): 177–78; (September 1855): 277; 52 (January 1856): 83; (May 1856): 468; (June 1856): 558–59; 60 (January 1860): 80–81.

32. "A Calendar. November: *Thanksgiving Festival,*" *Ladies' Magazine* 4 (November 1831): 519–22; see also *The Juvenile Miscellany* (Boston), monthly series, Vol. 1–4, No. 3 (September 1834–March/April 1836); "Editors' Table," *Godey's* 15 (November 1837): 238–39; Alice B. Neal, "A Thanksgiving Record," *Godey's* 53 (December 1856): 508–13.

Hale proudly announced that 29 states had celebrated Thanksgiving on the last Thursday of November in 1851: "Editor' Table," *Godey's* 45 (October 1852): 338.

33. "Editors' Table," *Godey's* 60 (February 1860): 175; see also "Editors' Table," *Godey's* 45 (October 1852): 388; 53 (September 1846): 274; 60 (April 1860): 368–69; Entrikin, *Sarah Josepha Hale*, 115; Finley, *The Lady*, 197–98.

Hale became concerned with the philological implications of denigration in the use of "female" to refer to "woman"; she also developed a series of titles like "editress" and "directoress" to distinguish women's jobs from men's: "Editors' Table," *Godey's* 71 (December 1865): 537.

34. "Editors' Table," *Godey's* 67 (September 1863): 276; 95 (December 1877): 524. President Lincoln's Proclamation is reproduced in Finley, *The Lady*, 203.

For a summary and analysis of Hale's efforts on behalf of establishing this national holiday by executive authority until congressional statute set the annual date of the fourth Thursday of November as the national holiday, see "Thanksgiving," in Angela Howard Zophy, ed., *The Handbook of American Women's History* (New York, 1990), 599–600.

35. Entrikin, *Sarah Josepha Hale*, 128.

36. "Editors' Table," *Godey's* 83 (December 1871): 567. Hale's suggestion predates the development of the settlement house movement of the late nineteenth century.

37. "Editors' Table," *Godey's* 95 (December 1877): 522. See Bertha Monica Sterns, "New England Magazines for Ladies," *New England Quarterly* 3 (1930): 627–56.

Hale's publisher had announced his retirement earlier in that year: "Godey's Arm Chair," *Godey's* 95 (July 1877): 87; (August 1877): 175.

38. "Editors' Table," *Godey's* 95 (December 1877): 522–23.

III

CIVIL WARRIORS AND POSTBELLUM REFORMERS

9

A Critical Moment and Its Aftermath for George H. Thomas

John Cimprich

The Battle of Nashville marked a climactic point in the American Civil War and in the life of Major General George H. Thomas. In late 1864, Thomas, recently promoted to the command of most federal forces in the central South, had the responsibility of halting a Confederate invasion into occupied territory that threatened to reverse the rising tide of federal victory. As the Confederates dug in on the high ground south of Nashville, Tennessee, a major federal base of operations, frigid winter weather interfered with action by either side. Because the Confederates had already captured many outpost garrisons and damaged a federal force at the bloody Battle of Franklin, Thomas had difficulty gathering enough men to defend Nashville. For the first time in his career, a reluctant Thomas needed to use black troops in the front lines.[1]

Six African-American regiments contributed significantly to victory on December 15 and 16. These soldiers participated in a series of uphill, frontal charges against fortified positions. The blacks' final charge helped to smash the Confederates' last line of defense and to complete the rout. In that critical moment, an impressed Thomas underwent a permanent change in his racial attitudes and announced to his staff: "The question is settled; the negro will fight." Later he elaborated that "this proves the manhood of the negro."[2]

A typical white southerner of the nineteenth century, Thomas previously had not seen blacks as having a humanity equal to that of whites. The general had grown up within a slaveholding family in Southampton County, Virginia, where during Thomas's fifteenth year Nat Turner's slave rebellion, one of the largest ones in the United States, took place. Killings by the rebels and their quick defeat by authorities probably convinced him that armed blacks were dangerous but undisciplined and irresolute. Members of the master class had commonly believed so, and one recent study found that traditional attitudes predominated in the specific neighborhood where Thomas grew up. Unverifiable stories that as a boy Thomas taught reading to several of his family's slaves and that he once considered freeing a female slave he bought to help his wife are hints, albeit the only ones in his prewar record, of a paternalistic interest in black advancement. Once Thomas became a career army officer, serving mostly away from the plantation South, slavery played but a small role in his life.[3]

By the outbreak of the Civil War, George Thomas's personality had long been formed. An unostentatious stocky man with a full salt-and-pepper beard, he projected solidity and seriousness. A cautious yet determined leader, he would prefer to gain battlefield victories through systematic planning and strength. Integrity and decency also marked the man. Thomas did not anger easily, but long service as a professional military officer had made him a staunch supporter of law and order. That service as well as marriage to a northerner had diluted his southern identity.[4]

In 1861 Thomas's nationalism won out after some emotional turmoil, and he took the Union's side in the Civil War. Soon he rose to the rank of general. Unwavering support of the Union cause made him accept President Abraham Lincoln's emancipation policy in 1863 but without deep commitment. The army's adjutant general stopped Thomas when he tried to exclude runaway slaves from his lines and again when he revoked a post commander's order requiring masters to pay slaves who continued to work for them. Still, Thomas succeeded in diverting to owners the pay allotted to several runaway slaves who labored on federal fortifications. His traditional racial attitudes hedged his cooperation with the changes underway.[5]

Thomas also reacted with a lack of enthusiasm to the new practice of enlisting blacks in the federal army: "It is perhaps far better for the negro to become a soldier, and be gradually taught to depend on himself for support, than to be thrown upon the cold charities of the world." When a recruiter complained, "That the negro is to be made a man first by being made a soldier does not seem to be comprehended yet by Commanding Generals," General Thomas had the author held under arrest until he issued an apology and a retraction. After attending a dress parade by some of the new black regiments, Thomas questioned whether or not they could do more than put on a show. Not believing that black troops would fight, he assigned them only labor duty and threatened to dismiss any officers who complained about this. In the words of one black soldier, "when dey wents to battle I was always left in camp ter helps take care of de supplies. General Thomas calls me a coward."[6]

Everything changed with the Battle of Nashville. Nationalism and a career officer's habitual obedience to superiors had made Thomas a nominal supporter of new federal policies on race relations, but the battle forced him to rethink private attitudes that he had accepted as correct from his upbringing. Afterward, Thomas would believe in racial equality, although he thought slavery had harmed black personalities and "it will take time for the regeneration." As a former master, he hired the one slave family he had owned. As postwar commander of the Military Division of the Tennessee (Tennessee, Kentucky, Mississippi, Alabama, and Georgia), he participated in the larger process of social change. The continuation of martial law in occupied areas required military forces to play a significant role in securing emancipation and restoring peace. He potentially could have much influence on those matters because he had worked very well with Tennessee's military governor, Andrew Johnson, who became president at the war's end. As conservative southern Unionists, the two had found they had much in common.[7]

Underneath the issues of Reconstruction lay an obvious conflict between most southern whites' commitment to slavery and the blacks' drive for freedom. According to Thomas, the army could act as the neutral mediator for promoting trust between the two sides. Then, regular wages from whites and diligent work from blacks could reinforce a new relationship. Thomas asserted that military courts could evenhandedly enforce state laws — excluding the "barbarous black codes" — while curing freedmen of the dishonesty that he believed slavery had made "second nature" to them. The general entered the process with some optimism, although his own statements revealed the enormous challenge of changing white attitudes. Events had stimulated that small part of his generally cautious personality that held an interest in innovation. Thus, he had high hopes for "restoring perfect order" in Tennessee, Georgia, and Alabama but worried about hostility to emancipation in Mississippi and Kentucky.[8]

From the start, Thomas's conservative command style tended to emphasize reacting to problems. During the summer of 1865, several congressional candidates in Tennessee openly questioned the legality of their state's Unionist government and the emancipation amendment to its constitution. At Governor William G. Brownlow's request, President Johnson ordered Thomas to uphold the state government with military force. When Thomas arrested Emerson Etheridge, a prominent proslavery candidate, the others quit challenging the new state administration.[9]

On the same day as Etheridge's arrest, General Thomas intervened in a Columbia, Tennessee, court case. Two lawyers there had initiated trespassing, assault, and battery charges against two black schoolgirls. Virginia Cox, Haley Trotter, and a white friend had entered a garden to carry off some plums. Catching them, the white owner angrily threw a rock, and one of the black girls responded in kind. Neither hit anyone. At the indictment, the white girl became a witness; the two blacks were jailed in solitary confinement with bail set at $500 each. Upon learning that $500 exceeded the bail allowed under state law, local officials reduced the rock thrower's bail to $250 and released her colleague. In a widely published order, an indignant Thomas tried to shame the lawyers and officials before the public: "By the malignant rebellious spirit which they have displayed by their persecution of the weak and helpless . . . they have shown themselves to be persons dangerous to the peace of the community." He speculated that their ultimate goal was to close the local freedmen's school, which the black girls attended. To send a strong message about the principle at stake, Thomas had the two lawyers confined and two Columbia officials suspended from office until "they possess some little humanity and show a willingness to conform to the laws."[10] Columbia grew quiet for a time, but racial clashes continued elsewhere.

Other public lessons from Thomas followed. He ordered the Methodist district around LaGrange, Georgia, to reinstate the Reverend John H. Caldwell as presiding elder after it fired him for preaching critically about slavery. When the church's state conference upheld the dismissal, however, the general abandoned the effort. Throughout the summer, he strongly supported the new Freedmen's Bureau as a key means of improving relations between white employers and black employees. Through careful investigations, he cleared the agency of several allegations of bias against whites.[11] By means of such interventions, Thomas sought to uphold both federal authority and egalitarian principles. He began to realize the army's power to affect events as well as its limitations.

Reconstruction inherently involved politics, something Thomas found uncomfortable. In late 1865, the president sent him to Mississippi to lobby for cooperation with Johnson's reconstruction program. The general urged the newly elected state legislators to ratify the proposed Thirteenth Amendment, which would write nationwide emancipation into the U.S. Constitution, and to grant blacks basic civil liberties, including the right to give testimony in court. For the most part, the legislature rejected these requests.[12]

Thomas had more success in defending black troops against political attacks. President Johnson had tried to moderate his personal racial biases since endorsing emancipation, but they were inflamed by a tale that black soldiers had "taken my own house [in Greeneville, Tennessee] and converted it into . . . a negro brothel." In several furious messages to Thomas, the president demanded the removal of black troops not just from Greeneville but from all of East Tennessee. Alleging that they had no discipline and might aid a black insurrection, Johnson also wanted as many as possible mustered out of their volunteer regiments. Thomas's investigation found black troops generally innocent of the charges against them. No brothel existed in Johnson's home; a relative had placed a white family there instead. Black regiments could not leave East Tennessee because of both a troop shortage and a need to restrain violence between returning Confederate and Union veterans. The general emphasized that "I do not believe that there is the least foundation for fearing an insurrection."[13]

Thomas firmly defended his forces:

As a general rule the negro Soldiers are under good discipline. . . . I believe that in the majority of cases of collision between whites and negro Soldiers that the white man has attempted to bully the negro, for it is exceedingly repugnant to the Southerners to have negro Soldiers in their midst.

He had constantly encouraged strict discipline in these regiments and even ordered them not to forage, because that often led to charges of property depredation. He concluded that the tales that stirred the president must have come from society's minority of "evil-minded persons . . . always ready to misrepresent and exaggerate." To a large extent, Thomas's input calmed Johnson. A more respectful tone marked all the president's recorded comments on racial matters through the rest of 1865.[14]

Many white southerners besides Andrew Johnson worried about a freedmen's insurrection. Anxieties rose in late 1865 as whites tried to sign up black laborers before the customary contracting time after the Christmas season. Thomas tried to calm fears by sending white troops to supposed hotspots. When Mississippi militiamen began disarming freedmen in the northern part of the state and frightening a number of them out of the area, Thomas ordered it stopped. No rebellion occurred, and most freedmen signed new contracts at the traditional time.[15]

Also in late 1865, Congress convened and raised questions about Johnson's reconstruction program. Called to testify before the newly created Joint Committee on Reconstruction, Thomas painted a mixed picture. The nation, he held, could rely upon freedmen to stay peaceful, seek education, and work well when granted fair treatment and opportunity. According to the general, who had modified his views since the war's end, white acceptance of emancipation was developing in the Upper South, but not yet in the Deep South. Only the continuing efforts of the occupation forces and the Freedmen's Bureau restrained violence against blacks, in his opinion.[16]

By early 1866, military protection of the freedmen increasingly aggravated new civil governments that Johnson had instituted in ex-Confederate states. General-in-Chief Ulysses S. Grant urged occupation commanders to continue upholding the blacks' liberty. Thomas trusted Governor Robert M. Patton of Alabama enough to allow the state militia to replace federal troops there, but a doubtful Grant cancelled this order. Thomas subsequently refused a politician's request for the removal of black troops from Sumner County, Tennessee, on the ground that the locality was too "rebellious." President Johnson, who had entered into a bitter conflict with Congress over his desire for a quick and mild reconstruction, issued in April 1866 a proclamation ending the state of insurrection that Lincoln had declared in 1861. Because Congress had not readmitted the ex-Confederate states, Johnson's decree created ambiguity regarding the acceptable types of military interference in civil affairs.[17]

Thomas feared that Johnson's proclamation ended martial law in occupied areas and that more violence against blacks would result. Although Grant took the position that martial law remained in effect, the matter remained unclear. At the same time, postwar demobilization of volunteer regiments undercut the strength of military occupation. Beginning in 1866 with 25,682 men (mostly blacks), Thomas's forces by late May fell to 4,047 regular troops (all whites). The general warned one subordinate that the officer would now have to rely exclusively on the "moral effect of your presence and opinion."[18] Thomas realized, with considerable pain, his inability to maintain both order and blacks' rights: "The General regrets . . . the state of affairs . . . but he is powerless to correct it. It is and has been the policy of the President to restore to the people of the Southern States *all* their privileges." He advised a number of complainants that "the only remedy exists in the action of the people themselves" and referred them to their state governments. He made an exception for African-American veterans, however, and in one case ordered the Freedmen's Bureau to intervene if two of them failed to receive a fair trial in a Murfreesboro, Tennessee, case.[19] Generally, though, Thomas felt forced by presidential policy and troop reductions to act less boldly.

As a result, southerners did not know what to expect from the army. One unionist planter in Mississippi's Yazoo Valley wanted to arm his black laborers against threatening nightriders. Thomas admitted the planter's right to do so but urged nonviolence and the use of civil processes, because "the only way to correct the evil is by the exercise of firmness and discretion." After the assassination of Lieutenant J. P. Blanding, a Freedmen's Bureau agent in Mississippi, the general tried to encourage effective state action on the case by offering military support. At the same time, Thomas warned a sheriff in Tennessee that "the surest way to avoid military interference is to execute the laws faithfully and impartially." Appeals came from numerous localities for removing, sending, keeping, or withholding troops, but troop allocations changed little right after demobilization. When Governor Charles P. Jenkins of Georgia complained about uncontrollable lawlessness in the northwest corner of his state, Thomas requested an additional cavalry regiment for the area, but Grant judged that no such force could be spared. Thomas clearly would have preferred to continue military interventions against racial violence.[20]

In July 1866, an increasingly concerned Grant directed the army to arrest and hold violators of blacks' civil rights when state authorities did not act. Under this often-cited General Order 44 and some specific directions from Grant, Thomas sent troops to arrest nightriders in northern Mississippi and had Brigadier General George Stoneman attempt to find the parties guilty for a bloody riot against blacks in Memphis, Tennessee. The Johnson administration canceled both initiatives, much to Thomas's dissatisfaction. The president stressed that he did not consider military intervention in such civil matters necessary. Perhaps sarcastically, he suggested instead that the victims initiate court cases using the Civil Rights Act that Congress had just passed over his veto.[21] Contested boundaries between civil and military jurisdictions constantly caused major problems during Reconstruction. The United States had traditionally idealized military subordination to civil authority, but the Civil War had greatly expanded military powers over rebellious civilians. The challenges of Reconstruction often seemed to call for similar exercises of military might.

Presidential pressure made Thomas act more cautiously for a time. To provide some aid for Governor Jenkins, he ordered one of his cavalry companies into northwest Georgia and took the position that military arrests under General Order 44 would "compel civil authorities to perform their duties."[22] Possibly emboldened by the defeat of many Johnson supporters in the congressional elections of 1866, Thomas subsequently sent out a few more cavalry companies against nightriders; one went to Morgantown, Georgia, and another to Grenada, Mississippi. He grumbled that "I am constantly hampered for want of cavalry." The horse soldiers had the best chance of beating the nightriders, but Thomas had only one regiment for his entire command, now downgraded from a military division to a department. These patrols could at least quiet a neighborhood, though they caught neither nightriders nor Lieutenant Blanding's assassin in 1866.[23]

Much easier to remedy was the forced contracting of black inmates from the Nashville workhouse to an Arkansas planter. Thomas drew public attention to this matter by assigning the investigation to Brigadier General William D. Whipple, his chief-of-staff. Only the threat of military arrests got action from city officials. Several children, falsely arrested as vagrants, were returned to their parents, and a group of adult freedmen also came back to Nashville.[24]

The workhouse incident was made more sensitive by Tennessee's readmission to Congress, which ended Reconstruction in the state. Like officials in the former slave state of Kentucky, which never lost its congressional seats because it did not secede, Tennessee's leaders now would sometimes perceive military interference as violating the state's rights. For his part, Thomas admitted that he should make military arrests in those two states only when requested and supervised by their governments. Knowing that racial violence continued there and that blacks rarely received justice in the state courts, he asked Grant for guidance, only to be advised that civilians should keep trying the state courts. Suspecting that state militias could eliminate nightriders, if motivated for the task, Thomas turned down Governor Brownlow's request for more federal troops to deal with racial violence. This led Brownlow to call out the militia.[25]

Thomas continued to try to improve popular attitudes. Two of his investigations involved nightrider violence against blacks near Columbus and Lebanon, Kentucky. Another sought to identify those who posted numerous placards threatening blacks in the area around Russellville, Kentucky, and Gallatin, Tennessee. The general also used a congratulatory letter to a new Mississippi judge to encourage leaders to "educate the people of Mississippi to a proper standard of nationality . . . that the rights of freed people will not be restricted."[26]

Likewise, Thomas supported the Freedmen's Bureau in most matters. When the agency's head in Georgia used Grant's Order 44 to protect freedmen by placing a garrison in Henry County, he gave the action his approval. Thomas also ordered military arrests when some Tennesseans attacked Bureau agents.[27] Although he granted military guards to Bureau officials at Pulaski and Columbia, he reprimanded those officials for acting "in a very summary, impolitic and unjust manner . . . [showing] a want of that judgement which should characterize the official conduct of persons charged with a delicate and responsible trust." In addition, he had one of them investigated. To avoid such problems, Thomas tried to recruit prudent agents for the Bureau from his officer ranks. He disapproved of the Bureau policy of providing inexpensive train transportation for freedmen, probably because of the cost and the appearance of special treatment. In his opinion, both public order and white acceptance of black rights depended upon the evenhandedness of federal actions.[28]

Federal policy dramatically changed in early 1867 with the passage of the Military Reconstruction Act for the ten states still excluded from Congress. Reconstruction issues had not ended the once close relationship between Thomas and Johnson, although the general sadly felt it was strained and thought the president "deprecated" some of his decisions. Johnson, unhappy with Thomas's egalitarianism but liking his cautiousness, twice tried to assign him command of a Military Reconstruction District. Thomas resisted because of "how repugnant such politico-military duties were to my mind." He believed that his efforts to win ex-Confederate acceptance of Reconstruction had failed, possibly because he was a southern Unionist. Major General Philip H. Sheridan, a very assertive northerner whom Johnson once wanted to replace with Thomas, looked to Thomas like the ideal man for the job. General Thomas began to think that only force and an influx of northerners into the South could resolve sectional problems.[29] In the reorganization of commands, Johnson assigned him to a new Department of the Cumberland, which included Tennessee, Kentucky, and West Virginia. Although not under Military Reconstruction, these states still were adjusting to slavery's end. The new command had 3,257 men, about 1,000 fewer troops than his previous department.[30]

Despite the paucity of his forces but probably encouraged by the start of Military Reconstruction elsewhere, Thomas got tougher. When white terrorists, calling themselves "Ghouls," began attacking blacks near Fort Donelson, Tennessee, he ordered the garrison to arrest them under Grant's General Order 44. He sent small forces to Franklin and LaGrange, Tennessee, to suppress nightriders. Furthermore, he suggested a new tactic: military trials of any Confederate veterans involved in racial violence. Although such an extraordinary action would have fit better under Military Reconstruction, the general tried to justify it on the ground that those veterans had violated their parole obligation to stay peaceful. When Grant approved a test of the tactic, Thomas expressed great hope for its success: "Only when a people are convinced that there is no way of evading the law will they abide by it."[31]

Thomas also sent members of his staff to investigate racial violence in Middle and East Tennessee, as well as the effectiveness of the state militia's response there. The Tennessee militia's domination by white and black Unionists had made it a controversial peacekeeping tool. It struggled with great difficulty to contain the tensions that resulted from the state legislature's 1867 decision to enact black male suffrage while continuing ex-Confederate disfranchisement.[32] As the August congressional election approached, Thomas carefully planned to use his men to help the militia, which he continued to favor after the investigations. Because Kentucky had no controversial suffrage laws, the general could move some troops south just for Tennessee's election. The largest force went to Memphis, because he believed it "contains more turbulent elements, and consequently greater danger of bloody riots." He ordered troops to be in camp ready for action during political rallies and the election, but on election day they would neither approach polls nor in any way interfere with balloting. He publicly announced his plan together with reassurances that he hoped Tennesseans themselves would keep the election peaceful.[33]

All the same, hostilities grew during the campaign. Thomas quickly sent a detachment to Franklin after a riot broke out against blacks there. When requested to send troops to Jackson, Thomas did so reluctantly, because friction between militia and civilians in that town seemed to put his own men in an "impossible" situation. After posting still other contingents at Humboldt, Brownsville, Sommerville, Nashville, LaGrange, Gallatin, Murfreesboro, and Columbia, Thomas had none left to meet subsequent requests from Greeneville and other communities. Upon Grant's orders, Thomas went to Memphis, negotiated a truce between the feuding police chief and the sheriff, and supervised federal forces in the city on election day. As a result of his efforts, Tennessee's African-American voters cast their first ballots in peace, and he proudly reported that the public seemed "entirely satisfied with the impartial conduct of the troops."[34]

Nashville's municipal election in September later kept the franchise issue boiling. Rejecting the legitimacy of the postwar laws, the mayor sought to conduct his own election and bar blacks from the polls. After Governor Brownlow called for federal troops to uphold state authority, General Thomas conducted lengthy and delicate negotiations that ultimately resulted in the mayor's decision to abandon his scheme. Thomas worried that the franchise acts had instilled "utter contempt" for law in Tennessee.[35] Although he did not record his personal opinion of black suffrage, this comment indicated for the first time a fear that black rights and public order might not always be compatible.

A clash over black suffrage during the congressional election subsequently led to Thomas's first application of his parole violation tactic. In LaGrange, William A. Milliken, a Confederate veteran, perceived the march of a group of armed blacks to the polls as a grave menace to whites' lives. Waving a gun, he threatened a northern businessman whom he blamed for the blacks' action. Milliken quickly attracted an angry mob of men agreeing with him. The federal soldiers posted in the town arrived in time to keep the peace and to arrest Milliken. They turned him over to town officials, who fined him $5. Soon afterward, Thomas had him rearrested for parole violation. Nevertheless, the U.S. District Court in Memphis granted Milliken a writ of habeas corpus, primarily on the ground that the war's end had made paroles irrelevant. When Johnson's attorney general refused to appeal the decision, Thomas had to abandon this experimental tactic.[36]

Other frustrating experiences soon followed Thomas's success in the elections. Much racial violence occurred in rural areas. In Tennessee, he feared some county officers supported the nightriders; in Kentucky, he judged local officials as well-meaning but ineffective. By now it was clear that small federal patrols could intimidate but not stop the troublemakers, many of whom by early 1868 had coalesced into what Thomas called the "rebel order of the Ku Klux Klan." In Pulaski, Tennessee, the reputed place of its founding, the group was "in full blast." He assigned one officer to investigate it there and had the head of the Freedmen's Bureau in Tennessee conduct a statewide study in the hope that these efforts would stimulate state court cases and federal action. President Johnson, now embroiled in his impeachment crisis, not surprisingly took a narrow and legalistic stand in responding to Thomas's reports. Pointing to Article IV, Section 4, of the U.S. Constitution, Johnson held that the army could act against domestic violence only when a state legislature or a governor requested it. In addition to lacking presidential support, Thomas did not have enough troops to meet the need uncovered by his investigations of the Klan. He only managed to move an infantry company to Columbia at Governor Brownlow's urgent request. He hoped that his garrisons "may have a moral effect . . . but under existing orders they can be of little service," because they had to obey local authorities "who do not appear to be zealous in their duties."[37]

Matters changed little after Johnson escaped conviction in his Senate trial. With his troops unreinforced and widely dispersed, Thomas had to reject numerous requests for military intervention and encourage the efforts of the Tennessee militia upon which Brownlow largely depended. In September, Johnson ordered federal commanders to get his permission before aiding civil officials, whenever time permitted it; the administration even restricted military help for federal marshals. That same month the Department of the Cumberland's force fell to 1,857 men, almost half its original troop strength. Most importantly, Grant dispatched all of its cavalry to the Great Plains to fight Indians.[38]

When an additional infantry regiment finally arrived about a month before the 1868 presidential election, Thomas headquartered it at Columbia, Tennessee, and then scattered detachments to Johnsonville, Brownsville, Memphis, and Grand Junction. He allocated a small force to the last place in response to a false report of black rioting because he consistently sought to appear evenhanded. On election day, the troops kept their assigned posts calm, but black voters suffered much violence elsewhere in Tennessee.[39]

The election of Grant, the Civil War hero who had kept a distance from Johnson's policies, at first seemed to pose a threat to racist nightriders. Grant's victory, as well as joint action by a few federals and many militia, quieted West Tennessee. At about the same time, Thomas discovered that mounted infantry made a workable substitute for cavalry in the campaign against racial violence. However, his problems soon increased. The new administration sent more of Thomas's forces to the Indian wars so that the total number of military posts in the department fell from 17 to 7 by the summer of 1869. When Klansmen shut down a freedmen's school in Mayfield, Kentucky, Thomas decided against sending a force there. He explained that the teachers would not reopen the school and that an intervention would only increase racial tensions without accomplishing anything. In another area, a disgruntled officer "betrayed a great want of discretion" by publicly expressing contempt for his peacekeeping assignment and by revealing the names of those who had requested military protection. Most seriously, wherever local authorities favored the Klan, nightriders rapidly lost their fear of federal troops.[40]

Thomas's original hopefulness regarding the reconstruction of American race relations had slowly dissolved into despair. He thought that most whites in the ex-slave states had simply abandoned traditional respect for law and order in matters involving the new legal status of blacks. Having never expected this of his fellow white southerners, the general commented, "It is mortifying to acknowledge that the state and local laws which should do so, and the more powerful force of public opinion, do not protect the citizens." Thomas considered the root cause to be what today's historians call the Cult of the Lost Cause, the unification of southern whites around a false belief in northern persecution of the South. Because of this belief, Thomas thought they exempted themselves from obedience to the national majority. Economic damages from the war as well as personal grudges against white and black unionists hardened resentment in the South, while the inconsistent course of Reconstruction during the Johnson administration facilitated resistance. Thomas believed that federal troops, despite limited numbers and restricting rules, "to some extent . . . prevented personal collisions and partisan difficulties." All the same, he concluded that "the evil done [by racist whites] has been great, and it is not discernable that an immediate improvement may be expected."[41]

Four frustrating years of Reconstruction led Thomas in 1869 to seek command of the very quiet Division of the Atlantic, which had a choice location in the northeastern states. Instead, the Grant administration reassigned him to the Division of the Pacific. Shortly afterward in 1869, Thomas died from a stroke.[42] Reconstruction, thus, largely shaped the last chapter of his life.

Thomas had joined the generals who worked for a new racial order in the South through his experience of the Battle of Nashville, a critical moment in his life. Like the battle, Reconstruction would include much black bravery and death but, unlike the battle, would not end in triumph. Because most other white southerners shared neither Thomas's new racial attitudes nor his unionism, he misjudged the chances for change at first. Restrained by a cautious personality, limited military means, and little direct contact with African Americans, he might not have done as much as he could. Still, he experimented with new peacekeeping tactics and remained idealistically committed to the cause.

Thomas's analysis of Reconstruction fits well with the conclusions in recent historical studies. Southern whites' hostility to change in race relations certainly fomented widespread and extralegal resistance, which President Andrew Johnson's policies facilitated in practice if not in original intent. Breaking up that resistance, even if possible, would have required tremendous force by 1869. Thomas's perception of the problem in southern attitudes toward law and social order, although a typical view for professional U.S. Army officers of his time, had depth and provides new insight into Reconstruction. Idealists such as Thomas could not help but leave their work on Reconstruction pleased with the sincere striving for change but saddened by the brutal opposition.[43]

NOTES

1. Francis F. McKinney, *Education in Violence: The Life of George H. Thomas and the History of the Army of the Cumberland* (Detroit, 1961), 373–403. The author wishes to thank Thomas More College for financial support of this project.

2. McKinney, *Education in Violence*, 403–14; Thomas J. Morgan, *Reminiscences of Service with Colored Troops in the Army of the Cumberland, 1863–65* (Providence, 1885), 48–49; Thomas B. Van Horne, *The Life of Major-General George H. Thomas* (New York, 1882), 347. The best works on Thomas and the battle are McKinney's *Education in Violence* and Wiley Sword's *Embrace an Angry Wind, The Confederacy's Last Hurrah: Spring Hill, Franklin, and Nashville* (New York, 1991), but neither deals with the change in Thomas's racial attitudes.

3. McKinney, *Education in Violence*, 3–8, 23–85; Daniel W. Crofts, *Old Southampton: Politics and Society in a Virginia County, 1834–1869* (Charlottesville, 1992), 206–7.

4. William F. G. Shanks, *Personal Recollections of Distinguished Generals* (New York, 1866), 61–65, 75–77, 80; Edward M. Coffman, *The Old Army: A Portrait of the American Army in Peacetime, 1784–1898* (New York, 1983), 235–36; Crofts, *Old Southampton*, 206.

5. McKinney, *Education in Violence*, 88–91; John Cimprich, *Slavery's End in Tennessee, 1861–1865* (Tuscaloosa, 1985), 38–39, 66–68, 92.

6. George H. Thomas to ?, 18 November 1863, George H. Thomas Papers (Historical Society of Pennsylvania); R. D. Mussey to George B. Halstead, 8 June 1864, Letters Received by Adjutant General L. Thomas Relating to Colored Troops, Record Group (hereafter RG) 94 (National Archives [hereafter NA]); W. D. Whipple to R. D. Mussey, 19 June 1864, Letters Sent by the Department of the Cumberland, vol. 223/431 DC, 128, RG 393 (NA); Morgan, *Reminiscences*, 22–25; George P. Rawick, ed., *The American Slave: A Composite Autobiography* (41 vol., Westport, 1972–79), supp. ser. 2, 3:818.

7. Van Horne, *Thomas*, 347; McKinney, *Education in Violence*, 83, 447–54.

8. W. D. Whipple to John E. Smith, 3 July 1865, Letters Sent by the Military Division of the Tennessee, vol. 33 DT, 10–11, RG 393 (NA); John Y. Simon, ed., *The Papers of Ulysses S. Grant* (18 vol. to date, Carbondale, 1976–), 15:241.

9. Cimprich, *Slavery's End in Tennessee*, 119; Paul H. Bergeron, ed., *The Papers of Andrew Johnson* (9 vol. to date, Knoxville, 1967–), 8:413.

10. Nashville *Press and Times*, 24 July 1865; W. W. Barrett et al. to W. D. Whipple, 21 August 1865, Letters Received by the Military Division of the Tennessee, RG 393 (NA).

11. Bergeron, ed., *Papers of Johnson*, 8:585, 9:281; *Report of the Joint Committee on Reconstruction* (Washington, 1866), pt. 1, 109, 112; pt. 3, 27.

12. Bergeron, *Papers of Johnson*, 9:400.

13. Ibid., 26, 27, 41, 48, 57.

14. Ibid., 57, 58ff (for Johnson's subsequent statements); Robert H. Ramsay to I. S. Donaldson, 18 July 1865; same to ?, 31 July 1865; same to William Shafter, 22 September 1865, Letters Sent by the Military Division of the Tennessee, vol. 33 DT, 35, 63, 165, RG 393 (NA).

15. W. D. Whipple to John E. Smith, 26 December 1865, Letters Sent by the Military Division of the Tennessee, vol. 33 DT, 284, RG 393 (NA); James E. Sefton, *The United States Army and Reconstruction, 1865–1877* (Baton Rouge, 1967), 43.

16. *Report of the Joint Committee on Reconstruction*, pt. 1, 109–11; pt. 3, 27–28.

17. Sefton, *Army and Reconstruction*, 71, 79, 193; Simon, *Papers of Grant*, 16:54, 141; W. D. Whipple to L. S. Mulloy, 31 March 1866, Letters Sent by the Military Division of the Tennessee, vol. 34 DT, 123, RG 393 (NA).

18. Sefton, *Army and Reconstruction*, 193; Simon, *Papers of Grant*, 16:150; C. W. Foster to George H. Thomas, 29 September 1865, Letters Received by the District of Middle Tennessee, RG 393 (NA); W. D. Whipple to T. J. Wood, 10 April 1866; George H. Thomas to George K. Leet, 12 November 1866, Letters Sent by the Military Division of the Tennessee, vol. 34 DT, 137, 366–67, RG 393 (NA).

19. W. D. Whipple to John A. Jackson, 14 April 1866; same to John W. Bowen, 11 April 1866; same to John E. Williams, 28 April 1866; George H. Thomas to Clinton B. Fisk, 8 June 1866; same to George K. Leet, 12 November 1866, Letters Sent by the Military Division of the Tennessee, vol. 34 DT, 141, 137, 156, 204, 368, RG 393 (NA).

20. George W. Howard to T. J. Wood, 25 June 1866; W. D. Whipple to T. J. Wood, 5 June 1866; same to A. L. Polk, 24 May 1866; same to Charles P. Jenkins, 24 May 1866, ibid., 225, 198, 187.

21. Sefton, *Army and Reconstruction*, 73; Simon, *Papers of Grant*, 16:230–231, 235.

22. George W. Howard to E. H. Leib, 1 September 1866; W. D. Whipple to T. J. Wood, 23 September 1866, Letters Sent by the Department of the Tennessee, vol. 34 DT, 286, 307, RG 393 (NA).

23. George H. Thomas to George K. Leet, 12 November 1866; same to Ulysses S. Grant, 28 November 1866; W. D. Whipple to T. J. Wood, 4 September 1866; A. L. Hough to T. J. Wood, 17 November 1866, ibid., 368, 374, 403, 290, 357.

24. W. D. Whipple to J. J. Smiley, 18, 24 October 1866; same to E. A. Cheatham, 20 October 1866; George H. Thomas to E. D. Townsend, 30 September 1867, ibid., vol. 34 DT, 321, 325, 328, vol. 35 DT, 317.

25. George H. Thomas to Ulysses S. Grant, 16 November 1866; same to Edwin Stanton, 19 November 1866; A. S. Hough to Horace Harrison, 7 December 1866; W. D. Whipple to C. R. Comstock, 5 October 1866, ibid., vol. 34 DT, 357, 360, 409, 311; Thomas B. Alexander, *Political Reconstruction in Tennessee* (Nashville, 1950), 149.

26. *House Executive Documents* (serial 1324), 205; W. D. Whipple to Charles E. Brady, 9 February 1867; same to Sidney Burbank, 7 March 1867; George H. Thomas to Robert A. Hill, 13 December 1866, Letters Sent by the Department of the Tennessee, vol. 35 DT, 29, 64, vol. 34 DT, 415, RG 393 (NA).

27. Nashville *Union and American*, 23 October 1866; W. D. Whipple to Davis Tillson, 28 October 1866; A. L. Hough to Thomas Duncan, 24 December 1866; same to J. H. Bridgewater, 24 May 1867, Letters Sent by the Department of the Tennessee, vol. 34 DT, 331, 425, vol. 35 DT, 133, RG 393 (NA).

28. George H. Thomas to M. C. Meigs, 7 December 1866; same to O. O. Howard, 1 December 1866, and 11 January 1867; W. D. Whipple to W. P. Carlin, 29 March 1867, Letters Sent by the Department of the Tennessee, vol. 34 DT, 408, 404, vol. 35 DT, 11, 87, RG 393 (NA).

29. George H. Thomas to Ulysses S. Grant, 16 November 1866; W. D. Whipple to George Baker, 22 February 1867; same to Edwin Stanton, 4 July 1867, ibid., vol. 34 DT, 357, vol. 35 DT, 42, 349–50; Sefton, *Army and Reconstruction*, 114, 156–57; Henry Coppee, *General Thomas* (New York, 1898), 292.

30. McKinney, *Education in Violence*, 464–66; *House Executive Documents* (serial 1324), 183.

31. Simon, *Papers of Grant*, 17:238–39; W. D. Whipple to Fred Rosenkrantz, 6 May 1867; same to E. D. Townsend, 6 August 1867; R. W. Johnson to Thomas Duncan, 11 July 1867; George H. Thomas to Marland Perkins, 21 September 1867, Letters Sent by the Department of the Cumberland, vol. 35 DT, 120, 248, 203, 288, RG 393 (NA); Brooks D. Simpson, *Let Us Have Peace: Ulysses S. Grant and the Politics of War and Reconstruction, 1861–1868* (Chapel Hill, 1991), 300, misinterprets the origin of the parole violation tactic.

32. W. D. Whipple to George H. Thomas, 7 June 1867, Letters Sent by the Department of the Cumberland, vol. 35 DT, 158, RG 393 (NA); *House Executive Documents* (serial 1324), 232; Alexander, *Reconstruction in Tennessee*, 75, 130–31, 149–53.

33. Simon, *Papers of Grant*, 17:607; W. D. Whipple to Thomas Duncan, 16 July 1867; same to E. D. Townsend, 18 July 1867; George H. Thomas to W. Watt Brown and Thomas B. Jennings, 19 July 1867; same to S. B. Beaumont, 20 July 1867, Letters Sent by the Department of the Cumberland, vol. 35 DT, 209, 212, 216, 220, 236, RG 393 (NA).

34. R. W. Johnson to Thomas Duncan, 11 July 1866; W. D. Whipple to A. W. Campbell and H. Jackson, 19 July 1867; same to A. W. Walker, 30 July 1867; George H. Thomas to Thomas Duncan, 29 July 1867; same to E. D. Townsend, 5 August 1867, Letters Sent by the Department of the Cumberland, vol. 35 DT, 203, 217, 237, 245, RG 393 (NA).

35. Sefton, *Army and Reconstruction*, 229; *House Executive Documents* (serial 1367), 151 (quoted).

36. Memphis *Post*, 3 August, 23 October 1867; Simon, *Papers of Grant*, 18:396.

37. W. D. Whipple to Thomas J. Harrison, 9 March 1868; A. L. Hough to W. P. Carlin, 21 March 1868; same to J.Q.R. Reeves, 25 March 1868, Letters Sent by the Department of the Cumberland, vol. 35 DT, 69, 79–80, 123, RG 393 (NA); Simon, *Papers of Grant*, 18:567; *House Executive Documents* (serial 1324), 183, (serial 1367), 144–45, 149–50.

38. George H. Thomas to William G. Brownlow, 24 June 1868; same to E. D. Townsend, 11 September 1868, Letters Sent by the Department of the Cumberland, vol. 178 DC, 134, 180, 184, RG 393 (NA); *House Executive Documents* (serial 1367), 142, 147; General Order 65, 1 September 1868, Department of the Cumberland General Orders, RG 393 (NA).

39. W. D. Whipple to George P. Buell, 1 October 1868; same to Wager Swayne, 9 October 1868; same to Gordon Granger, 25, 30 October 1868; George H. Thomas to E. D. Townsend, 15 May 1869, Letters Sent by the Department of the Cumberland, vol. 178 DC, 196, 220, 230, 231, 236–38, RG 393 (NA).

40. W. D. Whipple to Lucien Anderson, 13 January 1869; same to Henry M. Whiting, 22 January 1869; George H. Thomas to E. D. Townsend, 25 March, 15 May 1869, ibid., 283, 288, 332, 337–39.

41. *House Executive Documents* (serial 1367), 151–52; Charles R. Wilson, *Baptized in Blood: The Religion of the Lost Cause* (Athens, 1980), 40–46.

42. McKinney, *Education in Violence*, 467–71.

43. Roberta Sue Alexander, "Presidential Reconstruction: Ideology and Change," in Eric Anderson and Alfred A. Moss, eds., *The Facts of Reconstruction: Essays in Honor of John Hope Franklin* (Baton Rouge, 1991), 29–57; Coffman, *Old Army*, 235–36.

10

James Redpath in South Carolina: An Abolitionist's Odyssey in the Reconstruction Era South

John R. McKivigan

On April 14, 1877, James Redpath (1833–91) published his answer to a black Mississippi Republican who had asked him how southern blacks should respond to President Rutherford B. Hayes's withdrawal of the final detachments of federal troops and abandonment of Republican Reconstruction state governments in the South. A former abolitionist and veteran advocate for African-American rights, Redpath once was the leading journalistic partisan of John Brown and had served as the first superintendent of public schools for blacks in Charleston, South Carolina. Consequently, it was startling when Redpath advised that southern blacks

Should be taught that the men who fought for their freedom are now in a helpless minority in the Republican Party; that the blacks owe it no allegiance whatever now; and that its recognized leaders, who wield the power of the Government, are to-day the recreants who advocate and defend and decree their abandonment. . . . There is absolutely no difference whatever, now, between the Democratic Party and the Republican Party, (as represented by Hayes) on the question of the rights and condition of the negro, excepting in one important particular. That exception is a vital one. It points out the path of safety to the black voter. It points out, also the path of duty. We owe allegiance where we receive protection. The Democrats protect the democratic negro; the Republicans abandon the republican negro.[1]

Redpath then said he would "urge the black men of the South, if my voice could reach them, to join the democratic party."[2]

Redpath's disenchantment with the Republican Party's Reconstruction program had been evolving through more than a decade of personal involvement in and observation of Reconstruction. First a reporter and then a school administrator in Charleston, South Carolina, from February to June 1865, Redpath pursued his career as a journalist and Radical Republican partisan until 1869, concluding it with a brief period as an aide to Congressman Benjamin Butler. In the years from 1869 to 1876, Redpath wrote occasional articles on conditions in the South but largely devoted his time to managing a booking agency for lecturers. At the time of the final collapse of southern Reconstruction in 1876–77, Redpath briefly returned to his role as a journalist, minor government official, and Republican partisan. The demise of the last Republican state governments in the South, however, provoked Redpath's famous outburst, which marked his total disgust with the Republican party and the end of his active political involvement. Redpath's political and intellectual odyssey during Reconstruction casts revealing light on the frustration and disillusionment of many abolitionists who lived to see much of their work undone.[3]

Born in Scotland, Redpath emigrated to the United States in 1849 and found employment as a reporter for Horace Greeley's New York *Tribune*. While working for that newspaper, he developed a strong curiosity concerning the institution of slavery. In 1854 and 1855, he made two extensive journeys through the South "to see slavery with my own eyes, and personally to learn what bondsmen said and thought of their condition."[4] What Redpath witnessed and what slaves told him in secret interviews made the young Scottish immigrant a radical opponent of slavery. To expose true conditions, Redpath published an account of his travels in abolitionist newspapers under the pseudonym "John Ball, Jr." In 1859 he edited and republished these interviews with the slaves in a volume entitled *The Roving Editor*.[5]

From 1855 to 1858, Redpath resided in Kansas, where he reported on the sectional controversy in that territory for the St. Louis *Daily Missouri Democrat*, the New York *Tribune*, the *Chicago Tribune*, and other papers and briefly edited his own newspaper, the Doniphan *Crusader of Freedom*. His highly partisan coverage of the feuding between proslavery and antislavery factions in Kansas enhanced his reputation as a militant abolitionist. In Kansas, Redpath also befriended John Brown and became part of the Harpers Ferry conspiracy. After Brown's execution, Redpath published the first biography of Brown, in which he defended abolitionist instigation of slave uprisings as the only feasible means to end slavery.[6]

In the early years of the Civil War, Redpath was preoccupied with serving as an agent for the Republic of Haiti. In 1860 he toured Haiti as a reporter and returned to the United States as the official Haitian minister plenipotentiary to lobby for U.S. diplomatic recognition. Enlisting the assistance of his long-time friend, antislavery Senator Charles Sumner, Redpath secured this recognition within two years. At the same time, Redpath served as director of Haiti's campaign to attract free black emigrants from the United States. Redpath hoped that selective emigration of skilled blacks to Haiti would elevate conditions on the island nation and, thereby, help to dispel racial prejudice in the United States. He abandoned the scheme in the fall of 1862, however, when he recognized that North American blacks preferred to remain at home once the Civil War seemed to promise a new day of freedom for their race.[7]

In 1863 and 1864, Redpath redirected his energies to publishing cheap paperbound "Campfire Books," aimed at a reading audience of bored soldiers. This series featured a mixture of religious, historical, and humorous works by such authors as Louisa May Alcott, Wendell Phillips, and Victor Hugo. A particularly noteworthy title published by Redpath was William Wells Brown's *Clotelle, A Tale of the Southern States*, the first novel published by an African American. Redpath's firm was only sporadically profitable, and when he failed to obtain further advances of capital from abolitionist friends, it ceased operation in the summer of 1864.[8]

Experiencing serious financial difficulties from the failure of his publishing business, Redpath located employment as a war correspondent for the Boston *Daily Journal*. He joined General William Tecumseh Sherman's army in Georgia during the summer of 1864, and after the fall of Atlanta in September, Redpath covered General George H. Thomas's campaign against the Confederate army in Tennessee that culminated with the Union victory at Nashville in December 1864. Soon after the battle at Nashville, Redpath accepted an assignment from the New York *Tribune* to cover the campaign of General Sherman's army along the Atlantic coast. Accompanying one of the first Union detachments to enter Charleston in February 1865, he sent the *Tribune* the first descriptions of the fall of the symbolic cradle of southern secession.

Redpath's activities as a war correspondent reveal the concern of antebellum abolitionists for the future of the emancipated blacks and the political destiny of the former slave states. Redpath used his position as a war correspondent with the Union army in the South to report principally on events related to those concerns, rather than to describe the advance or retreat of military forces.

Transportation problems cost Redpath his biggest potential scoop of the war. He was at Hilton Head, South Carolina, when news arrived that Sherman's maneuvers had just forced the Confederates to evacuate their garrison in Charleston rather than allow it to be cut off. Hoping to be the first northern reporter to enter the fallen enemy citadel, Redpath immediately boarded a steamer to Charleston harbor, where he hurriedly transferred to a navy ship. To his chagrin, instead of landing at Charleston, the latter ship steamed on to Hilton Head. Redpath finally arrived in Charleston two days later in the company of numerous other reporters.[9] Soon after, Redpath failed in his assignment to join Sherman's army as it rapidly pushed on toward North Carolina.[10] Instead, Redpath used his time in Charleston to report on conditions in the captured city; the extent of damage stunned him.[11]

Despite the sufferings he witnessed, Redpath protested against any leniency toward former Confederate sympathizers. The devastation of the city, Redpath claimed, was solely the fault of the slaveholders. In a preening fashion, he recalled that the Charleston he had visited in the mid-1850s "was the high carnival of despotism in America, the Belthassar's Feast of the Slaveholder. The writing on the wall was visible to but one eye in all the delirious city" — Redpath's own.[12] He advised that those proud southern slaveholders must be humbled if they ever were to become loyal again, noting that "this war is saving the South in spite of itself."[13]

Redpath's self-righteous reporting soon reached the desk of the editor of the Richmond *Enquirer*, who branded it "wild intoxication" and reassured his Confederate readers that Redpath had forgotten that "Lord Cornwallis and the British also occupied the city of Charleston for a while."[14]

Although his writing outraged the southern press, Redpath was warmly supported by his own newspaper, the New York *Tribune*. Sydney Howard Gay, the paper's managing editor, had been a Garrisonian abolitionist since the 1830s and first published articles by Redpath while editor of the New York *National Anti-Slavery Standard* in the mid-1850s. Gay granted his war correspondents far more latitude than most northern editors, especially when the reporter's sentiments accorded with Gay's own proemancipation views. When Redpath considered resigning over disputed reimbursement vouchers in March 1865, an exchange of letters with Gay convinced him that he "wd rather work for the Tribune than for any other paper."[15]

Redpath reported that Charleston whites were sullen under occupation and reluctant to accept either defeat by the North or emancipation of their slaves. He did locate a few seemingly sincere individuals, mainly German and Irish Americans, who claimed to have been "compelled to talk secession to save themselves."[16] Redpath voiced strong skepticism, however, about the growing number of "Rip Van Winkle" Unionists who began emerging from the native white population as the hopes for the Confederacy declined. He predicted that "the best of the white Unionists here would be regarded as the worst of Copperheads in the Northern States, and that unless we encourage the negro, we will have trouble with this State again."[17]

According to Redpath's estimate, there were no more than 500 genuine white Unionists in the city, although 4,000 had signed the loyalty oath by the end of March. He warned, "That policy . . . only [encourages] perjury, and is slowly and surely digging the grave of the Republican party. It is the farce that comes before the tragedy. You will see."[18]

Redpath's appraisal was seconded by other northern reporters, including Whitelaw Reid, who declared that "few could be found less treasonable than the majority of South Carolina."[19]

Redpath's reports for the *Tribune* also described the conditions of the city's blacks. He observed a great movement of blacks attempting to reunite families divided by slavery and declared such sights put to a lie slaveholders' claims that blacks had "no enduring affection for their children."[20] Visiting numerous black churches in the company of the military, he witnessed joyous celebrations of the official announcement of emancipation.[21] As conditions became more settled, he noted that the city's black population was playing a large and respectable role in all of Charleston's public demonstrations. In a telling contrast, Redpath observed that when news of General Lee's surrender reached the city in mid-April, blacks turned out to celebrate victory of the Union while whites heralded the restoration of peace.[22]

Redpath also praised the black military units, such as the Fifty-fourth and Fifty-fifth Massachusetts Infantry Regiments, for their disciplined behavior as garrison troops in Charleston after its capture. He noted that "They are well behaved gentlemen, and contrast very favorably with some of the rebel citizens."[23] He added that the federal army commander's public presentation of an award to the Twenty-first United States Colored Troop spurred several dozen of Charleston's blacks to enlist in the unit.[24]

Redpath used his reporting to encourage northern public opinion to demand a thoroughgoing "reconstruction" of the South when the Confederacy was defeated finally. He recommended "throwing the port [of Charleston] and the State open to the Northern enterprise, intelligence, and virtue, which will flock here if the needed encouragement were given."[25] During his travels with Sherman's and Thomas's armies in Georgia and Tennessee, he already had endorsed large-scale land redistribution. Now, after observing the whites of South Carolina, he advised the mass enfranchisement of blacks as the only hope of creating a loyal majority in the state. Redpath argued that — in addition to Yankee emigration, land redistribution, and black suffrage — a free public educational system was essential to the creation of a New South. "Ignorance," he reported, had been the "mental Fort Sumter" of slavery.[26]

Support for freedmen's education was a common theme for wartime abolitionists, but it had an additional personal attachment for Redpath. His father, Ninian Redpath, had operated an academy in his native Scotland before migrating to the United States. Young James had been educated at his father's academy, which had adhered to the Lancasterian method of pupil-teacher monitoring of instruction. Having assisted his father in the classroom as a young man, Redpath hoped to transplant these economical yet effective techniques of basic education to the soil of the South.[27]

Redpath's career took an unexpected turn when, perhaps because of his strong public advocacy of black education, federal military occupation authorities asked him to take charge of creating schools for the newly liberated slaves of Charleston. After Redpath rejected the army's initial plan to open separate public schools for black and white students, the military officials permitted him to take possession of all public school buildings in the city and "to open them on a basis of equality."[28] Later that spring, Colonel Stewart L. Woodford, the military commander of the city, was prepared to turn the school buildings back to their white trustees, but Redpath successfully appealed to General John P. Hatch, commander of the northern district of South Carolina, to leave them under his control.[29]

Redpath reopened five public schools on March 4, 1865, and during the first week enrolled over 1,500, "all white, black, and yellow students, alike."[30] Eighty percent of the initial enrollees were black, however, because the former teachers at those schools encouraged white parents to keep their children at home. On the day the schools reopened, most white pupils were from the city's immigrant community.[31]

Because of "considerable opposition" from native whites, Redpath had to stop short of the total integration of the public schools. He reported to northern friends that "I am obliged to have separate rooms, and white teachers for the white children, — but all our friends here regard it as a great victory in getting the two classes into the same building."[32] He defended his limited action as "a great step toward destroying the prejudice against the colored people. All the colored people are delighted at this arrangement, — or rather they are in ecstacy [sic] about it."[33]

The initial rush of blacks to the schools surprised even Redpath. At the end of March, he reported to one freedmen's aid group that "the colored people are a unit in favor of learning at once at all together. Everybody from six to sixty is already out, or ready to turn out as soon as I can handle them."[34] A persistent problem for the schools that spring, however, was the rapid turnover of black students as many moved through the city with their parents on the way to the Sea Islands or other destinations.[35]

By May, Redpath had more than 100 instructors at work. Of them, 30 were from the North, 25 were southern blacks, and 45 were southern whites.[36] Redpath voiced displeasure at many of the latter two groups and actively recruited replacements from the North. Aided by his assistant Kane O'Donnell, another former northern newspaper reporter, Redpath supervised nine schools with a total enrollment of nearly 4,000 students of both races.[37]

Three northern philanthropic societies paid the salaries of Redpath's teachers: the National Freedmen's Aid Association, the New England Freedmen's Aid Society, and the American Missionary

Association. According to one local observer, Redpath's "sagacity and firmness" brought about cooperation among the freedmen's groups, rather than the competition that flared in many other southern states.[38]

To supplement the regular school program, Redpath organized evening classes for adults. By the end of April, over 500 students, mostly blacks, attended these sessions in basic literacy, which were taught by army officers and local free blacks as well as Redpath's regular cadre of teachers.[39] In addition, Redpath soon created a "normal school" to train older local blacks to be teachers.[40]

The northern teachers recruited for the Charleston schools gave tribute to Redpath's labors. A teacher paid by the New England Freedmen's Aid Society reported that "Mr. R. has done all in his power to make our situation pleasant. I think he is doing a great work here, and deserves much praise."[41] Redpath also drew compliments from supporters in the North. The New England Freedmen's Aid Society's monthly magazine applauded him for maintaining "the principle, that the negroes should share equally with the whites in the occupation of the schoolhouses, and in all the benefits of education."[42] A visiting reporter for a Boston newspaper claimed that Redpath and his teachers in just four months had created the most effective freedmen's schools in the entire South, "literally bringing order out of chaos."[43]

Throughout Redpath's tenure as superintendent, black and white students continued to attend the same school buildings but in separate classrooms. At the largest school on Morris Street, black and white pupils had their classrooms on separate floors but played together in the schoolyard during recess.[44] One observer praised Redpath's efforts to integrate the Charleston school system: "The successful working of the schools, and the harmony with which white and colored teachers work together in the same schools, will be a powerful aid in bringing about a feeling of social harmony in this community, and a disposition to acknowledge the great principle of political equality."[45] A scandalized native white teacher, however, complained that "The place is now an African Heaven, Redpath, a John Brown desiple [sic] has all the Schools open and the negro and whites Pell Mell altogether, his zeal in behalf of this race is remarkable a low ill bread [sic] person both in manners and appearance."[46]

Redpath defended the important role of the public schools, especially the night schools for adults, in the reconstruction of the South. He traced the political dominance of the South by the former slaveowning aristocracy to "the enslavement of the poor blacks, and the ignorance of the poor whites. By educating everybody we will take care to prevent a war of races, which the old ignoblesse would bring about, if they dared and could, by prohibiting Free Schools for all."[47]

Nevertheless, Redpath founded other institutions in addition to schools to assist the freedmen. Receiving permission from military authorities to start an orphanage for black infants, Redpath repaired a damaged dwelling and named the new institution the "Col. Shaw Orphan House." Possibly because of the well-selected name, General Hatch enthusiastically supported the project and ordered it supplied with military rations.[48] Perhaps the most significant organization that Redpath helped create for the Charleston black community was its own "home guard" battalion. Hatch authorized Redpath to found the unit and to select its original white officer corps. Then, when the newly appointed military commander of the city, Colonel William Gurney, responded to local white protests against arming blacks by trying to disband the battalion of black home guards, Redpath's appeals to Hatch saved the symbolically important organization.[49]

In May 1865, Redpath gained national attention by sponsoring public ceremonies that were widely copied and evolved into today's Memorial Day observances.[50] At the city race course, which had been the site of a prison for captured Union army soldiers, Redpath held services where over 250 deceased prisoners had been buried in four long, unmarked trenches.[51]

After he had visited the site in late March, he related to *Tribune* readers his outrage at the accounts he heard of the prisoners' mistreatment and at the "disrespect shown to the resting place of the bodies of our martyrs."[52] Redpath immediately founded a committee to arrange for enclosing the graveyard and erecting a suitable monument. Two newly formed local black groups, the "Friends of the Martyrs" and the "Patriotic Association of Colored Men," soon built and painted a fence for the graveyard with materials donated by the U.S. Army.[53]

On May 1, Redpath and his wife, Mary, who had joined him from Massachusetts, arranged a public dedication of the gravesite. Over 10,000 persons, mostly blacks, attended. Redpath led a two-mile procession from the downtown area to the race course. First in the line of marchers were nearly 3,000 students from the public schools, followed by members of several newly formed Charleston black associations, and then the general citizenry. One of the northern teachers, Elizabeth G. Rice, later recalled that each "person in passing threw flowers, which had been brought for the purpose of decorating the burial-ground, till it was entirely covered."[54]

While standing around the graves, the students sang patriotic songs such as "John Brown's Body," which they learned at Redpath's schools. After an invocation, the assembly elected Redpath chair of the proceedings, and he made a short address that was followed by those of several military officers and a number of local blacks. A brigade composed of three black regiments, including the Fifty-fourth Massachusetts, concluded the official services by marching past the graves of their fallen comrades; Redpath then led the crowd to a nearby site for a picnic, which lasted until dusk.[55]

The prominent role of blacks in this first Memorial Day celebration was typical of Redpath's initiative in encouraging them to participate in Charleston's civic events. When a delegation of leading antislavery northerners — including William Lloyd Garrison, Henry Ward Beecher, Theodore Tilton, Henry Wilson, and William D. Kelley — visited the city in mid-April, Redpath brought more than 2,000 of his students to a mass outdoor public reception. With the city seemingly aswarm with abolitionists, he playfully told his *Tribune* readers, "Babylon has fallen!"[56]

Redpath's unswerving support for the right of blacks to attend and participate in political meetings ultimately led him into heated clashes with local whites and with some Union army officers. The most serious of these occurred on May 11, 1865, when Colonel William Gurney, the military commander of the city, gave permission for a public meeting to be held at Hibernian Hall to discuss the reorganization of the South Carolina state government. A dispute later arose about whether Gurney had instructed that black citizens should be excluded from the meeting. In any case, the meeting's white organizers expelled those blacks in attendance from the hall. The only Union army officer in the building, a Lieutenant A. S. Bodine in command of a small military detachment sent to guard the meeting, echoed that order to the blacks. Redpath arrived a few minutes later and led the blacks, now congregated outside, back into Hibernian Hall. He confronted Bodine and demanded that blacks be allowed to participate in the meeting. While the officer equivocated, most of the whites abandoned the idea of holding the meeting and departed. Ultimately, the 40 remaining whites and 150 blacks passed a series of resolutions, pledging loyalty to the Union.[57]

The complaints of Redpath and others ultimately forced the military to conduct a court-martial of Lieutenant Bodine, who was an officer of the One Hundred Twenty-seventh New York Volunteers, the regiment formerly commanded by Gurney. Redpath was the principal witness against Bodine, and the military court found the officer guilty of disobeying his orders from Gurney to permit a public meeting open to all citizens. Bodine's punishment, however, was only a written reprimand that military authorities subsequently withdrew.[58] Redpath later reported that Gurney and most of the white units under his command actively harassed public meetings of blacks. He also complained that Gurney hesitated to punish members of white units for assaults on black soldiers in the city's garrison.[59]

The long hours of the superintendent's post began to tell on Redpath. At the close of the regular school year, he and his wife decided to escape the summer's heat by returning to Massachusetts for what was announced as a "vacation."[60]

Shortly after the Redpaths sailed for Boston in mid-June, an assemblage of students, teachers, and blacks was held in Charleston's Zion

Church to pass resolutions of praise for Redpath. It unanimously resolved "that the loyal citizens of Charleston, owe a debt of gratitude to him, for his labors of love and mercy in their behalf, which language cannot express, and which gold and silver can never cancel." The meeting also declared that Redpath's "return to us again will be hailed by us all as an omen of future good, and a guaranty for the perpetuation of the exalted privileges which we have enjoyed at his hands."[61] A contradictory review of Redpath's performance came from the office of the city military commander Gurney, who issued an order on June 30 relieving Redpath and O'Donnell of their responsibilities for Charleston's schools.[62]

All indications are that Redpath planned to return to Charleston in time for the reopening of public schools on October 1. In his absence, however, the Bureau of Refugees, Freedmen, and Abandoned Lands, better known as the Freedmen's Bureau, was moving to give centralized direction to the myriad efforts to educate the former slaves. After less than a month at his home at the Boston suburb of Malden, Redpath wrote the head of the Bureau, Major General O. O. Howard, to request an official commission. Howard replied that Secretary of War Edwin Stanton refused to allow him to commission civilians for Bureau posts as long as there were so many military men seeking them. Nonetheless, Howard promised to seek some other way to reemploy Redpath in South Carolina. Furthermore, Howard promised that if the Bureau's commander in that state, General Rufus Saxton, would fund a post for Redpath, he would approve that action.[63]

In the next few months, Redpath inadvertently undercut his chances of returning as head of Charleston's schools through both his private correspondence and his public writing. On July 21, Redpath wrote Howard to complain about reports that the white soldiers in the One Hundred Twenty-seventh New York Infantry Regiment continued to mistreat Charleston's freedmen. Redpath noted that he had complained of such behavior to local military authorities before he had sailed north, claiming that he had threatened to seek the court-martial of General Gurney, if necessary, to force him to discipline white troops for such actions. Redpath recommended the replacement of Gurney and several other Union commanders he deemed "unfriendly to the only loyalists whom S.C. has produced."[64]

Also in July, Redpath used the northern press to praise Union officers who had been supportive in Charleston and to expose those who had not. To the Boston *Liberator*'s readers, Redpath declared Saxton "as radical as any of us [abolitionists] in theory, and none of us are more brotherly in our intercourse with the freedmen than he."[65] In the same issue, he went public with his complaints about General Gurney and noted that officers who had shown friendship for the freedmen, such as Colonel Edward N. Hallowell of the Fifty-fourth Massachusetts Infantry Regiment, had been passed over for promotion. For the New

York *National Anti-Slavery Standard*, Redpath similarly wrote that General Hatch had been of major assistance to him in integrating Charleston's schools and protecting the rights of freedmen; however, a week later, Redpath wrote a second letter to complain that he had just learned that Hatch had denied Charleston blacks the right to participate in celebrations of the Fourth of July.[66]

The following month, Redpath raised his sights to attack the first steps by President Andrew Johnson to reconstruct the former Confederate states. While a reporter covering the war in Tennessee, he had criticized Johnson, as head of the state's military government, for lacking respect for the rights of freedmen. Redpath now warned Johnson against too hastily pardoning planters for their treasonous secession.[67]

As time approached for the reopening of schools, Redpath again corresponded with Freedmen's Bureau officials. On September 5, Redpath wrote Howard that although the New England Freedmen's Aid Society had elected him their secretary, he preferred to return to Charleston in the position of superintendent for schools of South Carolina and Georgia. He claimed that the commander of that military district, General Saxton, was "anxious that I shd [*sic*] go." Redpath also noted that the Bureau was paying the salary of a civilian as superintendent of schools for North Carolina and inquired why the same arrangement could not be made for him.[68]

Howard replied that he had decided to leave the selection of superintendents to district commanders and that Saxton could pay him if he chose. Howard also warned Redpath that financial problems in the Bureau meant that "in most cases the Supts. will have to be military men, for the present, at any rate."[69] Perhaps sensing Howard's misgivings about him, Redpath then changed tack. Although again noting that the Bureau was paying a civilian $1,500 a year as school superintendent in North Carolina, he expressed his willingness to accept any salary Howard or Saxton deemed appropriate. He also requested a pass for military transportation to Charleston, probably hoping to confer in person with Saxton. An aide to Howard wrote back that a pass was out of the question until Saxton had sent an endorsement for Redpath's appointment. On the same day, Howard advised Saxton to reject Redpath's entreaties because "from the difficulties we are now contending with, and from what I know of him, I think him the worst man to put in as Superintendent of schools."[70]

Although cryptic, Howard's advice was clear to Saxton, and Redpath's appointment to any position in the South Carolina schools was effectively blocked. Howard and Saxton ultimately did select a civilian for the South Carolina school superintendency, the less controversial Pennsylvania Quaker Rufus Tomlinson, a veteran teacher of blacks on the Sea Islands.[71]

A possible explanation for Howard's action toward Redpath comes from his modern biographer, William S. McFeely. In the summer of 1865, Howard was struggling to avoid confrontation between his young Bureau and the southern-born President Andrew Johnson. At that time, Howard hoped that Johnson might endorse the Bureau's plan to redistribute farmland from the ex-Confederate planters to the freedmen. Howard recognized that if Redpath was given an official position with the Bureau, his racial views and practices would inevitably irritate the president; therefore, Howard used Congress's failure to appropriate money for nonmilitary agents to exclude Redpath and other "radical" civilians, such as Abraham Lincoln's son Robert, from his agency.[72]

Redpath's banishment ended many of his practices that had offended local racial mores. As early as November 1865, a reporter from the *Nation* found the student body of the Freedmen's Bureau schools in Charleston all black, except for the children of several white teachers.[73] Moreover, military sanction for black participation in public political meetings remained a matter of contention between African Americans and various district commanders appointed by President Johnson until the beginning of Congressional Reconstruction in 1867.[74]

Redpath's experiences in South Carolina were an early sign of the serious social and political struggle over the status of the newly freed slaves that would dominate the postwar scene. The efforts of prewar abolitionists such as Redpath to win equal rights for African Americans very quickly ran into the hostility of white southerners, the indifference of many white northerners, and the inadequate educational preparation of most slaves.

The refusal by the Freedmen's Bureau to employ Redpath once again left him in a difficult financial situation. In what became a life-long pattern, he attempted to solve the problem by returning to journalism. To General O. O. Howard's chagrin, Redpath returned to South Carolina before the end of 1865 as a reporter for the New York *Tribune*.[75] Redpath's abolitionist ally Sydney Gay, supported by his employer, Horace Greeley, had rapidly soured on Andrew Johnson's policies and now sought eyewitness evidence of the need for a more thoroughgoing Reconstruction policy.[76] Redpath's new series of dispatches detailed the actions by South Carolina blacks to win equal political and civil rights, denounced the local white "Chivalry" for resisting such moves, and excoriated as "Legree[s] in Uniform" the numerous occupation officials who sided with the ex-Confederates.[77] In particular, Redpath described the efforts of Freedmen's Bureau officers to coerce the freed blacks back onto the plantations to labor in conditions not far removed from servitude. After his return to South Carolina, Redpath concluded, "I have lately more than questioned the utility of the Freedmen's Bureau under its present imperfect and inadequate organization. I have now no doubt that, feeble as it is and almost penniless, it is the only protection that the negro can have, in this unholy state."[78]

Perhaps Redpath's softened attitude toward the Bureau was a product of visits to its schools in Virginia and South Carolina. Although he found no more integrated schools, he was cheered by the increasing number of black teachers and even principals. The education of the freedmen, Redpath believed, would hasten the day "when capacity not color, experience not the epidermis, the sharpness of the faculty not the sharpness of the nasal feature, shall determine position."[79]

Back in his suburban Boston home by spring 1866, Redpath wrote articles condemning the accommodation of the Johnson administration to the racism of southern whites. He soon resumed his criticism of the failure of the army and the Freedmen's Bureau to protect the freedmen adequately, concluding that "there are several States in which it would be better for all parties, black and white, for the Bureau to be abolished." He especially blamed Howard for not resisting Johnson's systematic replacement of Rufus Saxton and other officers sympathetic to the freedmen with more conservative ones, concluding that "Johnson has a certain brutal courage which entitles him to respect; but Howard seems willing to lose his character rather than his place."[80] During this period, Redpath also produced a long series of semischolarly articles detailing the history of Brazilian slavery and implicitly calling for its abolition.[81]

Already a friend of Senator Charles Sumner and Governor John A. Andrew, Redpath moved further into Massachusetts Radical Republican circles by fostering a close association with former Union army general Ben Butler. Redpath traveled as a reporter with Butler as the politician shadowed and harassed Andrew Johnson's famous "Swing around the Circle."[82] Redpath wrote a series of articles seconding Butler's calls for the impeachment of Johnson on at least 13 counts of unconstitutional actions. In the same articles, Redpath called for "another forward movement" by "the Radical skirmish line" to "abolish the Regular Army, the entrenched Supreme Court, and the Senate of the United States." He claimed that "as long as these three standing menaces to popular rule, these three fortified garrisons of aristocracy, are permitted to exist, we will constantly be called on to waste our time and strength and opportunities in doing battle against them."[83]

When Butler won a seat in Congress in fall 1866, he had Redpath named clerk for a special congressional committee formed to investigate Lincoln's assassination. Although this "smelling committee" searched for evidence to tie Johnson to Lincoln's murder,[84] it failed to turn up any that was sufficiently incriminating and never issued a report. It did, however, add to the intense acrimony in the capital that finally led to the unsuccessful impeachment drive.[85] Little information has survived about the personal relationship between Redpath and

Butler, but the journalist always tried to find ways to support his financial obligations and his political principles simultaneously.

In mid-1867, Redpath returned to Boston as a feature writer for the Boston *Daily Advertiser*. He rarely wrote on political subjects, preferring instead travel, photography, literature, and the stage.[86] These articles proved an important bridge to the next phase of Redpath's career.

In 1869, with financial backing from veteran reformer Samuel Gridley Howe, Redpath launched the first professional booking agency for lecturers. By 1871 the Redpath Lyceum Bureau had offices in Boston, New York, and Chicago and provided its services to hundreds of lecture halls and lyceum committees across the nation. Among his earliest clients, Redpath numbered Ralph Waldo Emerson, Frederick Douglass, Wendell Phillips, Charles Sumner, and Susan B. Anthony. He later added magicians, musicians, and, especially, humorists, including Mark Twain, Josh Billings, and David R. Locke ("Petroleum V. Nasby"). Further expanding the forms of entertainment he offered, Redpath personally organized operatic and dramatic companies and sent them on successful national tours. Along with his close friend Phineas T. Barnum, Redpath introduced the figure of the "impresario" into American popular culture.[87]

In October 1875, Redpath sold his lyceum bureau to two longtime business associates, James Pond and George Hathaway. His reasons remain unclear, but the simultaneous dissolution of his nearly 20-year marriage might have prompted him to relocate from Boston.[88] Soon after, Redpath returned to the political arena to advocate reinvigorated federal efforts to protect southern freedmen's rights. In the early 1870s, many surviving abolitionists had abandoned an aggressive Reconstruction policy and joined the Liberal movement, which stressed sectional reconciliation over freedmen's rights. In the middle of the decade, northern visitors to the South, including former abolitionists and free soilers such as James Freeman Clarke, William Dean Howells, and James S. Pike, published reports that the freedmen lacked the abilities to sustain honest governments in that region.[89] Redpath knew the importance of northern public support to the survival of Reconstruction. In articles for the New York *Independent*, he warned that the doctrine of state sovereignty had been resurrected by ex-Confederates and their doughface allies, who now were plotting to win the fall 1875 election by deceiving and dividing the North while simultaneously extinguishing black suffrage in the South.[90]

In spring and early summer 1876, Redpath served as the secretary of a joint congressional committee Massachusetts Senator George S. Boutwell headed to investigate intimidation and violence in the recent state elections in Mississippi. Redpath travelled with the committee to various southern states before returning to Washington for further public hearings. Redpath subsequently published a controversial series of articles for the New York *Times* in which he detailed and denounced in strong language the campaign of violence the Mississippi Democrats had employed the previous year to keep blacks away from the polls.[91]

A concurrently published series of letters by Redpath to the New York *Independent* reveals that the investigation of conditions in the Deep South had produced grave despair in Redpath about the future of Reconstruction. His first letter repeated criticism of the southern Democrats' campaign of political terror, but it also blamed southern blacks and their northern allies for the deplorable conditions. Redpath presented a bleak account of government in Mississippi: "our reconstruction policy is a failure; . . . the illiterate Negro of Mississippi is as corrupt as the illiterate Irishman of New York; . . . the county governments there were burlesques of republican rule." The North, according to Redpath, had failed the freedmen: "We ought never to have given the Negro a vote, or we ought to have forced him to learn to read and built a school for him in every township. He has shown that he is not fit to rule in Mississippi." Redpath expressed grave doubts about further use of the federal military to keep blacks in power unless the blacks were quickly elevated by compulsory education: "If we give complete military protection to the Negroes in all elections in South Carolina, Mississippi, and Louisiana where there is a large black majority we shall establish a system of government which no white race on the face of the earth either ought to endure or will endure." Acknowledging that his diagnosis would not please northern friends of the blacks, Redpath, nonetheless, argued that "We must do something. Masterly inactivity means dastardly surrender. To begin with, we must comprehend the situation, and, above all, we must not lie about it."[92]

Redpath's analysis appeared so bleak that the editors of the *Independent* declared that he had "no hope for the Negro voter."[93] This led Redpath to compose a second letter on the "Lessons of Mississippi" for that paper, in which he declared,

Sentimental abolitionism was well enough in its day; but Mississippi owes its present condition as much to sentimental abolitionists as to fiendish Negro-haters. The blacks were ruined as good citizens by the chronic prattle about their rights, and they were never roused to a noble manhood by instructions to their duties.

Redpath retained hope in the power of education: "It is not by denunciations even of the Mississippi assassins, but by earnest and vigilant efforts to educate [the black man], that we shall ever be proud of him as a Republican citizen."[94] To Redpath's chagrin, within weeks, Democrats were quoting his *Independent* articles as justifications for the repression in the South.[95]

Despite his evident despair, Redpath joined in one last battle to preserve southern Reconstruction. During the presidential election in fall

1876, Redpath moved to western North Carolina to campaign on behalf of the Republican Party. In North Carolina, white former Unionists in the state's western mountains and blacks in the eastern counties stood by the Republican banner. Desperation forced these groups to work together, according to Redpath, because "the election of Tilden does not mean reform, but expulsion, as far as they shall be affected by such a disaster."[96] However, Redpath labored in vain, because the Democrats carried the state and national elections in North Carolina by comfortable margins.

Redpath then returned to Washington, D.C., and produced a second series of articles for the New York *Times*, documenting the unfair and coercive tactics that the Democratic Party had used to sweep the South. Dubbing this the "New Rebellion," Redpath claimed that the Democratic "victory" in the presidential election in Mississippi, Louisiana, and Georgia "was characterized by fraud and terrorism as universal and unblushing as the infamous election of 1875."[97] In his articles, Redpath called for an investigation to invalidate these election returns: "Order can come only from justice; prosperity can come only from security; and we must put down the banditti in order to bring order and justice [to the South]. Let her banditti vote be thrown out."[98] He also complained that the only signs of "military interference" in this election had been the endorsement of the Democratic ticket by many high-ranking army officers.[99] Redpath's reports were cheering to old abolitionists, such as Garrison, who were striving to rally northern support for the validity of the surviving Republican state governments in the South.[100]

In January 1877, Redpath accompanied a U.S. Senate committee to South Carolina, where it held hearings on the recent election. He returned to Washington after three weeks without a doubt that the election had been stolen by "the South Carolina Rifle-club Democracy."[101] Surprisingly, however, his reports on these hearings for the New York *Times* did not call for federal authorities to use force to sustain the Republican administration of Republican Governor Daniel H. Chamberlain against the superior armed force of its Democratic rivals. Privately, Redpath expressed growing despair about the viability of the few remaining southern Republican state governments in a letter to Whitelaw Reid, editor of the New York *Tribune*. In that letter, Redpath proposed to travel to New Orleans to gather evidence about frauds in Louisiana's 1876 election. Rather than attempt to salvage the outcome of that state's election for the Republicans, Redpath told Reid that he hoped his reports would "advise the antislavery element in the North to acquiesce in white supremacy in Louisiana *for the sake of the blacks.*"[102]

The presidential election of 1876 ultimately was resolved by an Electoral Commission that saved the White House for the Republicans. By a strict partisan vote, the commission awarded the disputed electoral votes of South Carolina, Louisiana, and Florida to the Republican candidate. The new president, Rutherford B. Hayes of Ohio, already had discreetly assured the South that federal troops no longer would be used to sustain the remaining Republican state governments there. Holding a futile belief that a conciliatory policy would win over large numbers of former Whigs to the Republican Party, Hayes extracted no solid assurances from southern whites that the rights of African Americans in the region would be respected.[103]

After the Electoral Commission ruled for Hayes, Redpath answered a letter from Merrimon Howard, a deposed Mississippi Republican sheriff, also sending the reply to numerous newspapers. Despite the despair he had voiced over the ongoing viability of Reconstruction, Redpath denounced the "New Southern Policy" of Hayes and the Republican leadership. Considering the tenor of the new administration and the uneven balance of forces in the South, he advised Howard and other southern blacks to make the best available terms with their new Democratic political masters. Redpath recommended that the remaining Republican governors in South Carolina and Louisiana turn over authority to the Democrats, arguing, "It is better for the sake of the blacks that the surrender should be made quietly and quickly."[104]

For the final collapse of southern Reconstruction, Redpath blamed the new president's capitulation to the Democrats.

One word, constantly in Hayes' mouth, reveals his character. That word is — Policy. That word is the shibboleth of his motley horde of scamp-followers. Once the inspiration of the Republicans was — Principle. The party was a warrior of the Lord then with a light from God's Throne on its forehead. As far as Hayes represents it, the party, now, is a leprous lazarus, whining for the votes that fall from the Southern Democratic table.[105]

Redpath acknowledged the need for some compromise with responsible Democrats. He did not criticize Hayes's appointment of southern Democrat David M. Key to his cabinet but asked why neither native southern white Republicans nor black Republicans, such as Frederick Douglass, were included as well. Redpath argued:

No man opposes conciliation. Every decent man desires it. That is Part the First of Hayes' *Policy*. But Part the Second is Surrender. It means the acquiescence of the National Government in the rule of the majority by the minority; because that minority of citizens has a majority of property, intelligence and military power. . . . Republicanism means not the rule of respectability but the rule of the majority; and Hayes' Gulf State policy is the suicide of republicanism. . . . Hayes says, or is reported to have said, that "if the rebels do not act in good faith he will soon change his policy." This is boy's talk, or worse. How *can* he change his policy after he yields his power?[106]

Redpath concluded his letter to Howard with thoughts about future political action.

For myself, being a white man, and a Northern Man, I propose to remain in the Republican party to do my part to purge it from the thieves on the one hand and the pedagogues on the other hand who now infest it; but if I were a negro and in the South, I should join the democratic party at once and vote for its candidates whenever they were reputable men. Whenever they were bandits I should refuse to vote at all.[107]

Redpath's advice contained elements of the compromise Booker T. Washington would advocate at the end of the century:

Pay less attention to politics and seek power through business. . . . Cease to array yourselves against the whites in politics, but, at the same time quietly and everywhere and always insist on the right of securing an education for your children. Securing that right, your children will secure all others, by and bye.[108]

In his unabating faith in education, Redpath remained a true son of his schoolmaster father.

Publishing his letter destroyed whatever opportunities Redpath might have had for preferment from the new Republican administration. In fact, office seekers wrote to Hayes denouncing Redpath's "gross and uncalled for attack" on the president and enclosing their own published rebuttals. One southerner wrote the new president that Redpath was "one of the original Exeter Hall agents of Abolitionism sent to this country in the British East-India interests, to foment fratricidal strife, and to destroy the organised system of labour in the Southern states then successfully applied to the production of rivalling staples to those of the East Indies."[109]

In 1877 Redpath joined a small band of similar-minded veteran abolitionists, including Wendell Phillips and William Lloyd Garrison, in denouncing the Republican Party's leadership for abandoning the freedmen, but little unity existed among the steadily dwindling ranks of former radical emancipationists, though many eventually came to Redpath's position that economic and educational assistance, rather than political or military intervention, would best serve the freedmen's long-range elevation to genuine equality.[110]

In a sense, the Howard letter also marked Redpath's abandonment of the freedmen. In his remaining 14 years, he shifted his journalistic and reformist efforts to other causes, such as Irish land reform, the rights of organized labor, and Henry George's "Single Tax" crusade. In the last years of his life, Redpath even developed a warm friendship with Jefferson Davis, whom he served as a ghostwriter, and called on other northerners to give up their antagonism to the ex-Confederates.

Redpath's journey from champion of John Brown in the 1850s to associate of Jefferson Davis in the 1890s is final evidence that witnessing the failure of Reconstruction had greatly transformed the vision of this aging exabolitionist.

NOTES

1. James Redpath to M[errimon] Howard, 14 April 1877, Published Circular Letter, Rutherford B. Hayes Papers (Rutherford B. Hayes Presidential Center).

2. Ibid.

3. James M. McPherson, *The Abolitionist Legacy: From Reconstruction to the NAACP* (Princeton, 1975), 6–10, 112–15, 391–92.

4. James Redpath, *The Roving Editor; or, Talks with Slaves in the Southern States* (New York, 1859), 3.

5. Boston *Liberator*, 4, 11 August, 1, 8 September 1854; *National Anti-Slavery Standard*, 14, 21, 28 October, 11, 25 November, 2, 9, 16, 23 December 1854, 27 January, 10 February, 17, 31 March, 7, 14 April 1855; Redpath, *Roving Editor*, passim.

6. Jim A. Hart, "James Redpath, Missouri Correspondent," *Missouri Historical Review* 57 (1962): 70–78; Bernard A. Weisberger, "The Newspaper Reporter and the Kansas Imbroglio," *Mississippi Valley Historical Review* 36 (1950): 633–56; Jeffrey Rossbach, *Ambivalent Conspirators: John Brown, the Secret Six, and a Theory of Slave Violence* (Philadelphia, 1982), 71, 86, 175–78, 226; James Redpath, *The Public Life of Capt. John Brown* (Boston, 1860).

7. John R. McKivigan, "James Redpath and Black Reaction to the Haitian Emigration Bureau," *Mid-America: An Historical Review* 69 (1987): 139–53; Willis D. Boyd, "James Redpath and American Negro Colonization in Haiti," *The Americas* 12 (1955): 169–82.

8. Madeleine B. Stern, "James Redpath and His 'Books for the Times,'" *Publisher's Weekly* 148 (1945): 2649–53; Madeleine B. Stern, *Publishers for Mass Entertainment in Nineteenth Century America* (Boston, 1980), 261–66; David Kaser, *Books and Libraries in Camp and Battle: The Civil War Experience* (Westport, 1984); Redpath to Louisa May Alcott, 13 August 1864, Louisa May Alcott Papers (University of Virginia Library).

9. New York *Tribune*, 22 February 1865; Charles Carleton Coffin, *The Boys of 1861; or, Four Years of Fighting* (Boston, 1901), 482–507; J. Cutler Andrews, *The North Reports the Civil War* (Pittsburgh, 1955), 621–24.

10. Redpath to Sydney Howard Gay, 6 March 1865, Sydney Howard Gay Papers (Columbia University Library).

11. New York *Tribune*, 2 March 1864; also reprinted in *National Anti-Slavery Standard*, 11 March 1864.

12. New York *Tribune*, 2 March 1865.

13. Boston *Daily Journal*, 14 November 1861; see also 3 November 1864.

14. Richmond *Enquirer*, n.d., as quoted in New York *Tribune*, 16 March 1865.

15. Gay to Redpath, 6 March 1865 and 25 February 1866; Redpath to Gay, ca. July 1865, June 1866, Gay Papers; Richard Kluger, *The Paper: The Life and Death of the New York Herald Tribune* (New York, 1986), 97–120; John R. McKivigan, "John Ball, Jr., Alias the Roving Editor, Alias James Redpath," *Manuscripts* 40 (1988): 309–10.

16. New York *Tribune*, 2 March 1865; see also Dale Rosengarten et al., *Between the Tracks: Charleston's East Side during the Nineteenth Century* (Charleston, 1987), 141.

17. New York *Tribune*, 11, 28 March 1865; see also 18 March, 18 April 1865.

18. New York *Tribune*, 13 May 1865.

19. As quoted in Francis Butler Simkins and Robert Hillard Woody, *South Carolina during Reconstruction* (Chapel Hill, 1932), 26–28.

20. New York *Tribune*, 2 March 1865.

21. Redpath recalled being allowed to make the announcement at one such service and being "suddenly hugged by one old colored lady." New York *Tribune*, 10 March 1865.

22. New York *Tribune*, 18 April 1865; see also 4 April 1865.

23. New York *Tribune*, 2 March 1865; see also 10 March 1865, *National Anti-Slavery Standard*, 11 March 1865. Redpath received more information about the performance of the Fifty-fifth Massachusetts regiment from one of its lieutenants, George Thompson Garrison, a son of the abolitionist William Lloyd Garrison. Francis J. Garrison and Wendell P. Garrison, *William Lloyd Garrison, 1805–1879* (5 vol., 1879; New York, 1960), 4:134.

24. New York *Tribune*, 11 March 1865.

25. New York *Tribune*, 28 March 1865; also reprinted in *National Anti-Slavery Standard*, 1 April 1865.

26. New York *Tribune*, 2 March 1865; also reprinted in *National Anti-Slavery Standard*, 11 March 1865.

27. G. F. Bartle, "The Agents and Inspectors of the British and Foreign School Society, 1826–1884," *Bulletin of the History of Education Society* 19 (1984): 19–30; Janet D. Crowe, "The Development of Education in Berwick upon Tweed to 1902" (M.E. thesis, University of Durham, 1969), 419–26, 543–46.

28. Redpath to the Editor of the *Standard*, 12 July 1865, in *National Anti-Slavery Standard*, 22 July 1865; see also Redpath to Mrs. Pillsbury, 9 March 1865, in (Boston) *The Freedmen's Record* 1 (1865): 61.

29. Redpath to the Editor of the *Standard*, 12 July 1865, in *National Anti-Slavery Standard*, 22 July 1865.

30. Redpath to Mrs. Pillsbury, 9 March 1865, in (Boston) *The Freedmen's Record* 1 (1865): 61.

31. New York *Tribune*, 18 March 1865.

32. Ibid.

33. Ibid.

34. (Boston) *The Freedmen's Record* 1 (1865): 73.

35. Charleston *Daily Courier*, 17 May 1865.

36. Ibid., 6 April 1865; Robert C. Morris, *Reading, 'Riting, and Reconstruction: The Education of Freedmen in the South, 1861–1870* (Chicago, 1976), 131.

37. Charleston *Daily Courier*, 2 March, 6 April, 17 May 1865; New York *Times*, 16 April 1865; New York *Tribune*, 16 April 1865; Walter J. Fraser, Jr., *Charleston! Charleston!: The History of a Southern City* (Columbia, 1991), 272; Martin Abbott, "The Freedmen's Bureau and Negro Schooling in South Carolina," *South Carolina Historical Magazine* 57 (1956): 68.

38. Charleston *Daily Courier*, 6 April 1865; W. F. Allen to ?, 23 May 1865, as reprinted in (Boston) *The Freedmen's Record* 1 (1865): 112–13; Charleston *Daily Courier*, 17 May 1865.

39. Redpath to William Gurney, 30 April 1865, in Charleston *Daily Courier*, 17 May 1865; (Boston) *The Freedmen's Record* 1 (1865): 97; *National Anti-Slavery Standard*, 29 July 1865.

40. W. F. Allen to ?, 23 May 1865, in (Boston) *The Freedmen's Record* 1 (1865): 112–13.

41. "M. C." to ?, 25 April 1865, reprinted in (Boston) *The Freedmen's Record* 1 (1865): 99–100.

42. (Boston) *The Freedmen's Record* 1 (1865): 70–71.

43. "Mazeel" to the Editors of the Boston *Daily Advertiser*, 30 June 1865, in Boston *Daily Advertiser*, 7 July 1865.

44. Joel Williamson, *After Slavery: The Negro in South Carolina during Reconstruction, 1861–1877* (Chapel Hill, 1965), 216.

45. William F. Allen to Editor of the *Freedmen's Record*, May 1865, as quoted in Morris, *Reading, 'Riting, and Reconstruction*, 131.

46. T. P. O'Neale to R. H. Gourdin, 3 June 1865, R. H. Gourdin Papers, as quoted in Williamson, *After Slavery*, 216.

47. Redpath to William Gurney, 30 April 1865, in Charleston *Daily Courier*, 17 May 1865.

48. New York *Tribune*, 8 April 1865; (Boston) *The Freedmen's Record* 1 (1865): 97; Redpath to the Editor of the *Standard*, in *National Anti-Slavery Standard*, 22 July 1865.

49. Redpath to the Editor of the *Standard*, 12, 20 July 1865, in *National Anti-Slavery Standard*, 22, 29 July 1865.

50. Mary R. Dearing, *Veterans in Politics: The Story of the G.A.R.* (Baton Rouge, 1952), 177; Paul H. Buck, *The Road to Reunion, 1865–1900* (Boston, 1937), 116; Lloyd Lewis, *Myths after Lincoln* (New York, 1941), 304–7; Elizabeth G. Rice, "A Yankee Teacher in the South: An Experience in the Early Days of Reconstruction," *Century Magazine* 62 (1901): 154.

51. Buck, *Road to Reunion*, 116.

52. New York *Tribune*, 8 April 1865.

53. Charleston *Daily Courier*, 2 May 1865; Redpath to the Editor of the *Standard*, in *National Anti-Slavery Standard*, 22 July 1865.

54. Rice, "Yankee Teacher in the South," 154; see also Charleston *Daily Courier*, 2 May 1865; New York *Tribune*, 13 May 1865.

55. Charleston *Daily Courier*, 2 May 1865; New York *Tribune*, 13 May 1865; Fraser, *Charleston! Charleston!*, 273.

56. New York *Tribune*, 20 April 1865; see also 17, 18, 22 April, 22 May 1865.

57. New York *Times*, 22 May 1865; Charleston *Daily Courier*, 8 July 1865.

58. Charleston *Daily Courier*, 8 July 1865.

59. Redpath to Editor of the *Standard*, 20 July 1865, in *National Anti-Slavery Standard*, 29 July 1865.

60. John C. Chavis to James Redpath, 20 June 1865, John C. Chavis Papers (University of South Carolina, Columbia).

61. Charleston *Daily Courier*, 17 June 1865.

62. Charleston *Daily Courier*, 1 July 1865.

63. O. O. Howard to James Redpath, 15 July 1865, O. O. Howard Papers (Bowdoin College Library).

64. James Redpath to O. O. Howard, 21 July 1865, Records of the Bureau for Refugees, Freedmen and Abandoned Lands (hereafter BRFAL) (National Archives).

65. Redpath to William Lloyd Garrison, n.d., published in Boston *Liberator*, 21 July 1865.

66. Redpath to Editor of the *Standard*, 12 July 1865, in *National Anti-Slavery Standard*, 22 July 1865; Redpath to Editor of the *Standard*, 20 July 1865, in *National Anti-Slavery Standard*, 29 July 1865.

67. (New York) *The Nation*, 17 August 1865.

68. Redpath to Howard, 5 September 1865, Howard Papers; see also Redpath to Howard, 15 September 1865, BRFAL.

69. Howard to Redpath, 13 September 1865, Howard Papers.

70. Howard to Rufus Saxton, 15 September 1865, Howard Papers; see also Redpath to Howard, 15, 18 September 1865, BRFAL; Joseph A. Selden to Redpath, 15

September 1865, Howard Papers.

71. Morris, *Reading, 'Riting, and Reconstruction*, 39; William S. McFeely, *Yankee Stepfather: General O. O. Howard and the Freedmen* (New York, 1968), 39; Williamson, *After Slavery*, 211.

72. McFeely, *Howard*, 65, 132; see also Morris, *Reading, 'Riting, and Reconstruction*, 39.

73. (New York) *The Nation*, 21 December 1865, as noted in Williamson, *After Slavery*, 217.

74. Thomas Holt, *Black over White: Negro Political Leadership in South Carolina during Reconstruction* (Urbana, 1977), 10–14.

75. James Redpath to Sydney Howard Gay, [undated] 1865, Gay Papers.

76. Gay to Redpath, 25 July 1866; Kluger, *The Paper*, 121, 124.

77. For examples, see New York *Tribune*, 25 November, 2, 16 December 1865, 20 January 1866; *National Anti-Slavery Standard*, 23 December 1865.

78. New York *Tribune*, 2 December 1865; see also 28 October, 25 November 1865. In these articles, Redpath repeated his earlier calls for confiscation of the lands of ex-Confederates and its distribution to the blacks.

79. New York *Tribune*, 28 October 1865; see also 2 December 1865.

80. Redpath to Editor of the *Standard*, 18 June 1866, in *National Anti-Slavery Standard*, 7 July 1866; see also Redpath to Editor of *The Nation*, 30 March 1867, in (New York) *The Nation*, 4 April 1867; *National Anti-Slavery Standard*, 14 September 1867; New York *Tribune*, 20 January 1866; (New York) *The Nation*, 28 March 1867.

81. New York *Tribune*, 31 March, 21 June 1866; *National Anti-Slavery Standard*, 23, 30 March, 13, 20 April, 11 May, 29 June, 6, 13 July 1867.

82. Boston *Evening Traveller*, 25, 27, 28, 29 September 1866; Charles Lowe to Benjamin F. Butler, 7 June 1865, in *Private and Official Correspondence of Gen. Benjamin F. Butler during the Period of the Civil War* (5 vol., n.p. 1917), 5:629; Hans L. Trefousse, *Ben Butler: The South Called Him BEAST!* (New York, 1974), 186–88; Robert S. Holzman, *Stormy Ben Butler* (New York, 1965), 161–63; Howard P. Nash, Jr., *Stormy Petrel: The Life and Times of General Benjamin F. Butler, 1818–1893* (Rutherford, 1969), 224–29; Murray M. Horowitz, "Ben Butler: The Making of a Radical" (Ph.D. diss., Columbia University, 1955), 306–8.

83. *National Anti-Slavery Standard*, 26 January 1867; see also 10 November 1866, 2 March, 14 September 1867; Boston *Daily Advertiser*, 7 December 1866; New York *Times*, 25 January 1867; (New York) *The Nation*, 28 March, 4 April 1867; Horowitz, "Ben Butler: The Making of a Radical," 308–11.

84. Boston *Daily Advertiser*, 3, 6, 26 November, 4, 7 December 1866, 9 July 1867; *National Anti-Slavery Standard*, 10 November 1866, 20 July 1867; *Congressional Globe*, 1st Sess., 40th Cong., 515–17, 522; Robert Werlich, *"Beast" Butler: The Incredible Career of Major General Benjamin Franklin Butler* (Washington, 1962), 127–28; Nash, *Stormy Petrel*, 231–32; Holzman, *Stormy Ben Butler*, 163–64.

85. David Miller DeWitt, *The Impeachment and Trial of Andrew Johnson* (1903; Madison, 1967), 237–39, 280–81; Lately Johnson, *The First President Johnson: The Three Lives of the Seventeenth President of the United States of America* (New York, 1968), 53–31, 550–51; Trefousse, *Ben Butler*, 191–92.

86. For examples of these articles, see Boston *Daily Advertiser*, 13, 14 February, 16 April, 6, 17, 20 June 1868. An important exception to the apolitical tone of Redpath's writings in this period was a lengthy three-part defense of Charles Sumner's Reconstruction record. *National Anti-Slavery Standard*, 4, 11 April 1868; David Donald, *Charles Sumner and the Rights of Man* (New York, 1970), 301–2.

87. Charles F. Horner, *The Life of James Redpath and the Development of the Modern Lyceum* (New York, 1926), 119–302; J. B. Pond, *Eccentricities of Genius:*

Memories of Famous Men and Women of the Platform and Stage (London, 1901), 533ff.

88. Strong circumstantial evidence exists that Redpath's marriage collapsed on account of a possible affair with the young southern-born novelist Sherwood Bonner. Hubert Horton McAlexander, *The Prodigal Daughter: A Biography of Sherwood Bonner* (Baton Rouge, 1981), 62–72, 79–80, 130–31, 97, 115–16, 151.

89. Robert F. Durden, *James Shepherd Pike: Republicanism and the American Negro, 1850–1882* (Durham, 1957), 183–219; Eric Foner, *Reconstruction: America's Unfinished Revolution* (New York, 1988), 524–28; McPherson, *Abolitionist Legacy*, 24–34, 41–42.

90. New York *Independent*, 2, 23 March 1876; McPherson, *Abolitionist Legacy*, 24–34, 41–42.

91. New York *Times*, 3, 8, 27, 31 July, 5, 8, 14, 21, 28 August, 1, 2, 11 September 1876; *Mississippi in 1875, Report of the Select Committee to Inquire into the Mississippi Election of 1875*, Senate Reports, #527, 44th Cong., 1st Sess. (2 vol., Washington, 1876); James Wilford Garner, *Reconstruction in Mississippi* (1901; Baton Rouge, 1968), 408–10; McPherson, *Abolitionist Legacy*, 51.

92. New York *Independent*, 3 August 1876; *American Missionary* 20 (1876): 205–6.

93. Ibid.; see also *American Missionary* 20 (1876): 204–5.

94. New York *Independent*, 31 August 1876.

95. New York *Independent*, 28 September 1876; McPherson, *Abolitionist Legacy*, 52.

96. New York *Tribune*, 6 November 1876.

97. New York *Times*, 17, 20, 22, 25 November, 1, 4, 11, 26 December 1876.

98. New York *Times*, 20 November 1876.

99. New York *Times*, 1 December 1876.

100. McPherson, *Abolitionist Legacy*, 84–86.

101. New York *Times*, 15, 16 January 1877; Alfred B. Williams, *Hampton and His Red Shirts: South Carolina's Deliverance in 1876* (Charleston, 1935), 435.

102. Redpath to W. Whitelaw Reid, 24 March 1877, W. W. Reid Collection (Library of Congress).

103. Foner, *Reconstruction*, 575–82.

104. Redpath to M[errimon] Howard, 14 April 1877, Hayes Papers; Vernon Lane Wharton, *The Negro in Mississippi, 1865–1900* (1947; New York, 1965), 169.

105. Ibid.

106. Ibid.

107. Ibid.

108. Ibid.

109. Donald C. Henderson to Rutherford B. Hayes, 30 April 1877, John Tyler, Jr., to Rutherford B. Hayes, 19 April 1877, Hayes Papers; Chicago *Inter-Ocean*, 18 April 1877.

110. McPherson, *Abolitionist Legacy*, 84–139.

11

George H. Moore — "Tormentor of Massachusetts"

John David Smith

A school of "romantic nationalists," according to David D. Van Tassel, dominated American historical scholarship in the three decades before the Civil War. Inspired by the European romantics, George Bancroft, Francis Parkman, and Jared Sparks used their histories to evangelize the ideology of American freedom and spread the message of America's rise and progress. As influential as these historians' works were in fostering American nationality, however, the Civil War era gave rise to a new generation of scholars who viewed the work of their forebears with considerable skepticism. Such now-little-known historians as Charles Deane, Edmund B. O'Callaghan, and Nathaniel B. Shurtleff focused largely on local studies to test the findings of their hero-worshipping predecessors. The new "critical" breed of historians scrutinized "often-repeated stories and burrowed into accumulated documents to verify and correct older histories." This transitional group of historians — falling between the romantic and the "scientific" historians who emerged later in the century — contributed significantly to the revisionist tradition in American historiography. According to Van Tassel, they "not only raised the general standard of scholarship but also improved current methods of collecting, evaluating, and editing documents."[1]

New Hampshire native George H. Moore (1823–92) stands as one of the most talented and controversial of the unsung school of critical historians. Joking about his origins, Moore admitted that although he was a New Englander, "my ancestors were *not* Puritans — but among those who came to 'catch fish.'"[2] His father, Jacob Bailey Moore, was himself a pioneer historian, antiquarian, and librarian of the historical societies of New Hampshire and New York.[3] The younger Moore earned his bachelor's and master's degrees in 1842 and 1845, respectively, from the University of the City of New York and was awarded a LL.D. from that institution in 1869. Although he never actually taught, for a decade Moore held a professorship in legal history and literature at the same university. He is best known, however, as librarian first of the New-York Historical Society (1849–76) and then of the Lenox Library (1876–92), which later served as the core collection of the New York Public Library. As a librarian, Moore supplied copies of documents, pamphlets, and rare books to some of the most important historians of his day, including Parkman, O'Callaghan, and Justin Winsor.[4] In addition, he corresponded about his own scholarship with several persons who later significantly influenced the course of U.S. history. Most notably, in 1839, while Moore attended Dartmouth College, Captain Robert E. Lee assisted him with his research on Charles Lee, U.S. Attorney General (1795–1801).[5] Moore ultimately wrote nine monographs and many articles and ranked as one of the country's most distinguished historians of colonial and Revolutionary America.[6]

Although a New Englander by birth and education, Moore felt compelled to distance himself intellectually from his region in order to write the section's history fairly, accurately, and critically. He believed in overturning what he called "the myths and traditions" of "the old school" of New England history. For too long, Moore said, Massachusetts had magnified men such as John Winthrop, Increase and Cotton Mather, and John Endicott. Instead, Moore was determined to examine under a microscope Massachusetts's "historical reputation," especially its alleged "early and consistent zeal against slavery."[7] Not surprisingly, he welcomed Brooks Adams's iconoclastic view of Massachusetts's past. It illustrated Moore's "theory of social evolution, which," he said, "likens the inner court of the New England Theocracy, the association of the elders of Massachusetts, to the sacred caste of the Zuni Indians."[8] On another occasion, Moore remarked to historian George Bancroft that Massachusetts natives could view things only through "Mass-spectacles."[9]

Moore's critical spirit transcended his historical work. In 1852, for instance, he judged both Franklin Pierce and Winfield Scott so weak as presidential candidates that he threatened not to vote at all. He informed Daniel Webster's private secretary G. J. Abbot:

Southern treachery and Northern cowardice have opened a new chapter, not only in the history of the Whig Party, but of the Country; what its final record will be, no human being can foresee. For my part, I am so thoroughly sickened of Whig Politics that I am inclined to believe I should vote the Democratic Ticket had they nominated anybody but a N. H. Loco Foco [Pierce].[10]

Nearly 40 years later, Moore declared, "Politicians have as much interest in history as hogs and generally about the same amount of knowledge thereof. Perhaps I am doing injustice to the animals, who are said to be very sagacious."[11]

For all his self-professed iconoclasm, however, in his political thought, Moore lined up with the old New England Federalists. He claimed never to have "held any spark of sympathy" for the Antifederalists because they valued "subserviency to the popular will" over "principle." Had the country followed the Federalism of Washington and Hamilton, Moore said, it would have been spared "the folly and wickedness of those who have perverted their teachings and yielded to . . . 'the madness of the people.'" This attitude spilled over into Moore's view of history as he ridiculed those who believed "that *facts* of history are *not true* and the *opinions* which the majority favor *are* true." Writing to Bancroft, Moore complained that Bancroft had given "*the enemies of the Constitution* too much credit for honesty as well as patriotism. The greatest misfortunes and disgraces of our government have been due, in all its history, to the fact that its administration was so easily transferred to the hands of its enemies."[12]

Despite his admitted Federalist bias, Moore considered himself a member of "the new school of historical criticism" that rejected all partisanship and hero worship. "Much of our earlier history," he informed Charles Deane, "is open to criticism, for errors which I am sorry to admit, have not always been due to ignorance or want of material." Moore argued that it was "high time to expurgate the mythical element from the treatment of a history which is so recent and for which the documents are so abundant as our own." He complained that too few of his fellow historians were "really patient and critical." Also, Moore was shocked by the "ignorance" that passed as history — for example, the uncritical flag-waving nationalism of the 1876 Philadelphia Centennial celebration. "I believe in the truth of history," Moore declared, "and unpleasant as the truth may be — intend to draw all my lines with a single purpose for absolute fidelity to what I regard as the first canon of historical criticism — 'above all things — truth.'" According to pioneer African-American historian George Washington Williams, Moore's contributions shined "with an energy and perspicuity of style" and "his refined sarcasm, unanswerable logic, and critical accuracy give him undisputed place amongst the ablest writers of our times." Moore's blend of Federalism, skepticism, cynicism, and determination to get the facts straight set him on a collision course with the venerable traditions of Massachusetts.[13]

In 1866 Moore published the controversial book that established his reputation as "the tormentor of Massachusetts."[14] *Notes on the History of Slavery in Massachusetts* merged critical historical methodology with an intense antislavery ideology into a broadside attack on what he deemed Massachusetts's hypocrisy on the slavery question.[15] The irony of condemning the state long considered the cradle of abolitionism for its gross complicity with the evil of slavery was not lost on Moore.

Moore's historical views were closely related to his political beliefs. His devotion to Federalism led Moore first to join the Whig party and, after its demise, to become an ardent Republican. Unlike most white Republicans, however, Moore favored the emancipation of blacks early in the Civil War. During that conflict, Moore published a pamphlet that underscored the resistance to the recruitment of blacks as soldiers and their emancipation during the American Revolution and singled out Massachusetts's persistent "conservative policy" on the question.[16] Four years later, Moore announced that his *Notes on the History of Slavery* contained nothing "to comfort proslavery men anywhere." For almost a century, supporters of Massachusetts had "drawn" the "curtains" on slavery's ignoble history in the state, Moore wrote. Now it was his responsibility as a historian to "let in the light upon them."[17]

In the best tradition of the critical historians at midcentury, Moore reprinted scores of official records from Massachusetts archives as well as extracts, travelers' accounts, inventories, supply bills, newspaper advertisements, church records, and petitions to underscore the "tough black knot" that slavery and racism held on Massachusetts for more than a century. He was determined to rest his argument "on facts rather than opinions," employing the calm judgment of the historian, "without disparagement and without exaggeration." The records of slavery everywhere, he insisted, showed "the same disregard of human rights, the same indifference to suffering, the same contempt for the oppressed races, the same hate for those who are injured." Moore sought to allow the documents themselves to trace the origins of the institution in Massachusetts. As narrator, he stood back and let his arsenal of primary sources indict Massachusetts before the world for greed and hypocrisy. Then, Moore stepped in to conclude that the "stains which slavery has left on the proud escutcheon *even* of Massachusetts, are quite as significant of its hideous character as the satanic defiance of God and Humanity which accompanied the laying of the corner-stone of the Slaveholders' Confederacy."[18]

Colonists in Massachusetts, Moore showed, enslaved Indians during the Pequot War and imported black slaves as early as 1638. Moore charged that, subsequently, the Atlantic slave trade, "since known and branded by all civilized nations as piracy, . . . continued to flourish under the auspices of Massachusetts merchants down through the entire colonial period, and long after the boasted Declaration of Rights in 1780 had terminated (?) the legal existence of slavery within the limits of that State." He also cited a 1639 Massachusetts account of "one of the earliest, if not, indeed, the very first attempt at breeding of slaves in America." When narrating a 1644–45 case concerning slave stealing along the African coast, Moore identified "not a trace of anti-slavery opinion or sentiment, still less of anti-slavery legislation; though both have been repeatedly claimed for the honor of the colony." Moore blamed the success of slavery and the slave trade in Massachusetts on the greed and racism of the colony's officials.[19]

Moore argued further that the Bay colony's officials in fact passed the first positive legislation establishing slavery in America, the 1641 *Body of Liberties of the Massachusetts Colony in New-England.* Although guaranteeing the fundamental rights of some persons, Massachusetts leaders protected the institution of slavery "as an existing, substantial fact." In assessing the 1641 code and its revisions, Moore declared that self-righteous defenders of Massachusetts no longer could preach that slavery was forced upon unwilling colonists by England. He was particularly outraged by Senator Charles Sumner's speech of June 28, 1854, which asserted that "'In all her annals, no person was ever born a slave on the soil of Massachusetts,' and 'If, in point of fact, the issue of slaves was sometimes held in bondage, it was never by sanction of any statute-law of Colony or Commonwealth.'" "Never," Moore complained, "were the demands of a free people eluded by their public servants with more of the contortions as well as wisdom of the serpent." On the contrary, Moore wrote, to Massachusetts's shame, the colony preceded "any and all the other colonies" in sanctioning slavery by law, years ahead of even the most notorious of the southern slaveholding colonies and states.[20]

Massachusetts whites, Moore explained, drew a clear distinction between the legal and social status of Christian (white) indentured servants and the status of Indians and black slaves. Early in the eighteenth century, when Bostonians sought to end black slavery in favor of white servitude, the resulting legislation riveted slavery more firmly on the colony than ever before. A 1703 law requiring security bonds to be posted for all manumitted blacks remained on the books as late as 1807. Other laws restricted slaves in much the same manner as the slave codes of the Old South and the Black Codes of Presidential Reconstruction. Moore noted that Massachusetts slaveholders frequently freed sick or elderly slaves, "to relieve the master from the charge of supporting them," a practice for which abolitionists had commonly attacked southern slaveholders.[21]

Moore argued further that slavery remained an important element in Massachusetts's economic and social fabric until the decade before the American Revolution. Individual blacks filed successful "suits for liberty," but these had no cumulative impact on the institution of slavery in Massachusetts. In discussing one of these suits, Moore challenged the notion that *James* v. *Lechmere* (1769) declared slavery unlawful in Massachusetts. It, in fact, was settled by the parties in question and, consequently, led to no legal precedents. Although one of the "cherished fancies" of defenders of Massachusetts was the idea that *James* v. *Lechmere* prefigured *Somerset* v. *Stewart* (1772), Moore maintained that in the *Somerset* case, Lord Mansfield prohibited only the forced removal of slaves, not the institution of slavery.[22]

Like many later historians, Moore credited the Revolution with unveiling "the inconsistency of maintaining slavery with one hand while pleading or striking for freedom with the other." However, he insisted, even then, that public opinion in Massachusetts was reluctant to emancipate the slaves and favored only gradual change.[23] This was the hypocrisy that so irked Moore. "If there was a prevailing public sentiment against slavery in Massachusetts — as has been constantly claimed of late," Moore argued, "the people of that day, far less demonstrative than their descendants, had an extraordinary way of not showing it." In no way did Massachusetts take the lead in freeing its slaves, even after ties were severed with England. Not until the authority of the U.S. Constitution was established, he said, did an end to the "pernicious commerce" in human flesh come to pass.[24]

To be fair to Massachusetts, Moore commended attempts — albeit unsuccessful ones — by the legislature and by individuals, white and black, to kill slavery in the state during the Revolution. Nevertheless, the failure of the legislature to do so when it was hammering out a state constitution in 1777 resulted from a lack of overall sympathy for blacks and from the growing assumption that abolition would fall under the province of the new national government. Consequently, the Massachusetts Constitution and Form of Government of February 1778 recognized slavery's existence and excluded blacks, Indians, and mulattoes from the rights of citizenship.[25]

Moore found not "the slightest trace of positive contemporary evidence" to support the assertion that the first article of the Declaration of Rights of Massachusetts 1780 Constitution was intended to abolish slavery in the state. Rather, that claim was yet another Massachusetts tradition that "will not stand the test of historical criticism." Only lawsuits and "bold judicial construction" gradually transformed the first clause of the Declaration of Rights into an "instrument of *virtual* abolition" because the Massachusetts legislature had never met "the subject [of abolition] fairly and fully" but operated instead with all the "cupidity" of Massachusetts's "slave-trading merchants." The most tragic and "humiliating" part of the sad story was that Massachusetts even failed to support its indigent former slaves.[26]

Finally, in 1788, Massachusetts passed legislation "directly and positively hostile to slavery," the prohibition of the slave trade to Massachusetts. Moore, ever suspicious of motives of Massachusetts politicians, believed that his cynicism was borne out by another bill passed in 1788 requiring the removal from the state of virtually all blacks who could not prove U.S. citizenship. Although this act allegedly was intended to prevent fugitive slaves from becoming a burden on the state, Moore interpreted it as the racist response of whites to fears of slave revolt and the presence of uncontrolled free blacks. He doubted "if anything . . . can be found which comes nearer branding color as a crime!" Aghast at the subsequent "arbitrary and illegal extension of the statute" to citizens of African-American ancestry, Moore wrote that the law disgraced Massachusetts until its repeal in 1834.[27]

By 1834, of course, Massachusetts was conspicuously in the forefront of the abolitionist movement. Although Moore was careful to note that the abolitionists themselves had "little if any historical connection with the existence of Slavery," his overriding message was that despite its meritorious accomplishments in battling slavery and later in fighting to preserve the Union, Massachusetts still had to acknowledge its long identification with slavery. Indeed, because slavery in Massachusetts had been abolished only *virtually*, not formally by legislation, only after the passage of the Thirteenth Amendment in 1865 did slavery come to cease in point of law.[28]

Given the racial, political, and sectional tensions of Presidential Reconstruction, Moore's book attracted controversy like a lightning rod. Critics greeted Moore's book with mixed reviews. New York's Henry B. Dawson, a biting critic who at one time or another had taken virtually all of the leading contemporary American historians to task, welcomed *Notes on the History of Slavery* with unrestrained praise. In the *Historical Magazine*, critical history's foremost journal,[29] Dawson proclaimed, "No Roundhead ever performed his iconoclastic labors with more zest or more thoroughly" than Moore. "He has labored patiently, . . . dispassionately, . . . [and] effectively, as is proved by . . . the extreme backwardness of all competent Massachusetts men in the work of disproving" it. Finally, Dawson doubted that "the claimants to superiority, throughout the Bay State, can maintain the elevated position, . . . which they have so long and so insolently attempted to occupy."[30]

The Democratic press, as might be expected, also lavished praise upon Moore's book, but not because of any commitment to critical scholarship. Rather, the New York *Herald* cited *Notes on the History of Slavery* as a timely reminder of "the inherent hypocrisy and baseness" of the Republican party. The reviewer held New Englanders accountable for "the worst features of slavery" and added that the Republicans — through the Freedmen's Bureau — were now engaged in a plot to establish "a system of negro servitude infinitely more heartless and grinding than any that has ever been charged to the Southern planter." In his own column, editor James Gordon Bennett also used discussion of Moore's book to attack the Republicans' efforts to guarantee civil rights for the freedmen. Bennett accused the "firebrand agents" of the Freedmen's Bureau with extorting the blacks and "trading in their labor — which is only another kind of slavery." "These modern Pharisees of New England," who first enslaved the blacks, wrote Bennett, "now say they would not have done what their fathers did" and threaten the nation with black revolution and race war. "Truly, they are the children of the old Puritan Pharisees."[31]

The Springfield *Republican* surprisingly welcomed *Notes on the History of Slavery* with a generous and balanced critique. The newspaper warned readers that although Moore's work "spoils a great deal of our virtuous brag," it would provide for "most a new revelation and to many a mortifying one." Indeed, the reviewer emphasized that because Massachusetts historians and orators had, unlike Moore, failed to consult original records, they had perpetrated the myth that no slaves had ever been born on Massachusetts soil. While accepting Moore's allegations, the reviewer noted that not all Massachusetts slaveholders were wicked men and that they only subscribed to the "prevailing ideas and spirit of the age in which they lived." Still, he declared defensively, Massachusetts not only was the first colony to emancipate its slaves but also led the nation in the abolitionist crusade. "We do not therefore feel the least inclination to be angry with Mr. Moore for having given us the first true account of slavery in Massachusetts," he wrote. "We may not brag henceforth as largely as before, but we shall do it more intelligently and to better purpose." Moore found the *Republican*'s review of his book gratifying and remarked to George Bancroft that the reviewer had "met it manfully."[32]

Other friends of Massachusetts, blacks, and the Republican party, however, trained their guns on Moore. The *Nation*, for example, charged that Moore "distorted" his reading of the 1641 *Code of Fundamentals*, which, it said, *sanctioned*, not *established*, slavery. "His conclusions will, of course, comfort the enemies of emancipation," explained the reviewer, who went on to condemn Moore's "apparent jealousy of New England's pre-eminence" and his "aversion to Puritanism."[33] The *Independent*, noting Moore's "intrepidity," his "rare degree of courage . . . [and] audacity," predicted, quite correctly, that his book would please the Copperheads. However, the critic said, Moore naively assumed that because black children were held as slaves, they were enslaved legally; rather, they were enslaved by "an ignorant and vicious custom," which "does not affect the fact that they were illegally so entreated." Unlike Moore, the *Independent*'s reviewer praised the 1641 *Body of Liberties* because it "limited and restrained" the slavery then current. Never establishing slavery, it proclaimed that those "then held as slaves . . . should be lawfully so held, freeing all other persons by its necessary interpretation."[34]

Some critics leveled personal attacks at Moore. George T. Davis charged him with carelessly accusing an innocent Massachusetts slaveholder of murdering his bondsman and incorrectly reporting the slaveholder's conviction and execution.[35] Charles F. Dunbar, editor of the Boston *Daily Advertiser*, who reportedly spent five months researching his criticism, intimated that Moore wrote his book "to gratify 'the personal resentments of [his] literary friends.'"[36] Dunbar blasted Moore as "a layman, not of conspicuously judicial instincts," who selected his evidence only with an eye toward bolstering his arguments. "There are few parts of his book," Dunbar wrote, in "which . . . it is safe for the reader to follow the author upon trust." Not only did he accuse Moore of "suppressing inconvenient authorities," but Dunbar also asserted

That where this process will not avail, he does not lack assurance in coolly setting aside their opinion or statements; and that his assumptions, not few in number nor unimportant in effect, have a single purpose, — to make out a case against this Commonwealth, in a matter better adapted to practice in the criminal courts than to historical discussion.

Specifically, Dunbar denied that Massachusetts authorities encouraged the slave trade and, like other reviewers, argued that because slavery existed in Massachusetts prior to 1641, it was not established by the *Body of Liberties*. Concerning hereditary slavery, Dunbar discredited Moore's "liberal interpretation" of the 1641 law, accusing him of dishonestly suppressing evidence that proved unequivocally that children of slaves were not held as slaves. Finally, Dunbar attacked Moore's allegation that slavery was not abolished by the 1780 Declaration of Rights but remained law until the Thirteenth Amendment.[37]

Moore's contention that the 1780 Massachusetts Convention never intended to abolish slavery remained under debate as late as 1875. Justice Charles Doe of the New Hampshire Supreme Court wrote that although "as, a matter of law, slavery could not exist under that constitution," he assumed that "Moore was right in concluding that neither the convention nor the people understood they were abolishing slavery by adopting the constitution." Doe, hoping "to give practical legal effect to the general declaration of freedom and equality and the right of life, liberty and property," asked to see George Bancroft's evidence to support his claim in volume ten of *History of the United States* that the Massachusetts convention specifically added a clause to abolish slavery. For his part, Moore remained convinced that he, not Bancroft, was right. "I must renew my regrets that you have committed yourself to so serious an error as that respecting the *intention* in the Mass. Convention to abolish slavery," Moore wrote to Bancroft. "I *know* you are wrong — and the position cannot be maintained."[38]

Moore enjoyed his controversial reputation as "the Devil's advocate, opposing the canonization of Massachusetts." He warned anyone who challenged Massachusetts's "threads of tradition and history" to expect the "ugly storm of reproaches" that had descended upon him.[39] In responding to his critics, Moore surrendered no ground, defended himself from charges of suppressing and misrepresenting sources, and launched new attacks. He gave Davis's criticisms short shrift, arguing that a master's cruelty toward a slave who ultimately died was no less than murder. Moore accused Davis and other defenders of Massachusetts's reputation of misrepresenting "how slow and gradual was the amelioration of the conditions of servitude. Impatient at the sluggish movement of humanity, they seem determined to bridge over the long valleys, the deep chasms and perilous gulfs through which their fathers actually struggled to reach the heights of Liberty and Equality." Davis, he said, had an "untimely sensitiveness in regard to the honor of his ancestry or his native State."[40]

Referring to Dunbar as "the 'great gun' of Boston" who sought his "annihilation," Moore dismissed Dunbar's arguments point by point in a lengthy rejoinder. Moore emphasized that he had no quarrel with Massachusetts per se but rather with "her self-righteous historians." Massachusetts was "far more likely to suffer from the cowardice of her friends than the courage of her enemies." Moore claimed that although he never asserted that the 1641 statute "originated" slavery, it was literally the earliest law "establishing slavery in America." Concerning hereditary slavery, Moore found Dunbar's "reasoning . . . utterly futile and worthless," fully in keeping with "the new school of Puritans." The legal status of hereditary slavery in Massachusetts never was formally challenged, Moore explained, mocking "the art with which the champions of Massachusetts have . . . contrived to conceal the truths with which they have always been so familiar."[41]

Modern scholars have sided with Moore in the issues raised by his critics. They credit him with uncovering the legalization of hereditary slavery in Massachusetts in the seventeenth century and the persistence of the institution and the slave trade after 1780. As historian William M. Wiecek has commented, Moore correctly perceived that the *Somerset* case concerned only the removal of slaves from England and, as a result, had no impact on slavery in Massachusetts.[42] Indeed, Moore prefigured by a century Jerome Nadelhaft's revisionist interpretation of the *Somerset* case. According to Robert M. Cover, the ambiguous nature of the records, differing interpretations of "constitutionality" and judicial review, and the absence of judicial opinion have made the history of slavery and abolition in Massachusetts "a historian's perennial football."[43] However, Moore's contemporaries used his book in a dramatically different game.

Published during Reconstruction, Moore's *Notes on the History of Slavery* armed white southerners with ammunition to challenge what they deemed the North's self-righteous position on slavery. New Englanders, "whose pious hands are uplifted in horror over the wrongs of the poor negro," were hypocrites, charged *De Bow's Review*. They retained slavery while it was profitable to do so but freed their slaves when it no longer paid. Northerners, then, had no right to berate southerners who "*happened to remain a few years longer in the practice which they introduced and taught.*"[44] To be sure, some white northerners got the message. The old abolitionist Parker Pillsbury, for example, was shocked by Moore's revelations. In 1883 he judged *Notes on the History of Slavery* "one of the most surprising volumes ever issued by the American press." Others, upon discovering that their families once had held slaves, mocked their own false pride and admitted their embarrassment. Writing in the *Nation* in 1886, one New Englander recounted his recent dismay upon learning that ancestors on both sides of his family had been slaveholders. "These evil results of hereditary slaveholding," he wrote, "so apparent (to the New Englander) in the Southern character — was their 'vicious quitch' even in us, also, all 'unbeknownst?'" "May we hope," the writer added jokingly, "that the news of the Emancipation Proclamation" had reached his ancestors in the next world.[45]

There was nothing humorous, however, about race relations in the South in 1866. The controversy over Moore's book raged soon after reports reached the North that the South's Black Codes had reduced the freedmen to a form of quasi-slavery. A few months earlier, the Joint Committee on Reconstruction had paraded the South's unwillingness to free the blacks in deed a well as in word before the American public.[46] Now, Moore charged that even in Massachusetts in 1866, "those disabilities which so strongly mark[ed] the social status of the negro still linger." On the race question, then, Massachusetts continued to preach more than it practiced.[47] This argument, moreover, came from a respected northern intellectual and librarian. From Reconstruction until well into the new century, southerners cited *Notes on the History of Slavery* to document northern hypocrisy regarding racial matters. "Massachusetts," the editor of the *Confederate Veteran* explained in 1897, "had always carried herself with a prudish dignity in the family of States." Moore, however, exposed "the pretty pranks she played when a girl."[48] The message was clear. At the very moment that one southern state after another was passing Jim Crow legislation — riveting blacks into a second-class legal status — northerners should not preach race relations to the South.

There is little evidence to support David Van Tassel's assertion that Moore was motivated by jealousy and determined in "justifying and increasing the reputation of New York state." The intensity of Moore's animus against Massachusetts per se was more apparent than real. Rather, *Notes on the History of Slavery* represents the emergence of a school of historical research bent on "exposing unmerited reputations" and revising the filiopietistic national past.[49]

Anticipating the scientific historians and breaking with the romantic historians, Moore viewed history as a factual chronicle. Because he was conscious of what later generations of historians would label "historical relativism," Moore argued,

It would be to misread history and to forget the change of times, to see in the Fathers of New England mere commonplace slavemongers; to themselves they appeared as the elect to whom God had given the heathen for an inheritance; . . . and for their wildest and worst acts they could claim the sanction of religious conviction.

However, just as the scientific historians of slavery later failed in their attempts to excise partisanship and bias from their writings, so, too, did Moore succumb to the frailties of the historian. In spite of his quest for objectivity, *Notes on the History of Slavery* was decidedly Whiggish in orientation, imposing the author's progressive nineteenth-century vision of liberalism and democracy on seventeenth- and eighteenth-century Massachusetts. The book also falls clearly into the ideological camp of neoabolitionist historians such as James Ford Rhodes, who gained prominence three decades later. Although Rhodes, like Moore, emphasized New England's role in the Atlantic slave trade, Rhodes blamed the South for the evils of slavery while Moore censured Massachusetts for clutching onto slavery for so long, as well as for its sanctimoniousness.[50]

Moore's writing echoed the abolitionists, old and new, when he attacked slavery's "brutal customs," its "utter wickedness," and its justifications based on "miserable pretences." Passionate in his language, Moore referred to the captains of slave ships as "pirates" and censured the kidnapping of blacks in Boston in February 1788 as "outrageous" and "atrocious." Moore held Massachusetts slaveholders accountable for what he termed "the looseness" of slave marriages in the colony, lamenting that the slaves' "marriage was not a matter of choice with them, [no] more than any other action of their life." Again speaking of white interference with slave marriages, Moore wrote that "it was as true then as it is now that the institution of slavery was inconsistent with the just rules of Christian morality."[51]

Moore differed from the later neoabolitionist historians, however, when he did not distance himself from the slaves as persons. Instead, Moore sympathized openly with the "poor Negroes" and "unfortunate creatures." He praised the creativity and contributions of skilled slaves and insisted that in no sense had the blacks been a "deadweight" on Massachusetts society. Moore, in fact, identified black self-assertion as an important force that ultimately worked toward the destruction of slavery. He cited advertisements for runaway slaves that mentioned their "notions of Freedom" and pointed out that as a form of protest, free blacks resisted paying taxes. Slave insurrection always loomed as a possibility in Massachusetts, Moore said, but in reality, slaves filed liberty suits and freedom petitions. In 1787, for example, some petitioned the Massachusetts legislature for aid to return to Africa. The next year, black abolitionist Prince Hall wrote a petition on behalf of three kidnapped Boston blacks, protesting their seizure and demanding abolition of the slave trade. At a time, then, when many whites in the Reconstruction North viewed blacks in overtly racist ways, Moore championed "the negro's capacity for intellectual improvement."[52]

On another level, Moore's book illustrates the uses of history in the crucible of legal and social change. Armed with the weapons of the historian, Moore exposed not only slavery's long history in Massachusetts but also the Bay State's lengthy tradition of racial intolerance and pro-scription. In *Notes on the History of Slavery*, Moore openly attacked the legacy of racism and hypocrisy that lay in slavery's wake. He recognized the ever-present forces of "localism, laissez-faire, and racism" that, according to Eric Foner, "reasserted themselves" at the close of the Civil War.[53] During the war, Moore had documented the glacial speed with which the Continental Congress had moved to consider the arming and freeing of black troops during an earlier conflict — the American Revolution. Hinting that the Lincoln administration should move swift-ly toward emancipation, Moore declared, "It requires little ingenuity to invent historical parallels — not very profound research to find histor-ical precedent — but it is the highest wisdom to know how to apply the lessons of the Past."[54] There were lessons to be applied. As late as June 1864, the Thirteenth Amendment failed to pass the U.S. House of Representatives by a vote of 93 to 65, and not until January 1865 could President Abraham Lincoln twist enough congressional arms to enable the amendment to pass the House 119 to 56.[55] At the very moment, then, that the South was expected to seek forgiveness for its sins, the North was demonstrating the longstanding hypocrisy and shoddy treatment of blacks that Moore's book was about to expose.

Moore's *Notes on the History of Slavery* took an important step for-ward in redefining U.S. nationality. Whereas the old romantic nation-alists had glorified the American past, Moore's new critical perspective found plenty of blame on both sides of the Mason and Dixon line. The post–Civil War United States was emerging as a pluralistic society caught up in the throes of an industrial revolution. Simplistic, moralis-tic notions of good-versus-bad would no longer suffice. Perhaps with a smirk on his face, Moore concluded his book by taking a final slap at Massachusetts. Slavery was not *legally* abolished there, he reminded his readers, until passage of the Thirteenth Amendment late in 1865, the votes of eight former Confederate states having been crucial in the amendment's ratification.[56] Ironically, slavery's "actual prohibition . . . in Massachusetts" was "accomplished by the votes of South Carolina and Georgia."[57] Moore's history reminded victorious northerners that there were limits to their own virtue, even as they began to tailor the bloody shirt.

NOTES

1. David D. Van Tassel, *Recording America's Past: An Interpretation of the Development of Historical Studies in America, 1607–1884* (Chicago, 1960), 111, 121.

2. Moore to Charles Deane, 28 February 1868, Charles Deane Papers (Massachusetts Historical Society).

3. The elder Moore "combined journalism, publishing, mill operations, and landowning." He "left New Hampshire in 1839," reportedly, "a bankrupt man." David J. Russo, *Keepers of Our Past: Local Historical Writing in the United States, 1820s–1930s* (Westport, 1988), 36–37.

4. See, for example, Moore to Parkman, 27 February 1846, 2, 3 March 1857, 8 January 1874, Francis Parkman Papers (Massachusetts Historical Society); Moore to O'Callaghan, 13 September 1860, Edmund Bailey O'Callaghan Papers (Manuscript Division, Library of Congress); Moore to Justin Winsor, 15 April 1880, in Lenox Library Memorial to James Lenox (Houghton Library Reading Room, Harvard University).

5. Lee to Moore, 25 November 1839, James Freeman Clarke Papers (Houghton Library, Harvard University).

6. Robert W. G. Vail, *Knickerbocker Birthday; a Sesqui-centennial History of the New-York Historical Society, 1804–1954* (New York, 1954), 97–98; Pamela Spence Richards, *Scholars and Gentlemen: The Library of the New-York Historical Society, 1804–1982* (Hamden, 1984), 34–42, 44; Rush C. Hawkins to the editor, New York *Times*, 19 May 1892, 4:7. Moore's best known work was *"Mr. Lee's Plan — March 29, 1777": The Treason of Charles Lee* (New York, 1860).

7. Moore to Charles Deane, 24 January 1887, Deane Papers; George H. Moore, *Notes on the History of Slavery in Massachusetts* [hereafter *Notes*] (New York, 1866), 14, 23. I have silently edited Moore's spelling and capitalization in line with modern usage.

8. Moore to Charles Deane, 24, 29 January 1887, Deane Papers.

9. Moore to Bancroft, 15 July 1875, George Bancroft Papers (Massachusetts Historical Society).

10. Moore to Abbot, 28 June 1852, George Jacob Abbot Papers (Yale University).

11. Moore to Henry H. Edes, 6 July 1889, H. H. Edes Papers (Massachusetts Historical Society).

12. Moore to Bancroft, 17 August 1877, 19 June 1882, Bancroft Papers.

13. Moore to Deane, 27 January 1868, Deane Papers; Moore to George Bancroft, 5 August 1875, 19 June 1882, Bancroft Papers; George Washington Williams, *History of the Negro Race in America* (2 vol., New York, 1882), 1:173n. Moore assisted Williams with his research, according to John Hope Franklin, *George Washington Williams: A Biography* (Chicago, 1985), 106.

14. "Personal," New York *Times*, 27 March 1869, 6:7.

15. Sections of Moore's book appeared during the Civil War years under his pseudonym "E. Y. E." See "Historical Notes on Slavery in the Northern Colonies and States — Parts 1–4," *Historical Magazine* 7 (November, December 1863): 342–45, 363–67; *Historical Magazine* 8 (January, June 1864): 21–30, 193–200; and "Additional Note on the History of Slavery in Massachusetts," *Historical Magazine* 9 (February 1865): 57.

16. George H. Moore, *Historical Notes on the Employment of Negroes in the American Army of the Revolution* (New York, 1862), 4–5.

17. Moore, *Notes*, 1, 224. In his book, Moore did not differentiate between the Plymouth Colony and Massachusetts Bay. He held them equally culpable for the origins of slavery. "In this connection," Moore wrote, "they may justly be regarded as one." (32).

18. Moore, *Notes*, 110, 98, 124, 68–69, 1–2, emphasis added.

19. Moore, *Notes*, 1, 5–6, 9, 29, 65–66, 7–8, 30, 10.

20. Moore, *Notes*, 11, 12, 16, 21, 11, 18–19. The wording, but not the content, of Sumner's quote appears in a slightly different form in *The Works of Charles Sumner* (15 vol., Boston, 1871), 3:384. George Washington Williams remarked that in *Notes on the History of Slavery in Massachusetts*, Moore "summoned nearly all the orators and historians of Massachusetts to the bar of history. He leaves them open to one of three charges . . . evading the truth, ignorance of it, or falsifying the record." Williams, *History of the Negro Race in America*, 1:173n.

21. Moore, *Notes*, 49, 52, 52–53, 54–55, 53.

22. Moore, *Notes*, 111–24, 132, 115–16. Moore added that "the absurdity of the claim set up for Massachusetts is not diminished by the fact that no case in the history of English Law has been more misunderstood and misrepresented than the Somerset case itself." See 115n.

23. Moore, *Notes*, 71.

24. Moore, *Notes*, 59, 111, 142, 144.

25. Moore, *Notes*, 153, 162–63, 176–200, 180, 191, 200.

26. Moore, *Notes*, 203, 203–4 (emphasis added), 209, 224, 221–22.

27. Moore, *Notes*, 224, 227, 230, 237, 229, 230, 240.

28. Moore, *Notes*, 241, 224, 242.

29. Van Tassel, *Recording America's Past*, 161; Peter Novick, *That Noble Dream: The "Objectivity Question" and the American Historical Profession* (Cambridge, 1988), 59.

30. Van Tassel, *Recording America's Past*, 161; [Dawson], review of Moore, *Notes on the History of Slavery in Massachusetts*, in *Historical Magazine* 10 (December 1866 [Supplement 2]): 48, 57. For another favorable review, see *The Spectator* (London) 39 (22 September 1866): 1063.

31. "Notices of New Publications," *New York Herald*, 3 June 1866, 5:2; "New England Negroism and Hypocrisy," ibid., 4:3.

32. "Slavery in Massachusetts," Springfield *Weekly Republican*, 16 June 1866, 3:1; Moore to Bancroft, 29 June 1866, Bancroft Papers.

33. "A Touchstone for Massachusetts," *Nation* 2 (22 May 1866): 645.

34. "Was Massachusetts the Mother of Slaves?" *Independent* 18 (7 June 1866): 4:2–3.

35. See *Correspondence Concerning Moore's Notes on the History of Slavery in Massachusetts: Two Letters from the Historical Magazine* (New York, 1866), 2. This letter, and Moore's response, appeared originally in the *Historical Magazine* 10 (September, October 1866 [Supplements 2 and 3]): 81–82, 105–8.

36. Moore to Bancroft, 24 September 1866, Bancroft Papers.

37. "Slavery in Massachusetts," *Boston Daily Advertiser*, 18 September 1866, 2:3–5. Dunbar's criticism also appeared as "Slavery in Massachusetts: The Boston Critics on Mr. Moore's *Notes*," *Historical Magazine* 10 (December 1866 [Supplement 2]): 138–43, and in *Slavery in Massachusetts: The Boston Critics and Mr. Moore* (n.p.), 1–17.

38. Doe to Bancroft, 13 July 1875; Moore to Bancroft, 22 November 1875, Bancroft Papers.

39. "Mr. Moore's Reply to His Boston Critics," in *Slavery in Massachusetts: The Boston Critics and Mr. Moore*, 22; Moore to Deane, 27 January 1868, Deane Papers. Moore's response also appeared in *Historical Magazine* 10 (December 1866 [Supplement 6]), 186–98.

40. Moore, "Letter from George H. Moore to the Editor," in *Correspondence Concerning Moore's Notes on the History of Slavery in Massachusetts*, 10, 6–7, 12.

41. Moore to George Bancroft, 24 September 1866, Bancroft Papers; "Mr. Moore's Reply to His Boston Critics," 19, 25, 33, 21, 29–31, 55.

42. Lorenzo Johnston Greene, *The Negro in Colonial New England* (New York, 1942), 16–17, 64–68, 382; Lawrence William Towner, "A Good Master Well Served: A Social History of Servitude in Massachusetts, 1620–1750" (Ph.D. diss., Northwestern University, 1955), 134, 247; William M. Wiecek, *The Sources of Antislavery Constitutionalism in America, 1760–1848* (Ithaca, 1977), 44n; Wiecek, "Somerset: Lord Mansfield and the Legitimacy of Slavery in the Anglo-American World," *University of Chicago Law Review* 42 (Fall 1974): 115.

43. Jerome Nadelhaft, "The Somerset Case and Slavery: Myth, Reality, and Repercussions," *Journal of Negro History* 51 (1966): 193–208; Robert M. Cover,

Justice Accused: Antislavery and the Judicial Process (New Haven, 1975), 44–45.

44. "The Massachusetts Slave Trade," *De Bow's Review*, a. w. s., 2 (August 1866): 296.

45. Parker Pillsbury, *Acts of the Anti-Slavery Apostles* (1883; reprint Freeport, 1970), 72; E.R.S. to the editor, *Nation* 43 (21 October 1886): 329–30; H.W.S. to the editor, ibid., (4 November 1886): 371–72.

46. See *Report of the Joint Committee on Reconstruction at the First Session Thirty-Ninth Congress* (Washington, 1866).

47. Moore, *Notes*, 111.

48. Sister Sallie, *The Color Line Devoted to the Restoration of Good Government Putting an End to Negro Authority and Misrule, and Establishing a White Man's Government in the White Man's Country, by Organizing the White People of the South* (n.p., [1868?]), 65; Thomas Nelson Page, *The Old South: Essays Social and Political* (1892; reprint Chautauqua, 1919), 292–96; Robert F. Campbell, *Some Aspects of the Race Problem in the South* (Asheville, 1899), 1; Mrs. Andrew M. Sea [Sophie Irvine Fox], *"Slavery in Massachusetts," A Brief Synoptical Review of Slavery in the United States* (Louisville, 1916), 3–12; "Slavery in Massachusetts," *Confederate Veteran* 5 (January 1897): 21. The editor of the *Confederate Veteran* quoted a review of Moore's book published in the New York *Commercial-Advertiser*.

49. "Mr. Moore's Reply to His Boston Critics," 34; Van Tassel, *Recording America's Past*, 122.

50. Moore, *Notes*, 204, 71. On the Whig interpretation of history, see Herbert Butterfield, *The Whig Interpretation of History* (1931; reprint New York, 1965), 24, 62, 94–95. On Rhodes, the neoabolitionist school of historians, and the inadequacies of "scientific" historical methodology as applied to the study of slavery, see John David Smith, *An Old Creed for the New South: Proslavery Ideology and Historiography, 1865–1918* (1985; reprint Athens, 1991), 117–30, 155–57, 190–91.

51. Moore, *Notes*, 9, 72, 87, 226, 227, 225, 227, 27–28, 56, 55.

52. Moore, *Notes*, 109, 63, 230, 198, 208, 129, 111, 135, 225, 226, 63n. On anti-black sentiment in the North during Reconstruction, see Forrest G. Wood, *Black Scare: The Racist Response to Emancipation & Reconstruction* (Berkeley, 1968).

53. Eric Foner, *Reconstruction: America's Unfinished Revolution, 1863–1877* (New York, 1988), 34.

54. Moore, *Historical Notes on the Employment of Negroes in the American Army of the Revolution*, 24.

55. Mark E. Neely, Jr., "Thirteenth Amendment," *The Abraham Lincoln Encyclopedia* (New York, 1982), 308.

56. Moore, *Notes*, 242; J. G. Randall and David Donald, *The Civil War and Reconstruction* (Boston, 1961), 396–97. Randall and Donald considered it "one of the many anomalies of reconstruction" that Arkansas, Tennessee, North Carolina, Virginia, Louisiana, Alabama, Georgia, and South Carolina were "considered competent to ratify the antislavery amendment, such ratification being essential to its enactment, and yet be rejected by Congress and not considered states in the Union."

57. Moore, *Notes*, 242.

Bibliography of Merton L. Dillon

BOOKS

Elijah P. Lovejoy, Abolitionist Editor (Urbana: University of Illinois Press, 1961).

Benjamin Lundy and the Struggle for Negro Freedom (Urbana: University of Illinois Press, 1966).

The Abolitionists: The Growth of a Dissenting Minority (De Kalb: Northern Illinois Press, 1974; Paperback edition, New York: W. W. Norton, 1979).

Ulrich Bonnell Phillips, Historian of the Old South (Baton Rouge: Louisiana State University Press, 1985).

Slavery Attacked: Southern Slaves and Their Allies, 1619–1865 (Baton Rouge: Louisiana State University Press, 1990).

ARTICLES

"Elizabeth Chandler and the Spread of Antislavery Sentiment to Michigan," *Michigan History* 39 (1955): 481–94.

"Captain Jason W. James, Frontier Anti-democrat," *New Mexico Historical Review* 31 (1956): 89–101.

"Sources of Early Antislavery Thought in Illinois," *Journal of the Illinois State Historical Society* 50 (1957): 36–50.

"John Mason Peck: A Study in Historical Rationalization," *Journal of the Illinois State Historical Society* 50 (1957): 385–90.

"The Failure of the American Abolitionists," *Journal of Southern History* 25 (1959): 46–62.

"Benjamin Lundy in Texas," *Southwestern Historical Quarterly* 63 (1959): 159–77.

"Abolitionism Comes to Illinois," *Journal of the Illinois State Historical Society* 53 (1960): 389–403.

"A Visit to the Ohio State Prison in 1837," *Ohio Historical Quarterly* 69 (1960): 69–72.

"Religion in Lubbock," in Lawrence Graves, ed., *A History of Lubbock* (Lubbock: West Texas Museum Association, 1962), Chap. IV, pp. 449–516.

"The Politics of Abolition — Vision and Revision: A Review Essay," *Wisconsin Magazine of History* 51 (1967–68): 164–67.

"The Antislavery Movement in Illinois: 1824–1835," in Harry N. Scheiber, ed., *The Old Northwest, Studies in Regional History* (Lincoln: University of Nebraska Press, 1968), pp. 296–311.

"The Abolitionists: A Decade of Historiography, 1959–1969," *Journal of Southern History* 35 (1969): 500–22.

"Three Southern Anti-Slavery Editors: The Myth of the Southern Antislavery Movement," *East Tennessee Historical Society Publications* 42 (1970): 47–56.

"Elijah Parish Lovejoy" and "Benjamin Lundy," in *Encyclopedia Americana*, 1970 edition, Vol. 17: 809, 852.

"White Faces and Black Studies," *Commonweal* 91 (1970): 476–79.

"Jame M. Cazneau," "Elizabeth Chandler," "Clara Driscoll," "Laura Smith Haviland," and "Mary Austin Holley," in Edward T. James et al., eds., *Notable American Women: A Biographical Dictionary* (Cambridge: Harvard University Press, 1971).

"Polk, Expansion, and Morality," *Reviews in American History* 2 (1974): 389–93.

"Integrating Southern History," *Reviews in American History* 6 (1978): 219–24.

"Elihu Embree" and "Benjamin Lundy," in David C. Roller and Robert W. Twyman, eds., *The Encyclopedia of Southern History* (Baton Rouge: Louisiana State University Press, 1979), pp. 407, 759.

"Benjamin Lundy, Quaker Radical," *Time Line* 3 (1986): 28–41.

"Slave Patrols" and "Benjamin Lundy," in Randall M. Miller and John David Smith, eds., *Dictionary of Afro-American Slavery* (Westport: Greenwood Press, 1988), pp. 424–26, 562–64.

"Gilbert H. Barnes and Dwight L. Dumond: An Appraisal," *Reviews in American History* 21 (1993): 539–52.

Selected Bibliography

Boles, John B. and Nolen, Evelyn T., eds. *Interpreting Southern History: Historiographical Essays in Honor of Sanford B. Higginbotham*. Baton Rouge, 1987.

Brock, William R. *Parties and Political Conscience: American Dilemmas, 1840–1850*. New York, 1979.

Capers, Gerald M. *John C. Calhoun — Opportunist: A Reappraisal*. Gainesville, 1960.

Chitwood, Oliver P. *John Tyler: Champion of the Old South*. New York, 1939.

Cooper, William J. *Liberty and Slavery: Southern Politics to 1860*. New York, 1983.

____. *The South and the Politics of Slavery, 1828–1856*. Baton Rouge, 1978.

Dillon, Merton L. *The Abolitionists: The Growth of a Dissenting Minority*, De Kalb, 1974.

____. *Slavery Attacked: Southern Slaves and Their Allies, 1619–1865*. Baton Rouge, 1990.

Faust, Drew Gilpin. *A Sacred Circle: The Dilemma of the Intellectual in the Old South, 1840–1860*. Baltimore, 1977.

Finley, Ruth E. *The Lady of GODEY'S*. Philadelphia, 1931.

Foner, Eric. *Reconstruction: America's Unfinished Revolution*. New York, 1988.

Fredrickson, George M. *The Black Image in the White Mind: The Debate on Afro-American Character and Destiny, 1817–1914*. New York, 1971.

Freehling, William W. *The Road to Disunion: Secessionists at Bay, 1776–1854*. New York, 1990.

Friedman, Lawrence J. *Gregarious Saints: Self and Community in American Abolitionism, 1830–1870*. New York, 1982.

Genovese, Eugene. *The World the Slaveholders Made: Two Essays in Interpretation*. New York, 1969.

____. *Roll, Jordan, Roll: The World the Slaves Made*. New York, 1974.

Ginzberg, Lori D. *Women and the Work of Benevolence*. New Haven, 1991.

Goodheart, Lawrence B. *Abolitionist, Actuary, Atheist: Elizur Wright and the Reform Impulse*. Kent, 1990.

Greenberg, Kenneth S. *Masters and Statesmen: The Political Culture of American Slavery*. Baltimore, 1985.

Hewitt, Nancy. *Women's Activism and Social Change: Rochester, New York, 1822–1872*. Ithaca, 1984.

Jenkins, William S. *Pro-Slavery Thought in the Old South*. Chapel Hill, 1935.

Keir, A. E. Nash. "A More Equitable Past? Southern Supreme Courts and the Protection of the Ante-Bellum Negro." *North Carolina Law Review*. 48:197–242 (1970).

Loveland, Anne C. *Southern Evangelicals and the Social Order, 1800–1860*. Baton Rouge, 1980.

McKenney, Francis F. *Education in Violence: The Life of George H. Thomas and the History of the Army of the Cumberland*. Detroit, 1961.

McPherson, James M. *The Abolitionist Legacy: From Reconstruction to the NAACP*. Princeton, 1975.

Morris, Robert C. *Reading, 'Riting, and Reconstruction: The Education of Freedmen in the South, 1861–1870*. Chicago, 1976.

Nagel, Paul C. *Descent from Glory: Four Generations of the Adams Family*. New York, 1983.

O'Toole, Patricia. *The Five of Hearts Club: An Intimate Portrait of Henry Adams and His Friends 1880–1918*. New York, 1990.

Peterson, Norma L. *The Presidencies of William Henry Harrison and John Tyler*. Lawrence, 1989.

Remini, Robert V. *Henry Clay, Statesman for the Union*. New York, 1991.

Russo, David J. *Keepers of Our Past: Local Historical Writing in the United States, 1820s–1930s*. Westport, 1988.

Samuels, Ernest. *Henry Adams*. Cambridge, 1989.

Sefton, James E. *The United States Army and Reconstruction, 1865–1877*. Baton Rouge, 1967.

Senese, Donald J. "The Free Negro and the South Carolina Courts, 1790–1860." *South Carolina Historical Magazine*. 68:140–153 (1967).

Simpson, Brooks D. *Let Us Have Peace: Ulysses S. Grant and the Politics of War and Reconstruction, 1861–1868*. Chapel Hill, 1991.

Stewart James B. *Wendell Phillips: Liberty's Hero*. Baton Rouge, 1986.

———. *William Lloyd Garrison and the Challenge of Emancipation*. Arlington Heights, 1991.

Tise, Larry. *Proslavery: A History of the Defense of Slavery in America, 1701–1840*. Athens, 1987.

Tolson, Jay. *Pilgrim in the Ruins: A Life of Walker Percy*. New York, 1992.

Van Deusen, Glyndon G. *The Jacksonian Era, 1828–1848*. New York, 1959.

Van Tassel, David D. *Recording America's Past: An Interpretation of the Development of Historical Studies in America, 1607–1884*. Chicago, 1960.

Wakramanayake, Marina. *A World in Shadow: The Free Blacks in Antebellum South Carolina*. Columbia, 1973.

Williamson, Joel. *After Slavery: The Negro in South Carolina During Reconstruction, 1861–1877*. Chapel Hill, 1965.

Index

About the Contributors

John Cimprich is Associate Professor of History at Thomas More College. He is the author of *Slavery's End in Tennessee, 1861–1865* and articles in the *Journal of American History, Civil War History*, and elsewhere. He presently is writing a biography of George H. Thomas.

Hugh Davis is Professor of History at Southern Connecticut State University and the author of *Joshua Leavitt: Evangelical Abolitionist*. He presently is working on a biography of Leonard Bacon.

Peter P. Hinks is Associate Editor of the Frederick Douglass Papers at Yale University. His book *"We Must and Shall Be Free": David Walker, Evangelicalism, and the Problem of Antebellum Black Resistance* is forthcoming.

Sylvan H. Kesilman, who formerly taught at Old Dominion University and other colleges, now teaches history and coordinates social studies in the school district of Philadelphia. He has written for *Ohio History*.

John R. McKivigan, Associate Professor of History at West Virginia University and Associate Editor of the Frederick Douglass Papers at Yale University, is the author of *The War against Proslavery Religion: Abolitionism and Northern Churches, 1830–1865*. He currently is writing a biography of James Redpath.

Randall M. Miller, Professor of History at Saint Joseph's University, is the author and editor of numerous books, including *"Dear Master"*:

(with John David Smith) *The Dictionary of Afro-American Slavery* (Greenwood, 1988).

Jane H. Pease and **William H. Pease**, Professors Emeriti at the University of Maine, are both associates in history at the College of Charleston. They have collaborated on numerous books. Among their recent works are *The Web of Progress: Private Values and Public Styles in Boston and Charleston, 1828–1843* and *Ladies, Women & Wenches: Choice & Constraint in Antebellum Charleston & Boston.*

John David Smith is Alumni Distinguished Professor of History at North Carolina State University. Among his many works are *An Old Creed for the New South: Proslavery Ideology and Historiography* (Greenwood 1985), (with Randall M. Miller) *The Dictionary of Afro-American Slavery* (Greenwood, 1988), and studies of the historian Ulrich B. Phillips.

James Brewer Stewart is Professor of History at Macalester College. He is the author of numerous works, including the highly acclaimed *Holy Warriors: The Abolitionists and American Slavery.* His most recent book is *William Lloyd Garrison and the Challenge of Emancipation.*

John B. Weaver teaches history at Sinclair College in Dayton, Ohio. He has published articles on various aspects of nineteenth-century reform and politics.

Bertram Wyatt-Brown is Milbauer Professor of History at the University of Florida. Among his many works are *Lewis Tappan and the Evangelical War against Slavery, Yankee Saints and Southern Sinners,* and the award-winning *Southern Honor: Ethics and Behavior in the Old South.* He currently is writing a book on the Percy family.

Angela Howard Zophy is Associate Professor of History at the University of Houston, Clear Lake. Among her works is *The Handbook of American Women's History.* She presently is writing a biographical study of Sarah Josepha Hale.